IDENTITY CRISIS

John Sides, Michael Tesler,
and Lynn Vavreck

IDENTITY CRISIS

The 2016 Presidential Campaign and the
Battle for the Meaning of America

PRINCETON UNIVERSITY PRESS

Princeton and Oxford

Published by Princeton University Press

41 William Street, Princeton, New Jersey 08540

6 Oxford Street, Woodstock, Oxfordshire OX20 1TR

press.princeton.edu

LCCN 2018947736

ISBN 978-0-691-17419-8

British Library Cataloging-in-Publication Data is available

Jacket design by Faceout Studio, Lindy Martin

This book has been composed in Minion Pro and Ideal Sans

Printed on acid-free paper. ∞

Printed in the United States of America

10 9 8 7 6 5 4 3 2 1

To Henry Brady, Jack Citrin, Dick Fenno, and David Sears:
Without them, there is no us.

CONTENTS

FIGURES AND TABLES

IDENTITY CRISIS

CHAPTER 1

Fayetteville

Rakeem Jones didn't see the punch coming.

He had been part of a group protesting at a rally for presidential candidate Donald Trump in Fayetteville, North Carolina. It was March 9, 2016, and Trump was leading the race for the Republican presidential nomination. After Trump began speaking, one of the group started shouting at Trump. A Trump supporter screamed at the group, "You need to get the fuck out of here!" The group was soon surrounded by sheriff's deputies, who began to escort them out. Jones gave the audience the finger. Another member of the group, Ronnie Rouse, said that someone shouted, "Go home, niggers!" (Both Rouse and Jones are black.)

As police led Jones out, seventy-eight-year-old John McGraw, who uses the nickname "Quick Draw McGraw," moved to the end of his row and sucker-punched Jones as he walked past. Jones was then tackled by the deputies, who said they had not seen McGraw's punch. McGraw, who is white, was able to leave the event and was interviewed afterward by a reporter from the program *Inside Edition*. When asked if he liked the rally, he said, "You bet I liked it." When asked what he liked, McGraw said, "Knocking the hell out of that big mouth." Then he said, "We don't know who he is, but we know he's not acting like an American. The next time we see him, we might have to kill him." The day after, McGraw was identified, arrested, and charged with assault and battery and disorderly conduct.

The incident went viral. One reason was Rouse's cell phone footage of the attack. Another was Trump's reaction. In his speech in Fayetteville, Trump appeared to excuse violence against the protesters, saying, "In the good old days this doesn't happen because they used to treat them very, very rough." Two days later, Trump said, "The audience hit back and that's what we need a little bit more of." Two days after that he offered to pay McGraw's legal fees. That never came to pass. McGraw appeared in court nine months later and pleaded no contest to both charges. He was sentenced to a year's probation.[1]

The attack on Rakeem Jones was just one of several violent incidents involving protesters and attendees at Trump rallies. Two days after the Fayetteville rally, the Trump campaign canceled a rally planned for the University of Illinois at Chicago when violence erupted between Trump supporters and protesters. And Trump's reaction to the attack on Jones was just one of many times when he condoned violence against protesters. After a Black Lives Matter activist was attacked and called "nigger" at a November 2015 rally in Birmingham, Trump said, "Maybe he should have been roughed up because it was absolutely disgusting what he was doing." On other occasions, referring to protesters, he said, "Knock the crap out of them" and "I'd like to punch him in the face" and "I'll beat the crap out of you."[2]

What happened in Fayetteville, Birmingham, and other places revealed something else about the election. McGraw's comment "We know he's not acting like an American" distills what the election was fundamentally about: a debate about not only what would, as Trump put it, "make America great again," but who is America—and American—in the first place. It was a debate about whether the president himself, Barack Obama, was an American. It was a debate about how many immigrants to admit to the country. It was a debate about how much of a threat was posed by Muslims living in or traveling to the United States. It was a debate about whether innocent blacks were being systematically victimized by police forces. It was a debate about whether white Americans were being unfairly left behind in an increasingly diverse country.

What these issues shared was the centrality of *identity*. How people felt about these issues depended on which groups they identified with and how they felt about other groups. Of course, group identities have mattered in previous elections, much as they have in American politics overall. But the question is always *which* identities come to the fore. In 2016, the important groups were defined by the characteristics that have long divided Americans: race, ethnicity, religion, gender, nationality, and, ultimately, partisanship.

What made this election distinctive was *how much* those identities mattered to voters. During Trump's unexpected rise to the nomination, support for Trump or one of his many rivals was strongly linked to how Republican voters felt about blacks, immigrants, and Muslims, and to how much discrimination Republican voters believed that whites themselves faced. This had not been true in the 2008 or 2012 Republican primaries. These same factors helped voters choose between Trump or Hillary Clinton in the general election—and, again, these factors mattered even more in 2016 than they had in recent presidential elections. More strikingly still, group identities came to matter even on issues that did not have to be about identity, such as the simple question of whether one was doing okay economically.

In short, these identities became the lens through which so much of the campaign was refracted. This book is the story of how that happened and what it means for the future of a nation whose own identity is fundamentally in question.

The Political Power of Identity

That identity matters in politics is a truism. Getting beyond truisms means answering more important questions: which identities, what they mean, and when and how they become politically relevant. The answers to these questions point to the features of the 2016 election that made group identities so potent.[3]

People can be categorized in many groups based on their place of birth, place of residence, ethnicity, religion, gender, occupation, and so on. But simply being a member *of* a group is not the same thing as identifying or sympathizing *with* that group. The key is whether people feel a psychological attachment to a group. That attachment binds individuals to the group and helps it develop cohesion and shared values.

The existence, content, and power of group identities—including their relevance to politics—depends on context. One part of the context is the possibility of gains and losses for the group. Gains and losses can be tangible, such as money or territory, or they can be symbolic, such as psychological status. Moreover, gains and losses do not even need to be realized. Mere threats, such as the possibility of losses, can be enough. When gains, losses, or threats become salient, group identities develop and strengthen. Groups become more unified and more likely to develop goals and grievances, which are the components of a politicized group consciousness.

Another and arguably even more important element of the context is political actors. They help articulate the content of a group identity, or what it means to be part of a group. Political actors also identify, and sometimes exaggerate or even invent, threats to a group. Political actors can then make group identities and attitudes more salient and elevate them as criteria for decision-making.

A key question about identity politics is how much it involves not only an attachment to your own group but also feelings about other groups. Identities can be "social," with direct implications for how groups relate to each other. These relationships do not have to be competitive, and thus group loyalties do not have to create hostility toward other groups. But group loyalties can and often do. Hostility can arise because groups are competing over scarce resources. It can also arise not out of any objective competition but because group leaders identify another group as a competitor or even the enemy. Both the "us" and the "them" of group politics can depend on what political leaders do and say.[4]

A Changing America

The social science of group identity points directly to why these identities mattered in 2016. First, the context of the election was conducive. The demographics of the United States were changing. The dominant majority of the twentieth century—white Christians—was shrinking. The country was becoming more ethnically diverse and less religious. Although the terrorist attacks of September 11, 2001, no longer dominated the nation's consciousness, there were other terrorist attacks in the United States and elsewhere. The civil rights of African Americans were newly salient, as the Black Lives Matter movement coalesced to protest the deaths of unarmed blacks at the hands of police. Indeed, several high-profile incidents between the police and communities of color made Americans more pessimistic about race relations than they had been in decades.[5] Moreover, there was no recession or major war, either of which tends to dominate an election-year landscape, as the Great Recession and financial crisis did in 2008 and the Iraq War did in 2004. This created more room for different issues to matter.

Another crucial part of the context: even before 2016, group identities and attitudes were becoming more aligned with partisanship. Racial and ethnic minorities were shifting toward the Democratic Party and voting for its candidates. Meanwhile, whites' attitudes toward racial, ethnic, and religious minorities were becoming more aligned with their partisanship. People who expressed favorable attitudes toward blacks, immigrants, and Muslims were increasingly in the Democratic Party. People who expressed less favorable attitudes toward these groups were increasingly in the Republican Party.

This growing alignment of group identities and partisanship is crucial because it gives these group identities more political relevance. It helps to orient partisan competition around questions related to group identities. It gives candidates a greater incentive to appeal to group identities and attitudes—knowing that such appeals will unify their party more than divide it. It makes the "us and them" of party politics even more potent.

A Racialized Campaign

But none of this context was new in 2016. The country's growing diversity was a long-standing trend, and its mere existence did not ensure an outsize role for group identities in 2016. Certainly this trend cannot itself explain differences between the 2016 election and presidential elections only four or eight years prior. Something else was necessary: *the choices of the candidates.* That the candidates talked so much about these issues, and disagreed so sharply, helped make these issues salient to voters.

First there was Trump himself. Trump was a real estate developer and a fixture of New York City society and its tabloids, which chronicled his marriages, affairs, and business dealings throughout the 1980s and 1990s. In 2004, he became a reality television star, hosting NBC's *The Apprentice* and *Celebrity Apprentice*, in which contestants competed for positions in his businesses. It was an unusual biography for a presidential candidate. But as Trump positioned himself to run for office, he did so with a strategy that has been anything but unusual in American politics: focusing on racially charged issues.

Even before he ran for office, Trump was no stranger to racial controversies. In 1973, the government accused him and his father, who was also a real estate developer, of refusing to rent apartments they owned to minorities and steering African Americans toward other properties where many minorities lived. The Trumps would later settle the case without admitting wrongdoing.

In 1989, there was the case of the Central Park Five: four black men and one Hispanic man who were wrongfully convicted of raping a white jogger in Central Park. Within days of the incident, Trump took out a full-page ad in New York City newspapers that declared, "BRING BACK THE DEATH PENALTY! BRING BACK THE POLICE!" The men's convictions were vacated in 2002 after another man confessed to the crime, although Trump continued to insist that the men were guilty and would do so again during the 2016 campaign.[6]

As Trump elevated his political profile during the Obama administration, racially charged rhetoric was central. He rekindled the long-discredited claim that Obama was not a native American citizen and became a virtual spokesperson for the "birther" movement. The strategy worked: when Trump flirted with running for president in 2011, his popularity was concentrated among the sizable share of Republicans who thought that President Obama was foreign born or a Muslim or both.[7]

Obama eventually released his long-form birth certificate, but Trump made similar insinuations throughout the 2016 campaign. This was only one of Trump's many claims during the campaign that played on racial and religious anxieties and fears and brought elements of the election-year context—undocumented immigrants, terrorism, Black Lives Matter, and others—to the fore.

Trump's tactics by themselves were not enough to make racial issues central to the campaign. Had his opponents taken the same positions as him, then voters' own views on these issues would not have helped them choose among the candidates. But for the most part Trump's opponents took different positions and condemned his controversial statements. In the Republican primary, many of Trump's Republican opponents—and many Republicans, period—broke with him when he proposed things like banning travel by Muslims to the United States.

Then, in the general election, Hillary Clinton fashioned her campaign as a direct rebuke of Trump. One part of that involved a different social identity: gender. Of course, because she was the first woman major-party nominee, Clinton's gender was already significant. But she also emphasized the historic nature of her candidacy and targeted Trump for his mistreatment of women.

Moreover, Clinton distinguished herself from Trump on issues related to race and ethnicity. She took sharply different positions on civil rights, policing, and immigration. She accused Trump of catering to white supremacists and hate groups. Ultimately, she ran as Obama's successor and the curator of the coalition that had put him in the White House—a coalition predicated on ethnic minorities, young people, and others who were relatively liberal on racial issues. Clinton did not embrace every aspect of Obama's record; indeed, on some racial issues she took more liberal positions than Obama. But her candidacy was clearly meant to cement and expand his legacy as the first African American president.

How Identity Mattered in 2016

Because Trump, Clinton, and the other candidates focused so much on issues tied to racial and ethnic identities, it is no surprise that those identities and issues mattered to voters. But how? It was *not* because those identities and attitudes changed much in the aggregate. In the years immediately before 2016, there was no clear secular increase or decrease in the strength of ethnic identities—with the possible exception of a modest increase in the strength of racial identity among white Americans. Similarly, there was no secular increase in prejudice against ethnic or religious minorities. The metaphor of a wave was sometimes used to describe what was happening in the United States and many European countries. This was fundamentally misleading, as the political scientist Larry Bartels argued based on European survey data, which showed no change in, for example, attitudes toward immigration between 2002 and 2015.[8]

The better metaphor, Bartels argued, was a reservoir. Among Americans, there is a range of sentiments about ethnic and other groups. Some people strongly identify with their group and some people do not. Some people have favorable attitudes about other groups and some people do not. It is not that these sentiments never change, or that the balance of people with different sentiments is unimportant. But the key question for elections is whether and how these sentiments actually matter for voters. In 2016, the candidates tapped into these reservoirs of opinion and helped "activate" ethnic identities and attitudes, thereby making them more strongly related to what ordinary Americans thought and how they voted.

How did the activation of identities and attitudes matter in 2016? The story begins even before the election itself (chapter 2). As the campaign got under way, much was made of Americans' "anger" and anxiety about their economic circumstances. But levels of anger and anxiety were no greater in 2016 than in recent years. In fact, economic anxiety had been *decreasing*, not increasing, in the eight years before 2016. What economic and political dissatisfaction did exist was powerfully shaped by political identities. With a Democrat in the White House, Republicans had much less favorable opinions about conditions in the county. But dissatisfaction also reflected racial attitudes: under Obama, white Americans' feelings about blacks became associated with many things, including whether and how they felt about the economy. "Racial anxiety" was arguably driving economic anxiety. Moreover, during Obama's presidency, there was an even stronger alignment between partisanship and identities and attitudes tied to race, ethnicity, and religion. The party coalitions were increasingly "racialized" even before the 2016 campaign began.

The upshot was not an electoral landscape heavily tilted toward the opposition Republicans, as would typically happen had economic anxiety been increasing. Instead, the landscape implied both a toss-up election and one that was ripe for racially charged divisiveness.

Then, in the Republican primary, the party was forced to confront its own divides (chapter 3). These divides had to do with racial and ethnic issues, particularly immigration. Ultimately, the party was so fractured before and during the 2016 election that party leaders could not agree on any frontrunner. This opened the door for Trump. From the moment he entered the race, Trump garnered extraordinary media coverage, which helped propel him to the top of the polls and helped ensure that he stayed there (chapter 4). That coverage amplified his unusually vitriolic message. Although many Republican leaders believed that the party needed to moderate on issues like immigration, many Republican voters were not so sure. These voters helped propel Trump to the nomination (chapter 5). Attitudes toward African Americans, Muslims, and immigrants more strongly related to support for Trump than support for the previous Republican nominees John McCain and Mitt Romney. Moreover, support for Trump was also strongest among white Americans with racially inflected grievances. This activation of whites' own group identity was an uncommon pattern in GOP primaries—and it showed again how economic anxieties came to matter more when they were refracted through social identities. The important sentiment underlying Trump's support was not "I might lose my job" but, in essence, "People in my group are losing jobs to that other group." Instead of a pure economic anxiety, what mattered was racialized economics.

In the Democratic primary, party leaders were more unified behind Hillary Clinton than leaders have been behind any nonincumbent presidential candidate in years (chapter 6). But Clinton still faced an unexpectedly strong challenge from Senator Bernie Sanders, an independent who, while caucusing with Democrats in the Senate, stood firmly outside the party. Sanders's appeal, like Trump's, depended on extensive and often positive media coverage. Although many believed that the divide between Clinton supporters and Sanders supporters was fundamentally ideological—with Sanders supporters much more liberal—Clinton and Sanders supporters were largely in agreement on many policy issues. Similarly, Clinton and Sanders supporters were not much divided by gender, gender identity, or sexism, even though Clinton's campaign routinely emphasized the historic nature of her bid to become the first female president. More important were partisan and racial identities. Clinton's status as a longtime Democrat allowed her to build support among primary voters who themselves identified as Democrats. Similarly, Clinton's embrace of Obama and her racially progressive message helped her build support among racial minorities and especially African Americans. The prevalence of Democrats and African Americans among primary voters propelled Clinton to the nomination.

In the general election campaign, Clinton and Trump continued to clash on issues tied to race, ethnicity, and gender (chapter 7). But now, Trump's controversial statements and behavior—and the media attention that they generated—hurt him in ways that they did not during the primary. The more news attention Trump received, the more his poll numbers dropped. Trump also seemed disadvantaged by his unorthodox campaign organization, which raised far less money than a typical presidential campaign and lagged behind Clinton's in televised advertising and field organizing. It made sense, then, that Clinton had a durable lead in the polls even though she continued to face extensive media attention to her use of a private email server as secretary of state, which in turn helped make voters' views of her on several dimensions as negative as, if not more negative than, views of Trump. Nevertheless, her controversies seemed to pale compared to Trump's. By the end of the campaign, it seemed almost impossible for Trump to win.

Then he did. To be sure, Clinton's narrow lead in the national polls was borne out in her victory in the national popular vote (chapter 8). Her victory was also in line with the growing economy and Obama's increasing approval rating. Indeed, Clinton arguably exceeded what would be expected from the candidate whose party was seeking the rare third consecutive term in the White House. These facts made it difficult to interpret the election as center-ing on economic anxiety or a desire for "change."

Instead, the election turned on the group identities that the candidates had activated—and these identities help explain why Trump won the Elec-toral College and, thus, the White House (chapter 8). First, partisan identi-ties ensured that Trump ultimately faced little penalty within a Republican Party that had often failed to embrace his candidacy. Despite Trump's many controversies, Republican Party leaders and voters rallied to him at the end of the campaign. Indeed, Trump did about as well among Republicans as Clin-ton did among Democrats.

Second, attitudes concerning race, ethnicity, and religion were more strongly related to how Americans voted in 2016 than in recent elections. By contrast, the apparent impact of economic anxiety was much smaller and not particularly distinctive compared to earlier elections. This activation of racial attitudes helped Trump more than Clinton. Despite the ongoing alignment of racial attitudes and partisanship, as of 2012 a substantial minority of white Obama voters still expressed less favorable views of immigration, undocu-mented immigrants, African Americans, and other minority groups. Trump's appeal to these voters helped ensure that Obama supporters in 2012 who voted for Trump in 2016 outnumbered Romney supporters who voted for Clinton. And because these voters were disproportionately represented in battleground states such as Michigan, Ohio, Pennsylvania, and Wisconsin, they helped Trump win the Electoral College—especially when the coalition that elected Obama did not show up for Clinton in comparable numbers.

Before the election, the prevailing wisdom was that the country's grow-ing diversity would help the Democrats continue to win the White House. Trump's victory showed that the backlash against that diversity could be a winning issue too.

What Is the Identity Crisis?

It is one thing to say that identity mattered in 2016. It is another to call it an "identity crisis." When that term was coined by the psychologist Erik Erikson, it referred to the individual's struggle, particularly in adolescence, to develop a sense of self—that is, his or her true identity. Analogous crises were the preconditions, and arguably the legacy, of this election.

There was, for instance, the ongoing identity crisis within the Republican Party—one that the party's unexpected victory in November did little to remedy. Party leaders were already divided on issues like immigration, and many of these leaders rejected Trump's inflammatory comments during the campaign. But his victory raised the question of whether the GOP would now embrace his views. Trump also called into question the party's apparent unity on economic issues. During the primary, he took heterodox positions—expressing support for entitlement programs and raising taxes for the wealthy—and then became the Republican nominee anyway. Trump revealed that many Republican voters were not movement conservatives or even particularly ideological. This raised a deeper question about what it truly meant to be a Republican or a conservative in the era of Trump.

The Democratic Party faced its own internal debate in the months after the election. The party's ranks in Congress, state legislatures, and governors' mansions had already taken a serious hit during Obama's presidency. But many blamed this on Republican gerrymandering and believed that an ascendant Obama coalition would continue to deliver the White House. With that theory now in tatters, the party began the same soul-searching that Republicans had engaged in after 2012. A key question was whether the party needed to moderate the progressive stance on racial issues that Clinton had embraced—and thereby try to win back white voters who had voted for Obama but then Trump.

The election was also symptomatic of a broader American identity crisis. Issues like immigration, racial discrimination, and the integration of Muslims boil down to competing visions of American identity and inclusiveness. To have politics oriented around this debate—as opposed to more prosaic issues like, say, entitlement reform—makes politics "feel" angrier, precisely because debates about ethnic, racial, and national identities engender strong emotions. It is possible to have a technocratic discussion about how to calculate cost-of-living increases in Social Security payments. It is harder to have such a discussion about whether undocumented immigrants deserve a chance for permanent residency or even citizenship. It is even harder when group loyalties and attitudes are aligned with partisanship, and harder still when presidential candidates are stoking the divisions. Elections will then polarize people not only in terms of party—which is virtually inevitable—but also in terms of other group identities.

The upshot is a more divisive and explosive politics.

CHAPTER 2

"Whaddaya Got?"

In the 1953 film *The Wild One*, a woman approaches Marlon Brando's character, Johnny Strabler. He is the leader of a gang called the Black Rebels Motorcycle Club. She asks, "What are you rebelling against, Johnny?" His famous reply: "Whaddaya got?"

When the film debuted, Brando's line—and the character's entire persona, with his sideburns and black leather jacket—evoked something dangerous. It seemed like contempt or frustration, but even Johnny couldn't say exactly what it was.

When the 2016 presidential campaign got under way, most Americans were not wearing black leather or riding motorcycles. But in the minds of many observers, Americans were feeling an inchoate rebelliousness that sounded an awful lot like "Whaddaya got?"

Americans were said to be angry, anxious, fearful. They were said to "be poised for a major reset."[1] In an October 2015 NBC News/*Wall Street Journal* poll, 69 percent of Americans agreed with this statement: "I feel angry because our political system seems to be working for the insiders with money and power like those on Wall Street or in Washington, rather than it working to help everyday people get ahead." And 54 percent agreed with the statement, "The economic and political systems in this country are stacked against people like me." In a different poll from the same time, almost half of Americans said that "America's best days are behind us," and just over half said that the "American culture and way of life" had changed for the worse since the 1950s.[2]

But this focus on voter anger was misleading in two respects. First, any anger coexisted with positive feelings. Thanks to the slow but steady economic recovery after the Great Recession of 2007–9, Americans felt as favorably about the economy as they had in over ten years. In the same October NBC News poll, 58 percent said they were "cautiously optimistic about where things are headed." Second, there was about as much displeasure and distrust in 2012 when the incumbent president was reelected—suggesting that Americans' mood in 2016 did not clearly presage any "reset." In fact, the economic and political conditions in the country pointed to a toss-up race with no clear favorite.

The election's outcome would not just hinge on trends in the economy, however. There were two other trends—one long standing and one more recent—that were reshaping the American electorate and the Democratic and Republican coalitions. The long-term trend was strengthening partisan-ship. Republicans and Democrats have become more divided on how they evaluate political leaders, perceive the economy, feel about political issues, and even evaluate the truth of well-established facts. In 2016, "voter anger" was disproportionately a Republican phenomenon. This helped ensure that Obama's approval rating remained relatively low despite growing optimism about the economy.

The second trend involved the alignment of partisanship and identities tied to race, ethnicity, and religion. The administration of Barack Obama was not only eight years of a Democratic president—in which partisan po-larization continued to grow—but also eight years of a black president. As a result, Americans' racial identities and racial attitudes became even more potent political forces and helped transform the party coalitions. Non-whites increasingly identified as Democrats. Whites—and particularly whites who did not have a college degree and had less favorable views of racial and ethnic minorities—increasingly identified as Republican. The party coalitions became more divided by race and ethnicity after Obama took office and before the 2016 presidential campaign was seriously under way.

Just as conditions in the country did not clearly favor either party, these shifts in the party coalitions did not either. Although many analysts and pol-iticians believed that the country's growing ethnic diversity posed challenges for Republicans, others argued that the Republicans could benefit, at least in the short term, from appeals to their growing base of white voters. Ulti-mately, an electorate divided by party and race set the stage for an election that played directly on these divisions and whose outcome appeared far from certain.

"Morning Again in America," Again?

Obama took office amid the worst recession since the Great Depression. This "Great Recession" was especially punishing because its pairing with a financial crisis led to an even more sluggish recovery.[3] For example, the deep recession that occurred in 1981–82—during Ronald Reagan's first term—saw unemployment peak at a higher level than it did in the 2007–9 recession. But after the 1981–82 recession was over, the economy grew at a much more rapid pace. Unemployment returned to its prerecession value in just under three years. By contrast, this took almost eight years after the Great Recession began.[4]

Despite this sluggish pace, an economic recovery did occur. The overall economy, as measured by the gross domestic product, grew in nearly every quarter between 2009 and 2016. Meanwhile, unemployment fell and disposable income increased. By the end of 2015, the unemployment rate of 5 percent was below its median value over the sixty years from 1948 to 2008. Disposable income was nearly $2,000 above its prerecession peak in the second quarter of 2008. Falling unemployment, combined with the low inflation rate, meant that the so-called misery index—which peaked during the high unemployment and high inflation of the late 1970s—was close to a sixty-year low.[5]

One persistent question, however, was whether the economic recovery was helping average Americans. Indeed, for many years preceding the recession, most of the gains in income had gone to the wealthiest Americans.[6] However, Census Bureau data on family incomes showed increases in every income quintile, especially in the two years before the election (figure 2.1).[7] To be sure, family incomes in the lowest quintile had not returned to their pre-recession level. The point is just that the economic recovery helped all income groups, not just the wealthy.

What is more, the economic recovery registered in how voters themselves saw the economy. This was quite contrary to a lot of commentary in 2015 and early 2016, which described the middle or working class as "losing ground," "falling behind financially," or just "feeling screwed" and asserted that "economic blues define campaign[s]."[8] But the longest-standing measure of Americans' views of the economy suggested otherwise.

The Index of Consumer Sentiment, which dates to the late 1950s, captures people's views of their current financial circumstances and economic conditions in the country, as well as their expectations about the near future (figure 2.2).[9] After Obama took office, consumer sentiment increased initially before dropping sharply in the summer of 2011, when the possibility that Congress might not raise the debt ceiling and thereby cause the United

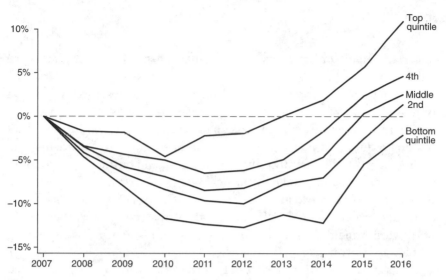

Figure 2.1.
Changes in real average family incomes compared to 2007 levels, by income quintile.
Dollar amounts measured in $2016.
Source: Census Bureau Historical Table F3, https://www.census.gov/data/tables/time
-series/demo/income-poverty/historical-income-families.html.

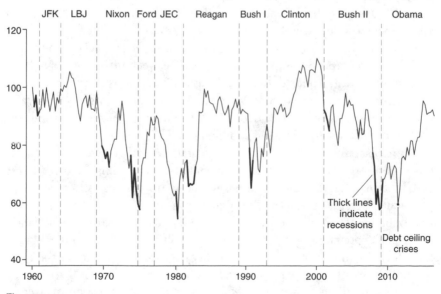

Figure 2.2.
The Index of Consumer Sentiment, 1960–2016.
The data stop in the third quarter of 2016.
Source: University of Michigan, Survey Research Center.

States to default on its debts worried financial markets and Americans alike.

But after that crisis passed, consumer sentiment resumed its upward trajectory. By 2016, consumer sentiment was nearly as positive as it had been during the recovery from the recession of 1981–82.[10] To put this in terms of the survey questions that gauge consumer sentiment, more Americans were saying that both their family's financial situation and business conditions in the country would be good over the next year. More Americans were saying that it was a good time to purchase expensive items like furniture or a refrigerator. Americans actually felt as good about the economy as they did in 1984, when Ronald Reagan ran for reelection in 1984 with a slogan saying that it was "morning again in America."

This growing optimism was not limited to the wealthy or well educated (figure 2.3). Although people with higher incomes have nearly always had more positive views of the economy than have those with lower incomes, all income groups became more positive after the end of the Great Recession. While middle- and lower-income households may have experienced the economic recovery differently than those with higher incomes, it was not evident in their own evaluations of the economy. The same parallel trends are evident when people are broken down by their level of formal education (see the appendix to this chapter). Consumer sentiment improved among those with and without a college degree.

Indeed, what is distinctive about the Obama years—especially compared to the Reagan years—is how *small* the gap was between income groups. From 2009 until the third quarter of 2016, the average gap was lower than during the administrations of George H. W. Bush, Bill Clinton, George W. Bush, and Ronald Reagan.[11] Americans with different incomes were more similar in their evaluations of the economy under Obama.

It may seem myopic to focus on short-term economic trends, given the longer-term trends toward economic inequality. But the impact of economic inequality on U.S. election outcomes has been ambiguous. Americans support equality in the abstract and say that they are concerned about the growth in economic inequality, but growing inequality has not clearly shifted Americans' policy preferences in the progressive direction that many observers anticipated. This may explain why inequality's steady increase since the 1970s has not made either party politically dominant.[12]

Less ambiguous, however, is the impact of short-term economic trends, which are strongly related to presidential election outcomes and do help explain oscillating party control. The only debate involves how short the short term is: the six months or the two years before the election. The political scientists Christopher Achen and Larry Bartels characterize economic voting

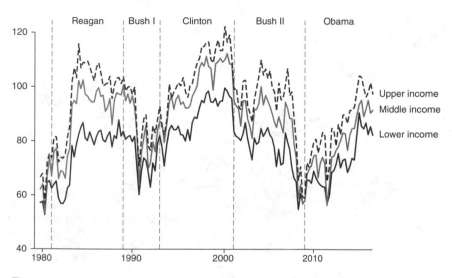

Figure 2.3.
The Index of Consumer Sentiment among income groups, 1980–2016.
The data stop in the third quarter of 2016.
Source: University of Michigan, Survey Research Center.

with this pungent metaphor: "Like medical patients recalling colonoscopies, who forget all but the last few minutes, the voters' assessments of past pain and pleasure are significantly biased by 'duration neglect.'"[13] As a result, economic trends in 2015 and 2016 were the most consequential for understanding who would win the White House.

The Wrong Track

Despite the economic recovery and rising consumer sentiment, however, the zeitgeist of 2016 was hardly "morning again in America." There were significant currents of dissatisfaction with the country, the federal government, and Barack Obama. But this dissatisfaction was generally *not* worse in 2016 than in the previous several years, despite the ongoing narrative about "angry" voters. Instead, 2016 stood out not because voters were angrier but because their improving views of the economy had not much affected their views of Obama and the country.

Early in the election year, commentators often focused on the fact that most Americans told pollsters that the country was on the "wrong track." But this is the norm: in thousands of polls since 1981, the percentage saying "wrong track" has outnumbered the percentage saying "right direction" 88 percent

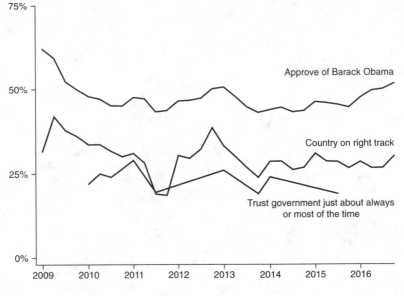

Figure 2.4.
Presidential approval, trust in government, and evaluations of the country's direction,
2009–16.
All data aggregated to the quarterly level except political trust. The data include only
polls taken before November 8, 2016.
Sources: Pew Research Center surveys (trust), Pollster.com (presidential approval,
right direction).

of the time. Indeed, saying "wrong track" is virtually a ritual without clear
political consequences—and that was especially true in 2016, when polls
showed that the people who said "wrong track" did not even agree on whom
to blame. This is why the "wrong track" question is not a good predictor of
who will win presidential elections.[14]

Moreover, there had been no increase in dissatisfaction or anger
(figure 2.4). Indeed, if anything, approval of Obama was *improving* somewhat in late 2015 and 2016. Other polls showed a similar trend. For example, a
fall 2015 Pew Research Center poll asked respondents whether they were
"basically content," "frustrated," or "angry" with the federal government. The
most common response was "frustrated" (57%). Only 22 percent said "angry,"
and this was lower than in the fall of 2013, when anger was more prevalent
during the federal government's partial shutdown.[15] In short, Americans
were no more "angry" than in 2012, when a comfortable majority reelected
the incumbent president.

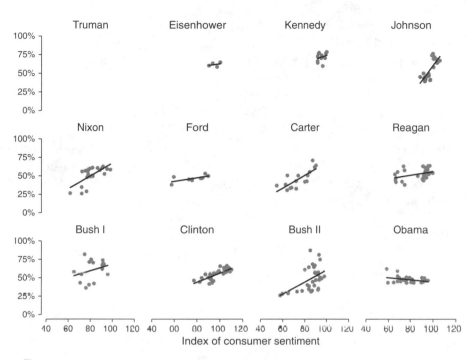

Figure 2.5.
The relationship between consumer sentiment and presidential approval.
For Obama, the data end in the third quarter of 2016.
Source: University of Michigan, Survey Research Center.

More distinctive was the divergence between perceptions of the economy
and political evaluations. Typically, the economy looms large in many different political attitudes. When people perceive that the economy is doing well,
they evaluate elected officials more favorably, trust the government more, and
are more likely to think that the country is going in the right direction.[16] But
by 2016, people's increasingly favorable economic evaluations had not translated into more favorable political attitudes. For example, even though economic evaluations were as positive as in the mid-2000s, *fewer* people said that
the country was going in the right direction: 26 percent in the last quarter of
2015 as opposed to 40 percent in the third and fourth quarters of 2004.

Obama's approval rating was also lower than expected given the public's
positive evaluations of the economy. Indeed, Obama was the only president
since John F. Kennedy whose approval ratings did not increase alongside consumer sentiment (figure 2.5). In fact, in Obama's case, the relationship between consumer sentiment and his approval rating was actually *negative*.[17] If

presidential approval were a function of consumer sentiment and nothing else, Obama should have been more popular than he was—approximately 5 percentage points more popular in the third quarter of 2016. But his approval ratings proved stickier than consumer sentiment alone predicted.[18]

This put Obama and the Democratic Party in a different position from four years before. As 2011 came to an end, views of Obama were more positive than objective economic conditions and other factors would have predicted. Voters tended to blame George W. Bush more than Obama for the state of the economy, perhaps because the Great Recession began when Bush was in office.[19] But even if Obama escaped some of the blame for that recession, in his second term he seemed to have escaped credit for the recovery.

A Toss-Up Election

What did these trends—or lack thereof—portend for the presidential election? As far back as 2014, many political observers and even some Republicans were bullish on the Democrats' chances. There were headlines like "The Republican Party's Uphill Path to 270 Electoral Votes in the 2016 Elections" and "The Most Likely Next President Is Hillary Clinton." In a January 2016 survey of academic experts, sixteen out of the seventeen expected the Democrats to win the White House.[20]

Early optimism for the Democrats was justified in this sense: the economic recovery and the public's assessment of Obama advantaged the Democratic Party. Incumbent parties tend to do better when the economy is improving, especially during the election year. Politicians themselves know this. Richard Nixon, for example, blamed a late economic downturn for his loss in the 1960 presidential election. In his book *Six Crises*, he wrote, "In October, usually a month of rising unemployment, the jobless rolls increased by 452,000. All the speeches, television broadcasts, and precinct work in the world could not counteract that one hard fact."[21] And even though Obama's approval had not increased as much as expected given growing optimism about the economy, neither was it clearly a drag on the Democrats' chances.

A simple statistical model of presidential elections from 1948 to 2012 demonstrates that these two factors favored the Democrats in 2016. The model includes changes in the gross domestic product from the first quarter to the third quarter of the election year and the president's approval rating as of June of the election year (see this chapter's appendix for more details). In 2016, the economy's nonannualized growth rate was 1.1 percentage points in the first two quarters of the year, and Obama's approval rating in June 2016 was 50 percent. Economic growth was solid but not spectacular compared to other elections when the incumbent party was seeking a third consecutive term. For example, in 1960, the growth rate was slightly negative, just as Nixon noted. But in 1988 and 2000, growth was about a point higher than in 2016. Obama's June approval rating was the same as Reagan's in 1988, though lower than Clinton's in 2000 (58%) and Eisenhower's in 1960 (61%).

It makes sense, then, that these two factors forecasted a Democratic victory but still gave Republicans a significant chance. The Democratic candidate was estimated to receive 51.8 percent of the major-party vote. Factoring in the uncertainty underlying the forecast, this translated into a 72 percent chance of a Democratic victory—a real, but hardly definitive, advantage.[22]

Other factors, however, made the election's outcome less certain. For one, there was no incumbent on the ticket. This matters in two ways. First, there is an incumbency advantage in presidential elections. One study of American presidential elections from 1828 to 2004 found that incumbents receive an average of 2.5 points of additional vote share in presidential elections. As the political scientist James Campbell noted, incumbency is no guarantee of victory, but it is "an opportunity that can usually be converted to an advantage." It is an advantage that the Democrats did not have in 2016.[23]

Second, the impact of the economy and presidential approval on presidential elections appears to be larger when the incumbent is on the ticket. Voters tend to assign more credit or blame to the actual incumbent than to any potential successor.[24] A different model, which allowed the impact of presidential approval and the GDP growth to vary based on whether an incumbent was running, produced a less favorable forecast for the Democrat: just under 50 percent of the major-party vote (see again this chapter's appendix).

The forecast was also more favorable for Republicans after accounting for the fact that the Democrats were running for a third consecutive presidential term. Across established democracies, the longer a party has been in power, the less likely citizens are to vote for its candidates. The political scientist Alan Abramowitz has shown that parties are penalized more after holding the White House for two or more terms than when they have held it for only one term. The political scientist Christopher Wlezien has called this "the cost of ruling" and shown that it may stem partly from the tendency of presidents to push policy in one ideological direction even as the public shifts in the opposite direction.[25]

Even before 2016, the Democrats had suffered from the cost of ruling, losing a large number of seats in Congress and state legislatures. In 2016, the potential cost of ruling was substantial: even after accounting for presidential approval and economic growth in the 1948–2012 presidential elections, an incumbent party that had already served at least two terms received an average of 3.8 points fewer of the vote, compared to a party that had served only one term. A model with these three factors predicted that each party had almost exactly a 50 percent chance of winning (see this chapter's appendix).

These simple forecasting models are not perfect predictors. They do not tell us everything about presidential elections. They do not imply that the campaign itself is irrelevant. They assume that the candidates are evenly matched in their capabilities and resources. They produce forecasts with substantial uncertainty.[26]

Nevertheless, these models provide a useful baseline. In 2016, aspects of the electoral landscape were favorable to the Democrats, particularly a growing economy and a Democratic president whose popularity was growing as the election year proceeded. Still, the disjuncture between Obama's approval and public sentiments about the economy—combined with Obama's absence from the ticket—made it less than certain that Democrats would get credit for a growing economy. Conditions also seemed ripe for the Democrats to suffer the "cost of ruling" and Republicans to benefit accordingly.

The sum of these factors suggested that the election was a toss-up. This conclusion was consistent with a broader range of forecasting models—some of which predicted a Republican victory and others of which predicted a Democratic victory. A statistical averaging of these models showed that the election was, again, essentially a toss-up. Bettors in election forecasting markets had a similar view: as of January 2016, they gave Democrats only a 60 percent chance of winning, a narrow advantage at best.[27]

In short, the election-year conditions in the country did not support the early confidence in the Democrats' chances. The presidential race was either party's race to lose.

Bitter Partisans

The impact of election-year conditions shows how presidential elections depend on short-term forces in the country. But long-term forces are also at work, ones that do not shift as quickly from election to election. Of these forces, none is more important than Americans' abiding loyalty to a political party. In 2016, party loyalty meant that voter "anger" was most prevalent in the Republican Party. Republicans manifested the most dissatisfaction, distrust, and disapproval. Although these Republican sentiments were not any worse than in the previous few years, they were crucial to understanding why Obama's approval ratings lagged the growing economy and how and for whom dissatisfaction would matter in 2016.

Partisan divisions in political attitudes are nothing new. More than fifty years ago, the authors of the seminal political science book *The American Voter* wrote, "Few factors are of greater importance for our national elections than the lasting attachments of tens of millions of Americans to one of the parties." These divisions have sharpened even since then. Polarization among political leaders has made partisanship among ordinary Americans a more potent force. Americans have become better "sorted" in terms of party and ideology: Democrats increasingly describe themselves as liberals and Republicans increasingly describe themselves as conservatives. Americans have become more hostile toward the opposite party and toward its presidential candidates. Americans are now more concerned that their son or daughter might marry someone in the opposite party. Americans appear willing to discriminate against members of the opposite party and even find them less physically attractive. This does not mean that the parties have become monoliths or that people have become orthodox liberals or conservatives. But it does mean that partisan antagonisms are growing. Unsurprisingly, then, more Americans today see differences between the parties. In fact, a politically inattentive American today is as likely to perceive important differences between the parties as a politically attentive American was in 1960.[28]

Partisanship is also a lens through which Americans perceive the objective world. As the authors of *The American Voter* wrote, "Identification with a party raises a perceptual screen through which the individual tends to see what is favorable to his partisan orientation."[29] For example, Americans tend to think the economy is doing better when their party controls the White House. This partisan bias in economic perceptions increased between 1985 and 2007, particularly during the Bush administration, and then declined during the Great Recession, when the downturn was so severe that most Americans—including both Democrats and Republicans—evaluated the economy unfavorably.[30]

But by 2016, this partisan bias had reasserted itself. YouGov/*Economist* polls conducted from June to December 2015 found that, among Democrats, 27 percent said they were better off financially than a year ago, 48 percent said that their finances were about the same, and 20 percent said they were worse off financially. By contrast, only 11 percent of Republicans said they were better off financially, while 43 percent said they were worse off.[31]

Republicans were even more pessimistic about the economy when its performance was directly linked to President Obama. In a May 2016 survey, some respondents were asked to evaluate the economy and their personal financial situation relative to "the year 2008," and others were asked to evaluate these things relative to "when President Obama was first elected." Republicans were about 20 points more likely to say that both the national economy and their own finances had "gotten worse" when the question mentioned Obama.[32]

This partisan divide was important enough to override the impact of income. Class cleavages in financial satisfaction paled in comparison to the partisan cleavage. According to YouGov/*Economist* polls, Republicans in the highest income quintile, those making more than $100,000 per year, were actually slightly *less satisfied* than Democrats in the lowest income quintile, those making less than $20,000 per year. Economic dissatisfaction was in large part a partisan phenomenon.

It is hardly surprising, then, that Republicans and Democrats had very different views of Barack Obama. Partisan differences in assessments of Obama were larger than they had been for any previous president. On average, Obama's approval rating among Democrats was almost 70 points higher than his approval rating among Republicans. This difference was even larger than the partisan differences during the administrations of George W. Bush (60 points) and Bill Clinton (55 points), both of whom held office when partisan polarization was increasing.[33]

Partisan polarization also helps explain why increasingly positive evaluations of the economy did not appear to improve Obama's approval rating. It is not only that partisans saw the economy differently but also that in a polarized age, Americans may give little credit to a president not of their own party. A good comparison is again to the last quarter of 1983, when consumer sentiment was essentially the same as at the end of 2015. At that point in time, 87 percent of Republicans approved of Reagan and so did 30 percent of Democrats. By June 2016, Obama's support in his own party was almost as high as Reagan's, but it was much lower among Republicans (14%)—about where it had been for almost six years.

The growing salience of partisanship is also manifest in voting behavior. Fewer voters split their tickets. There are fewer true swing voters who might vote for one party's candidate in one election and the other party's candidate in the next election. It is typical for a presidential candidate to attract the support of 90 percent or more of his or her party's supporters.[34]

Presidents are obliged, of course, to state their righteous opposition to partisanship. George W. Bush pledged to be a "uniter, not a divider," and Obama inveighed against the "bitter partisanship and petty bickering that's shut you out, let you down and told you to settle." But the behavior of Americans—and perhaps presidents themselves—undercuts these promises, and partisanship in the American political system has ratcheted ever upward.[35]

Race, Ethnicity, and the Changing Party Coalitions

In an interview late in his presidency, Obama lamented "the suspicion between the races" and said that it "has shaped an entire generation of voters and tapped into their deepest anxieties."[36] Indeed, the racial divides that were already salient to American politics became even larger during Obama's presidency, and this provided one of the most important ways in which his presidency shaped the 2016 election.

Political divides in American politics have increasingly become racial and ethnic divides—ones that touch on feelings about groups such as African Americans, immigrants, and Muslims. The Democratic Party has become increasingly attractive to nonwhites and to whites with more formal education, who tend to have more favorable attitudes toward racial and ethnic minorities. The Republican Party has become increasingly attractive to whites and especially whites with less formal education, who tend to have less favorable views of minorities.

The "racialization" of partisanship was under way even before Obama became a national figure. Americans' partisan attachments became more closely aligned with racial attitudes in the post–civil rights era as politicians from the two parties increasingly diverged in both their policies and their rhetoric about race.[37] But eight years of an African American president accelerated and intensified racialization. This meant that the outcome of the 2016 election would depend not only on election-year fundamentals like the economy but also on how successfully the candidates could navigate these racial dynamics and mobilize a winning coalition.

The first major change in the party coalitions was the increasing Democratic advantage among nonwhites (figure 2.6). This was not preordained: for years, many nonwhites—especially Latinos and Asians—had not consistently aligned with one political party. But that changed. Although there was no secular trend in Asian American partisanship from 2007 to 2016, the longer-term trend was clear: in exit polls, Asian Americans' support for Democratic presidential candidates increased from 31 percent in 1992 to 73 percent in 2012. Latinos also came to identify more with the Democratic Party. Among Latinos, Democrats outnumbered Republicans by 23 points in 2002 but 36 points in 2016.[38]

African Americans' identification with the Democratic Party strengthened as well, even though blacks had long been Democratic. Figure 2.6 understates this shift because it does not capture how strongly blacks identified with the Democratic Party. But in the American National Election Studies, the percentage of blacks who said that they were "strong" Democrats increased from 31 percent in 2004 to 55 percent in 2012.

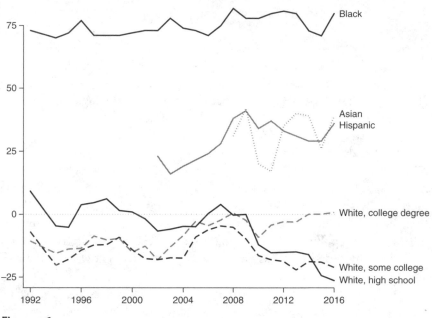

Figure 2.6.
Democratic advantage in partisanship, by race and education.
The figure presents the percent of respondents who identify with or lean toward the Democratic Party, minus the percent who identify with or lean toward the Republican Party. Positive numbers indicate a Democratic advantage.
Source: Pew Research Center surveys through August 2016.

For whites, the trend was exactly opposite: during the Obama era, whites were leaving the Democratic Party. In Pew Research Center surveys from 2007, whites were just as likely to call themselves Democrats as they were to call themselves Republicans. But by 2010, whites were 12 points more likely to be Republicans than Democrats (51% versus 39%).

White flight from the Democratic Party occurred almost entirely among whites without a college degree. Although these voters were widely believed to have fled the Democratic Party years earlier, that was confined to the South. What transpired under Obama was broader. Whites who did not attend college were evenly split between the two parties in Pew surveys conducted from 1992 to 2008. But by 2015, white voters who had a high school degree or less were 24 percentage points more Republican than Democratic (57% versus 33%). White voters with some college education but no four-year degree were 19 points more Republican (55% versus 36%). Meanwhile, whites with a college degree shifted toward the Democratic Party. Thus, the increasing alignment between education and whites' party identification—also known as the "diploma divide"—was largely a phenomenon of the Obama era and preceded the 2016 campaign itself.[39]

Why did this diploma divide in party identification emerge—and why did it emerge when it did? A key reason was race. For many years, whites with less formal education had not mapped their views about race onto their broader political views. Because they tended to follow politics less closely, they had not fully learned or internalized the long-standing divisions between the Democratic and Republican Parties on civil rights and other issues related to race. But once Obama was in office, whites with less formal education became better able to connect racial issues to partisan politics. There was a large increase in the proportion of non-college-educated whites who knew that the Democratic Party was more supportive of liberal racial policies than was the Republican Party.[40]

Then racial attitudes became more connected to whether whites identified as Democratic or Republican. Whether whites attributed racial inequality more to the country's legacy of racial discrimination or more to blacks' lack of effort increasingly came to distinguish Democrats from Republicans (top left panel of figure 2.7). These beliefs about racial inequality—measured by asking respondents how much they agreed with statements like "It's really a matter of some people not trying hard enough; if blacks would only try harder they could be just as well off as whites" and "Generations of slavery and discrimination have created conditions that make it difficult for blacks to work their way out of the lower class"—capture a central debate about race in America and especially how much white Americans subscribe to the common stereotype that blacks themselves do not try hard enough.[41]

Some of this racialization occurred before Obama took office, particularly between 1990 and 1994, when the partisan balance among whites who attributed racial inequality to blacks' lack of effort shifted from near parity to a 22-point advantage for the Republicans. But the polarization among whites increased sharply when Obama first ran for president. In 2012, there was a 15-point Democratic advantage among those emphasizing racial discrimination and a 42-point Republican advantage among those emphasizing blacks' lack of effort.

The same pattern was visible when comparing whites by their support for interracial dating (upper right-hand panel of figure 2.7). This time, however, the trend is entirely confined to the Obama era, when even racial issues that had never divided white Democrats from white Republicans suddenly did so. About 17 percent of people opposed interracial dating in 2009, and 13 percent did so in 2012. These people shifted sharply to the Republican Party while Obama was in office.

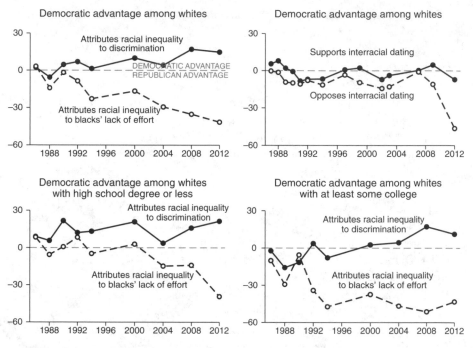

Figure 2.7.
Racial attitudes, education, and whites' party identification.
The figure presents the percent of whites who identify with or lean toward the Democratic Party.
Source: American National Election Studies and Pew Research Center (interracial dating graph).

This polarization during Obama's presidency was most pronounced among whites who did not have a college education (bottom left-hand panel of figure 2.7). The Republican advantage in this group increased from 15 points in 2004 to 39 points in 2012. Whites who did not have a college education but emphasized racial discrimination became more Democratic. There was no similar pattern during the Obama era among whites with at least some college education (bottom right-hand panel of figure 2.7). Among these more politically attentive whites, polarization along racial lines occurred earlier.

The growing alignment between racial attitudes and white partisanship was not due to some other factor, such as ideology or religiosity. In fact, no other factor predicted changes in white partisanship during Obama's presidency as powerfully and consistently as racial attitudes. Nor was the racialization of partisanship simply a by-product of whites' changing their racial attitudes to match their views of Obama. Racial attitudes that were measured before Obama became president predicted subsequent changes in party identification when these individuals were reinterviewed during his presidency.[42]

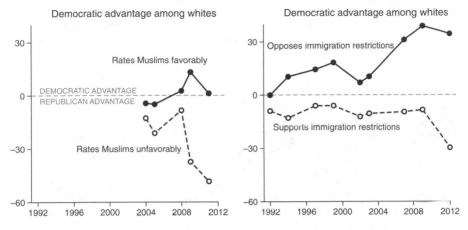

Figure 2.8.
Muslims, immigration, and whites' identification with the Democratic Party.
Sources: Pew Global Attitudes Project (favorability toward Muslims) and Pew Values
Surveys (immigration).

The partisanship of whites became aligned not only with views of racial inequality but also with views of Muslims and immigration. Because Obama was repeatedly characterized as Muslim or foreign born, a general aversion to all minority groups, and to Muslims in particular, became more strongly correlated with white Americans' vote preferences in both the 2008 and 2012 presidential elections.[43] Consequently, whites who rated Muslims unfavorably became more likely to identify as Republican once Obama took office (figure 2.8). Similarly, whites who wanted stricter immigration restrictions (around 75%) moved toward the Republicans while whites who opposed these restrictions increasingly identified as Democrats. Partisan polarization on immigration predated Obama's presidency but strengthened during it. Regardless of whether people were switching parties based on their attitudes toward Muslims and immigrants or changing their attitudes about these groups to reflect the growing partisan divisions on Islam and immigration, the implications for the 2016 election were the same: the two parties were more divided on issues of race, ethnicity, and religion than they were before Obama's presidency.[44]

Of course, these Obama-era trends also coincided with the onset of the Great Recession. But it is unlikely that economics was driving defections from the Democratic Party among whites with less formal education or less favorable views of racial and ethnic minorities. For one, the recession began under a Republican president, George W. Bush, and both he and his party received most of the blame—which is exactly why Obama won so handily in 2008. Moreover, rising unemployment has historically favored the Democratic Party in presidential and gubernatorial elections, perhaps because Democrats are

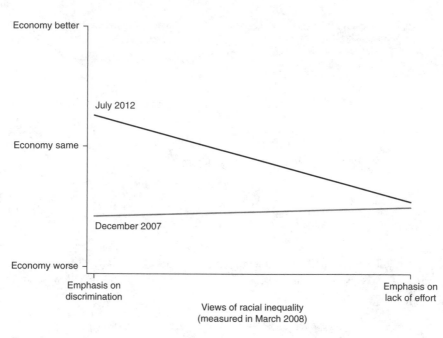

Figure 2.9.
Racial attitudes and whites' evaluations of the national economy, 2007 versus 2012.
The analysis includes 1,904 white respondents who were interviewed in both December 2007 and July 2012. The results are based on a model that accounts for party and ideology. Predicted values calculated by setting partisanship and ideology to their averages among white respondents.
Source: Cooperative Campaign Analysis Project.

perceived as caring more about the issue of jobs and employment than do Republicans.[45] If anything, then, the Great Recession should have driven the voters experiencing economic hardship to Obama and the Democratic Party. And even if voters did blame Obama, one would then expect defections from the Democratic Party to reverse themselves as the economic recovery took hold, but instead the defections accelerated over the course of Obama's presidency. This is why racial attitudes appear the more likely culprit.

Racialization affected more than partisanship, too. Opinions about many issues linked to Obama became influenced by both racial attitudes and race—a phenomenon called "the spillover of racialization." Particularly relevant was how racialization spilled over into evaluations of the economy. In December 2007, beliefs about racial inequality were not related to whites' perceptions of whether the economy was getting better or worse, after accounting for partisanship and ideology (figure 2.9). But when these exact same people were reinterviewed in July 2012—nearly four years into the Obama administration—these racial attitudes were strongly correlated with economic perceptions. Along with partisanship, racial attitudes appeared to fuel economic anxiety during Obama's presidency.[46] This presaged the "racialized economics" of the 2016 campaign.

Conclusion

In early 2016, two *Washington Post* writers, David Maraniss and Robert Samuels, set out to gauge the mood of Americans by traveling the country for over a month. What they found was much more than an all-consuming anger:

> For every disgruntled person out there who felt undone by the system and threatened by the way the country was changing, caught in the bind of stagnant wages or longing for an America of the past, we found someone who had endured decades of discrimination and hardship and yet still felt optimistic about the future and had no desire to go back. In this season of discontent, there were still as many expressions of hope as of fear. On a larger level, there were as many communities enjoying a sense of revival as there were fighting against deterioration and despair.[47]

This is precisely what the quantitative evidence shows. The economy had improved since the Great Recession and voters realized it, but their assessments of Obama and the country were less favorable than the economy alone might have predicted. At the same time, however, there was little evidence of any increase in "voter anger" leading into the election year—and no clear signs of a "change election" predicated on growing anger.

Simple narratives about voter anger also obscured who was angry and why. Anger clearly depended on partisan and racial identities. This was visible in the polarization of Democrats and Republicans in their approval of Obama, their perceptions of the economy, and, increasingly, their views of racial, ethnic, and religious minorities. And because racial attitudes evoke angry emotions in ways that other political attitudes do not, racialization may help explain why some whites appeared angry despite positive trends like a growing economy.[48]

If racial and ethnic identities were reshaping American politics and the party coalitions, the obvious question was which party would benefit. To many observers, these trends gave Democrats the advantage. The white fraction of eligible voters was shrinking—from 84 percent in 1980 to an estimated 70 percent by 2016. Some Republicans believed the party needed to move quickly to court nonwhite voters. As Republican senator Lindsey Graham put it in June 2015, "My party is in a hole with Hispanics." Other analysts saw little chance that Republicans could counter a growing Democratic Party advantage in the Electoral College. In that 2014 article about the GOP's "uphill path to 270 electoral votes," the *Washington Post*'s Dan Balz wrote, "A recent conversation with a veteran of GOP presidential campaigns raised this question: Which, if any, of the recent battleground states are likely to become more Republican by 2016? The consensus: very few."[49]

But a more racialized politics can cut in many directions, especially in the short term. For this reason, at least some strategists and political scientists argued that Republican candidates could gain from catering to their base of white voters.[50] Some evidence supported that argument. Drawing attention to the country's changing demographics in a survey significantly increased the percentage of whites who identified as Republicans. Similarly, drawing attention to the Democratic Party's outreach to Latino voters made white Democrats view their party less favorably. And increased contact with racial and ethnic minorities in Chicago and Boston led whites to express more ethnocentric attitudes, turn out to vote in higher numbers, and support Republican candidates at greater rates. Identity politics certainly cut both ways in down-ballot races during Obama's presidency. The Democrats' majority in the House of Representatives when Obama entered the White House had turned into a paltry minority. Those Democratic defections were most prevalent among voters with less favorable views about racial and ethnic minorities. The question for 2016 was whether increased Democratic support from nonwhites would again be offset by greater Republican support and higher turnout among whites.[51]

Regardless of which party would benefit, one thing was clear: racially charged issues were increasingly central to American party politics. That these issues would be central to the 2016 campaign itself became clearer on the morning of June 16, 2015.

CHAPTER 3

Indecision

After eight years of the Obama administration, Republicans had lots of ideas about how to win back the White House. Some wanted the party to woo the constituencies that seemed crucial to Obama's victories, including women and ethnic minorities. Some wanted the party to embrace an orthodox conservatism and stop nominating candidates whom they deemed too moderate. Others wanted candidates who would just stick to a script. As Republican National Committee (RNC) chair Reince Priebus put it right before the 2014 election, "I'd rather have candidates being careful to a fault than, you know, having a fountain of blabber coming out of their mouth that's not disciplined."[1]

On the morning of June 16, 2015, a candidate who would do none of those things entered the Republican primary: Donald Trump. At first glance, Trump seemed like the sort of marginal candidate that the GOP could quickly shunt to the side. After all, the party had successfully coordinated on more mainstream front-runners in earlier nomination battles—a phenomenon documented in a widely discussed political science book, *The Party Decides*.[2] Less than a year later, however, Trump stood alone as the last remaining Republican presidential candidate. He had defeated sixteen others, including candidates with more political experience and support among Republican leaders. He defied the predictions of many politicians, political observers, pundits, and political scientists.

Trump's count of delegates to the national convention shows the relative ease with which he won (figure 3.1). He won early and often, building a

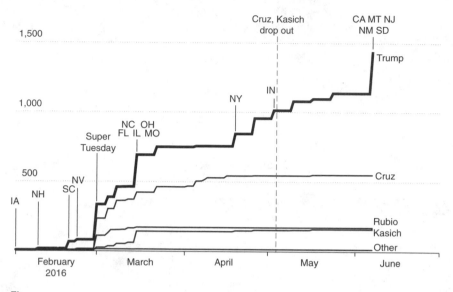

Figure 3.1.

Delegates won by the Republican presidential candidates.

The graph does not include the 130 delegates who were not bound by state primaries or caucuses to vote for a candidate. Data courtesy of Josh Putnam of Frontloading Headquarters.

sizable lead by the middle of March 2016, only six weeks after the first contest in Iowa. None of the other candidates put a dent in that lead. The last to drop out, Senator Ted Cruz of Texas and Governor John Kasich of Ohio, were hundreds of delegates behind, with little chance of catching up.

How Trump beat the odds to secure the nomination is perhaps the most important story of the 2016 election. After all, growing partisan polarization, combined with equivocal conditions in the country, made this an election that Republicans could win. Almost any candidate they put forward would have a reasonable chance of winning the White House.

Trump's appeal was predicated on three factors. The first was the fractured ranks of Republican Party leaders even before the 2016 election. They were divided on policy, particularly on issues like immigration, and divided on tactics, with a more moderate "establishment" faction frequently at war with a conservative "insurgent" faction over basic questions like whether to allow a government shutdown. This factionalism made it difficult for Republican leaders to coordinate on a single front-runner among the party's many presidential aspirants. There were various candidates competing within different factions of the party, instead of one candidate serving to unify these factions. Therefore, voters got no clear signal from Republican leaders about which candidate to support.[3]

This void was filled in part by the second factor helping Trump: media coverage (see chapter 4). Media coverage has frequently pushed presidential primary candidates to the front of the pack. That coverage can be fleeting, however, as some candidates in 2016 discovered. But for Trump, it was not. Trump's ability to generate conflict and controversy—and thereby extraordinary ratings and profits for news organizations—helped him dominate news coverage for much of the primary campaign, and this coverage in turn helped propel him to a lead in the polls and ensure that he stayed there. And even though some coverage was critical—of his personal life, business record, views on issues, and so on—much of it was not. Republican candidates, leaders, and interest groups facilitated Trump's ascendance by failing to attack him early and in earnest.

Finally, Trump succeeded by tapping into long-standing, but often unappreciated, sentiments among Republican voters (see chapter 5). Although many Republican leaders wanted to appeal to racial and ethnic minorities, Trump went in the opposite direction—and capitalized on deep concern about immigration, Islam, and racial diversity among rank-and-file Republicans. Although many Republican leaders wanted cutbacks or dramatic reforms to entitlement programs such as Social Security and Medicare, Trump defended those programs—and capitalized on the underappreciated strain of economic liberalism among many rank-and-file Republicans. On both issues, Trump was actually closer to the views of Republican voters than were other Republican leaders and some other Republican candidates. Rather than trying to move the party—for example, toward an embrace of immigration reform—Trump simply met many Republican voters where they were. In short, the divide between Republican leaders and voters on these issues became a divide on Trump himself, whom few leaders supported but many voters did.

The result was a convincing victory for Trump—and an intensifying identity crisis for the Republican Party.

The "Lessons" of 2012

Election night 2012 shocked many Republicans. Even though conditions in the country and the public polls favored Obama—as did the Romney campaign's own internal polls, for that matter—many Republicans believed that the polls would be wrong. In a Gallup poll conducted ten days before the election, almost three-fourths of Republicans expected Romney to win. Romney himself had written a victory speech but no concession speech. On that night, Fox News anchor Megyn Kelly responded to Karl Rove's bullishness on Romney's prospects with this pointed question: "Is this just the math you do as a Republican to make yourself feel better or is this real?"[4]

Obama's comfortable win then catalyzed a debate within the Republican Party about what it should do next. According to a study by the political scientist Philip Klinkner, losing parties in presidential elections have addressed one or more of three things: their platform, their organization, and their procedures for nominating candidates. Changes to the platform are hardest, as this necessitates navigating ideological shoals within the party. Instead, losing parties tend to focus on procedures or organization.[5]

After 2012, the GOP's response did center on its party and campaign organization. This can be summarized as "doing better math." For example, in the RNC's postmortem report on the 2012 election—entitled the *Growth and Opportunity Project*—the longest section is on "campaign mechanics." The goal was to close the gap between the Democratic and Republican Parties in how they used data and analytics to increase the efficiency of their fund-raising and voter contact. The RNC's report emphasized the need for "a commitment to greater technology and digital resources" and "a deeper talent pool that understands and can deploy data and technology/digital campaigning."[6]

The Republican Party also revisited the procedures for nominating candidates, just as it had after its loss in 2008. For example, the RNC created a committee to manage the primary debates, which had proliferated. (There were twenty in 2012.) Reince Priebus said, "While I can't always control everyone's mouth, I can control how long we have to kill each other." In 2015–16, there would be twelve debates. The RNC also required that states holding their primaries before March 15 allocate delegates in proportion to each candidate's share of the vote and not on a winner-take-all basis.[7]

But there was little consensus when it came to revisiting the party's policies and platform. Moderates within the party pushed for changes that acknowledged the country's changing demography. The *Growth and Opportunity Project* argued, "The Republican Party must focus its efforts to earn new supporters and voters in the following demographic communities: Hispanic, Asian and Pacific Islanders, African Americans, Indian Americans, Native Americans, women, and youth. . . . Unless the RNC gets serious about tackling this problem, we will lose future elections; the data demonstrates this." The report said that the party "must embrace and champion comprehensive immigration reform" to appeal to Hispanic voters. One of the report's authors, former George W. Bush press secretary Ari Fleischer, said, "We couldn't talk about inclusiveness . . . and then ignore immigration. Otherwise, it would've rung hollow, I think."[8] In short, the report was trying to push the party toward a more liberal position on immigration—even though Republican voters had little desire to do so.

Other Republican leaders echoed these sentiments. Romney's campaign manager said he regretted Romney's position on immigration; at one point during the 2012 Republican primary, Romney had suggested that undocumented immigrants "self-deport" to their countries of origins. Two days after the 2012 election, House Speaker John Boehner said that immigration reform was "long overdue." Even the conservative media personality Sean Hannity advocated for immigration reform: "I think you control the border first. You create a pathway for those people that are here. You don't say you've got to go home. And that is a position that I've evolved on."[9]

But many conservatives rejected the *Growth and Opportunity Project*, perhaps illustrating why bromides about "big tents" are easier than the spadework of changing platforms. To these conservatives, the problem wasn't that Romney was too conservative, it was that he wasn't conservative enough—a "meandering managerial moderate," as the conservative writer Ben Domenech put it. Rush Limbaugh said, "The Republican Party lost because it's not conservative." Texas senator Ted Cruz said, "It is amazing that the wisdom of the chattering class to the Republicans is always, always, always 'Surrender your principles and agree with the Democrats' . . . every time Republicans do that we lose."[10]

This divide within the party appeared to grow during Obama's presidency, casting a shadow on Republican successes in midterm elections. Republicans won a remarkable sixty-three House seats in the 2010 election and thirteen House seats in 2014, earning its largest majority since 1928. After 2014, Republicans also controlled the Senate for the first time since 2006. Although these victories helped Republicans stymie Obama's legislative agenda, they also illuminated, and even exacerbated, divisions within the party.

The "Knuckleheads"

These divisions emerged soon after the 2010 election. That election saw the rise of the Tea Party, a loose congeries of grassroots groups and national advocacy organizations that vehemently opposed the Obama administration and advocated for conservative policies. Tea Party activism helped push congressional Republicans further to the right. Most of the Republicans newly elected in 2010 were more conservative than the typical Republican who had served previously—and they and many Republican activists opposed many of the workaday compromises typical to legislative life.[11] One of those compromises was raising the debt ceiling—a frequent and necessary occurrence because the federal government continually borrows money. In the summer of 2011 the threat that Congress would not raise the debt ceiling gave rise to concerns that the United States might default on its debt obligations and plummeting economic confidence among Americans (see chapter 2). Ultimately, a compromise measure passed, but it split the Republican caucus.[12]

Another prominent battle involved the signature issue of the Growth and Opportunity Project: immigration reform. The effort to pass immigration reform had foundered in 2007, but the party's dismal showing among Latinos in the 2012 election gave the effort new momentum. A Senate bill did pass in June 2013 with the support of fourteen Republicans, but it was perceived as too liberal by some House Republicans. Representative Steve King of Iowa warned of immigrant drug mules with "calves the size of cantaloupes because they're hauling 75 pounds of marijuana across the desert." Work on a separate House bill then fell apart after the stunning primary defeat of the House majority leader, Eric Cantor, by a little-known economics professor, David Brat, who had attacked Cantor on immigration reform.[13]

A third battle came in October 2013, when the federal government shut down after Congress failed to appropriate funds for government operations. Conservatives like Ted Cruz wanted to use the threat of a shutdown to win changes or delays to the Affordable Care Act. A week before the shutdown, Cruz gave a twenty-one-hour speech to advocate for defunding "Obamacare." But ultimately Obamacare survived and a bill ending the shutdown passed the House, once again splitting Republicans.

As polls showed that Americans tended to blame Republicans for the shutdown, news accounts described a Republican "civil war" between business groups and the Tea Party. Republican representative Peter King of New York disparaged "Ted Cruz and his whole crazy movement." Cruz called the bill a "lousy deal," and conservatives mounted challenges to Republican Senate incumbents like Majority Leader Mitch McConnell of Kentucky and Thad Cochran of Mississippi in 2014. This was part of a broader pattern: in 2010–14 there was an increase in primary challengers who won at least 25 percent of the vote. And within the Republican Party, many challengers were from the ideological right. Although incumbents usually won—including McConnell and Cochran—the losses of candidates like Cantor commanded the most attention. These primary battles were further evidence of the GOP's divides.[14]

After 2014, the Republican Party's unified control of both the House and Senate did little to resolve its internecine battles. In the House, a new group—the Freedom Caucus—embodied Tea Party ideals and antagonized John

Boehner, who had allowed votes on bills that many Republicans opposed. Within a year, Boehner resigned from Congress. Boehner's departure set off a halting search for a new Speaker. Representative Paul Ryan of Wisconsin, who had been Mitt Romney's running mate in the 2012 presidential election, reluctantly agreed to serve. At that point, only a third of Republicans in the country approved of the Republican congressional leadership. Before long, Ryan also found himself sparring with the Freedom Caucus. Watching all of this from afar, Boehner called his House Republican opponents "the knuckleheads." For good measure, he called Ted Cruz "Lucifer in the flesh."[15]

Republicans on Capitol Hill were a microcosm of the party. There were, to be sure, important areas of consensus. Few Republicans advocated increases in taxes or a large-scale expansion of government entitlements. But the divides illustrated the party's inability to coordinate at the elite level. This was a harbinger of the Republican presidential primary.

The Mischiefs of Faction

Of course, the mere existence of factions within political parties is nothing new. Parties are collections of ambitious politicians whose goals often conflict. Parties are also collections of interest groups with different agendas. Presidential nominations often bring factional battles to the fore because the stakes are so high. William "Boss" Tweed captured these stakes when he said he did not care who "did the electing" as long as he "got to do the nominating."[16]

Political parties therefore need a way for factions to negotiate and arrive at some consensus on a presidential nominee. For a long time, this involved bargaining among party leaders, including at the nominating convention once it became a standard practice. After the 1968 election, reforms first in the Democratic Party and soon after in the Republican Party based the allocation of convention delegates to the candidates on voters' choices in primaries and caucuses rather than on deals made by party leaders in proverbial "smoke-filled rooms." As a result, leaders began to use the period before the first caucuses and primaries—the "invisible primary"—to try to coordinate on a nominee. Endorsements by party leaders during the invisible primary served as an important signal about which candidates were more promising. In presidential primaries between 1980 and 2004, endorsements were associated with who was leading the polls as the primaries began and ultimately who won the nomination. The apparent impact of endorsements was greater than that of fund-raising or news coverage. This was the evidence presented in *The Party Decides* and related research.[17]

Party leaders are typically seeking a nominee who is ideologically compatible with, or at least satisfactory to, multiple party factions and can win the general election. These two criteria may be in significant tension, as some factions may prefer a candidate whose beliefs make him or her a hard sell to swing voters in a general election. The challenge, then, is for party leaders to balance these competing considerations and coordinate on a candidate. As the invisible primary began in earnest in 2015, it became apparent that the Republican Party would struggle to do this.

This was visible in the sheer number of candidates running: former Florida governor Jeb Bush, surgeon Ben Carson, New Jersey governor Chris Christie, Ted Cruz, businesswoman Carly Fiorina, former Virginia governor Jim Gilmore, Lindsey Graham, former Arkansas governor and 2008 presidential candidate Mike Huckabee, Louisiana governor Bobby Jindal, John Kasich, former New York governor George Pataki, Kentucky senator Rand Paul, former Texas governor and 2012 presidential candidate Rick Perry, Marco Rubio, former Pennsylvania senator and 2012 presidential candidate Rick Santorum, Donald Trump, and Wisconsin governor Scott Walker. In one sense, this crowd was not surprising: potential candidates, particularly well-qualified ones, are choosy about when they run for higher office and will wait until conditions are favorable.[18] Because the 2016 presidential election was one that Republicans could win, lots of candidates threw their hats in the ring. Political observers marveled at what Priebus, among others, called the "deep bench" of the Republican Party.[19]

But this proliferation of candidates also suggested a problem. Perhaps the most invisible part of the invisible primary is the work that parties do to discourage candidates from running in the first place. In 2015, at least one prominent Republican—Mitt Romney—flirted with running but did not enter the race because his donors and staffers were lukewarm or supporting other candidates. Nevertheless, the signals being sent by party leaders seemed equivocal enough that many other candidates felt it was worthwhile to run.[20]

The candidates who ran represented distinct party factions or simply stood outside those factions. Moreover, in at least two of the GOP's most prominent factions, there were multiple candidates running—further complicating the task of coordination. Paul was the lone representative of a more libertarian philosophy within the party. He had made waves with a March 2013 filibuster protesting the Obama administration's national security policy, prompting Senator John McCain to call him a "wacko bird."[21] Ultimately, the libertarian faction in the GOP is small, which helps explain why Paul did not make much headway during the primary.

Several other candidates stood squarely in the more conservative wing of the party, particularly on issues such as abortion and gay rights. Both Huckabee and Santorum had run for president previously on this platform and had won caucuses or primaries in states, such as Iowa, with more religious and social conservatives. In 2016, Cruz seemed the most prominent candidate from this faction.

Members of the largest group of candidates were somewhat less conservative and better connected to the "establishment"—that is, to other parts of the party's traditional base, such as business groups. Early on, Jeb Bush was the most prominent of these candidates. Given his family lineage—his father and brother were, of course, the forty-first and forty-third presidents, respectively—and his connections within the party, he was an early front-runner. He announced his "active exploration" of a candidacy on December 16, 2014, and his campaign quickly sought to establish his dominance by locking in supporters and donors in a below-the-radar effort named "shock and awe" after the military doctrine that advocated early and overwhelming force on the battlefield. The early signs for Jeb Bush were good: he and his affiliated political action committee, or super PAC, raised $114 million in the second quarter of 2015.[22]

Challenging Bush were candidates like Christie, Graham, Jindal, Kasich, Rubio, Pataki, and Walker. They were not all similar to Bush or necessarily "establishment" candidates, but their appeal was potentially broader than just to social conservatives. Some of these candidates faced the simple challenge of being unknown to many Republicans. In July 2015, about half or more of Republican voters were not familiar enough with Graham, Kasich, Jindal, Pataki, and Walker to have an opinion about them. This shows how difficult it can be for statewide officeholders to break into the national consciousness. Even Walker, who had made headlines outside Wisconsin after successfully battling to end collective bargaining rights for public-sector unions and then surviving a recall attempt, was familiar to only 52 percent of Republicans.[23] Christie was better known but not better liked: he faced questions about his role in "Bridgegate," a scandal in which members of his staff had ordered lane closures in Fort Lee, New Jersey, to tie up traffic trying to access the George Washington Bridge and punish the mayor of Fort Lee for not supporting Christie. To many in the party, Christie was "damaged goods."[24]

Rubio, by contrast, was better liked. The question, however, was whether he would be able to challenge Bush, whose pedigree was similar in some respects, including not only their Florida home base but also their support for immigration reform. Bush and Rubio had had a decent relationship before the campaign: after Rubio's Senate victory in 2012, Bush stood at his side and said, "Marco Rubio makes me cry for joy!" But now, Bush and his team regarded Rubio as a threat, and Rubio found that most Florida political insiders were on Bush's side.[25]

Candidates without experience in elective office—Carson, Fiorina, and Trump—seemed to be in another category, sometimes labeled "the outsiders." This label actually understates how much these candidates had sought to ingratiate themselves with insiders. Carson, after retiring from a storied career as a neurosurgeon, polished his bona fides within the party by becoming a prominent critic of Obama—something that had additional resonance because Carson was himself black—and speaking to conservative groups and writing for conservative outlets. Fiorina, the former CEO of Hewlett-Packard, had advised John McCain's 2008 campaign, worked for the RNC and American Conservative Union Foundation, and run unsuccessfully for the U.S. Senate in California in 2010.

Trump had not been a loyal partisan of any kind. As Trump said about his real estate projects, "When you need zone changes, you're political. . . . You know, I'll support the Democrats, the Republicans, whatever the hell I have to support." Bill and Hillary Clinton were even guests at his wedding to Melania Trump in 2005.[26] But in 2009, Trump registered as a Republican and tried to win Republicans' support. Amid his "birther" crusade against Obama in 2011, Trump flirted with a presidential run and even briefly led in the polls for the Republican nomination. He spoke at the Conservative Political Action Conference. He was a frequent guest on Fox News. He eventually endorsed Mitt Romney in 2012, although he was irked that Romney did not do more to embrace him. After 2012, he started meeting with Republican strategists and donating more to Republican candidates and party organizations. To be sure, Trump was no Republican regular—and would routinely criticize the party and threaten to run as an independent in 2016—but nevertheless he worked to build his appeal within the party ahead of his presidential campaign.[27]

In many previous Republican presidential primaries, a fractious and diverse field produced a more moderate or "establishment" candidate as the nominee, even if other candidates won some individual caucuses and primaries. Nominees who fit this pattern include Bob Dole in 1996, George W. Bush in 2000, John McCain in 2008, and Mitt Romney in 2012. But there was no coalescing around such a candidate for the 2016 nomination.

This was perhaps most visible in whether and whom Republican Party leaders endorsed during the invisible primary. Endorsements during the invisible primary are particularly telling. It is easy for a party leader to wait and see who is leading after the first few caucuses and primaries and then jump on that candidate's bandwagon. It is costlier for leaders to stick out their necks and endorse before voters have begun to weigh in.

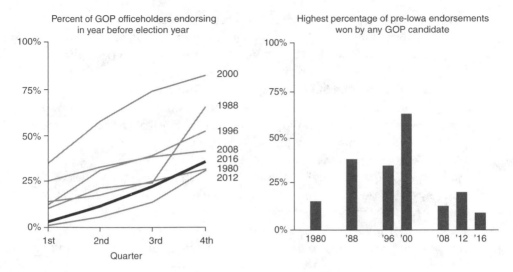

Figure 3.2.
Endorsements of Republican presidential candidates by Republican governors, senators, and U.S. House members.
Any endorsements received before the year preceding the election year are counted in the first quarter of that year. Any endorsements that came in the election year, but before the Iowa caucus, are counted in the fourth quarter of the prior year.

What distinguished 2016 was, first, the relatively slow pace of endorsements (see left-hand panel of figure 3.2). By the eve of the Iowa caucus, only 35 percent of sitting Republican governors, senators, and U.S. House members had endorsed any of these Republican candidates. This was slightly higher than in the period preceding the Iowa caucus in both 1980 and 2012, but it was lower than the average. And because there were far more Republican candidates running in 2015 than in 1979 or 2011, it arguably should have been easier for Republican leaders to find a candidate to endorse. But most stayed on the sidelines.

There was also no consensus on which candidate to endorse, which is captured by the percent of endorsements won by the candidate with the most pre-Iowa endorsements (see right-hand panel of figure 3.2). In earlier years, there was never complete consensus, of course. George W. Bush stands out in 2000 for having won almost two-thirds of the possible endorsements. But in 2008, 2012, and especially 2016, the Republican Party did not coalesce as fully around a single candidate. All of this was unusual. In previous primaries, Republican elites were more likely than Democrats to make endorsements and unify around one or two candidates.[28]

What distinguished 2016 from 2012, however, was that no candidate got anything close to a majority of the endorsements (see this chapter's appendix for full endorsements data). In 2011, when even more Republicans were on the sidelines, most of the endorsements went to the eventual nominee, Romney. By contrast, 2016 looked more like 2008, with the endorsements spread more evenly across the candidates and no clear front-runner. In 2016, the three candidates with the most endorsements were Bush, Rubio, and Cruz. No Republican governor, senator, or member of the House endorsed Carson or Trump during the invisible primary; only three endorsed Fiorina. Of course, none of these candidates would say publicly that this was a problem. In October 2015, one of Carson's senior staff said, "We haven't gotten a single damn endorsement and we don't care." This is a typical refrain from candidates with few or no endorsements. In 2011, GOP candidate Jon Huntsman said that "nobody cares" about endorsements.[29]

Factionalism in the Republican Party was manifest even among the few members of Congress who did endorse a candidate (figure 3.3). On average, the members of Congress who endorsed Bush, Rubio, Cruz, or Paul were located at different places on the two dimensions underlying much of the roll-call voting in Congress: the standard liberal-conservative dimension and a dimension that helps capture the party's "insider" or "establishment" wing and the "outsider" or "insurgent" wing, which was visible on issues like the debt ceiling. Bush's supporters tended to be more moderate, based on their scores on the liberal-conservative dimension. Rubio's were clustered around the average Republican on both dimensions. Cruz's endorsers tended to be toward the right on the liberal-conservative dimension—although they were not as conservative as Cruz himself—and, like Cruz, tended to score as "outsiders" on the other dimension. Paul's endorsers were scattered across the ideological map. In short, the lack of an early consensus on a presidential front-runner was rooted in the same fissures that had divided the Republican Party before the primary campaign got under way.[30]

This indecision and lack of consensus in the Republican Party showed up among state legislators and donors as well. Only 20 percent of Republican state legislators endorsed a Republican presidential candidate before the Iowa caucuses, and no candidate was endorsed by more than 5 percent of state legislators. Donors also sat on their hands. As of the summer of 2015, many Republican donors had not given to any candidate. Among those who had, most were "hedging their bets" and giving to multiple candidates.[31]

Many Republican candidates were therefore able to raise enough money to be competitive. This illustrates one feature of the modern nominating system: the ability of candidates to raise money despite having little support from party leaders. Although it surprised no one that Jeb Bush and Marco Rubio raised plenty of money—$156 million and $163 million, respectively, combining their campaign committees and affiliated super PACs—even more striking

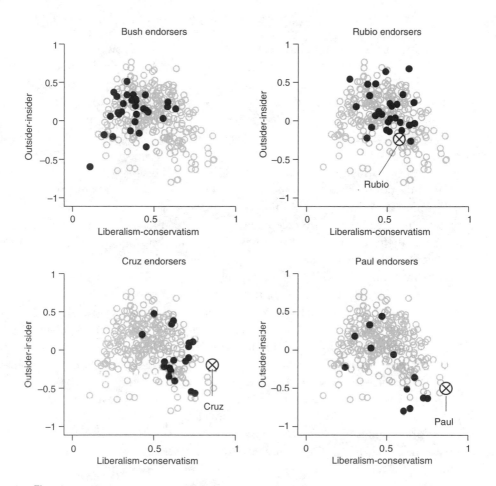

Figure 3.3.
The ideological location of presidential candidate endorsers in Congress.
The graph includes pre-Iowa endorsements by Senators and House members in
the 114th Congress. "Liberalism-conservatism" is measured with first-dimension
NOMINATE scores and "outsider-insider" status with second-dimension NOMINATE
scores. Dark circles indicate endorsers and gray circles indicate other members of
Congress.

was the fund-raising of candidates like Carson and Cruz. Carson raised $82
million, mainly from a network of small donors, often solicited via direct
mail and telemarketing. Cruz raised $143 million through a network of both
smaller donors and wealthy conservatives. Ultimately, campaign cash in 2016
resembled the endorsements: neither clearly favored a single presumptive
nominee. The pattern looked different in 2012, when both the early money
and endorsements suggested Romney was the front-runner.[32]

The upshot of the 2016 invisible primary was that party insiders could not identify one single candidate who stood above the others on both criteria: satisfactory on the issues and electable in November. This was different from four years earlier, when 2011 polls of Republican activists and party officials in Iowa, New Hampshire, and South Carolina showed that few candidates or potential candidates were viewed more favorably on both criteria compared to the eventual nominee, Romney—including Sarah Palin, Michele Bachmann, Newt Gingrich, and Rick Perry.[33]

In 2015, however, the picture was muddier. In a July 2015 national survey of the most politically active Republican voters, majorities or near majorities believed that Walker (61%), Rubio (58%), Bush (57%), Carson (47%), Perry (42%), and Cruz (40%) were acceptable to most Republicans. They were less confident in these candidates' ability to win the general election, but a majority believed that Walker or Rubio could win. Notably, only about a quarter said that Trump was acceptable to most Republicans or could win the November election. Ultimately, there seemed to be more candidates who could be acceptable to most party factions and capable of winning the general election—and no one candidate was the first choice of more than 18 percent of these activists. This presaged Republicans' struggle to identify an alternative to Trump once he was leading.[34]

Despite this indecision, the invisible primary still had some of its traditional consequences. It began the winnowing process, as five Republican candidates dropped out between September and December 2015: Jindal, Graham, Pataki, Perry, and Walker. Walker was the most surprising. Early in the campaign, he was described as "having a moment." But in the first debate, on August 6, 2015, Walker turned in what was deemed a "tentative performance," which in turn led to anemic fund-raising. His performance in the second debate was described as "not the breakthrough moment his supporters had hoped to see." His campaign had built a large operation that now it could not fund. Walker decided that he would not run "a deficit campaign."[35]

But even with the field narrowing, the party's factionalism made it harder for any single candidate to "win" the invisible primary. For a candidate like Trump, there was an opportunity that long-shot candidates in most previous primaries did not have. Republican voters had received no clear signal about who the front-runner was or should be.

The resulting uncertainty meant that this signal needed to come from somewhere else. It was news media coverage that would fill this void.

CHAPTER 4

"The Daily Donald Show"

Since I began covering presidential campaigns in 1980, I can think of nothing as unfair as the disproportionate media attention that has been lavished on Trump from the beginning.

—Walter Shapiro, *Roll Call*, January 14, 2016

It may not be good for America, but it's damn good for CBS.

—Les Moonves, chairman, president, and CEO of CBS Corporation

Someone watching CNN on the afternoon of March 19, 2016, would have seen an odd sight: an empty stage. It would eventually be the scene of a Donald Trump rally. But nothing was happening at that moment. The political commentator Josh Jordan tweeted, "Not only are the networks still covering the Trump rallies live and uninterrupted, they are showing the empty stage/ introductions live." *New York Times* reporter Jonathan Martin chimed in, tweeting, "How many Hillary events get this coverage?" His implication, of course, was that few did.[1]

This episode was not even the first time that week that cable news outlets had paid more attention to a Trump event, or even to the period before a Trump event, than to another candidate's event that was unfolding at the same time. Several days prior, cable networks did not carry a Bernie Sanders speech, instead featuring a panel of pundits while the chyron at the bottom of the screen said "AWAITING TRUMP" and "STANDING BY FOR TRUMP." And the week before, the same thing had happened to Hillary Clinton, whose speech was not aired in favor of extended coverage of a Trump press conference where he insulted other candidates and reporters and promoted Trump-branded steaks, wine, vodka, and water.[2]

This attention to Trump was hardly unusual. Trump dominated news coverage almost from the moment he entered the race, and news coverage helped make him the front-runner among Republican voters—even while he remained anathema to most Republican leaders. Trump did it by providing what news organizations and consumers wanted. He eschewed anodyne talking points and hackneyed anecdotes for braggadocio, verbal fisticuffs, and controversial policy stands. All of this made Trump consistently newsworthy. His Republican opponents often found themselves struggling for airtime, except when they tangled with Trump.

Trump was also helped by the focus of news coverage. Although some news stories scrutinized Trump's record and questioned his views on policy, more prevalent was typical "horse race" coverage of an unusual candidate beating the odds—or a "winner," as Trump might have said. Changing this narrative would have necessitated extraordinary measures from Trump's opponents. But instead of attacking Trump, they mainly sat on their hands, or perhaps clasped them to pray that Trump would simply go away. There were not sustained attacks on Trump until late in the primary campaign. Meanwhile, many party leaders continued to equivocate about an alternative to Trump, rallying only late to Marco Rubio.

The irony is that Trump was not invulnerable. Several of his controversial remarks hurt him with Republican voters, and as of the start of the caucuses and primaries, he was not even the most liked Republican candidate. But months of dominating the news with little pushback from his opponents left Trump at the front of the pack. From there, it was a relatively easy path to the nomination.

Conferring Status

The centrality of news coverage to presidential nominations is nothing new. The reforms that elevated the importance of voters' choices in primaries and caucuses made any channel of communication with voters more important. In 1983, the political scientist Nelson Polsby argued that "the proliferation of primaries weakens the influence of state and local politicians on the choice of delegates and increases the influence of the news media." This is particularly true when politicians and other party leaders do not send clear signals about the preferred nominee, as in 2016. It has become even truer as news coverage of the early invisible primary has increased.[3]

Clear signals are important because nominations often present a challenging task for voters. There can be lots of candidates, some of whom are familiar only to political cognoscenti. How, then, is a voter to know which candidates are "good"? Which candidates have adequate experience? Which candidates have beliefs that a voter shares? Which candidates can win the general election? Voters need information to answer these questions, and news coverage helps to supply it.

Scholars have long noted the importance of the media in situations very much like a presidential primary. In a classic 1948 paper, Paul Lazarsfeld and Robert Merton described how the media can "confer status" on individuals: "The mass media bestow prestige and enhance the authority of individuals and groups by legitimizing their status. Recognition by the press or radio or magazines or newsreels testifies that one has arrived, that one is important enough to have been singled out from the large anonymous masses, that one's behavior and opinions are significant enough to require public notice."[4] News coverage of primary elections today performs this precise function. Candidates who meet standards of "newsworthiness" garner coverage. Because news coverage of campaigns typically focuses on the horse race—which candidates are winning and losing, their campaign strategies, and the like—candidates will earn more coverage when they raise large sums of money or do unexpectedly well in preelection polls or early primaries and caucuses. News coverage also features events that are novel—such as when a candidate first announces his or her candidacy—and episodes that make for good stories, with compelling characters and conflicts. When candidates succeed by any of these metrics, even if they have been largely ignored to that point, they will be suddenly "discovered" by media outlets and, therefore, by the public. Their poll numbers will increase. For example, in the 2012 Republican primary, businessman Herman Cain's unexpected victory in a nonbinding straw poll of Florida Republicans catapulted him into the news, as news outlets judged this largely meaningless event a surprise "upset" over then-front-runner Rick Perry. Cain's poll numbers spiked.[5]

Of course, good poll numbers themselves justify further news coverage, which can create a self-reinforcing cycle. But for many candidates, this cycle is broken by coverage that is negative. New front-runners tend to attract additional scrutiny from news outlets, which seek to learn more about candidates who previously have been covered little if at all. For Cain, this meant scrutiny of his political views and coverage of accusations of sexual harassment and marital infidelity.

Many primary candidates, then, experience a cycle of "discovery, scrutiny, and decline" as their poll numbers fall, often for good. The decline can be the direct result of the scrutiny, but it is also sometimes the result of the next candidate's "discovery." To be sure, not every candidate may experience this cycle. Some are never discovered and languish in obscurity. Others, like Mitt Romney in 2012, have already been "discovered"—Romney had run in 2008—and never experience sharp ups or downs in news coverage or polls for much of the primary season.

In the 2016 Republican primary, the conditions described by Lazarsfeld and Merton were very much in place. A seventeen-candidate field is pretty close to a "large anonymous mass," which makes "singling out" all the more important. One candidate—Trump—benefited the most.

"He Made Great Copy"

Two sources of data show Trump's dominance of news coverage in the 2016 primaries. The first consists of stories collected from a set of twenty-four prominent news outlets, including major broadcast television networks (CBS, NBC, ABC, and PBS), cable news networks (CNN, Fox, and MSNBC), radio (National Public Radio and the *Hugh Hewitt Show*), websites (*Huffington Post*, *Politico*, and *Breitbart*), and twelve of the country's largest newspapers.[6] The social analytics firm Crimson Hexagon collected all stories that both mentioned at least one Republican candidate's name and used the phrase "presidential campaign." As a shorthand, call these data "news stories."

The second source of data consists of all mentions of the Republican presidential candidates that aired on a set of national cable networks: Al Jazeera America, Bloomberg, CNBC, CNN, Comedy Central, Fox Business, Fox News, LinkTV, and MSNBC. Although this set of outlets is perhaps less diverse, using mentions of the candidates within stories rather than the stories themselves allows us to measure more carefully the volume of attention each candidate received. These data stem from a partnership between the Internet Archive's Television News Archive and the GDELT (Global Database of Events, Language, and Tone) Project.[7] As a shorthand, call these data "cable mentions."

The most striking thing is how much coverage Trump received (figure 4.1). From May 1, 2015, to April 30, 2016, Trump's median share of cable mentions was 52 percent. In other words, he received about half of the mentions, on average, and the other Republican candidates split the rest. In the 305 days between July 1, 2015, and April 30, 2016, Trump received the most cable mentions on 295 of them. Trump was mentioned in about 25 percent of the "news stories," on average, and had the highest share of coverage for 280 of the 305 days. This 25 percent figure may undercount the attention Trump received because the news story data do not capture how much of the story focused on Trump as opposed to other candidates. It may also be true that cable net-

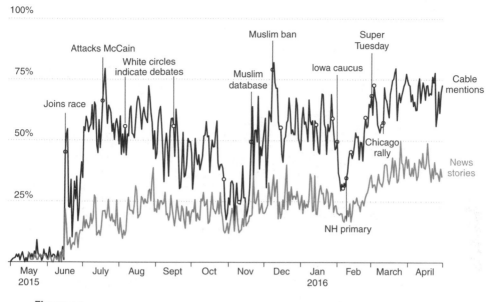

Figure 4.1.
Donald Trump's share of news coverage during the Republican primary.
White circles indicate debates.
Source: Internet Archive and GDELT; Crimson Hexagon.

works had a stronger incentive to devote attention to Trump, given the need to attract audiences across many hours of programming. But in both sources of data, Trump's dominance of coverage is clear.[8]

News coverage of Trump was powerfully correlated with his standing in national polls (figure 4.2). After smoothing both trends to remove day-to-day noise and focus on the underlying signal, the correlation was 0.94. (The maximum possible correlation is 1.0.) The correlation between Trump's poll standing and share of cable mentions was also high (0.80).[9]

Of course, this raises the question, Was the news driving Trump's poll numbers, or were Trump's poll numbers driving the news, or perhaps some of both? There is no doubt that the initial spike in Trump's poll numbers was driven by news coverage (see figure 4.2). Americans do not change their minds about a candidate for no reason or absent new information. In a YouGov/ *Economist* poll conducted between June 13 and June 15, 2015—immediately before Trump's announcement—only 2 percent of Republican registered voters supported him. In a YouGov/*Economist* poll conducted one week later, 11 percent did. But as the campaign proceeded, there was influence in both directions—from news coverage to poll numbers, and from poll numbers to news coverage. This is true for Trump and the other Republican candidates.

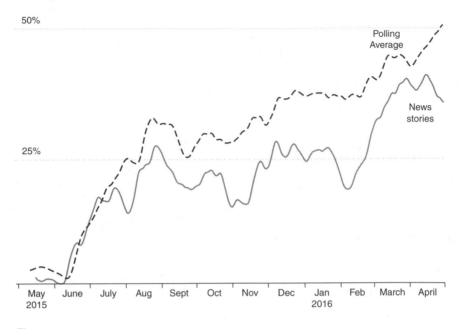

Figure 4.2.
Trends in Donald Trump's national polling average and news coverage.
Both trends have been smoothed using lowess (bandwidth = 0.05). This makes each
day's value roughly a three-week centered average, with days further "away" in that
three-week period counting for less than days closer to the day in question.
Source: Crimson Hexagon; Pollster.

Voters depend on the news for signals as to which candidates deserve attention and support—and, in turn, news outlets calibrate their coverage based
in part on how well candidates are doing in the polls. For Trump, his rise was
facilitated by the volume of coverage that he received, and the volume of
coverage was in turn influenced by Republican voters' increasing affinity
for him.[10]

    Why did Trump receive so much coverage? One answer is the self-
reinforcing cycle of news coverage and polls, but this is only part of the story.
After all, other candidates experienced that same cycle, albeit briefly. Another
part of the story is how Trump expertly played to the economic incentives
and news values of media outlets. News organizations are part of for-profit
companies, and Trump was good for business. The news media value things
that make for "good stories"—interesting characters, novelty, drama, conflict,
and controversy—and Trump supplied those in spades.[11] Indeed, Trump had
long understood how to generate news coverage. As he wrote in *The Art of*

the Deal, "Bad publicity is sometimes better than no publicity at all. Controversy, in short, sells."[12]

For years, Trump's exploits had been judged newsworthy. This began with his early business dealings and romantic relationships—for example, he was on the cover of the *New York Times Magazine* in 1984—and it continued when NBC gave him his own reality television show. Before he ran for president, news outlets, especially Fox News, put Trump on the air and helped validate him as a political figure. During the campaign, some commentators argued that Trump's preexisting celebrity means that news coverage could not have helped him that much. "The media didn't create Trump," the argument went. In fact, no person becomes a celebrity *without* media coverage. As one former New York tabloid writer, Susan Mulcahy, put it, "I helped make the myth of Donald Trump. We didn't see it at the time, but item by inky item we were turning him into a New York icon." Neil Barsky, who covered Trump's business career in the 1980s and 1990s as a reporter at the *Wall Street Journal,* said, "Then and now, we in the media helped enable the Trump myth. He made great copy. Early on, I noticed that any article I wrote about him—whether for the tabloid Daily News or the serious Wall Street Journal—would get great play. This invariably led me and others to dig deeper for Trump news."[13]

Trump's celebrity status ensured that the announcement of his candidacy would get more coverage than that of a more obscure candidate, even one with more conventional credentials. On the day Trump announced his candidacy, he was mentioned in 22 percent of these news stories and received 45 percent of the mentions of the Republican candidates on these cable networks. This spike was larger than what most other candidates received after their announcements, which may reflect the controversy that Trump stirred with his remarks that day, including a reference to "rapists" coming from Mexico.[14] This was Trump's moment of "discovery"—not in the literal sense but rather as a candidate for the nomination.

Once he was in the race, Trump was focused on getting the coverage he was accustomed to getting before running for president. There was some irony here, given that in 1980 Trump had said that television was bad for politics ("It's hurt the process very much"). But as a candidate, Trump sought media attention and monitored television coverage especially closely. One reporter chronicled how Trump spent most of a three-hour flight watching himself on television—flipping around the channels, judging cable news pundits based on whether they supported him, and commenting on rebroadcasts of his own speeches ("very presidential"). Trump also made himself available to media outlets in a way that other candidates would not.[15]

But arguably what mattered more than Trump's sheer availability was what he said on air. As one CNN source put it, "He'll throw a hand grenade in, and then will come on to talk to us about it."[16] The "grenades" reflected Trump's penchant for the controversial remarks and blistering attacks that aligned with news values such as novelty, drama, and conflict. Many spikes in coverage were not the result of Trump simply sitting for an interview but rather a consequence of what he had said specifically. For example, Trump's comments about "rapists" from Mexico led to a second round of news coverage in late June as corporations began severing their business relationships with him. Univision announced that it would not air the Miss USA or Miss Universe pageants, both produced by Trump. NBC announced that it would no longer air the pageants or Trump's show *The Apprentice*. Macy's dropped his clothing line. Naturally, Trump fired back on Twitter: "Why doesn't somebody study the horrible charges brought against @Macys for racial profiling? Terrible hypocrites!"[17]

The dustup with Macy's was, by the standards of Trump controversies, a relatively minor one. On July 18, Trump criticized Republican senator John McCain, who as a navy pilot in the Vietnam War had spent five harrowing years in Vietnamese prisons after his plane was shot down and he was captured. Trump said, "He's not a war hero. He's a war hero because he was captured. I like people who weren't captured." This drew widespread condemnation, including from many Republicans.[18] Two days after his comment, Trump commanded nearly 80 percent of the cable network mentions of the candidates (figure 4.1).

In the first televised debate, on August 6, 2015, Trump tangled with Fox News' Megyn Kelly, who was helping to moderate the debate and asked Trump a pointed question about his previous insults of women, such as "fat pigs." After the debate, Trump attacked Kelly, saying, "There was blood coming out of her eyes, blood coming out of her wherever"—a remark interpreted as implying that Kelly was menstruating. Trump's share of coverage shot up: on cable networks, from 44 percent the day before the debate to 64 percent five days later.

This pattern repeated itself. Trump would say something controversial, inflammatory, or insulting, and he would receive a spike in coverage. A week after terrorist attacks in Paris on November 13, 2015, Trump appeared to endorse a database of Muslims living in the United States, although at other times he suggested that the database would be for refugees from countries like Syria. After a terrorist attack in San Bernardino, California, on December 2, Trump went further, calling for a "total and complete shutdown of Muslims entering the United States"—a proposal that, again, attracted strong bipartisan criticism and, again, substantial news coverage.[19]

Over and over again, Trump's comments allowed him to, as Fox News anchor Bret Baier put it, "contort the day's media stories." Waiting for the next grenade, cable television outlets not only covered Trump rallies, and even the empty stage beforehand, but at times acquiesced to Trump's demands about how he was covered—allowing him to call in rather than appear in person and even dictate camera placement at his events. In short, a political junkie could do what Trump did himself: binge-watch the Trump campaign in real time.[20]

Those decisions occasioned not a little hand-wringing, including within the media. But it was harder to argue with the consequences: viewers, ratings, and profits. Ratings may have led Fox News to make peace with Trump after he attacked Megyn Kelly: Fox News hosts were worried their ratings would suffer if Trump boycotted the network. Other news executives were even more forthcoming about the economic value of covering Trump. Jim VandeHei, formerly of *Politico*, said that Trump was "great box office." CNN president Jeff Zucker "was beaming," according to one news report, and described the network's ratings by saying, "These numbers are crazy—crazy." The numbers were why Leslie Moonves said, "It may not be good for America, but it's damn good for CBS."[21]

Journalists sometimes did not like the argument that news coverage gave Trump a boost. For example, *Politico*'s Jack Shafer seemed to vacillate between acknowledging that "the press helped 'create' the surge that has carried Trump to his current status as the Republican Party's front-runner" (September 2015) and constructing an elaborate straw man by which the media could only help a candidate if there was a "media conspiracy" or a "candidate-promoting media cabal" (March 2016).[22] But there need not be any cabal at all—only a set of news outlets that, though not identical, made many decisions based on a common set of economic incentives and news values. In 2016, those incentives and values aligned nicely, and Donald Trump was the beneficiary.

Gasping for Air

And what about the other candidates? The reporter McKay Coppins put it well: "the daily Donald show sucked up the media oxygen," and "the rest of the Republican presidential candidates were left desperately gasping for air."[23] Most other candidates had, at best, limited success garnering news coverage and benefiting from the consequent rise in their poll numbers. This was often because the coverage was temporary, driven by one-off events like a good debate performance or a good poll in Iowa. The other candidates also faced this conundrum: they often made the most news because of a confrontation with Trump. Sometimes this happened when a candidate tried, usually unsuccessfully, to beat Trump at his own game of controversy and insults. At other times, Trump initiated the confrontation. Either way, the news environment revolved around Trump.

Trump's advantage is visible, for example, in cable network mentions of him and four of his competitors: Ben Carson, Jeb Bush, Rubio, and Ted Cruz (figure 4.3). Only Carson made a real dent in coverage of Trump, but not for long. Carson's trajectory was emblematic of "discovery, scrutiny, and decline."[24] After an initial spike in coverage when he announced his candidacy, Carson received little coverage until a spike in his Iowa poll numbers after an early blitz of television advertisements there. This constituted the "discovery" of Carson, and by the end of September, Carson was polling second behind Trump and occasionally even ahead of him. There was talk of Carson's "quiet surge."[25]

Then the scrutiny began. There was coverage of controversies involving Carson—such as when he said, "I would not advocate that we put a Muslim in charge of this nation." There was also scrutiny of Carson's record. Reporters noted his tenuous grasp of policy and questioned aspects of his biography, such as his claim that as a youth he tried to stab a friend in the stomach only to have the friend's belt buckle deflect the knife, or his claim he had received a "full scholarship" from West Point, even though he had never applied to the military academy, which does not give full scholarships anyway. At this point, Carson's coverage exceeded that of Trump for several days. Then came the decline. Carson received less news coverage. His polling numbers dropped. At the beginning of 2016, Carson overhauled his campaign, but he never performed exceptionally well in a caucus or primary and dropped out of the race on March 4, 2016.[26]

Meanwhile, Jeb Bush's campaign never lived up to the potential suggested by his pedigree, experience, and fund-raising. Bush stumbled in May 2015 when he struggled to say whether in hindsight he would have supported the Iraq War, which was begun and championed by his brother. One news report said, "Jeb Bush had a terrible, horrible, no good, very bad week." On the day he announced his candidacy in June, some reporting said that Bush was "sorely lacking in pep" and that "the ordeal" of campaigning "was wearing on him." Later Trump called Bush "low energy," a charge that was amplified by news accounts noting—and thereby ensuring—that this attack "stuck to Bush like glue." In fact, Bush's largest spike in news coverage came when he and Trump feuded after Trump criticized George W. Bush because the 9/11 attacks had occurred on his watch. By late fall, Bush's fund-raising and poll standing were ebbing. One news report summed it up: "No more 'shock and awe.'" At a campaign stop a week before the New Hampshire

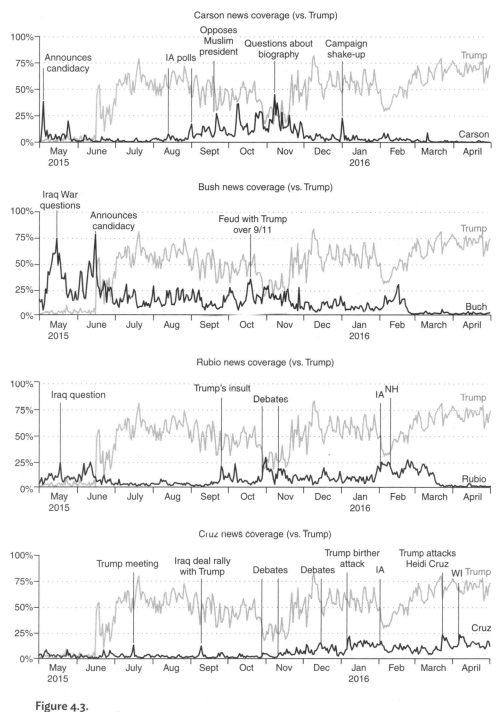

Figure 4.3.
Republican candidates' shares of cable mentions.
Sources: Internet Archive and GDELT.

primary, Bush resorted to asking his audience for applause, saying, "Please clap." He ultimately placed fourth. A late campaign stop by George W. Bush made little difference in the South Carolina primary. On February 20, Bush dropped out of the race. In March, he endorsed Ted Cruz.[27]

Trump's ability to dominate news coverage was a particular problem for Marco Rubio. His campaign was predicated less on building a top-notch ground campaign that could mobilize existing Rubio supporters and more on using news coverage—"free" media—to persuade voters to support him. His campaign used quantitative data and statistical models to determine the media markets where Rubio should schedule visits, in hopes that these visits would generate local news coverage and, ultimately, additional vote share and delegates. Trump upended all of that, preventing Rubio from getting the coverage his campaign was depending on.[28]

Like Bush, Rubio had early stumbles. Rubio also struggled to explain his position on the Iraq War—which the *Washington Post*'s Chris Cillizza called "the most painful 180 seconds of Marco Rubio's presidential campaign so far." Rubio faced scrutiny for his finances, including the patronage of a wealthy Florida businessman, and even his speeding tickets—creating spikes of coverage in June as these stories broke. Then, again like Bush, Rubio received less coverage and saw his poll numbers drop thanks to Trump's entry in the race. Rubio rebounded when his performances in the fall debates were judged favorably. He even appeared to benefit from a tangle with Trump, who criticized Rubio during a speech at the September 25 Values Voters Summit ("this clown, Marco Rubio") only to be booed. By the end of November, Rubio's poll numbers were back to where they were in May.[29]

Rubio then showed that something other than Ben Carson could knock Trump out of the news, at least relatively speaking: losing. In the Iowa caucus, Rubio beat the expectations set by late polls, while Trump underperformed. By placing second to Cruz while Trump came in third, Rubio got a bump in coverage and in his national poll numbers. Trump's share of news coverage dropped sharply. Rubio's odds of winning the nomination in the prediction markets jumped from 33 percent to 60 percent.[30]

However, Rubio struggled to build on this momentum—even though, finally, some Republican leaders got off the sidelines and endorsed him. After Iowa, Rubio picked up forty additional endorsements from Republican senators, governors, and members of the House, while Cruz picked up twenty-five and Trump picked up fifteen. This gave Rubio sixty-six total endorsements, which was more than any other candidate. But in the debate immediately before the New Hampshire primary, Chris Christie attacked Rubio for repeating scripted talking points—something Rubio then proceeded to do moments later by repeatedly using the exact same attack line against Barack

Obama. Christie's attack, plus others, led to headlines like "Did Marco Rubio Squander His Big Moment?"[31] Of course, headlines like that are often self-fulfilling prophecies, and Rubio ended up finishing fourth in the primary while Trump won handily. His news coverage then dropped, as did his polling numbers—from 15 percent to 10 percent in Morning Consult surveys conducted before and after the primary. Rubio rebounded somewhat, coming in second in the South Carolina primary and Nevada caucus, but on Super Tuesday, he won only one of the eleven contests. His polling numbers began to slide, and there was no obvious way for him to eat into Trump's delegate lead. After finishing a distant second to Trump in Rubio's own home state of Florida, he dropped out on March 15, 2016.

The experience of Ted Cruz also illustrated how candidates often needed to engage with Trump to get substantial news coverage. Early on, Cruz got little coverage except when he and Trump met on July 16—Cruz complimented Trump, saying, "Donald and I are friends," and, "I like Donald because he's brash, he's bold, and he speaks the truth"—and when he and Trump both spoke at a rally denouncing the Obama administration's deal to limit Iran's nuclear program. Cruz seemed to believe that if he made nice with Trump, he could win over Trump's supporters if Trump bowed out. When both spoke out against the Iran nuclear deal, they were described as having a "relatively cozy relationship."[32]

But that would change as Cruz's poll standing increased after his performances in the fall debates were judged favorably. Indeed, Cruz's experience showed that the debates often produced news coverage for other candidates more than for Trump. This was ironic, given that the Republican National Committee—no friend of Trump's—had reduced the number of primary debates, hoping to make the eventual nominee's path smoother. By December, there were headlines like "It's Cruz, Not Trump, Who Looks More like the Favorite to Win the GOP Nomination." Then two predictable things happened. One was additional scrutiny from the news media, such as about Cruz's unpopularity among his Senate colleagues. The other was attacks from Trump—and therefore more surges in coverage of Cruz. In early January, Cruz got news coverage because Trump questioned his citizenship status. (Cruz was born in Calgary to a Cuban father and American mother, making him a U.S. citizen by birth.) Trump later suggested that Cruz's father, Rafael, was somehow involved in a conspiracy to kill President John F. Kennedy. On March 23, after a group supporting Cruz made a campaign ad that featured an old photo of a scantily clad Melania Trump, Trump himself tweeted, "Be careful, Lyin' Ted, or I will spill the beans on your wife," to which Cruz replied via Twitter, "Donald, if you try to attack Heidi, you're more of a coward than I thought."[33]

Despite the scrutiny and attacks, Cruz had some successes, winning eleven caucuses and primaries. After Carson's withdrawal, Cruz consolidated a bit more support. His poll numbers hit 25 percent, and he won a few more primaries, most notably in Wisconsin. But despite these wins, and despite gambits like announcing Carly Fiorina as his running mate were he nominated, Cruz fell further and further behind Trump in the delegate count. Along with John Kasich, he was one of the last two candidates standing, and Cruz and Kasich even discussed a coordinated strategy to deny Trump the nomination. But the plan never came to fruition. Cruz withdrew his candidacy on May 3, as did Kasich the following day.[34]

Ultimately, the experiences of the Republican candidates other than Trump showed that it was possible to get media attention and chip away at Trump's dominance of the news and his lead in the polls. But this was often fleeting—the result of short-lived coverage of a debate or some other horse race metric. Moreover, several candidates experienced notable spikes in news coverage only because Trump had attacked them, showing again how reliably he could set the media's agenda.

Did Trump Receive Too Much Coverage?

Trump's dominance of news coverage gave rise to a heated debate about whether he received too much coverage. Certainly his Republican opponents thought so. In December 2015, Jeb Bush told reporters that Trump was playing them "like a fine Stradivarius violin," and John Kasich said, "Well, look, when the media just constantly drools over him and when he's—if I were on television as much as he was, I'd probably have 50 percent of the vote." Right before he dropped out, Ted Cruz said that "network executives have made a decision to get behind Donald Trump. Rupert Murdoch and Roger Ailes at Fox News have turned Fox News into the Donald Trump network." Ailes had already validated Cruz's point a few weeks prior, saying, "Did he get too much coverage? Yes." And others in the media agreed. CNN's Brian Stelter said, "Trump is the media's addiction. When he speaks, he is given something no other candidate gets. That's wall-to-wall coverage here on cable news. He sucks up all the oxygen." A *New York Times* headline described the challenge succinctly: "Television Networks Struggle to Provide Equal Airtime in the Era of Trump."[35]

There is no easy way to determine whether Trump got "too much" news coverage. One possible way to answer this is to compare 2016 to previous presidential primaries, but any comparison is complicated by differences in these elections in the number of candidates, their respective viability, and the competitiveness of the race—as well as by dramatic changes in the news media over time.

Nevertheless, several such comparisons suggest that Trump received an unusually large share of news coverage. For example, one study of the 1976–2000 presidential primaries counted every mention of the candidates in broadcast news coverage in both the year before the primaries and during the primary season itself. Across those elections, only one candidate garnered more than 50 percent of the mentions—Al Gore in 2000, who received 64 percent of mentions when he was one of only two candidates in the Democratic primary and coasted to an easy victory over his opponent, Bill Bradley. Other candidates who were somewhat close to 50 percent were Bob Dole in 1996 (48%) and George W. Bush in 2000 (42%). In the 2012 Republican primary, the most-covered candidate, Romney, received only 30 percent of mentions in news coverage.[36]

By comparison, between May 1, 2015, and April 30, 2016, Trump received 54 percent of the total cable network mentions. One thing that distinguishes Gore, Dole, and Bush from Trump is that they were dominant front-runners based on their support among party leaders. Even Romney was in a far stronger position than Trump. And these candidates were facing a smaller field too. That Trump received a level of coverage that was comparable if not greater—even though the 2016 field was larger, even though his early support in the party was weak, even though the 2016 race lacked a front-runner and was thus far more unsettled—suggests that he received an unusual amount of news coverage. In essence, Trump received the coverage a dominant front-runner usually receives, even though he was not one.

But perhaps Trump received more coverage simply because he was polling better, relative to his competitors, than did candidates in earlier primaries. However, in the last six months of 2015, Trump's share of newspaper coverage (54%) was much larger than his share of the polls (32%)—and the discrepancy was among the largest observed in any primary since 1980.[37] Of course, it is expected and arguably defensible that news coverage favors candidates who are polling well over those at the back of the pack. But Trump's share of coverage exceeded what his polling alone predicted.

How Negative Was Coverage of Trump?

Critics of the argument that news coverage helped Trump sometimes argued that the coverage was mostly negative and therefore could not have helped Trump. *Politico*'s Jack Shafer wrote, "Most of the attention directed toward Trump has been negative, speaking to his personal weaknesses, his professional weaknesses and his policy weaknesses." Certainly, Trump's ability to dominate news coverage did not mean that the news coverage was always positive. There were many examples of news coverage that scrutinized not only Trump's controversial remarks but also his personal life and business record.[38] But was "most of the attention directed toward Trump" negative? It is far from clear that it was.

During the campaign itself, numerous political commentators and writers raised the concern that Trump was not being scrutinized enough. Marc Ambinder said that the media "didn't take Trump seriously" and "didn't publicly vet him aggressively." *Vox*'s Ezra Klein described how Trump's rhetoric on taxes "fooled the media for a while." *Buzzfeed*'s Ben Smith fumed about the media's reporting Trump's (false) claim that he did not initially support the Iraq War. National Public Radio's David Folkenflik, who covers the news media, characterized coverage of Trump as "typically reactive and as a result generally insubstantial" and further argued that we "can't say coverage by most outlets treated Trump w[ith] sufficient thoroughness/seriousness."[39]

Moreover, three sources of data suggested that coverage of Trump was not particularly negative, either overall or relative to other candidates. First, for the news articles collected by Crimson Hexagon (see figure 4.1), the firm coded the overall tone of each article—how positive or negative it was—based on the general valence of words used in the article. The articles mentioning Trump were not systematically more negative than articles mentioning other candidates. However, many articles mentioned more than one candidate, making it harder to identify how Trump was covered.[40]

Second, *FiveThirtyEight*'s Nate Silver examined the most prominent articles in political news coverage between June 2015 and March 2016. Prominence was captured by the volume of links to the story from other news organizations, meaning that these were the stories that the news media itself considered most important. When those articles were about the GOP primary, Trump was the subject of the large majority (68%)—consistent with his overall dominance of news coverage. In these stories, however, the coverage was not necessarily unfavorable to Trump. The most popular topic was Trump's poll numbers. There were twice as many stories focused on polling as on Trump's controversial remarks. None of these leading stories was an investigative piece. These polling stories also tended to emphasize Trump's popularity. Typically, horse race coverage of campaigns, which focuses on metrics like poll numbers, will be positive for any candidate succeeding by those metrics. Thus, although these prominent news stories certainly contained valuable reporting—including into the views of Republican leaders alarmed by Trump's rise—a substantial number of these stories would not qualify as scrutiny and could even be considered positive for Trump.[41]

A third analysis of news coverage during the invisible primary reached a similar conclusion. This analysis was based on a collaboration between Harvard University's Shorenstein Center on Media, Politics and Public Policy and the firm Media Tenor, which employed trained human coders to categorize the topic and tone of hundreds of stories from eight major news outlets. In these stories, most Trump coverage was positive or neutral in tone and for the same reason identified in Silver's analysis: many stories were about horse race metrics. As the report's author, Thomas Patterson, noted, "The overall media portrayal of a 'gaining ground' candidate is a positive one." Even coverage of Trump's issue positions and personal characteristics—the very things that commentators believed needed more scrutiny—was often positive in tone because of favorable quotes from Trump supporters.[42]

None of this means that there was no important, thoughtful, or revealing reporting about Trump. Nevertheless, horse race stories were most prominent in news coverage and were arguably favorable to Trump's rise and dominance as the front-runner. As the *Washington Post*'s Dana Milbank put it, "News organizations apply to him the same type of horse-race reporting that they do to conventional candidates, driven by polls, defining who's up and who's down, who won the news cycle and who lost. Trump's moves are often described as 'brilliant.'"[43]

"Teflon Don"

Had Trump been scrutinized more rigorously, would it have made any difference? During the campaign, some commentators said that it would not. Trump was supposedly "unattackable," a "Teflon" candidate or a "Teflon Don" to whom no controversy would stick.[44] However, Trump's popularity among Republican voters *was* affected by the scrutiny that he did receive or brought on himself. Even though Trump had been a celebrity for a long time, people had not made up their minds about him. Opinions among Republican primary voters changed during the primary, and not always in Trump's favor.

Trump's "net favorability"—the percentage of Republicans with a favorable view of him minus the percentage with an unfavorable view—improved in the six polls after he announced his candidacy (figure 4.4). His net favorable rating increased from 0 (43% favorable, 43% unfavorable) to 27 (57% favorable, 30% unfavorable). This shows that views of Trump were not fixed in stone just because he was a celebrity. Republicans quickly warmed to him, despite the initial controversy surrounding his remarks about immigration.

But Trump's standing did suffer after other controversies. After his remark about John McCain's war record, his net favorable rating among Republicans dropped 16 points—despite Trump's later claim that his poll

Percent favorable minus percent unfavorable

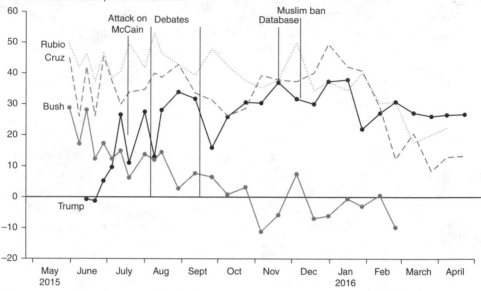

Figure 4.4.
Net favorable rating of Republican candidates among Republicans.
Net favorability is calculated as the percentage of Republicans with a favorable view
of a candidate minus the percentage with an unfavorable view.
Source: YouGov polls.

numbers had increased after he made this remark. His poll numbers also dropped after the August 6 debate, where he tangled with Megyn Kelly, as well as the September 16 debate. His poll numbers dropped again later in January, right about when he boycotted a Republican primary debate, leaving his rivals to poke fun at him for the night.[45] To be sure, Trump's standing with Republicans did not suffer much from certain controversies. Trump suffered at best a small drop in popularity after his proposals for a database of Muslims and a temporary ban on Muslims traveling to the United States. This is likely because Trump's proposals were not unpopular among Republican voters, many of whom did not have a favorable view of Muslims (see chapter 5). But it was entirely possible for controversy, and the resulting scrutiny, to hurt Trump's standing among Republican voters.

Two problems remained for those hoping to stop Trump. One was that many of these controversies were only in the news briefly. Nate Silver's study found that beginning in December 2015, no particular Trump story was prominent for more than about two days. The second, and arguably more important, problem for Trump opponents was that Trump led in most polls throughout the primary season even though he was not the most popular

Republican candidate. Trump's net favorable rating among Republicans, while better than that of the fading Jeb Bush, was lower than either Rubio's or Cruz's until the beginning of the caucuses and primaries.

"Other People's Problem"

If Trump was not "unattackable," the strategy for his Republican opponents was obvious: attack. But for the most part, Trump's foes did not do this. Just as many Republicans sat on their hands when it came to endorsing a candidate, many sat on their hands when it came to attacking a candidate they deemed anathema to the party's ideals. Without these attacks, there was less fodder for news coverage and less chance that potentially damning facts about Trump would be revealed early, when they could do the most damage.[46]

For one, few of Trump's primary opponents attacked him in the preprimary debates. According to a tabulation by the *National Journal*, there were only occasional shots at Trump from most of the candidates until the tenth debate, which took place on February 25, 2016, after Trump had already won decisively in New Hampshire, South Carolina, and Nevada. The notable exception was Jeb Bush. This was perhaps ironic: Bush was often viewed as out of his depth—ignorant of what modern campaigning entails and impotent in dealing with Trump. Indeed, back in 2012, Bush was complaining of "how immature and unstatesmanlike it was that these aspiring leaders of the free world were duking it out on Twitter with sarcastic hashtags and so-called memes." But for a long time, Bush was the only candidate routinely taking on Trump. The *National Journal* summed up the result in the headline "Donald Trump's Long, Easy Debate Ride."[47]

The same pattern emerged in candidate advertising. Initially, almost all the attack ads—those ads criticizing a candidate or criticizing a candidate while promoting the candidate sponsoring the ad—focused on candidates other than Trump (figure 4.5). It was, again, only after Trump's victories in South Carolina and Nevada that Trump's opponents—mainly Rubio and Cruz and their allied super PACs—began attacking Trump via paid advertising. This was yet another way in which Trump had a long, easy ride.

The decision to delay attacks on Trump seemed to reflect both indecision and miscalculation. Throughout the fall of 2015, Republican leaders repeatedly expressed concern about Trump's rise. The head of the National Republican Senatorial Committee, Ward Baker, called Trump a "misguided missile" who "is subject to farcical fits." Another leader likened a Trump nomination to a "hangover and then herpes."[48]

But despite this concern, there was little coordinated effort to take Trump down or settle on an alternative. From the *Washington Post*, November 13:

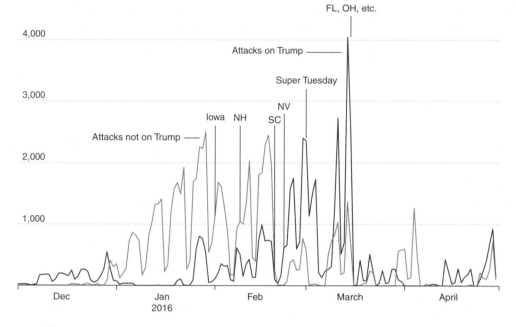

Figure 4.5.
Volume of Republican attack advertisements.
An attack ad is any ad that mentions another candidate in a critical fashion.
Source: Kantar Media/CMAG.

"The party establishment is paralyzed. Big money is still on the sidelines." The *Washington Post*, November 25: "Plan A for GOP Donors: Wait for Trump to Fall. (There Is No Plan B.)" The *New York Times*, December 1: "But in a party that lacks a true leader or anything in the way of consensus—and with the combative Mr. Trump certain to scorch anyone who takes him on—a fierce dispute has arisen about what can be done to stop his candidacy and whether anyone should even try." The *Washington Post*'s Chris Cillizza, December 7: "I asked one senior GOP strategist how the party establishment could somehow disarm Trump given his current status in the race and the lack of any leverage they have over the front-runner. His answer? 'Pray.'" *Buzzfeed*, January 14: "The Anti-Trump Calvary That Never Came." Party leaders were at such loose ends that they even considered drafting Romney as a late entry into the race.[49]

So why not simply denounce Trump? Some Republican leaders feared that taking down Trump would give rise to something even worse: the nomination of "Lucifer" himself, Ted Cruz. In January 2016, when Cruz was close on Trump's heels in Iowa polls, a spate of stories indicated the party's unease.

A *Politico* headline: "Trump and Cruz Send Shivers Down GOP Spines." The conservative commentator Michael Gerson: "For Republicans, the only good outcome of Trump vs. Cruz is for both to lose." Lindsey Graham likened the choice between Cruz and Trump to "being shot or poisoned." As one news account described it, "In Trump, most party leaders see a candidate who is unpredictable and controversial, but far less ideological than Cruz and, therefore, more likely to work with them. Several have reached out to Trump in recent weeks as their preferred candidates have stalled in the polls."[50]

All the while, the candidates were certainly attacking—but mainly each other, not Trump. Even after Cruz's "bromance" with Trump soured, most of his ads attacked or criticized candidates other than Trump, especially Marco Rubio. Before the Iowa caucus, 58 percent of Cruz's attack ads attacked Rubio, whereas only 24 percent attacked Trump. Rubio's strong finish in Iowa led Cruz to ratchet up the attacks: 76 percent of Cruz's attack ads that aired between Iowa and the New Hampshire primary targeted Rubio, as did 62 percent of his ads that aired between New Hampshire and the South Carolina primary. It was only after Trump's win in South Carolina that Cruz pivoted and began attacking Trump in earnest.

The so-called establishment candidates made a similar calculation. They apparently believed that they were each other's biggest threat, so they left Trump relatively unscathed. Right to Rise, Jeb Bush's super PAC, was sitting on the largest pile of money, but its chief, Mike Murphy, called Trump a "false zombie frontrunner" and said that Trump was "other people's problem." Instead, Murphy said that Bush needed to "consolidate" the supporters of the establishment candidates—the "regular Republican, positive-conservative lane." Bush's campaign had hatched a project called Homeland Security that sought to dig up dirt on Rubio.[51] On the airwaves, most of Bush's and Right to Rise's attack advertisements targeted Rubio. This included 62 percent of Bush's attack ads before the Iowa caucus and 87 percent that aired between the Iowa caucus and New Hampshire primary—exactly when Rubio was getting additional endorsements from Republican leaders and hoping to build on his good showing in Iowa.

Rubio's strategy was similar. His attack ads focused on Bush and to a lesser extent Cruz. Again, it was only after South Carolina that Rubio also began to take Trump on—but not without a significant backlash. At a rally on February 29, Rubio, whom Trump was calling "Little Marco," fired back by saying that Trump had a "spray tan" and "small hands." The latter, Rubio insinuated, meant that Trump had a small penis: "And you know what they say about guys with small hands . . ." This led to an exchange on the subject at the next Republican candidate debate, which CNN summarized with this headline: "Donald Trump Defends Size of His Penis." Commentators were aghast at what Bloomberg's Sasha Issenberg called Rubio's "declivitous descent into dick jokes." Only a few days later, Rubio backed down, saying that his children were "embarrassed" and that he was "not proud" of his comments. Rubio eventually apologized to Trump.[52]

The upshot is that Trump's path to the nomination was easier because his opponents helped make it so. This is all the more remarkable because Trump's major opponents had large, well-funded campaigns, whereas the Trump campaign was essentially the opposite of the sophisticated operation that the Republican National Committee's *Growth and Opportunity Project* report had recommended: Trump raised less money, struggled to recruit experienced staff, and was slow to do basic things like purchase voter files or build a field organization.[53] So Bush, Rubio, and Cruz could have used their advantage in fund-raising and television advertising to try to counter Trump's advantage in free media. Between December 1, 2015, and May 4, 2016—when the last of Trump's opponents dropped out—Trump aired about 33,000 ads, whereas Bush aired 39,000, Cruz aired 49,000, and Rubio aired 59,000. But the other candidates largely did not use their advantage to take on, or take down, Trump.

Conclusion

Of course, it is impossible to know what would have happened had Trump faced more attacks or earlier attacks. It is impossible to know what would have happened if Trump had received less attention from the news. Neither may have changed the outcome—particularly given how difficult it was for Republican leaders to coordinate on an alternative to Trump. However, it would be a mistake to treat Trump as a phenomenon that bubbled up purely from the grass roots. Trump's ability to command news coverage helped legitimate him as a serious candidate, enabled him to stand out in a crowded field, and gave Republican voters the signal that they were not getting from their party's leaders. The result was a significant divide between Republican voters and Republican leaders, few of whom supported Trump.

But neither a fractured field nor dominance of news coverage was enough for Trump to win. Not every candidate can build a durable coalition among Republican voters, even when they do get news coverage. (Ask Ben Carson.) That Trump could do so is even more remarkable given how late he came to the Republican Party. Trump's success in winning over voters illustrated another identity crisis—in this case, the Republican Party's.

CHAPTER 5

Hiding in Plain Sight

Our country is in serious trouble. . . .

When Mexico sends its people, they're not sending their best. They're not sending you. They're not sending you. They're sending people that have lots of problems, and they're bringing those problems with us. They're bringing drugs. They're bringing crime. They're rapists. And some, I assume, are good people. But I speak to border guards and they tell us what we're getting. And it only makes common sense. It only makes common sense. They're sending us not the right people. . . .

Save Medicare, Medicaid and Social Security without cuts. Have to do it.
—Donald Trump, announcing his candidacy on June 16, 2015

Donald Trump capitalized on a crowded Republican field and a party leadership that could not agree on any single alternative to him. He garnered massive news coverage, denying media oxygen to his competitors. He benefited when his Republican opponents underestimated his chances of winning and attacked him only late in the campaign. But which voters ultimately came to support him, and why?

Initially, Trump seemed an improbable candidate to appeal to Republican voters. He came lately to the party and to positions that were long-standing parts of the party's orthodoxy, such as opposition to abortion. On other issues, however, he rejected that orthodoxy outright and continued to do so throughout the campaign. Moreover, his personal life—his multiple marriages, his lack of any deep religious faith, his image as a Manhattan playboy—suggested he would alienate many Republicans, especially social conservatives.

One often-cited explanation for Trump's appeal—as well as that of other "outsider" candidates—was Republican voters' "anger." But anger is not an explanation. The question is what Republicans were angry about, and there was substantially less consensus on that question. Republicans were said to be angry about "the status quo," "traditional politics and politicians," Barack Obama, Republican leaders in Congress, "a concentration of wealth and power that leaves them holding the short end of the stick," and many, many other things.[1]

The reasons Republican primary voters came to support Trump were the direct consequence of what he campaigned on. A rich political science literature shows that the information voters acquire during a campaign can "activate"—or make more salient—their preexisting values, beliefs, and opinions. That is exactly how Trump won support: he activated long-standing sentiments among Republican voters—sentiments that were more prevalent among voters than among the Republican leaders that Trump often criticized. Trump simply went where many Republican voters were, despite denunciations from conservative intellectuals and party elders.

Trump's campaign message had three central themes, but two of them appeared to resonate most. The first—and least important—was dissatisfaction with politics and the economy. Although many Republicans were dissatisfied with aspects of both, such sentiments were less crucial to Trump's rise. Among Republican voters, Trump did not benefit much from any belief that ordinary people had little ability to influence politics. Trump did not appeal particularly to those who were less well off: most Trump supporters did not have low incomes or meet any conventional definition of "poor," and the size of people's incomes was not strongly related to whether they supported Trump or another Republican candidate. To the extent that economics mattered, Trump's support was tied more to people's economic dissatisfaction: how people felt rather than their actual income. But even economic dissatisfaction was secondary to other factors.

A more important factor was the liberalism on economic issues among Republican voters. Despite the caricature of Republicans and especially Republican primary voters, many are not conservative ideologues. For decades, they have maintained views about taxes and government programs that are moderate or even liberal. Although Republican leaders have pushed for lower taxes for wealthy Americans, reductions in discretionary spending, and far-reaching reforms to entitlement programs like Medicare and Social Security, many Republican voters have not followed along. Trump's heterodox opinions—such as "Save Medicare, Medicaid and Social Security without cuts"—appealed to these voters.

The final, and arguably most important, factor was attitudes about racial, ethnic, and religious groups and racially charged issues. As these attitudes became increasingly aligned with Americans' party identification (chapter 2), more Republican voters expressed views of blacks, Muslims, and immigration that were in line with Trump's views. On immigration in particular, the Republican electorate has for decades been less supportive than Republican leaders. Many Republicans also express a shared identity with white people and think whites are being treated unfairly relative to minority groups. All of these attitudes were strongly associated with support for Trump—and in ways that they were not associated with support for his Republican opponents or the party's recent presidential nominees. It was not the voters who changed in 2016 so much as the choices they were given.

Indeed, the importance of economic insecurity was most apparent when economic sentiments were refracted through group identities. Worries about losing a job were less strongly associated with Trump support than were concerns about whites losing jobs to minorities. There was a powerful idea that "my group"—in this case, white Americans—was suffering because other groups, such as immigrants or minorities, were getting benefits that they did not deserve. This idea, which was common among Republican voters, also predated Trump. He just leveraged it to his advantage.

Ultimately, Trump built a coalition that transcended some of the party's traditional divides. This caught many observers and Republican leaders by surprise, but the roots of Trump's appeal were hiding in plain sight. He capitalized on an existing reservoir of discontent about a changing American society and culture. That discontent about what America had become helped propel him to the nomination.

Political Activation in Presidential Primaries

One of the most venerable political science findings about political campaigns is that campaigns can affect the criteria voters use to make decisions. By emphasizing certain issues or speaking directly to certain groups, candidates can make those issues and group identities more salient to voters and more predictive of their choices. Appeals to group loyalties and antagonisms have proved especially likely to change voters' opinions of candidates.[2]

This is all the more true in presidential primary campaigns because voters' identification with a party does not help them choose among candidates from that party. This makes their opinions of the candidates more malleable. Although some voters may come to support a candidate just because of the pure buzz of media coverage, durable momentum usually requires more than buzz alone. As Larry Bartels puts it in his description of presidential primaries, "Through the din of horse race coverage, the hoopla of rallies, and the frantic chasing after 'Big Mo,' the enduring political identities of candidates and citizens gradually shape the perceptions and evaluations on which primary votes are based." This process of "political activation" implies that when voters acquire more information about candidates during the primaries, they evaluate candidates based on their long-standing political predispositions.[3]

For example, Bartels shows that in 1984, Colorado senator Gary Hart's momentum after his unexpected victory in the New Hampshire primary was concentrated among highly educated, white social progressives. These voters were more receptive to Hart's message of "new ideas" and less enthused about Walter Mondale's traditional New Deal policies. In the 1987 invisible primary, revelations about Hart's extramarital affair with Donna Rice activated opposition from Democrats with traditional views about sex and family values. In 2008, Barack Obama's momentum after winning the Iowa caucus was concentrated among people with liberal views on racial issues— the very people most likely to be attracted to an African American candidate. In 2012, Rick Santorum's unexpected primary victories produced a surge of support from social conservatives who agreed with his positions on abortion and same-sex marriage.[4]

In other words, jumping on a candidate's bandwagon is not purely a leap of faith: media coverage signals to voters whether the surging candidate is "their type," and those whose beliefs align with the candidate's then lead the surge. In 2016, the media's extensive coverage of Trump arguably provided voters with even more information about his campaign's message than they had had about prior candidates. Voters heard Trump in his own words, summarized by news outlets, and critiqued by commentators and even some Republicans. Each key element of Trump's message had the potential to resonate with many Republican voters.

Identifying the origins of Trump's appeal means confronting the perennial challenge that arises in social science research and political analysis: distinguishing cause and effect. If some belief is associated with support for Trump, that could mean one of two things: having that belief caused people to support Trump, or people who already supported Trump decided to adopt that belief (perhaps because they heard Trump say it). This latter possibility is a real risk because voters often change their positions and the importance they place on issues to match the positions and priorities of their preferred presidential candidates. When that happens, things that look like causes of a candidate's support are really consequences or rationalizations of that support.[5]

Fortunately, a novel and unusual survey helps address this issue. In July 2016, a month after the primary's conclusion, the Views of the Electorate Research (VOTER) Survey interviewed 8,000 respondents who were originally interviewed in 2011–12.[6] This 2011–12 survey captured respondents' views long before Trump's presidential candidacy, meaning that these views could not have been affected by his rhetoric in the 2016 campaign. In July 2016, this survey then asked Republican primary voters which of four Republican primary candidates—Trump, Ted Cruz, John Kasich, and Marco Rubio—they had supported. This survey thus identified whether Republican voters' opinions measured well before 2016 were associated with support for Trump in the primary—and which opinions appeared to matter most.

Economic and Political Dissatisfaction

One theme of Trump's campaign was encapsulated in his famous slogan, "Make America great again," and his refrain, "Our country doesn't win anymore." Trump argued that conditions in the country were terrible and far worse than they used to be. In his announcement speech, Trump said that the economy's growth rate was sluggish and that the "real" unemployment rate was 18–20 percent. Trump thought that the political system was not any better. He not only criticized Obama, as every Republican presidential candidate did, but also blamed both parties, calling Democratic and Republican leaders "incompetent." He proclaimed that he was not beholden to special interests, saying in his announcement speech, "I don't need anybody's money. I'm using my own money. I'm not using lobbyists. I'm not using donors. I don't care. I'm really rich."[7] Although Trump reneged on his pledge to strictly self-fund his campaign, he still vowed to be the voice of the American people against a rigged system dominated by powerful special interests.

Should this message have resonated? The political science literature suggests it had potential. In a famous essay on American public opinion, the political scientist Philip Converse showed that Americans often talk about political parties and candidates in terms of how well things are going in the country when a party or candidate is in power. Converse called this factor "the nature of the times." Key groups of voters, especially those with less formal education or who pay less attention to politics, reward or punish the incumbent party based on the state of the economy.[8]

Trump's message seemed poised to resonate particularly with Republicans, who were dissatisfied with the economic, political, and cultural direction of America (chapter 2). There was also a sense among some Republicans that the political and economic system was rigged. In a fall 2015 Pew Research Center poll, about half of Republicans said that "voting by people like me doesn't really affect how government runs things" and "there's not much ordinary citizens can do to influence the government in Washington." Similarly, in a March 2016 Pew poll, about half of Republicans said that the "economic system in the US unfairly favors powerful interests." These sentiments were not unique to Republicans: a similar fraction of Democrats expressed doubt that citizens could influence government, and a larger fraction of Democrats believed that the U.S. economic system favors the powerful. The question was whether Trump could tap into any discontent that did exist among Republicans.[9]

However, several measures of political and economic dissatisfaction were not tightly linked to support for Trump. Republican voters who agreed that "people like me don't have any say about what the government does" or that "ordinary citizens cannot influence the government in Washington" or that the U.S. economic system "unfairly favors powerful interests" were only a little bit more likely to support Trump than those who disagreed with those statements (figure 5.1). This modest influence of political dissatisfaction extended to disenchantment with the Republican establishment as well. In several primary exit polls, Republican voters who felt betrayed by their party's establishment were not especially likely to have voted for Trump. Interestingly, Trump himself believed that political dissatisfaction was not helping him as much as it should. He frequently complained that he was not getting credit for self-funding his campaign.[10] It appears that he was right.

Similarly, Trump support was not strongly associated with family income. According to YouGov/*Economist* surveys, the median Trump supporter reported an income in the $50,000–$60,000 range, right around the median income for American households overall. In the two January surveys, which captured opinion right before the primaries began, the income of the median Trump supporter was similar to that of the median supporter of some other Republican candidates, including Cruz and Rubio. On average, Trump did a bit better among those with lower incomes than those with higher incomes, but these differences waned during the primary season. By March 2016, for example, Trump support among those in the lowest income quartile—those making under $30,000 per year—was only slightly higher than among the highest tercile, those making $100,000 a year or more (middle right-hand panel of figure 5.1). Trump voters were not especially poor or especially likely to be poor.[11]

Trump supporters were more distinctive in how they felt about the economy. Throughout the primary campaign, Trump's support was higher among the 34 percent of Republicans who said that both their personal

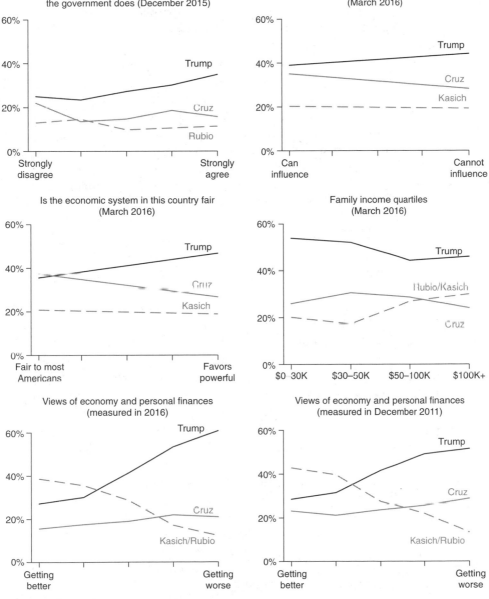

Figure 5.1.

Political and economic dissatisfaction and support for Donald Trump among Republicans. Sources: December 2015 RAND Presidential Election Panel Survey (top left); March 2016 Pew Research Center poll (top right, middle left); March 2016 YouGov/ *Economist* polls (middle right, bottom left); VOTER Survey (bottom right panel).

finances and the national economy had gotten worse over the past year, compared to the 30 percent of Republicans who said that their finances and the national economy were getting better (bottom panels of figure 5.1). The gap between those two groups was persistently around 20–25 percentage points. Trump's support from economically anxious Republicans came primarily at the expense of Marco Rubio and John Kasich.

Even Republican primary voters who said as of December 2011 that both their own personal finances and the national economy were getting worse were significantly more likely to vote for Trump in 2016, compared to those who thought that the economy was getting better.[12] Trump voters were not just parroting back Trump's argument about how badly things were going in the country. Nevertheless, assessments of the economy and one's personal finances did not appear to be the primary drivers of Trump's support.

Economic Liberalism

The second of Trump's themes put him, once again, opposite the party's leaders. Although Trump had adopted some planks of the Republican platform, his embrace of party orthodoxy was far from complete. On foreign policy, he questioned long-standing U.S. alliances, including the North Atlantic Treaty Organization. He criticized the administration of George W. Bush for prosecuting the Iraq War. He criticized free trade agreements. But particularly salient in the primary campaign were Trump's apostasies on economic issues. He rejected the party's enduring goal of entitlement reform, promising to protect Social Security, Medicare, and Medicaid benefits. He said he believed in raising taxes on the wealthy, including himself. He supported mammoth government spending on infrastructure. Of course, it was not clear whether Trump would follow through on any of this. His actual tax plan would have cut taxes for the wealthy. But his willingness even to say these things set him apart from typical Republican candidates.[13]

Trump's heterodox politics were especially notable given the growing conservatism of Republican Party leaders in Congress and the growing strength of conservative interests within the party, such as the network affiliated with the businessmen Charles and David Koch. Unsurprisingly, then, Republican leaders and conservative thinkers were aghast. Republican senator Ben Sasse said that Trump "waged an effective war on almost every plank of the Republican Party's platform." The *National Review*'s January 2016 issue, which was entitled "Conservatives against Trump," called him "a philosophically unmoored political opportunist who would trash the broad conservative ideological consensus within the GOP in favor of a free-floating populism with strong-man overtones."[14]

But although the *National Review* may have accurately described the consensus among pundits and politicians, it badly overestimated the consensus within the party's base. Most rank-and-file Republicans are not, nor have they ever been, pure conservatives. This is why Trump's message resonated with economically liberal Republican voters.

The idea that ordinary Americans are not orthodox ideologues is well established in political science. In the same essay in which he wrote about the "nature of the times," Philip Converse described Americans' "belief systems," or how people organize (or do not organize) their political ideas. Ideologies like liberalism and conservatism provide one mode of organization: they tell voters "what goes with what." For example, liberalism today usually means opposing the death penalty and supporting abortion rights. Conservatism means the opposite. However, after analyzing survey data from the 1950s, Converse found that the public was largely "innocent of 'ideology.'" When asked their likes and dislikes about the political parties and presidential candidates, relatively few used ideological concepts. The majority could not define terms like *liberal* and *conservative* or could define them only in vague terms. Moreover, people's views on various political issues often did not "go together" the way that liberalism or conservatism would predict.[15]

Since Converse's essay was published in 1964, this basic finding has not really changed. In a reevaluation of Converse's work based on 2000 data, a team of political scientists found that although a larger group used ideological concepts when describing the parties and candidates, this was still a small minority of voters (20%, compared to 12% in the 1950s). Similarly, although the political parties are better "sorted" on certain issues—with Democrats more consistently liberal and Republicans more consistently conservative—it is still common for voters to have political views out of step with their party. As political scientists Donald Kinder and Nathan Kalmoe concluded, "Ideological innocence applies nearly as well to the current state of American public opinion as it does to the public Converse analyzed."[16]

Republican voters might appear to be more ideologically orthodox than the electorate as a whole. Compared to Democratic voters, they are more likely to use ideological language when describing candidates and know that the Democratic Party is to the left of the Republican Party. But Republicans can be less ideologically consistent than Democrats because many self-identified conservatives, who make up the bulk of the Republican Party, take liberal positions on economic issues like the size of government, taxing the wealthy,

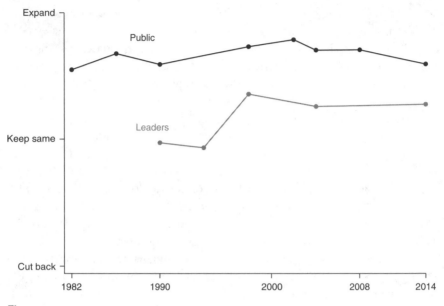

Figure 5.2.
Views of Republican voters and leaders on Social Security.
Source: Chicago Council on Global Affairs.

and the minimum wage. They are, as the political scientists Christopher Ellis and James Stimson argue, "symbolically conservative" but "operationally liberal." As a result, numerous Republicans, even Republican primary voters, have favored maintaining or increasing spending on government programs like Social Security, health care, education, and infrastructure. This is why, as Henry Olsen and Dante Scala have written, liberals, moderates, and those who identify as only somewhat conservative are crucial Republican voting blocs, even though much commentary portrays Republican primary voters as a strongly conservative monolith.[17]

One illustration of Republican voters' potential receptivity to Trump's message concerned Social Security. Republican leaders and voters had been divided on Social Security for decades, according to parallel surveys of voters and leaders conducted by the Chicago Council on Global Affairs (figure 5.2). The leaders surveyed are not typically elected officeholders but rather congressional aides, officials in the executive branch, think tank experts, academics, business leaders, labor leaders, religious leaders, military officers, and the like. On average, Republican voters were more supportive of expanding spending on Social Security. For example, in the 2014 survey, 62 percent of Republican voters, but only 26 percent of Republican leaders, said that spending on Social Security should be expanded. Most leaders were not advocating cuts to Social Security, to be sure, but nevertheless Trump's promise to protect Social Security was in line with long-standing views among Republican voters.

Unsurprisingly, then, once Trump got in the race, he attracted considerable support among more liberal Republicans. For example, Trump did better among Republicans who believed Social Security and Medicare were very important in this 2011 interview, even though those attitudes were measured five years earlier (top left-hand panel of figure 5.3). Trump also did better among Republicans who, as of late 2011, supported a tax increase on Americans making more than $200,000 per year (top right-hand panel). This was approximately 34 percent of Republicans—far from a majority but illustrative of the ideological diversity in the party.

Other surveys showed an even more powerful correlation between economic liberalism and support for Trump. In December 2015, respondents to the RAND Presidential Election Panel Survey (PEPS) were asked whether the government should pay "necessary medical costs for every American citizen," whether there should be a tax increase on individuals making more than $200,000 per year, whether the federal minimum wage should be increased, and how respondents felt toward "big business" and "labor unions." Among likely Republican primary voters, economic liberals were not a tiny minority: 30 percent favored the government's paying medical costs, 47 percent supported raising the minimum wage, 51 percent support increasing taxes on the wealthy, and 25 percent had more favorable views of unions than of big business. And it was these liberals who tended to support Trump most strongly (lower left-hand panel of figure 5.3). By contrast, Ted Cruz, who may have been the most conservative candidate to ever run for the Republican nomination, performed best among economic conservatives.[18] Cruz outperformed Trump by about 15 percentage points among the most economically conservative Republicans but lost to Trump by over 30 points among more liberal Republicans.

Other surveys showed a similar pattern. For example, in YouGov/*Economist* surveys conducted throughout the primary campaign, Trump's support was stronger among those who prioritized Social Security and Medicare, whereas Cruz's support was stronger among those who described themselves as "very conservative." By the end of the primaries, Cruz was winning a majority of these voters. But only 25 percent of Republicans described themselves as very conservative in the first place, so Cruz needed to expand his support beyond this group. He could not, perhaps because there are not enough committed ideologues in the party in the first place.

In sum, there have always been voters, and especially Republican voters, whose views could make them susceptible to a heterodox primary candidate like Trump. Such candidates usually struggle to succeed, however, because party elites and activists, who tend to be stronger ideologues, will not

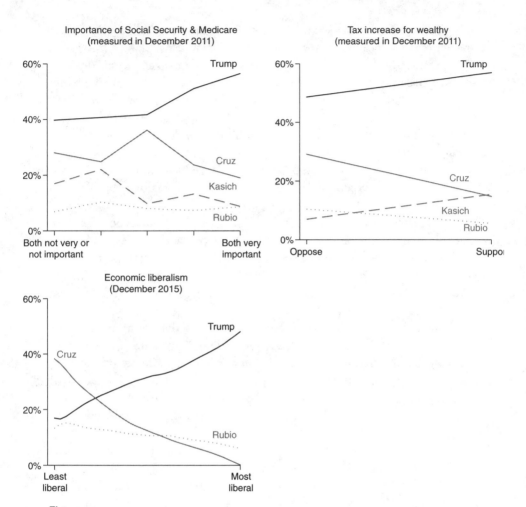

Figure 5.3.
Economic liberalism and support for Republican primary candidates.
Sources: VOTER Survey (top panels); December 2015 Presidential Election Panel
Survey (bottom panel).

support them. But when Republican elites failed to derail Trump's candidacy
early on, Republicans who had not adopted every plank of the party platform
had their own candidate.

Race, Immigration, and Islam

A third theme of Trump's campaign was even more widely discussed and
controversial: issues intimately tied to race, ethnicity, and religion—and
especially to blacks, immigrants from Latin America, and Muslims. These

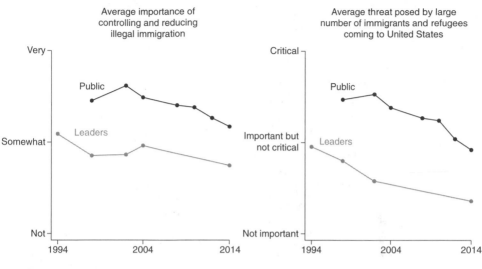

Figure 5.1
Views of Republican voters and leaders on immigration.
Source: Chicago Council on Global Affairs.

of many Republican voters. In the Chicago Council on Global Affairs surveys, Republican voters expressed much more concern about immigration than did Republican leaders (figure 5.4). Republican voters assigned more importance to "reducing illegal immigration" and were more likely to say that "immigrants and refugees coming to the U.S." posed a "critical threat." Those concerns became less prominent in later surveys, but even in 2014, 86 percent of Republican voters said that controlling and reducing immigration was somewhat or very important (versus 60% of Republican leaders) and 73 percent said that immigrants and refugees posed an important or critical threat (versus 22% of Republican leaders).

Most Republican voters also took positions on immigration policy that dovetailed with Trump's. Even before the primary campaign, majorities of Republicans supported building a fence along the Mexican border, said that "immigrants are a burden because they take jobs, housing and health care," and wanted tougher restrictions on immigration in general. Thus, it was not surprising that 68 percent of Republican primary voters believed that Trump's statement about Mexican immigrants being rapists who bring drugs and crime into the country was "basically right."[25]

At times, other polls suggested that most Americans, including most Republicans, would support a more lenient immigration policy, such as granting undocumented immigrants permanent residency or even citizenship. But there was less enthusiasm for how this would work in practice. For example, one survey of Californians found that 70 percent supported a path to citizenship. At the same time, however, 42 percent supported having undocumented immigrants return to their home countries first, and 51 percent said that undocumented immigrants must meet the typical criteria that legal immigrants must meet, such as having family in the United States, skills needed by U.S. employers, or a credible asylum claim. Immigration reform legislation typically required none of these, which raised concerns that it would give undocumented immigrants an unfair "inside track." The conclusion of the scholars who conducted this poll is striking: "The majority's negativity toward the details of any politically-viable reform package weakens the incentive for politicians to press forward, and the large and intransigent minority of the public overall (*almost half of the Republican electorate*) that categorically rejects any broad-based legalization program *stands as a potential group lurking and ready to mobilize against elected officials who back legalization.*"[26] Indeed, this "potential group" had already been mobilized before the 2016 campaign. In a 2012 study of the Tea Party, the political scientists Theda Skocpol and Vanessa Williamson quoted one Tea Party supporter who said that she wanted to "stand on the border with a gun." Another said, "I feel like my country is being stolen by people who have come here illegally." Donald Trump was well aware of such sentiments. In preparation for his presidential bid, he instructed his aides to listen to thousands of hours of conservative talk radio. They reported back to Trump that "the GOP base was frothing over a handful of issues," one of which was immigration.[27]

Trump's emphasis on immigration focused not only on undocumented immigrants from Latin American countries but also on Muslim immigrants. In August 2015, he made headlines for refusing to admonish a supporter who told him at a rally, "We have a problem in this country. It's called Muslims." In September, he suggested that large numbers of Syrian refugees were terrorists. He also falsely claimed that thousands of Muslims in New Jersey cheered the 9/11 attacks. Later that fall came his proposals for a national database to register Muslims, enhanced surveillance of mosques in the United States, and a ban on Muslims entering the United States.[28]

Trump's proposals were immediately rebuked by politicians from across the political spectrum, including many prominent Republicans. Jeb Bush said, "You talk about closing mosques, you talk about registering people—that's just wrong." Paul Ryan said that the Muslim ban violated the Constitution and was "not who we are as a party." Mitt Romney, Dick Cheney, and Reince Priebus also opposed Trump's proposal. Trump's future running mate, Mike Pence, tweeted, "Calls to ban Muslims from entering the U.S. are offensive and unconstitutional."[29]

But here again, Trump was arguably in line with public opinion. On average, Americans have less favorable views of Muslims, relative to most other social groups, and view Muslims especially unfavorably on dimensions like their proclivity for violence. Attitudes toward Muslims are less favorable among Republicans than among Democrats (see chapter 2). In a June 2014 Pew Research Center poll, two-thirds of Republicans thought that Islam was more likely than other religions to encourage violence, compared to 40 percent of Democrats. And even before Trump ran, negative views of Muslims already had political consequences: they were associated with support for the war on terror and negative views of Obama, especially the belief that he was not born in the United States.[30]

Thus, it was not surprising that, despite bipartisan condemnation of Trump's proposed Muslim ban, large majorities of Republican primary voters favored it. For example, a *Washington Post*/ABC News poll found that 59 percent of Republicans supported the ban, compared to only 15 percent of Democrats. In Republican primary exit polls, support for the ban ranged from a low of 63 percent in Michigan and Virginia to a high of 78 percent in Alabama. There appeared to be a clear constituency for Trump's message about the dangers that Muslims posed to the United States.[31]

Given Trump's rhetoric about blacks, immigrants, and Muslims, it is no surprise that views of those groups were strongly correlated with supporting him (figure 5.5). Support for Trump was associated with how much people attributed racial inequality to the legacy of discrimination as opposed to a lack of effort by African Americans—even when those views were measured in 2011 (upper left panel of figure 5.5). The 85 percent of Republicans who tended to emphasize blacks' work ethic were more than 50 points more likely to support Donald Trump in the primaries than were those who emphasized discrimination. Support for Trump was also correlated with 2011 evaluations of African Americans on a feeling thermometer (upper right panel).[32]

That racial attitudes measured five years before the 2016 campaign would be related to Trump support is not unexpected. Racial attitudes tend to be stable throughout adulthood, and campaign appeals to racial anxieties have often succeeded in activating support from some whites.[33] But these findings suggest which specific racial attitudes were especially important. It was less about a general dislike of blacks per se. Relatively few Republicans rated blacks unfavorably on the feeling thermometer—15 percent placed blacks at 40 or below on the 0–100 scale—and the correlation between these ratings and Trump support was modest. Trump's support had more to do with the racialized perceptions of deservingness captured in people's explanations of racial inequality. Of course, many argue that such explanations are

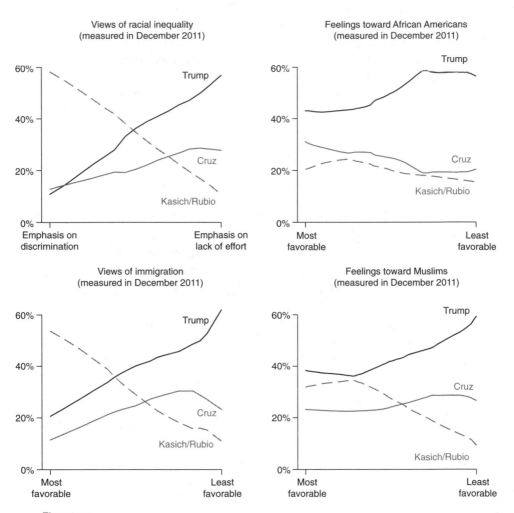

Figure 5.5.
Attitudes toward immigration, Muslims, and African Americans and support for Republican primary candidates.
The lines have been smoothed using lowess.
Source: VOTER Survey.

themselves rooted in racial prejudice, particularly views that African Americans are culturally inferior.[34] But that remains a hotly debated topic in the social science literature. Regardless, the measure captures the widespread notion that African Americans no longer face much discrimination and are receiving unearned special favors. Indeed, whites who hold these beliefs often cite "reverse discrimination" as being a more serious problem.[35]

Trump support was also strongly associated with views of immigration. Respondents to the VOTER Survey were asked in 2011 whether there should be a path to citizenship for undocumented immigrants, whether undocumented immigrants were mostly a benefit to or a drain on society, and whether it should be easier or harder to immigrate to the United States. Trump did much better among voters who were unfavorable to immigration, based on a scale combining these questions, while Rubio and Kasich did worse.[36] Trump's advantage over Cruz was also clear. Both candidates gained vote share at Rubio's and Kasich's expense among voters with moderate or conservative-leaning positions on immigration. But among those voters with the most conservative views according to this measure, Trump did especially well, and at Cruz's expense. Given that attitudes toward immigrants depend more on cultural than economic factors, the connection between concerns about immigration and support for Trump was likely undergirded by the sense that immigrants threaten the nation's identity and heritage.[37]

Other perceptions of threat—this time involving Muslims—were also associated with Trump support. Respondents to the VOTER Survey were asked in December 2011 to evaluate Muslims on a feeling thermometer that captured their overall views of Muslims. Trump performed significantly better with Republican voters who rated Muslims relatively unfavorably in 2011 than he did with Republican voters who rated Muslims relatively favorably (bottom right panel of figure 5.5). Views of Muslims were not strongly related to support for Cruz or Rubio, but they were related to support for Kasich, just in the opposite direction. Kasich condemned both Trump and Cruz for their rhetoric about Muslims.[38] The problem for Kasich was that in December 2011, most Republicans (64%) rated Muslims on the "cold" side of the feeling thermometer; the average rating for Muslims among Republicans was 37 (compared to 81 for Christians and 74 for Jews). The prevalence of negative views of Muslims helped sustain Trump's support among Republican voters despite harsh scrutiny of his position toward Muslims, including from prominent Republican leaders.

White Identity

Trump's primary campaign also became a vehicle for a different kind of identity politics—one oriented around some white Americans' feelings of marginalization in an increasingly diverse America. Affection for Trump emerged quickly among avowed white nationalists, including a community, mostly online, known as the alt-right. Trump was endorsed by the neo-Nazi website

Daily Stormer and by former Ku Klux Klan leader David Duke. A white nationalist super PAC made robocalls on behalf of Trump in Iowa and New
Hampshire that said, "We don't need Muslims. We need smart, educated,
white people." Richard Spencer, the president of the National Policy Institute,
which is "dedicated to the heritage, identity, and future of European people
in the United States and around the world," described "an unconscious
vision that white people have—that their grandchildren might be a hated minority in their own country" and said that Trump "is the one person who can
tap into it." Even some voters, few of whom were neo-Nazis, expressed concern about the plight of whites. One New York woman told a reporter, "Everyone's sticking together in their groups, so white people have to, too."[39]

Trump faced consistent criticism for fomenting these sentiments, for
example by retweeting supportive tweets from white supremacists, or failing to
condemn his white nationalist supporters swiftly and strongly enough. In an
essay entitled "Are Republicans for Freedom or White Identity Politics?," the
conservative writer Ben Domenech called Trump a "danger" to the party.
After Trump said that he "didn't know anything about" David Duke, a Rubio
spokesman said, "If you need to do research on the K.K.K. before you can
repudiate them, you are not ready or fit to be president." Mitt Romney
tweeted, "A disqualifying & disgusting response by @realDonaldTrump to
the KKK. His coddling of repugnant bigotry is not in the character of America." But some conservatives attacked the critics, with media personality
Tucker Carlson saying that "Obama could have written" Romney's tweet.[40]

It is unusual for white identity to be politically potent. Whites' solidarity
with fellow whites has been less prevalent and less powerful than solidarity
among minority groups, such as Latinos and especially African Americans.
This is because in-group identity arises from isolation, deprivation, and discrimination, and whites have long been less deprived and discriminated
against than minority racial groups.[41]

But all of this was changing, even before Trump's candidacy. In her book
Strangers in Their Own Land: Anger and Mourning on the American Right,
the sociologist Arlie Russell Hochschild details her extensive conversations
with whites in Louisiana bayou country and the resentment they felt over how
the beneficiaries of affirmative action, immigrants, and refugees were "steal-
ing their place in line," cutting ahead "at the expense of white men and their
wives." These sentiments were visible in surveys as well. In American National
Election Studies (ANES) surveys conducted in December 2011 and February 2012, 38 percent of Republicans thought that there was at least a moderate amount of discrimination against whites. That figure jumped up to
47 percent in the ANES study in January 2016. Similarly, in an October 2015
Public Religion Research Institute poll, nearly two-thirds of Republicans

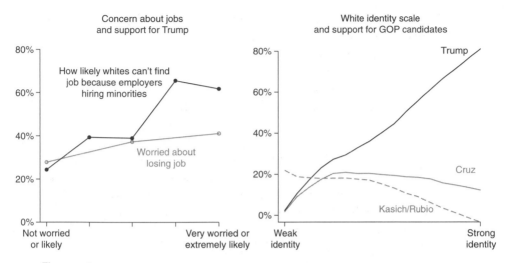

Figure 5.6.
White identity and support for Donald Trump in the primary.
Sources: January YouGov/*Economist* surveys for worried about job and 2016 ANES
Pilot Study for beliefs about whites' jobs (left panel); 2016 ANES Pilot Study (right
panel, with line smoothed using lowess)

thought that "discrimination against whites has become as big of a problem as discrimination against blacks and other minorities." In a 2016 survey, most Republicans agreed with this statement: "People like me are asked to make too many sacrifices that benefit people of another race." Research by political scientist Ashley Jardina and others has shown that a sense of discrimination or competition with minority groups increases whites' solidarity with other whites and opposition to minority groups.[42]

Trump's campaign appealed directly to this very sense of economic and cultural threat. Trump support was strongly correlated with whether Republicans thought that whites are unable to find a job because employers are hiring minorities. By contrast, Trump support was only weakly correlated with whether respondents were worried about losing their own jobs (left panel of figure 5.6). Consistent with a long line of research showing that group interests are more potent politically than self-interest, economic anxiety was channeled more through white identity politics than it was through Trump supporters' concern for their own personal well-being.[43]

The January 2016 ANES Pilot Study asked four questions that captured white identity: the importance of white identity, how much whites are being discriminated against, the likelihood that whites are losing jobs to nonwhites, and the importance of whites working together to change laws unfair to whites. A scale combining these questions was also strongly related to

Republicans' support for Donald Trump (right panel of figure 5.6). Moreover, this measure of white identity was not related to evaluations of any other political figure in this survey, including Barack Obama, after accounting for attitudes about African Americans, Muslims, and Latinos. Trump was distinctive in how he tapped into white grievances.

Of course, Trump's appeal to white identity in 2016 was not unprecedented. Both Pat Buchanan in 1996 and George Wallace in 1968 campaigned on threats to white Americans and thereby made white identity an important part of their electoral support.[44] But neither Buchanan nor Wallace won a major-party nomination, much less the presidency. Trump's success may mean that appeals to white identity, including the suggestion that white dominance is increasingly threatened by nonwhites, is a rising force in American politics.

The Preeminence of Identity over Economics

Compared to the supporters of other Republican candidates, Trump supporters were more dissatisfied with the economy, more liberal on economic issues, less supportive of immigration, less favorable toward Muslims, more inclined to attribute racial inequality to a lack of effort by African Americans, and more strongly identified with whites—even when some of these things were measured more than four years before Trump's candidacy. The major debate during the campaign, however, was which factor was preeminent—and especially whether "economic anxiety" or "racial anxiety" mattered more.

Disentangling these various factors is not straightforward, of course. Nevertheless, factors tied to race, ethnicity, and religion appeared more strongly related to Trump support in the primary than was voters' economic insecurity. This pattern emerged in three different surveys—the VOTER Survey, the December 2015 PEPS, and the January 2016 ANES Pilot Study. The results from the VOTER Survey are particularly important because each of these factors was measured well before Trump's candidacy. (See this chapter's appendix for further details.)

A concise visualization of findings from the VOTER Survey and the ANES Pilot Study is depicted in figure 5.7. After accounting for various factors simultaneously, the relationship of Trump support to "racial anxiety" is clear. In the VOTER Survey, the combined relationship of Trump support to views of immigration, Muslims, and racial inequality was large: people with the least favorable views—that is, most likely to oppose immigration, dislike Muslims, and attribute racial inequality to blacks' lack of effort—were 53 points more likely to support Trump than those with the most favorable views (all else held

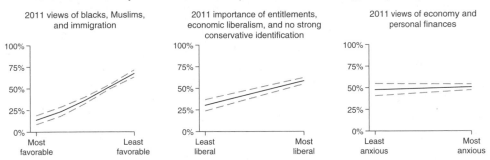

2016 VOTER Survey: Combined relationship between chance of supporting Trump and . . .

2011 views of blacks, Muslims, and immigration — 2011 importance of entitlements, economic liberalism, and no strong conservative identification — 2011 views of economy and personal finances

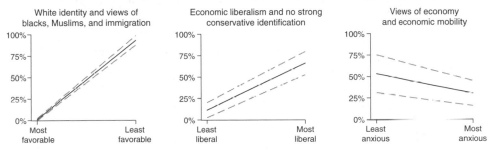

2016 ANES Pilot Study: Combined relationship between chance of supporting Trump and . . .

White identity and views of blacks, Muslims, and immigration — Economic liberalism and no strong conservative identification — Views of economy and economic mobility

Figure 5.7.

The combined relationship between Trump support and attitudes related to race, ethnicity, religion, liberalism, and economic anxiety.

This figure captures the relationship between support for Trump and the combination of various attitudes, holding other factors at their means. The dotted lines represent 95 percent confidence intervals.

Sources: VOTER Survey; 2016 ANES Pilot Study.

equal). In the ANES survey, accounting for white identity lessened the relationship between support for Trump and attitudes toward immigration and Muslims, suggesting again that a politicized white identity was a potent electoral force. The combination of a more politicized white identity and views of immigration, Muslims, and African Americans was very strongly related to support for Trump—implying a maximum shift of 93 points, largely because of the apparent power of white identity (see figure 5.6).

The relationship of liberalism to Trump support also stands out after accounting for other factors. In the VOTER Survey, the combined relationship of prioritizing Social Security and Medicare, liberal views on economic issues (supporting increased taxes on the wealthy and the government's role in providing health care and regulating business), and identifying as anything other than "strongly conservative" was notable—a maximum 28-point shift

in Trump support. In the ANES survey, the same relationship emerges: identifying as less than a "strong" conservative and supporting a hike in the minimum wage and increasing government spending on health care and child
care were collectively associated with a maximum 55-point shift in Trump
support.

By contrast, there was a much weaker relationship between support for
Trump and plausible measures of "economic anxiety." In the VOTER Survey,
the combination of perceptions of the national economy and one's personal
finances was not related to Trump support.[45] In the ANES survey, a mostly
different measure of economic anxiety was also weakly related to support for
Trump. The ANES included questions not only about whether the economy
was getting better but also about economic mobility: "How much opportunity is there in America today for the average person to get ahead?"; whether
it is harder "for you to move up the income ladder"; and "whether people's
ability to improve their financial well-being" is better than, worse than, or
the same as it was twenty years ago. If anything, the more that anxious Republicans were based on a composite scale of these items, the *less* likely they
were to support Trump in the primary. In short, although Americans' economic disaffection was a recurring theme of political analysis, it appeared less
important than other factors in explaining Trump's rise to the Republican
nomination.[46]

Other factors common to election-year commentary appeared less important as well. The importance attached to the issue of terrorism as of late 2011
was not associated with Trump support, even though Trump spoke frequently
about the need to fight ISIS (the Islamic State in Iraq and Syria) and "radical
Islamic terrorism." Similarly, despite Trump's frequent criticisms of free trade
agreements, opposition to increasing trade or to free trade agreements was
weakly associated with supporting him. There was also little apparent relationship between support for Trump and distrust of government.[47] Finally, despite
much election-year discussion of the concept of "authoritarianism"—valuing
traits like obedience and manners over self-reliance and curiosity—it too
was not consistently associated with support for Trump. Some research even
found that it was more associated with support for Ted Cruz in the primaries. To be sure, authoritarian worldviews have become increasingly
important in American politics. But Trump's playboy lifestyle and thin record of social conservatism may have weakened any connection between authoritarianism and support for him, especially given the competition from a
strong religious conservative such as Cruz.[48]

Of course, these surveys did not measure every conceivable factor that
undergirded Trump's appeal. There are undoubtedly other factors that were
important, at least for some voters. Nevertheless, these surveys tell a consis-

tent story: support for Trump was tied most strongly to white grievances; views of immigration, Muslims, and blacks; and liberal views about economic issues. These factors, more than economic anxiety, helped explain Trump's surprising path to the Republican presidential nomination.

The importance of attitudes related to race, ethnicity, and religion was even more striking because it was so unusual. Typically, the divides in party primaries are about ideology, with moderates squaring off against ideologues. Certainly that was true in recent Republican primaries. Sometimes more conservative Republicans prevailed, as they did in nominating Ronald Reagan over George H. W. Bush in 1980 or George W. Bush over John McCain in 2000. More often, the Republican nominee was more moderate than others in the field. Gerald Ford, Bob Dole, and Mitt Romney are examples.

Thus, the 2016 Republican divide over issues like immigration was less familiar. Typically, it has been the Democrats who have been more divided over race because the Democratic coalition has included African Americans, liberal whites, and conservative whites. Voters in the 1984, 1988, 2008, and 2016 Democratic primaries were all sharply divided by race. The Republican Party, by contrast, has been more unified around a "color-blind policy alliance" that calls for a diminished role of race in public policies. Few Republican candidates for president have attempted to distinguish themselves from their Republican rivals on issues connected to race and ethnicity—until Trump did exactly that.[49]

Trump was also unusual in how he talked about identity. Candidates have traditionally used implicit racial and ethnic appeals to win over sympathetic voters without appearing overtly prejudiced. These appeals have often activated support among voters with less favorable views of racial minorities. But Trump's appeals were explicit. He went where most Republican presidential candidates have not gone and became the first Republican in modern times to win the party's presidential nomination based in part on these attitudes.[50]

This is readily visible when comparing the 2008, 2012, and 2016 Republican primaries. Support for John McCain in 2008 or Mitt Romney in 2012 was at best weakly related to support for a path to citizenship for undocumented immigrants, views of racial inequality, or feelings toward Muslims (figure 5.8). But Trump was more popular than McCain or Romney among Republicans who opposed a path to citizenship, viewed racial inequality primarily in terms of blacks' lack of effort, and had less favorable attitudes toward Muslims.[51]

The perception of discrimination against whites was also more strongly associated with support for Trump than it was for Mitt Romney in 2012 (figure 5.8). Support for Romney was 8 points lower among Republicans who said that there was a great deal of discrimination against whites, compared to those who said there was none. Trump, however, performed about 22 percentage

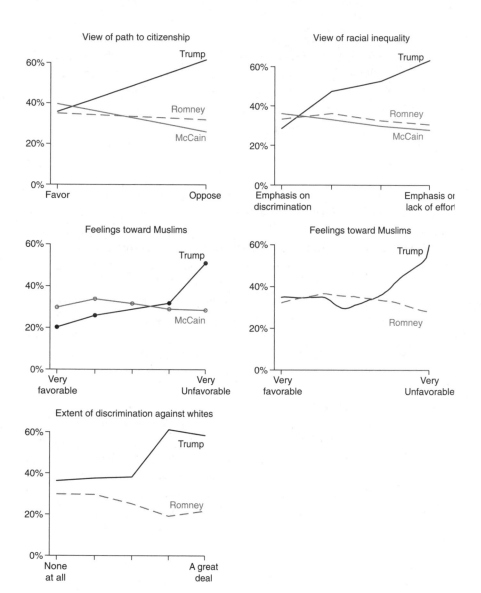

Figure 5.8.

White identity and views of immigration, African Americans, and Muslims and support for the Republican presidential nominees in 2008, 2012, and 2016.

The lines in the middle right-hand graph are smoothed using lowess (bandwidth = 0.8).

Sources: 2008 and 2012 Cooperative Campaign Analysis Project, 2016 YouGov/ *Economist* surveys (top panels); PEPS and 2008 Cooperative Campaign Analysis Project (middle left); ANES Pilot Study and 2012 Cooperative Campaign Analysis Project (middle right); 2016 ANES Pilot Study and 2011–12 Evaluations of Government and Society Study (lower left).

points *better* among Republicans who said that there was a great deal of discrimination against whites.

To be sure, Trump was not the first presidential primary candidate whose support was related to opposition to immigration. Pat Buchanan was another. Buchanan's presidential campaigns were frequently compared to Trump's because Buchanan also spoke out against immigration—even calling for a wall on the Mexican border—and also performed well among Republicans who shared his view.[52] For example, a CBS/*New York Times* poll conducted after Buchanan won the 1996 New Hampshire primary had him polling even with the eventual nominee, Dole, among Republicans who said both that immigrants take jobs from U.S. citizens and that the country cannot afford to open its doors to any more newcomers. The difference, however, is that opposition to immigration was less fervent in the Republican Party in the 1990s. Fewer than 20 percent of Republican voters agreed with both statements in that 1996 survey. That percentage would almost certainly be higher today.

Conclusion

In one sense, Trump's rise appeared entirely consistent with earlier presidential primaries and scholarship about them. Primary campaigns often activate the underlying beliefs and values of voters—in essence, telling voters, "If you believe X, then you should vote for candidate Y." In 2015–16, the Trump campaign signaled to voters which candidate they should choose if they favored entitlement programs or were concerned about the impact of immigration and the situation of white Americans. Although this seemed like an odd coalition on its face, it was not an unusual combination of ideas among Republican voters.

The political logic of Trump's campaign diverged sharply from the advice in the *Growth and Opportunity Project* report that was commissioned after the 2012 election. That report's support for immigration reform to broaden the party's appeal to Latino voters—a position shared by candidates like Bush and Rubio—sought to change how some Republican leaders and voters thought about immigration. Trump did something different. Rather than trying to change hearts and minds, he won over the many Republicans who were already doubtful about immigration's benefits for the country.

Trump's campaign surprised and dismayed many Republicans for another reason: it revealed that many rank-and-file Republicans were not movement conservatives. One conservative analyst, James Pethokoukis of the American Enterprise Institute, described how Republican leaders had often thought about their voters: "These are conservative voters, anti-Obama voters.

We'll give them the same policies we've always given them." What Republican leaders discovered, however, was that those policies were not what all Republican voters wanted. Most voters, even primary voters, are not ideologues. In 2016, those voters finally had someone to vote for.[53]

As Republican Party leaders dealt with the nomination of Donald J. Trump, they often looked inward—blaming themselves for failing to change the beliefs of Republican voters that supported Trump, or at least for failing to take action that would have defused these voters' concerns. Representative Raul Labrador blamed inaction on immigration: "The reason we have Donald Trump as a nominee today is because we as Republicans have failed on this issue." Others in the party saw an even broader failure. A former staffer from one of the organizations affiliated with the Koch brothers said, "We are partly responsible. We invested a lot in training and arming a grassroots army that was not controllable, and some of these people have used it in ways that are not consistent with our principles, with our goal of advancing a free society, and instead they have furthered the alt-right." A Koch donor said, "What we feel really badly about is that we were not able to educate many in the tea party more about how the process works and how free markets work. Seeing this movement that we were part of creating going off in a direction that's anti-free-market, anti-trade and anti-immigrant—many of us are really saddened by that."[54]

Those comments reveal the range of the Republican Party's frustrations. Trump flouted many Republican leaders' desire for a more conciliatory tone on immigration—and then became the standard-bearer for Republican voters on the issue: in a December 2015 CNN poll, 55 percent thought he was the best Republican candidate to tackle the issue. Trump also flouted many Republican leaders' desire for an orthodox conservative—and then became the candidate of the many Republican voters who never wanted an unfettered free market in the first place. Trump ignored the many Republicans who criticized him for emboldening fringe white nationalists—and then became the champion of white voters with racially inflected grievances.

What Republican leaders did not appear to understand, however, was just how long standing and potent this constellation of sentiments was. Trump tapped into beliefs, ideas, and anxieties that were already present and even well established within the party. His support was hiding in plain sight.

CHAPTER 6

Cracks in the Ceiling

On June 7, 2016, Hillary Clinton stood before a crowd of supporters in Brooklyn, New York, and said, "Tonight caps an amazing journey—a long, long journey." She had just clinched the Democratic nomination for president after months of campaigning against Vermont senator Bernie Sanders. It was a very different night from eight years before, when, as a New York senator, Clinton had lost a long nomination battle with Illinois senator Barack Obama. Now, after serving as Obama's secretary of state, she was poised to become his successor.

The Democratic nomination contest in 2015–16 stands out from the Republican contest—and from most recent nomination contests, Democratic or Republican—in one key respect: the unity of party leaders. More party leaders supported Clinton than had supported any candidate since at least 1980. These leaders manifested little of the factionalism and lack of coordination apparent in the Republican contest. Their early support of Clinton helped clear the field for her and sustain her campaign, even when Sanders became a challenger.

Clinton's success was visible in the share of delegates that she won (figure 6.1). Within a month of the Iowa caucus, she opened a 186-delegate lead that continued to grow for most of the campaign. To overcome Clinton's lead, Sanders needed lopsided victories in delegate-rich states, but those were hard to come by because the Democratic Party allocates delegates in proportion to primary and caucus outcomes. Thus, Sanders faced, as former Obama strategist David Plouffe put it, "what seems like a small but, in fact, is a deep

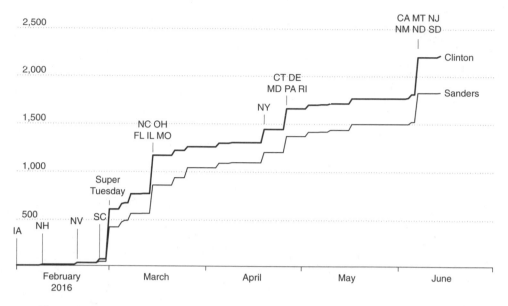

Figure 6.1.
Number of delegates won by Hillary Clinton and Bernie Sanders.
The graph includes only pledged delegates and not any Democratic "super-delegates." Data courtesy of Josh Putnam of Frontloading Headquarters.

and persistent hole." For this reason, Clinton was favored to win throughout the primary campaign. Betting markets, which fluctuated wildly on the Republican side, gave Clinton an 85 to 95 percent chance of winning the nomination for most of the period after the Iowa caucus.[1] Altogether she won 3.7 million more votes than Sanders.

But even if Clinton's victory was not really in doubt, Sanders's challenge was significant. When he announced his candidacy, Sanders said, "I think people should be a little bit careful underestimating me."[2] This was prescient. In terms of votes and delegates, Sanders arguably overperformed expectations while Clinton underperformed, especially given her extraordinary support among party leaders. Sanders's challenge was even more notable because he was an avowed "democratic socialist" from the small state of Vermont and had never even been a Democrat. Since 1991, he had served as an independent member of the House and Senate, where he was a frequent critic of the Democratic Party and its leaders.

Sanders's challenge to Clinton benefited from three things, however. The first was a set of tools, including social media, that helped him generate grassroots enthusiasm and large crowds at rallies and speeches. Second, fund-raising from small-dollar donors bankrolled a professional campaign even though he received little support from well-heeled donors and party leaders.

The third was media coverage. Sanders faced the perennial challenge of insurgent candidates: how to turn thousands of supporters at local rallies into millions of votes. Just as it did for Trump, media coverage brought Sanders to a wider audience and helped spur his long climb in the polls by conveying the familiar tale of the surprisingly successful underdog. Meanwhile, Clinton received more negative media coverage, in part because of questions about her use of a private email server while she was secretary of state and because of the Clinton campaign's inability to defuse the issue and engage more productively with the news media.

This pattern of news coverage was mirrored in how the voters saw the two candidates. Clinton started the campaign quite popular among Democratic voters—more popular than previous Democratic presidential candidates, including the Hillary Clinton who ran in 2008. But unlike in 2008, her popularity ebbed as Sanders supporters came to view her less favorably. Meanwhile, Sanders came to be seen more favorably, even among Clinton supporters.

What characteristics distinguished Sanders and Clinton supporters? To many election-year commentators, the two candidates were locked in an ideological battle royale. The Sanders campaign was supposedly a potential "watershed in the development of progressive politics," and Sanders supporters were said to "want the Democrats to be a different kind of party: a more ideological, more left-wing one."[3] But ideology was not the key divide among Democratic primary voters. Although they perceived Sanders as more liberal than Clinton, and Sanders voters themselves were more likely to identify as liberal, there were small differences between Sanders and Clinton voters on many policy issues. In 2016, it was Republican primary voters, not Democrats, who were more divided on public policy and especially economic issues.

Democratic primary voters were also not much divided by gender or attitudes about gender. Despite Clinton's historic achievement as the first woman to win a major-party nomination, she did not garner much additional support from women, even women with a strong gender consciousness. People with more sexist attitudes, especially men, were less likely to support Clinton, but relatively few Democratic primary voters expressed overtly sexist attitudes and the impact of these attitudes faded once other factors were accounted for.

Instead, the important divisions had to do with other identities: party, race, and age. Clinton voters were more loyal to the party, more racially and ethnically diverse, and older. Sanders voters were more likely to be independent, white, and younger. Clinton's coalition in 2016 was actually the racial inverse of her 2008 coalition: in 2016, she did much better with black primary voters but worse among whites and especially whites with less favorable attitudes toward blacks.

As a result, "identity" mattered in both the Democratic and Republican primaries but in different ways. The divisions in the Democratic primary electorate centered on which groups voters belonged to—Democrat, white, black, and so on. Republican divisions centered on how voters felt about the groups they did *not* belong to, including blacks, Muslims, and immigrants. Feelings about these minority groups did not differentiate Sanders supporters from Clinton supporters, which was no surprise: Sanders and Clinton largely took the same positions on racial issues and immigration.

Clinton's coalition helped her win because it was composed of groups that were simply more numerous in the Democratic electorate than were the groups supporting Sanders—especially because the party had become so racially and ethnically diverse. But her victory presaged a real challenge: expanding that coalition in the general election.

An Organized Political Party

The writer and humorist Will Rogers famously said, "I am not a member of any organized political party. I am a Democrat." This stereotype has stuck through the years. While Republicans supposedly marched in lockstep to an increasingly conservative drummer, Democrats were depicted as the fractious party of disparate interests—once upon a time, Northern liberals and Southern conservatives, and then, more recently, feminists, environmentalists, union members, civil rights activists, and so on. The phrase "Democrats in disarray" became a trope of political journalism and commentary. For some time, "disarray"—or at least "less consensus"—characterized presidential nominations in the Democratic Party too.[4]

But in 2016, it was exactly the opposite. This was visible in the pace of endorsements by prominent Democratic leaders during the period before the Iowa caucus (figure 6.2). Unlike in the Republican primary, the Democratic endorsements came swiftly. By the end of the 2016 invisible primary, nearly 83 percent of sitting Democratic governors and members of Congress endorsed a presidential candidate—much more than in any Democratic primary since 1980. The 2016 primary even outpaced 2000, when the sitting vice president, Al Gore, ran in what was a virtual coronation.

Fully 80 percent of these officeholders endorsed Hillary Clinton (see the appendix for this chapter). She received a greater percentage than any other Democratic candidate since 1980, including what she herself had received in

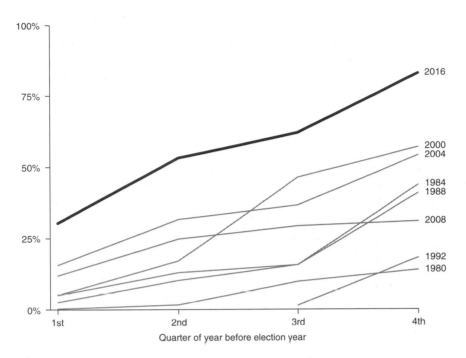

Figure 6.2.
Pace of invisible primary endorsements of Democratic presidential candidates by
Democratic governors, senators, and U.S. House members.
Endorsements that occurred earlier are assigned to the first quarter of the year
before the election. Endorsements that occurred in the election year but before the
Iowa caucus are assigned to the fourth quarter.

2007. In total, she received 201 endorsements from these Democratic leaders.
Vice President Joe Biden, who ultimately did not enter the race, received
3. Sanders received 2. Former Maryland governor Martin O'Malley received 1.
The other Democratic candidates—former Rhode Island senator and governor
Lincoln Chafee, Harvard Law School professor Lawrence Lessig, and former
Virginia senator Jim Webb—received none. This put Clinton in a very
different, and more dominant, position than she was in during her first pres-
idential bid.

Clinton's dominance can be attributed to several factors. She and her husband, former president Bill Clinton, had developed an extensive network of
supporters over their many years in politics. Clinton also had extraordinary
experience herself—as first lady, where she was involved not only in the cere-
monial aspects of the job but also in policy making and strategy, as a senator
from New York, and as secretary of state. For a time, her work as secretary of
state was widely admired and, as is common for political figures who are

outside electoral politics, her poll numbers soared. She even earned plaudits from Donald Trump, who said in 2012 that she was a "terrific woman" who "works really hard" and "does a great job."[5] By stepping down as secretary of state in early 2013, she gave herself plenty of time to build a campaign and advertise the potentially historic nature of her candidacy.

Clinton succeeded in scaring off many potential candidates. The Democratic field was smaller than in other Democratic primaries in which no incumbent president was running, such as in 1988, 2004, and 2008. Candidates whom some factions of the party urged to run—such as Massachusetts senator Elizabeth Warren, who was supported by many progressives—stayed out. The biggest nonentrant was arguably Vice President Biden himself. As members of the Obama administration, both Clinton and Biden could claim to be successors. But as vice president, Biden was more obviously "next in line."

Biden faced challenges, however. His previous presidential primary bids in 1988 and 2008 had not been particularly successful. As of 2013, commentators noted that Biden was less popular than Clinton in polls; many Democratic leaders and strategists believed that Clinton was "dominant."[6] Nevertheless, Biden thought seriously of running. Although Biden and his family were grieving after the untimely death of his son Beau from brain cancer in May 2015, reports that summer suggested that Beau and others in the family had urged Biden to run. In late August, Biden met with Warren, leading to more speculation that he would run—even though, at that point, Clinton already had 145 endorsements from Democratic governors and members of Congress.[7]

Ultimately, however, Biden declined. In a speech at the White House on October 21, 2015, he said, "Unfortunately, I believe we're out of time—the time necessary to mount a winning campaign for the nomination." Perhaps some of Clinton's supporters would have defected to Biden, but Biden's advisers—as well as Obama himself—believed that it was too late. Plouffe, channeling Obama's views, had told Biden, "Mr. Vice President, you have had a remarkable career, and it would be wrong to see it end in some hotel room in Iowa with you finishing third behind Bernie Sanders."[8]

This left Hillary Clinton virtually alone in the Democratic field. The other Democratic candidates were gaining little traction. The main opponent, Sanders, was not even a Democrat. No other, more prominent challenger entered the race. She was in a far stronger position than in 2008. Indeed, the last time there had been such a clear successor to a two-term Democratic president—Gore in 2000—he won handily with even less support in the form of endorsements than Clinton had.

But in 2016, Clinton's victory in the primaries was not as convincing. Even though she raised almost $128 million by January 2016—more than any other candidate, Democrat or Republican—Sanders raised a healthy $96 million despite his lack of support from elected party leaders and their fund-raising networks. Sanders depended instead on small donors: about 61 percent of the money he raised through January 2016 was in amounts of $200 or less, compared to 18 percent of Clinton's. More than half of Clinton's primary campaign funds were from donations of the maximum amount ($2,700), but only 8 percent of Sanders's funds were.[9]

Sanders also received a far larger percentage of the primary vote relative to how few endorsements he received during the invisible primary (figure 6.3). On average, candidates who win a higher percentage of the available endorsements also win a higher percentage of the vote, although this relationship flattens out as the percentage of endorsements increases, suggesting diminishing returns. The location of individual candidates relative to this line shows whether they received a higher- or lower-than-expected share of the vote, relative to their share of endorsements.

Sanders won a remarkable share of the vote (43%) for a candidate with almost no support from Democratic leaders. Sanders was similar to Trump, who won 44 percent of the vote despite a lack of support from Republican leaders during the invisible primary. By contrast, Hillary Clinton arguably underperformed. To be sure, no candidate had ever won as large a percentage of endorsements as Clinton did, so it was uncertain what her expected vote share should have been. But it was striking that Clinton won less of the vote than many other candidates who received fewer endorsements—George W. Bush in 2000, Gore in 2000, John Kerry in 2004, Bob Dole in 1996, and George H. W. Bush in 1988. Clinton won only a slightly higher percentage of the vote than she did in 2008 (55% versus 48%), even though far more Democratic leaders publicly supported her in 2016.

Of course, Sanders's vote share was arguably inflated by his remaining in the race to maximize his influence in the party even after it was clear Clinton would win. But Sanders's success was still extraordinary. Like Trump, Sanders managed to win many votes from members of a party with which he was barely identified, if at all. The question is how.

Taking the "Burlington Revolution" National

Sanders began his primary campaign as a virtual unknown. As of March 2015, he was less familiar than nearly every other candidate or potential candidate in either party: only 24 percent of Americans could provide an opinion of him, favorable or unfavorable, while nearly all (89%) expressed an opinion of Clinton. As of July 2015, a little over two months after Sanders announced his

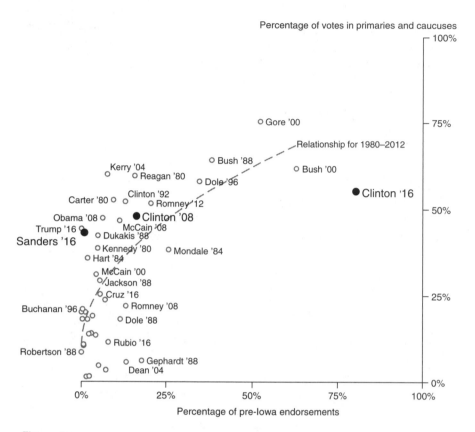

Figure 6.3.
The relationship of pre-Iowa endorsements and total primary vote share for leading presidential candidates, 1980–2016.

The graph includes all primary candidates who won a caucus or primary in at least one state. The graph excludes party primaries in which the incumbent president was running (GOP 1984 and 1992, Democrats 1996, GOP 2004, Democrats 1992). Endorsements are calculated as a fraction of all sitting governors, senators, and members of the U.S. House in a party. The dashed line is a fractional polynomial fit to the 1980–2012 data.

candidacy, 52 percent of Democrats still did not have an opinion of him.[10] For candidates like Sanders, the imperative is to make themselves known, and media coverage is therefore crucial. In 2015, Sanders benefited from increasing news coverage that was more positive than Clinton received.

As the primary campaign went on, a larger and larger percentage of stories about the Democratic primary mentioned Sanders, and a larger number of Democratic voters indicated their support for Sanders instead of Clinton

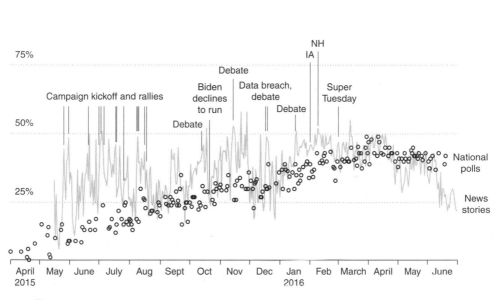

Figure 6.4.
Bernie Sanders's share of news coverage and national primary polls.
The line indicates the share of news stories mentioning Sanders. The dots indicate
individual polls, coded at the midpoint of their field dates.
Sources: Crimson Hexagon; Pollster.

(figure 6.4). Sanders's media coverage and polling numbers were strongly correlated: once smoothed to remove small bumps and wiggles, the correlation
between the data in figure 6.4 is 0.69—not as strong as the correlation between
Trump's media coverage and his poll standing, but still quite strong.[11]

The catalyst for coverage of Sanders was his official kickoff on May 21,
2015, in his hometown of Burlington, Vermont. What followed was a series of
Sanders rallies that attracted larger and larger crowds: an estimated 4,000 in
Minneapolis on May 31; 5,500 in Denver on June 20; 9,600 in Madison on
July 1; 11,000 in Phoenix on July 18; and then, from August 8 to August 10,
15,000 in Seattle; 28,000 in Portland, Oregon; and 27,500 in Los Angeles. In
the early going, at least some of these rally attendees showed up not only
because they had seen Sanders in the news but because they had been mobilized by the Sanders campaign and Sanders supporters via Facebook, Reddit,
emails, and other social media, or by low-tech strategies like paper flyers and
sidewalk chalk.[12] At this point in time, Sanders's share of news coverage far
exceeded his share in national polls.

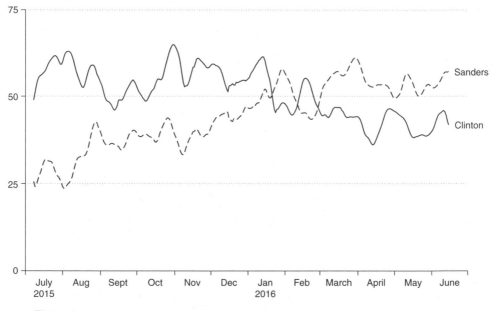

Figure 6.5.
Net favorable ratings of Hillary Clinton and Bernie Sanders among Democratic voters. The graph depicts the percentage of Democrats and Democratic-leaning independents with a favorable view of each candidate, minus the percentage with an unfavorable opinion.
Source: Gallup daily polls.

The question for Sanders was how to turn enthusiastic rallies into meaningful support on a national scale. Many candidates have done better at attracting crowds than winning votes. (Howard Dean in 2004 is one example.) Sanders was often holding rallies where he already had lots of supporters, which was frequently in places outside the crucial early primary or caucus states. So it was appropriate to ask, as an MSNBC headline put it the day Sanders kicked off his campaign, "Can Bernie Sanders take the 'Burlington Revolution' national?"[13]

This is where news coverage came in. Many of the spikes in coverage of Sanders came after days on which he held rallies (figure 6.4). This again served the function of "conferring status," whereby media coverage signals that someone's "behavior and opinions are significant enough to require public notice."[14] The crowds at the rallies were interpreted as evidence of a viable campaign, as is often true of horse race news coverage. For example, even before the big rallies, an overflow crowd of 300 at a Sanders event in rural Iowa was framed as a story of Sanders's "gaining momentum" and possibly mounting a "credible challenge." Of course, campaigns can orchestrate an "overflow crowd" by planning an event in a small venue. Nevertheless, Sanders's crowds contrasted with Clinton's small pop-in visits at diners and coffee shops. This translated into news coverage of Sanders that was largely favorable.[15]

This increasing and increasingly positive coverage helped give Sanders a national profile—one that Reddit groups and sidewalk chalk alone could not. By the end of August 2015, the percentage of Democrats who had no opinion about Sanders had dropped and the percentage with a favorable view had increased to 53 percent from 39 percent (figure 6.5). Notably, Sanders accomplished this even with Trump dominating news coverage. In fact, across the campaign, more coverage of Trump on cable networks was associated with *more* coverage of Sanders but less coverage of Clinton, Jeb Bush, Marco Rubio, and others. Attention to Trump did not come at Sanders's expense.[16]

For Hillary Clinton, the initial months of the campaign were quite different (figures 6.5 and 6.6). As Sanders began receiving more news coverage, she received less. As Sanders's poll numbers inched upward, hers fell. Compounding her challenge was the growing attention to Biden, particularly after reports that his family was encouraging him to run. Biden's poll numbers rose in tandem with the news coverage.

When Clinton did make news, it was often because of scandals. The biggest was the issue that dogged her throughout the campaign: her use of a personal email account and private email server, located at her home in Chappaqua, New York, while serving as secretary of state. This was first reported in the *New York Times* on March 2, 2015.[17] Subsequent coverage focused on whether Clinton had violated federal government rules about the use of personal email for conducting government business; why she had eventually turned over only some of her emails to the State Department; and whether her email account and server were secure enough to protect sensitive or even classified correspondence. Clinton's office said that "nothing nefarious was at play" and that they had turned over her official emails while deleting about 32,000 personal emails. As one Clinton aide put it, "If she emailed with her daughter about flower arrangements for her wedding, that didn't go in." Clinton's advisers also said that she had not used a personal email account for classified correspondence.[18]

In addition, Clinton faced scrutiny for the work of the Clinton Foundation, a charitable organization that had been established by Bill Clinton. The Clinton Foundation had accepted donations from foreign actors or governments who were also pursuing goals with the Obama administration. There had been contact between Clinton Foundation leaders and officials at the State Department that raised questions about whether Clinton, as secretary of state, had favored donors to the Clinton Foundation. The story emerged in the spring of 2015 with the publication of a book called *Clinton Cash* and a

New York Times article ("Cash Flowed to Clinton Foundation amid Russian Uranium Deal") published on April 23.[19]

These scandals, especially the email server, proceeded in what may be the worst possible way for a political candidate: a steady drip of revelations and news coverage throughout the campaign.[20] After a federal judge ordered the State Department to release portions of Clinton's emails every month, these releases created regular spikes of news coverage, as did the September 8 apology that Clinton released on Facebook. Systematic analysis of that coverage showed it to be very negative. In March 2015, when the email story broke, the percentage of negative references of Clinton outweighed the percentage of positive references by 85 points. Clinton's coverage became less negative in April, but from April to September there was still much more negative coverage than positive coverage.[21] The contrast between coverage of Clinton and Sanders was dramatic.

Unsurprisingly, Clinton's support among Democratic voters weakened. She had begun the campaign with very strong support: in an early March 2015 Gallup poll, 79 percent rated her favorably and only 13 percent rated her unfavorably.[22] This was better than her rating, as well as Obama's, at the same point in the 2008 campaign. It was also better than Al Gore's in March 2000. By early September, her favorability slipped (figure 6.5) and her support in primary trial-heat polls dropped 17 points (figure 6.6). Stories at this time wrote of "the latest piece of bad news for Hillary Rodham Clinton"; Clinton's "jittery supporters," "beleaguered candidacy," and "weakness in the polls"; how "top Democrats are increasingly concerned about her electability"; and the possibility of an "11th-hour rescue mission" by Joe Biden, John Kerry, or even Al Gore.[23]

Sanders still faced challenges, of course. In a late September poll of Democratic activists, 84 percent thought that Clinton could win the general election, but only 49 percent thought that Sanders could. Clinton also led Sanders on the question of who could win the Democratic nomination and who was acceptable to most Democrats. But Sanders's weaknesses were not the dominant narrative. Indeed, the *Washington Post*'s Philip Rucker and John Wagner noted that Sanders "had not faced the kind of media scrutiny, let alone attacks from opponents, that leading candidates eventually experience."[24]

In October, however, Clinton's fortunes improved. At the first Democratic debate on October 13, Clinton was judged the "clear winner" and was said to have "dominated the debate stage" while showing "experience and self-assurance." Sanders even defended Clinton from questions about her private email server: "Let me say something that may not be great politics, but I think the secretary is right—and that is that the American people are sick and tired of hearing about your damn emails." This prompted a standing ovation from

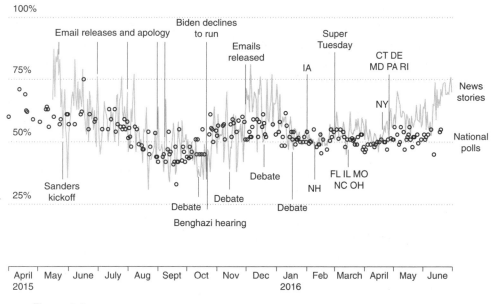

Figure 6.6.
Hillary Clinton's share of news coverage and national primary polls.
The line indicates the share of news stories mentioning Clinton. The dots indicate
individual polls, coded at the midpoint of their field dates.
Sources: Crimson Hexagon; Pollster.

the audience. Postdebate polls found that the majority of Democrats thought that Clinton had won. Even Trump declared her "the winner."[25]

Clinton also benefited when Joe Biden decided not to run on October 21. Clinton's poll numbers immediately jumped as pollsters stopped asking about Biden, and the race then became a de facto two-person race between Clinton and Sanders (figure 6.6). There was much less change, if any, in Sanders's poll numbers. The same analysis of news coverage that showed Clinton at such a disadvantage for all of 2015 found that in October her coverage was net positive, although only barely so. By the end of the month, her net favorable rating among Democrats had increased 14 points (figure 6.5).[26]

From that point until early January, little changed in the race—despite additional releases of Clinton's emails, two more debates, and an incident in which Sanders staffers had retrieved proprietary Clinton campaign information from a voter database maintained by the Democratic National Committee. (Sanders apologized for this in the December debate.) Sanders's poll numbers hovered around 30 percent for most of November and December, and news coverage of the polls shifted to emphasize Clinton's strengths.[27]

Then this changed quickly in Sanders's favor. The sequence began with a surge in televised advertising in Iowa, especially by Sanders. One of Sanders's ads—a minute-long montage of American images and footage from Sanders rallies, set to the tune of Simon and Garfunkel's "America"—elicited very positive responses when it was shown to a representative sample of Americans. Nearly 80 percent said that it made them at least a little bit happy or hopeful. No other ad in 2016 was rated so positively.[28]

The spike in Iowa advertising coincided with a Sanders surge in Iowa polls. A January 2–7 NBC News/*Wall Street Journal*/Marist Iowa poll showed Clinton leading Sanders by only 3 points. In December, Clinton had led by an average of 16 points. News coverage of this poll emphasized the "tight race" and that Clinton "could lose." In four subsequent polls, two showed Clinton narrowly winning and two showed Sanders winning. Only one poll in all of 2015 had shown Sanders ahead of Clinton in Iowa.[29]

There is no way to know for sure that the spike in Sanders's advertising helped his poll standing in Iowa. But given that many Democrats did not have an opinion of Sanders even as of early January—roughly 25 percent in national Gallup polls—there were clearly many Iowa Democrats who could be influenced by an advertising blitz. And this same pattern in Iowa had happened before. In late 2011 and early 2012, Rick Santorum surged in Iowa polls after a burst of local campaigning, as did Ben Carson in the summer of 2015.[30]

Just as it did for Santorum and Carson, an Iowa surge brought Sanders national attention. His share of overall news coverage increased. Sanders was mentioned in 35 percent of news stories in the first week of January, 39 percent in the second week, 44 percent in the third week, and 46 percent in the final week (figure 6.4). Meanwhile, Clinton's average lead in national primary polls shrank from 20 points to 13 points. Headlines said things like, "Hillary Clinton Gets Set for a Long Slog against Bernie Sanders."[31]

The tone of news coverage continued to favor Sanders for the rest of the primary.[32] In part, this was because Sanders won twenty-three caucuses and primaries and continued to exceed the expectations of political observers, which is the surest way to generate positive news coverage in a presidential primary. He never experienced a period of intense scrutiny like some Republican candidates received. Clinton herself did not even supply this scrutiny. Although the two had some sharp exchanges in candidate debates, neither attacked the other in television advertising. Altogether, 99.75 percent of the ads that Clinton and Sanders aired during the primaries were positive ads.

The polling trends matched the tone of news coverage. In the initial months of 2016, Sanders became more popular, while Clinton's popularity slipped (figure 6.5). By the end of the campaign, Sanders's net favorable rating was higher than Clinton's among Democrats (+57 versus +42). The decline in Clinton's favorability contrasts with what happened in 2008. Even after a bruising fight with Obama, her net favorable rating (+48) was the same as at the beginning of the 2008 primary and higher than at the end of the 2016 primary.[33]

This decline in Clinton's popularity among Democratic primary voters came about because Sanders supporters viewed Clinton less favorably as the campaign went on. In the RAND Presidential Election Panel Study (PEPS), which interviewed the same voters twice during the primary, 27 percent of Sanders supporters had an unfavorable view of Clinton in the initial interview (conducted December 14, 2015–January 6, 2016). When interviewed in March 2016, 37 percent did. By the end of May, nearly 60 percent of Sanders supporters rated Clinton unfavorably, according to YouGov/*Economist* polls.[34] Meanwhile, Clinton supporters grew to like Sanders *more*: in the PEPS, the percentage with a favorable view of Sanders increased from 58 percent in December 2015 to 73 percent in March 2016.

In other words, Sanders's success was not so much about capitalizing on an early reservoir of discontent with Clinton. It was about building support despite her popularity within the party. Clinton's favorability ratings were high early on and experienced no secular decline throughout 2015, even as Sanders's support in trial-heat polls increased. Instead, Sanders's challenge to Clinton appeared to shift the views of his own supporters, making them less favorable to Clinton in the winter and spring of 2016. This helps explain why Clinton's slog was long.

But a long slog did not mean that the race was a nail-biter. Clinton won three of the first four primaries—a narrow victory in Iowa, an unsurprising loss in New Hampshire, a 5-point win in Nevada, and a decisive victory in South Carolina—which gave her a delegate lead that would only grow. By April, Sanders's fund-raising was falling sharply, news coverage of Clinton was increasing, and her national poll numbers improved as well. Her lead over Sanders increased from its low of 6 points in mid-April to nearly 11 points in early June.[35]

Ultimately, Sanders's challenge, though significant, was never strong enough to put the nomination itself in much doubt. Clinton's coalition was more than large enough for her to win.

"I'm Not Even Sure He Is One"

Hillary Clinton's coalition depended on support from not only Democratic leaders but also Democratic voters. In general, presidential candidates supported by party leaders in the invisible primary do better in the primaries with

partisan voters than with independents, perhaps because party leaders provide cues for partisan voters.[36] In 2008, Clinton bested Obama in endorsements and beat him 51 percent to 45 percent among voters who identified as
Democrats.

In 2016, partisanship divided voters even more. Despite reliably voting
with the Democrats in Congress, Sanders had not invested in the Democratic
Party and once described it as "ideologically bankrupt." As Sanders pondered
a presidential run, his advisers told him that he would have to sacrifice some
of that independence and run as a Democrat. But when Sanders was asked
on the day of his presidential announcement if he was now a Democrat, he
replied, "No . . . I'm an independent." Throughout the campaign, Sanders
touted his independence, vowed to take on the political establishment, and
railed against the Democratic National Committee and the party's nomination rules for giving "superdelegate" votes at the party convention to party
leaders—who, unsurprisingly, preferred Clinton to Sanders by a margin of 609
to 47. Sanders also dismissed Clinton's endorsements, including from stalwart
progressive organizations such as Planned Parenthood and the Human Rights
Campaign, as "establishment politics."[37] By contrast, Clinton touted her party
endorsements and her history of working for the party and its candidates.
Clinton took Sanders to task for his criticism of the party and his reluctance
to raise money for down-ballot Democrats. "He's a relatively new Democrat,"
she said of Sanders, "and, in fact, I'm not even sure he is one."[38]

This battle between a quintessential party insider and an ardent political
independent made party identification strongly associated with support for
Clinton or Sanders even before Sanders's campaign picked up steam
(figure 6.7). In early June 2015, Hillary Clinton had the support of between 60
and 70 percent of Democratic voters, including those who described their partisanship as "strong" and those who described it as "not very strong" (labeled
"weak" in the figure). Her support among independent voters who leaned
toward the Democratic Party, however, was over 20 points lower. The effect
of partisanship then increased during the campaign as voters acquired more
information about the candidates. By the end of the primaries, two-thirds of
strong Democrats, half of weak Democrats, and only one-third of Democratic-
leaning independents preferred her to Bernie Sanders. The same pattern is
visible even in partisanship that was measured years before the 2016 primary:
in the Views of the American Electorate Research (VOTER) Survey, those who
strongly identified as Democrats in 2011 were 25 points more likely to support Clinton than independents who leaned toward the party.

This pattern advantaged Clinton more than Sanders. Democrats were
over 70 percent of the primary electorate in most states, according to exit polls.
In YouGov/*Economist* surveys, a majority of Democratic primary voters (54%)

popular among blacks and whites with more favorable views of blacks, whereas his opponents became less popular. In fact, Hillary Clinton was the first public figure to experience this "Obama effect." Before the 2008 primary, white Democrats with more sympathetic views of African Americans liked her more than whites with less sympathetic views. That pattern reversed itself in 2008, as blacks and racially sympathetic whites gravitated to Obama and less sympathetic whites to Clinton. But after Clinton joined the Obama administration, the original pattern reasserted itself.[47] Obama's tacit endorsement of Clinton's candidacy—he never officially endorsed her but made statements expressing his strong support—likely boosted her chances of winning the black vote.

The second factor was Sanders himself. To be sure, Sanders also staked out progressive positions on racial issues. But Sanders was a little-known senator from a mostly white state who had been criticized by African American activists for preaching a message of economic equality that ignored the intersection of race and class. In 2015, African Americans rated him nearly 60 points less favorably than they did Clinton.[48]

The Clinton campaign therefore viewed states with large minority electorates, particularly in the South, as a firewall that would protect her from potentially poor showings in the largely white states of Iowa and New Hampshire. So, after losing the New Hampshire primary, Clinton and her allies pressed their advantage with minority voters. Before the South Carolina primary, Clinton criticized Sanders's focus on economic inequality: "We have to begin by facing up to the reality of systemic racism because these are not only problems of economic inequality. These are problems of racial inequality." She tied herself to Obama, mentioning him twenty-one times in the February 11 Democratic debate, while chastising Sanders for his criticism of the Obama administration. The Congressional Black Caucus also endorsed Clinton before the South Carolina primary, and Representative John Lewis (D-GA), himself a civil rights icon, challenged Sanders's claims of civil rights activism.[49]

All these factors—Clinton's explicit racial appeals, her embrace of Obama, black voters' unfamiliarity with Sanders, her strong support from black politicians—ensured that race's impact on Clinton's primary bid in 2016 would be far different from the impact it had eight years earlier. Indeed, in twenty states that held primaries in both 2008 and 2016, Clinton's average support among black voters was over 60 points higher in 2016 than in 2008 (figure 6.8). In the same states where she had lost 84 percent of black voters to Obama, she took 77 percent of the black vote from Sanders. Clinton did particularly well among blacks who both rated Obama very favorably and said that race was a very important part of their identity.[50]

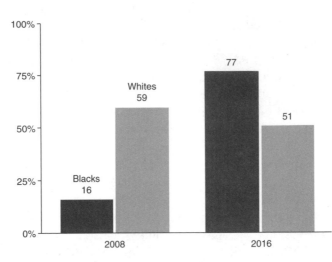

Figure 6.8.
Hillary Clinton's average two-candidate support among whites and blacks in the 2008 and 2016 Democratic primaries.
Clinton's support is calculated as her share of the vote for her and Obama in 2008 and her and Sanders in 2016. The averages are weighted by the number of primary votes for her and Obama or her and Sanders. The twenty states included in the analysis are: Alabama, Arkansas, Connecticut, Florida, Georgia, Illinois, Indiana, Maryland, Michigan, Mississippi, Missouri, New York, North Carolina, Ohio, Pennsylvania, South Carolina, Tennessee, Texas, Virginia, and Wisconsin.
Source: State exit polls.

At the same time, Clinton's average statewide share of the white vote was 8 points lower in 2016 than in 2008. In part, this is because the racial attitudes of white voters played a much different role in 2016 from in 2008 (figure 6.9). In 2008, white Democratic primary voters who attributed racial inequality to a lack of effort gravitated to Clinton instead of Obama. In 2016, when Clinton was Obama's ally and not his opponent, these white voters were less likely to support her. The loss of these white voters is one reason that Hillary Clinton performed worse among white voters overall.[51]

Clinton won despite this. Indeed, Clinton's 2016 coalition may be the one that Democrats must assemble to win the nomination of a party whose base has become increasingly progressive on matters of race and ethnicity. But this coalition may have come at a cost. After losing the Michigan primary to Sanders, Clinton reportedly felt that "she'd focused too heavily on black and brown voters at the expense of competing for the whites who had formed her base in 2008."[52] It was not just Michigan, either. In the Ohio and Pennsylvania primaries, both of which Clinton won, her vote margin among whites

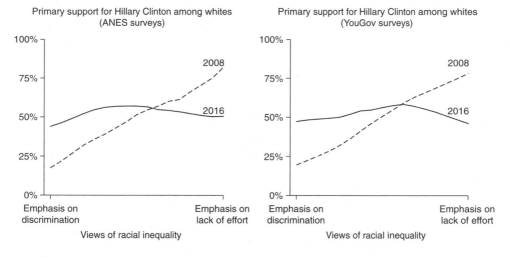

Figure 6.9.
Racial attitudes and support for Hillary Clinton in the 2008 and 2016 Democratic primaries.
Sources: American National Election Studies Time Series (left-hand panel); 2008 Cooperative Campaign Analysis Project and 2016 YouGov/*Economist* surveys (right-hand panel).

decreased by 10 points compared to eight years before. Clinton's path to the nomination in 2016 raised the question of whether she could win over the same white voters in November.

The Generation Gap

The other dominant divide in the Democratic primaries involved age. It might seem perplexing that the seventy-four-year-old Sanders could build such support among voters forty or fifty years younger, but it was hardly unprecedented. Age has often divided Democrats in presidential primaries. In 1968, 1972, 1984, 2004, and 2008, the Democratic presidential candidate who challenged party insiders with a "fresh" or "new" perspective garnered more support from younger voters than from older voters.

The attractiveness of new political perspectives to the young has historically derived more from style and rhetoric that appeal to youthful idealism than from policy positions. For example, since 1968, every major third-party candidate for president, regardless of their policy positions, has performed better with younger than older voters. The same has been true in Democratic primaries. In Larry Bartels's study of the 1984 primary, he attributes

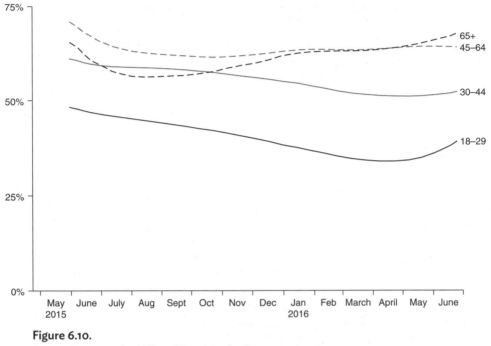

Figure 6.10.
Age and support for Hillary Clinton in the Democratic primary.
The lines are smoothed with lowess (bandwidth = 0.8).
Source: YouGov/*Economist* polls.

Gary Hart's strong support among younger voters to his style and "new ideas" rhetoric rather than his vague issue stands. Similarly, in the 2008 primary, Obama's support among younger voters had little to do with policies. Democratic voters' own policy positions were not associated with their preference for Clinton or Obama. Rather, Obama's popularity with younger primary voters stemmed more from his campaign messages of hope and change, which contrasted with Clinton's emphasis on the political experience that made her "ready to lead on day one."[53] Clinton's and Sanders's rhetoric and style were also quite different. Sanders called for a revolution that would fundamentally change politics. Clinton ran as a pragmatic incrementalist—or, as she put it, "a progressive who likes to get things done"—and criticized Sanders's approach as unrealistic, much as she had criticized Obama's "fantastical" message of hope and change in 2008.

Clinton's challenge with younger voters was evident early (figure 6.10). As the campaign went on, these age differences grew larger. By the end of the primaries, about two-thirds of Democratic voters over the age of forty-five supported Hillary Clinton, compared to half of Democrats between the ages of thirty and forty-four, and only a third of those under the age of thirty. The problem for Sanders, however, was that there just were not that many younger voters in the Democratic primary electorate. Analyses of voter file data in selected Democratic primary states showed that voters between the ages of eighteen and twenty-nine made up only 14 percent of the electorate in Michigan, 12 percent in Texas, and 11 percent in Ohio. This reflects the predictable pattern whereby younger voters turn out to vote at much lower rates than older Americans. Even in the 2008 primary, when Obama's candidacy was thought to have mobilized young voters, eighteen- to twenty-nine-year olds were still three times less likely than senior citizens to vote in the primaries.[54]

If Sanders faced the challenge of mobilizing young voters in the primary, Clinton would face a similar challenge in the general election. Young people certainly continued to lean toward the Democratic Party. Indeed, a Harvard Institute of Politics survey of young people conducted at the end of the primaries found that three-quarters had an unfavorable opinion of Donald Trump. But at the same time, 53 percent had an unfavorable opinion of Clinton. The question was whether young people would turn out to vote in November for a candidate whom many saw as the lesser of two evils.

The Woman Card

Hillary Clinton's bid to become the first female presidential nominee of a major party made gender a constant theme of the campaign. This was, in fact, Clinton's intention. In 2008, she repeatedly said, "I am not running as a woman." But in 2016, she openly embraced the historic significance of becoming the country's first woman president.

Strategizing effectively about gender was never easy for Clinton. Women in leadership roles often encounter a "double bind."[55] If they conform to masculinized notions of strong and competent leadership, they risk being called aggressive or overly ambitious—"a nasty woman," as Trump would later call Clinton. But if they show compassion or emotion, they risk being seen as ineffective and soft—lacking "the strength" for the position, as Trump said of Clinton in December 2015. The challenge for women is magnified when the office at stake has been held exclusively by men and the job description includes commander-in-chief of the military.[56]

The double bind was evident in Clinton's 2008 campaign, which sought to neutralize the issue of gender even at the expense of her likability. Her chief strategist, Mark Penn, suggested in an early memo that Margaret Thatcher should be the role model: "The adjectives used about her (Iron Lady) were not of good humor or warmth, they were of smart, tough leadership." The political scientists Regina Lawrence and Melody Rose found, with a few notable exceptions, that Clinton followed Penn's strategy by avoiding gendered appeals and engaging in "not so subtle efforts to 'outmale' her opponents." Perhaps consequently, voters perceived Clinton as a stronger leader than Barack Obama. But, just as the double bind would predict, voters perceived Clinton as less likable than him.[57]

Hillary Clinton's masculinized campaign was arguably one reason that gender had only a small effect on voting behavior in the 2008 primaries. Clinton did perform better with female voters than with men, but this gender gap was modest, particularly in contrast to the enormous racial divide. In Democratic primary exit polls, women were only about 8 percentage points more likely to support Hillary Clinton than men were, on average. Moreover, women who expressed solidarity with other women were not more likely to support Clinton, relative to women who expressed less solidarity. Voters who supported traditional gender roles and expressed resentment of women who demand gender equality were also no less likely to support Clinton. In fact, it was the opposite: those with traditional views of gender roles were more likely to support Clinton over Obama. This is because traditional attitudes about gender are correlated with less favorable views of African Americans.[58]

But a lot changed after 2008. Clinton had occupied the historically male-dominated position of secretary of state and seen her public image reach new heights. Many strategists believed that she could now embrace her gender because she had shown she was "tough enough" for the job during her time as secretary of state.[59] Clinton did exactly this. For example, in the October 2015 debate she said, "Finally, fathers will be able to say to their daughters, 'You too can grow up to be president.'" She answered a question about being an insider by saying, "I can't think of anything more of an outsider than electing the first woman president," and "Being the first woman president would be quite a change from the presidents we've had." Republicans regularly attacked her for playing the gender card. She always responded the same way: "Well, if calling for equal pay and paid leave and women's health is playing the gender card, then deal me in." After Trump said in April that "the only thing she has going for her is the woman card," the Clinton campaign issued donors a hot pink "woman card" with the phrase "Deal me in" at the bottom.

Did this strategy work? There was some evidence it did. In states that conducted Democratic primary exit polls in both 2008 and 2016, Hillary Clinton increased her vote share by 9 points among women (53 percent to 62 percent) compared to 5 points among men (45 percent to 50 percent), although it is not certain that the difference was due to gender per se. Clinton's argument about daughters may also have mattered: in YouGov/*Economist* polls, Clinton performed about 8 points better among parents of daughters than among similarly situated parents of only sons. Other studies have found that having daughters makes parents more supportive of feminist positions.[60] But at the same time, Clinton faced the double bind again despite the shift in her strategy. In a May 2016 YouGov/*Economist* poll, 49 percent said she was a "very strong leader," whereas only 29 percent said this of Sanders. But she lagged Sanders in likability: 40 percent said that they liked Clinton "a lot" and 21 percent disliked her, whereas 50 percent liked Sanders a lot and only 9 percent disliked him.

The negative consequence of Clinton's gender was visible in another way: Clinton lost votes among voters with more sexist attitudes, although these losses were mitigated by the fact that there were not very many Democratic primary voters with these attitudes in the first place. A measure of attitudes about gender—called "modern sexism" in the academic literature—helps capture subtle biases against women, such as the belief that there is no real discrimination against women and that women get undeserved special favors. Surveys tap into those beliefs by asking respondents to agree or disagree with statements like, "Women who complain about harassment cause more problems than they solve."[61]

Clinton did worse among the minority of Democratic primary voters who expressed more sexist attitudes, and especially among men (figure 6.11). There was also a strong association between sexism and views of Clinton among Sanders supporters. Male Sanders supporters who expressed some degree of sexism—men often described as "Bernie Bros" during the campaign—were most unfavorable to Clinton.[62] But the potential electoral impact of sexism in the Democratic primary was muted because there were not that many sexist voters who could penalize Clinton for her gender. Most Democrats and Sanders supporters gave responses that put them toward the progressive end of this modern sexism measure. Clinton lost support among only a small minority of roughly 10 percent or so.

One other way that gender could have mattered for Clinton was if women were attracted to her because of their own gender or feminist consciousness. But there was little evidence of this. For instance, women with the most egalitarian views of gender were not particularly likely to support Hillary Clinton in the primaries (figure 6.11). Moreover, in other surveys, women who said that gender was a very important part of their identity were not more likely to support Clinton than were women who said gender was not important. And women who described themselves as feminists—35 percent of female voters in the Democratic primaries—were no more likely than women who did not identify as feminists to support Clinton over Sanders.[63]

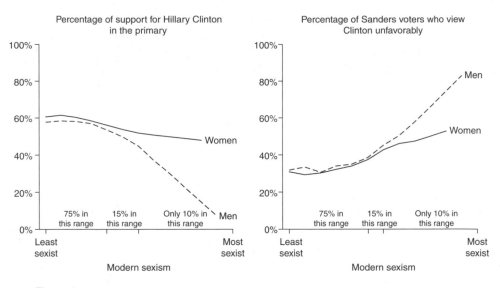

Figure 6.11.
Sexism and views of Hillary Clinton in the Democratic primary.
Modern sexism was measured in the December 2015 wave and primary vote and
Clinton favorability in the July–August wave. The lines have been smoothed using
lowess. The notation along the horizontal axis describes the share of voters along the
range of the modern sexism scale.
Source: PEPS.

    The weak effects of gender consciousness are not surprising. Unlike ra-
cial solidarity among African Americans or racial attitudes among whites,
gender consciousness has not typically been a substantial force in modern
American political behavior. As the political scientists Nancy Burns and
Donald Kinder have written, "The social organization of gender emphasizes
intimacy between men and women; the social organization of race emphasizes separation between whites and blacks. Separation fosters solidarity
among African Americans. Integration impairs solidarity among women."[64]
    In fact, at least some liberal women were offended by Clinton's appeals
to gender solidarity. Susan Sarandon voiced this sentiment when she tweeted,
"I don't vote with my vagina. It's so insulting to women to think that you
would follow a candidate JUST because she's a woman." One target of Sarandon's ire, the first female secretary of state, Madeleine Albright, ultimately had
to apologize for saying, "There's a special place in hell for women who don't
help each other," when she campaigned with Clinton in February 2016.[65] The
episode showed the challenge of galvanizing women with a message of gender solidarity.

Ultimately, then, gender was not the dominant divide in the Democratic primary. This raised concerns about the general election, where Clinton would need support from women to offset possible defections from voters who have more traditional views about gender roles than Democratic primary voters. Her two campaigns for the Democratic nomination suggested that this would be a challenge.

Identity More than Issues

To many observers, the Democratic nomination was not primarily a story of social identity. The story was the fight between the progressive and centrist wings of the party. Sanders supporters were supposed to be well to the left of Clinton supporters on taxes, trade, health care, and so on. But that was not the case: Clinton and Sanders supporters were mostly similar on these and other issues. The choice between Clinton and Sanders depended little on policy battles and more on identities grounded in partisanship and race.

To be sure, voters certainly perceived Clinton and Sanders as ideologically different—and increasingly so as the campaign went on and voters learned more. For example, in the December 2015 wave of the PEPS, 14 percent of Democratic primary voters called Clinton "very liberal," 43 percent called her "liberal," and 27 percent called her "moderate" (only 10% could not place her ideologically). Sanders was less well known at that point, with 24 percent unable to place him, but already 36 percent called Sanders very liberal. In March 2016, 48 percent called him very liberal. These perceptions of the candidates were reflected in how Democratic voters described themselves. Sanders voters were more likely to describe themselves as liberal or very liberal rather than moderate or conservative, even when asked five years before the primary itself (see table 6.1). Although identification as liberal usually goes together with identification as a Democrat, the two factors worked in opposite directions in the primary—with strong Democrats gravitating to Clinton and strong liberals to Sanders.

But although Sanders voters tended to describe themselves as more liberal than did Clinton supporters, the two groups differed little on economic policies. This was true when VOTER Survey respondents had been interviewed years earlier, in December 2011 (table 6.1). People who became Sanders supporters were no more likely than people who became Clinton supporters to favor government-provided universal health care or tax increases on the wealthy—although they were somewhat more likely to favor government regulation of business (table 6.1). Combining these three questions into an economic policy index showed Sanders and Clinton supporters to be only 0.02

Table 6.1.

Views of Clinton and Sanders Supporters

	Clinton Supporters	Sanders Supporters
Strength of identification as liberal (Dec. 2011)		
(0 = moderate or conservative; 0.5 = liberal; 1 = very liberal)	0.28	0.40
Views of economic policy (Dec. 2011)		
Economic policy index (0 = most conservative; 1 = most liberal)	0.78	0.80
Federal government provides universal health coverage	73%	74%
Increase taxes on those making $200,000 or more	84%	86%
Too little regulation of business	44%	58%
Views of economic policy (Jan. 2016)		
Economic policy index (0 = most conservative; 1 = most liberal)	0.79	0.81
Increase government services and spending	58%	61%
Increase government spending for health insurance	81%	83%
Raise the minimum wage	77%	83%
Increase government spending for child care	68%	76%
Favor increasing trade (Dec. 2011)	49%	48%
Views of economy (Dec. 2011)		
Economic anxiety index (0 = least anxious; 1 = most anxious)	0.43	0.48
Economy getting worse	14%	18%
Personal finances getting worse	22%	19%
Views of economy and economic mobility (Jan. 2016)		
Economic anxiety index (0 = least anxious; 1 = most anxious)	0.48	0.60
Economy getting worse versus one year ago	18%	19%
Economy will be worse one year from now	16%	16%
None or little opportunity for average person to get ahead	44%	70%
Compared to parents, harder for you to move up income ladder	42%	66%
Harder for people to improve finances versus twenty years ago	41%	75%

Source: December 2011 refers to the 2016 VOTER Survey, where primary vote preferences were measured in July 2016, and the other measures are from December 2011. January 2016 refers to the 2016 American National Election Studies Pilot Study.

points apart on a 0–1 scale. Sanders and Clinton supporters also had virtually identical attitudes regarding trade policy. Focusing on these earlier data is valuable because it guards against the very real possibility that voters adopted the views of the candidate they came to support for other reasons.

But even in January 2016, after months of campaigning, Sanders and Clinton supporters had similar views on key issues. In the American National Election Studies Pilot Study, Clinton and Sanders supporters did not differ much in their views of government spending overall, spending on health insurance or child care, or raising the minimum wage—as well as on an index combining these items. Large majorities supported these policies regardless of whether they supported Clinton or Sanders.[66]

Sanders supporters were more distinctive in their views of the economy and economic mobility. In both surveys, Sanders supporters expressed somewhat less positive views of the economy than did Clinton supporters. This was true even in December 2011, suggesting these differences were not purely a consequence of campaign rhetoric, including Sanders's critique of the economy's health and Obama's stewardship of the economy. Sanders supporters were also more likely than Clinton supporters to say that there was little or no opportunity for the average person to get ahead and that it was harder to "move up the income ladder." Of course, those are sentiments that Sanders had been expressing for months, which may mean that Sanders supporters in this survey were merely echoing him. But regardless, differences in concern about the economy and economic opportunity did not translate into distinctive policy preferences.

Other analyses showed the same thing. The political scientist Daniel Hopkins found at best small differences on policy issues between eventual Clinton and Sanders supporters when they had been interviewed in earlier years. Hopkins argued that the factors behind Sanders's support "do not suggest that it is grounded in an enduring liberalism." The political scientists Christopher Achen and Larry Bartels, who were the first to describe the findings from the January 2016 survey, wrote that "Mr. Sanders's support is concentrated not among liberal ideologues." Achen and Bartels also located the origins of Sanders's support in social and political identities.[67]

The important role of these identities stands out in statistical models of people's preference for Clinton or Sanders in the VOTER Survey (figure 6.12; see this chapter's appendix for details). The relationships involving partisanship, race, and age persisted: being more strongly identified with the Democratic Party, being nonwhite, and being older were all associated with support for Clinton. Identifying as liberal was associated with support for Sanders. There were also more modest associations between support for Sanders and both economic anxiety and political trust: Sanders did better among those

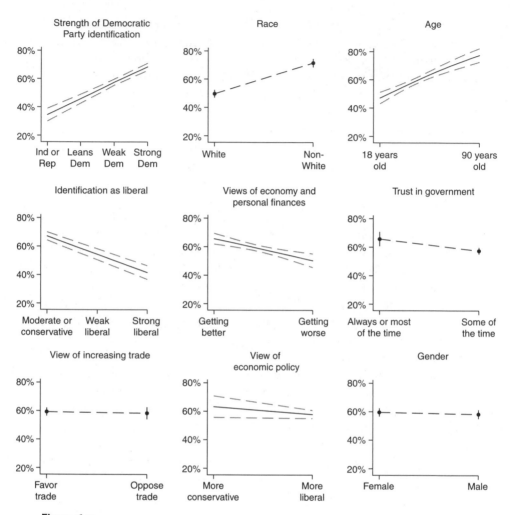

Figure 6.12.

The relationship between Clinton support and various factors.

The figure displays the predicted association between each factor and support for Hillary Clinton, with a 95 percent confidence interval. These are derived from the statistical models in the chapter appendix. Candidate preference was measured in July 2016; other factors were measured in December 2011.

Source: VOTER Survey.

with more concerns about the economy and those who expressed less trust in the government.[68] Similarly, other surveys showed that Sanders also did better among those who had more pessimistic views of economic mobility and agreed with the statement, "People like me don't have any say about what the government does" (see the chapter appendix). However, those beliefs were measured during the campaign and may be consequences, more than causes, of candidate support.

Other explanations received mixed or little support, however. There was little apparent impact of views on economic issues in the VOTER Survey (figure 6.12), and similar findings emerged in other surveys as well (see again the chapter appendix). Sanders and Clinton supporters may have been divided by whether they called themselves liberal, but they were not divided by their actual liberalism on economic policies. Similarly, views of trade had almost no relationship to support for Sanders or Clinton. Although trade was discussed and debated in both parties' primaries, voters' own opinions on the issue appeared to matter little, if it all. The role of gender did not emerge clearly either. Neither gender nor sexism was associated with primary vote preferences, once other factors were accounted for. Views of African Americans, Muslims, or immigration also had weak associations with support for Clinton or Sanders, likely because Sanders and Clinton did not disagree very much about immigration or racial issues.

Ultimately, the impact of partisan and racial identities in the Democratic primary was so strong that the results of the individual state contests could be explained in large part with only two factors: the percentage of African Americans in the state and the percentage of Democrats in the primary electorate (figure 6.13). Clinton performed about 50 percentage points better on average in the states with the largest share of black voters than she did in the whitest ones. This factor alone explained almost 70 percent of the variation in state primary outcomes. Clinton's advantage in these predominantly black states was dismissed by Sanders's advisers early on. They trumpeted Sanders's strength in the early primary and caucus states, such as Iowa, saying, "We're going to show that a prairie fire beats a firewall."[69] In this case, it did not.

Similarly, in the twenty-seven states that conducted exit polls during the 2016 primaries, Clinton performed over 30 percentage points better on average in states with large Democratic electorates than she did in states with the most independent primary voters. These two factors combined explain almost 80 percent of the variation in state primary outcomes.

Conclusion

Clinton's "long, long journey" to the Democratic nomination began in a very different place from Donald Trump's journey to the Republican nomination. Clinton had the strong support of Democratic leaders, while Trump had virtually no support among Republican leaders. She was perhaps the ultimate party insider, while Trump, like Sanders, was not. Thus, Trump's success in

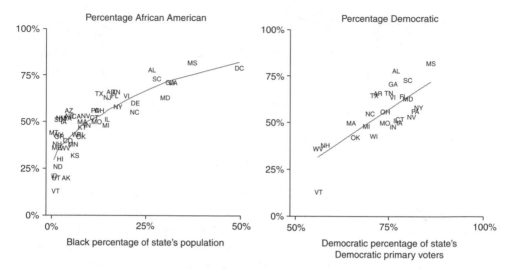

Figure 6.13.
Race, party, and Hillary Clinton's statewide share of the primary vote.
Sources: Democratic primary exit polls; U.S. Census (black population); Dave Leip's
Election Atlas (Clinton vote).

the primary, like Sanders's, depended on garnering media coverage and building support among those voters predisposed toward his candidacy.

The support for Trump and Sanders was often assumed to have similar roots. This was wrong in many respects. Trump drew support from people who had liberal views on economic policy and conservative views on immigration but not necessarily any greater economic anxiety. But Sanders's support depended little on views of economic policy and racial and ethnic minorities but somewhat more on economic anxiety.

This was a direct consequence of how the candidates campaigned. Trump defended entitlement programs and criticized the impact of immigration, which put him at odds with many of his competitors. But Clinton's and Sanders's policy differences were more a matter of degree than of kind. Both wanted to increase the minimum wage and taxes on the rich but disagreed about how much. Both wanted the government to ease the burden on college students but disagreed about how far the government should go. It was harder for Democratic primary voters to choose between them based solely on policy issues.

The larger role of economic anxiety in the Democratic primary also follows from what the candidates said on the campaign trail. Every Republican candidate for president railed against Barack Obama's stewardship of the economy, preventing Trump from separating himself from his rivals on this issue. But it was easier for Bernie Sanders to separate himself from Hillary Clinton. Clinton's connection to Obama made it harder for her to criticize how the country was doing, while Sanders did so freely by focusing on economic inequality and whether ordinary people were really getting ahead.

Social identities were the common force in both parties' primaries, just in different ways. In the Republican primary, Trump campaigned on issues deeply connected to racial, ethnic, and religious minorities, and thus his support depended on how voters viewed blacks, immigrants, and Muslims and whether whites were losing out to these groups. In the Democratic primary, views of racial and ethnic minorities mattered less because Clinton and Sanders took similarly progressive positions on issues like racial justice and immigration. Instead, other dimensions of identity mattered: racial identity (rather than views of racial minorities), partisanship, and age. Clinton's appeal to Democrats, African Americans, and older voters was the key to her victory.

But important questions remained as Clinton pivoted to the general election. Could she unify the party, even though many Sanders supporters viewed her unfavorably? Would she be able to build a coalition beyond just the Democratic base—including not only racial minorities and progressives but also the white moderates or even conservatives who had backed Obama? Many of these were the white, working-class voters that she had said you "have to win." That was in 2008. The question now was whether she could win them in 2016.

CHAPTER 7

The Trump Tax

My msg 2 GOP: Time 2 start nominating disciplined, principled, conservatives; men and women who will defeat their opponents, not themselves.
—Sean Hannity, tweet, November 9, 2012

It was early June 2016, and Hillary Clinton and Donald Trump had work to do. It had been clear for weeks that Clinton would win the nomination, but the news was hardly congratulatory. A *Washington Post* headline from May 15: "Even Supporters Agree: Clinton Has Weaknesses as a Candidate. What Can She Do?" A *New York Times* headline from May 28: "Hillary Clinton Struggles to Find Footing in Unusual Race."[1] Democrats were worried that Clinton was not likable and would struggle to make herself more likable.

Trump was in no better position. On May 28, he was widely condemned for attacking Gonzalo Curiel, the judge overseeing a case in which one of Trump's business endeavors, Trump University, was being sued. Trump said that Curiel was a "hater" and "Mexican" and argued that Curiel's ethnicity would prevent Trump from receiving a fair trial. Critics, including prominent Republicans, pointed out that Curiel was an American of Mexican ancestry and called Trump's statement racist. Trump was also feuding with the Republican National Committee with the party convention only a month away. Meanwhile, a poll of Republicans found that nearly half wanted a different nominee. A group of convention delegates was even planning to block Trump's nomination.[2]

Clinton and Trump faced a common challenge: how to rally their own parties and build a winning coalition on Election Day. They began the general election campaign as historically unpopular presidential candidates. In early June, 57 percent had an unfavorable view of Clinton and 62 percent had an unfavorable view of Trump. Four years earlier, only 43 percent had had an unfavorable view of Barack Obama and 42 percent an unfavorable view of Mitt Romney. In fact, about one in five Americans had an unfavorable view of *both* Clinton and Trump—twice as many as in 2012.[3]

Clinton and Trump responded to this common challenge with their same messages from the primaries. Clinton argued that the country was better—"stronger together"—when it was inclusive of all Americans. She attacked Trump for how he had treated minorities and women. Trump argued that the American way of life was in danger—from crime in urban areas to terrorist attacks by Muslims to crime and economic hardships caused by undocumented immigrants. To "make America great again" was not about "togetherness" but rather about protecting and defending certain Americans—and a certain conception of American identity—from these threats.

For virtually the entire summer and fall, Clinton appeared to be winning this argument. Trump's statements about and behavior toward immigrants, Muslims, women, and other groups generated controversy after controversy. These controversies enabled Trump to dominate the news, but the news coverage was often negative and cost him in the polls, even among Republicans. Only at the end of the campaign did Republicans rally to Trump. This was arguably his saving grace.

Trump's struggles did not mean that Clinton's path was easy. She faced continued questions about the private email server, culminating on October 28 in FBI director James Comey's bombshell announcement that they were reopening their investigation of her. Comey's announcement hurt her standing with voters—although whether it changed the election's outcome is less clear. Nevertheless, the issue of her emails garnered more news coverage than Trump's many scandals and became firmly lodged in the public's mind. Clinton wanted to make the election about Trump's character, but the campaign also brought her own character to the fore. Voters eventually rated Trump as more honest and a stronger leader than they did Clinton.

Still Trump's problems seemed to outweigh Clinton's, and Clinton led in most polls. Although the country's political and economic conditions had predicted a toss-up, a Clinton victory appeared likely—even a virtual certainty in some forecasts. A presidential race that was supposed to be close seemed like an anticlimax.

Whose America?

Clinton's and Trump's campaign messages were unusual. Typically, one presidential candidate focuses on the economy. When the economy is growing, the incumbent party candidate takes credit and promises further prosperity. When the economy is in decline, the challenger blames the incumbent. If economic indicators do not clearly advantage either side, candidates may avoid the subject or debate whether the economy is healthy or unhealthy.[4] The latter happened in 2012, with Obama emphasizing the economy's growth since the Great Recession and Romney arguing that the economy had not recovered enough. Clinton and Trump did talk about the economy, but they often focused more on the other's character and especially on their clashing visions of American identity.

Clinton did not fully embrace the economy as a campaign issue or the Obama administration's record. Although the video announcing her candidacy introduced middle-class Americans who had been left behind in the recovery from the Great Recession and whom she intended to champion, Clinton did not consistently emphasize this theme. The economy and jobs figured prominently in her campaign speeches, but only about 8 percent of the appeals in her television advertisements referred to economic issues. Moreover, when she discussed the economy, Clinton stopped short of endorsing the Obama administration's record. In her acceptance speech at the Democratic National Convention, Clinton acknowledged Obama and Biden, saying, "Our economy is so much stronger than when they took office." But then she said that "none of us can be satisfied with the status quo" and "we're still facing deep-seated problems."[5] In this way, Clinton's campaign resembled Al Gore's in 2000. Gore was wary of being linked to Bill Clinton's scandals and downplayed the robust economic growth of the Clinton years. At the Democratic National Convention, he said, "This election is not a reward for past performance," and then went on to emphasize other issues.[6] Clinton would later say she believed that economic conditions were not that favorable, despite positive trends (see chapter 2). After the election, she wrote, "The economy was definitely in better shape than it had been after the financial crisis, but incomes hadn't begun to rise for most families, so people still felt like their progress was fragile and could be ripped away at any moment."[7]

Trump's message about the economy was simple: it was terrible and he would fix it. In his convention speech, he cited statistics intended to portray the economy as weak and promised to "bring our jobs back." One of his television ads contrasted "Donald Trump's America" to "Hillary Clinton's America" and promised that Trump's America would see "millions of new jobs created" and "wages go up." Another ad described tax cuts that would help Americans and allow businesses to "create more jobs." The ad promised "prosperity for you." But like Clinton, Trump also focused mostly on issues other than the economy. In Trump's television advertising, only 34 percent of the appeals were about the economy.[8]

Rather than just debate the economy, Trump and Clinton debated American identity. Clinton envisioned America as a place where all people were welcome, regardless of race, ethnicity, or religion. At the convention, she spoke of fighting "systemic racism" and protecting the rights of blacks, Latinos, women, people with disabilities, and gay and transgender people. She celebrated the United States because it had "the most dynamic and diverse people in the world" and advocated expanding on that diversity by offering citizenship to undocumented immigrants. She rejected Trump's "mean and divisive rhetoric" and ideas like a wall on the Mexican border.[9]

Throughout the campaign, Clinton criticized Trump's behavior toward women and racial and ethnic minorities both during his campaign and before he ran for president. In a major speech in August, she said Trump was espousing "racist lies," taking "hate groups mainstream," and promoting an "emerging racist ideology known as the alt-right."[10] Her ad "Mirrors" depicted young girls looking at themselves in the mirror while soundbites of Trump's disparaging women played ("I'd look her right in that fat ugly face of hers," "A person who is flat-chested is very hard to be a 10," and so on). Another ad, "Role Models," showed pictures of children watching television as clips of Trump's controversial statements played, including his remarks about "rapists" coming from Mexico and Megyn Kelly's having "blood coming out of her whatever," as well as his mockingly pantomiming the movements and speech of a *New York Times* reporter, Serge Kovaleski, who has a congenital joint disorder. In short, Clinton argued that Trump's agenda would weaken the country by marginalizing the very same people Clinton wanted to bring together to strengthen the country. Unlike recent presidential candidates, Clinton focused not on policy but rather on distinguishing her character from Trump's. Two-thirds of the appeals in her ads were about Trump's personal attributes compared to hers. She rarely attacked Trump's policy proposals in these ads.[11]

Trump's vision was very different. He portrayed an American culture and nation in decline. Trump seized on statistics showing that violent crime had increased slightly in some cities and claimed that the country was experiencing historically high levels of crime—when in fact the national crime rate had fallen dramatically since the early 1990s. Trump also emphasized the threat posed by "radical Islam" and illegal immigrants. For example, after a Muslim man shot and killed forty-nine people at a gay nightclub in Orlando on June 12, Trump repeated his call for a ban on Muslims traveling to the United States. At the convention, Trump spoke of "illegal immigrant families" that were "being released by the tens of thousands into our communities" and told the story of a young woman killed by an undocumented immigrant who was driving drunk. In important respects, Trump echoed Richard Nixon's 1968 campaign, in which he also focused on black crime and promised to restore law and order.[12]

Trump portrayed Clinton as someone who would make these problems worse. He attacked her as not only corrupt—saying that she would "keep our rigged system in place" and accusing her of "pay to play politics" and "decades of lies and scandal"—but also weak on immigration and terrorism. He linked the Clinton Foundation to potential threats from Muslim countries, saying, "Crooked Hillary says we must call on Saudi Arabia and other countries to stop funding hate. I am calling on her to immediately return the $25 million plus she got from them for the Clinton Foundation!" One of his television ads would describe "Hillary Clinton's America" as a place where "Syrian refugees flood in" and "illegal immigrants convicted of committing crimes get to stay, collecting Social Security benefits, skipping the line."[13]

Clinton and Trump helped make immigration and Islam central to news coverage about the campaign. For example, on CNN, stories about the presidential campaign that also mentioned "immigration" or immigrant" increased more than threefold compared to 2012. Stories that mentioned "Islam" or Muslims" increased more than fivefold. A more systematic analysis of mainstream news organizations by Harvard University's Berkman Klein Center for Internet and Society found that coverage of immigration and Muslims, particularly as those issues involved Trump, outpaced coverage of every other issue. Conservative news outlets amplified these issues even more: widely shared stories from the conservative and distinctly pro-Trump site *Breitbart* included "More Than 347,000 Convicted Criminal Immigrants at Large In U.S." and "Immigration to Swell U.S. Muslim Population to 6.2 Million."[14]

Ultimately, both Clinton and Trump ensured that American voters saw a campaign that was not just about economic stewardship or wonky debates about fiscal policy, entitlement programs, and the like. Instead, the candidates made the campaign about something entirely different: whether the country's increasing ethnic, racial, and religious diversity was a strength or a threat.

Bad Publicity

Donald Trump had built a career on the theory that "bad publicity is better than no publicity." In the general election campaign, he was arguably wrong. Although both Clinton and Trump were damaged by their respective scandals and controversies, the damage to Trump was often more dramatic. Missteps by or revelations about Trump would drive news coverage, hurt his standing with voters, and widen Clinton's lead. In particular, Trump's attacks on immigrants and Muslims, as well as revelations of his treatment of women, hurt him and fueled further attacks by Clinton. Throughout the summer and fall, polls that asked whether respondents would vote for the Republican or Democratic candidate for president showed Trump underperforming this generic Republican candidate. It seemed as if Clinton would win handily, outperforming forecasts based on the country's economic and political conditions. The website *Vox* began referring to this divergence between the polls and the prediction as the "Trump Tax."[15]

The Trump Tax was visible in how Trump was covered in the media and how voters perceived him. Three different ways of capturing news coverage (figure 7.1) show the publicity that Trump received: the percentage of stories in prominent outlets that mentioned each candidate (the previous measure of "news stories"), each candidate's share of mentions on cable networks (the previous measure of "cable mentions"), and the percentage of stories in eight major outlets in which one candidate, but not the other, was mentioned in the headline ("solo-headlined stories"). Cable mentions and solo-headlined stories more precisely capture asymmetries in coverage, as most campaign news stories will mention both candidates but with varying degrees of emphasis.[16]

The perceptions of voters (figure 7.2) can be captured two ways. One is the candidates' net favorable ratings—the percentage with a favorable view minus the percentage with an unfavorable view—which come from daily surveys by the Gallup organization. Because Gallup was surveying roughly 500 individuals a day, their surveys provide a very sensitive measure of opinion change. Another measure is the trial-heat polls asking respondents whether they planned to vote for Clinton or Trump.[17]

Trump's dominance of news coverage was clear. He received more coverage than Clinton almost every day between June 1 and Election Day, including 63 percent of cable news mentions and 69 percent of the solo-headlined stories. This is very different from the historical pattern in presidential general elections, where both candidates tend to receive roughly equal amounts of coverage.[18]

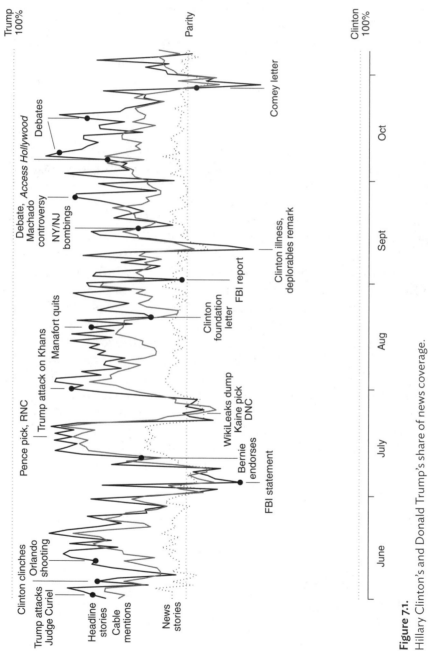

Trump 100%

Parity

Clinton 100%

Trump attacks
Judge Curiel

Clinton clinches   Orlando
                    shooting

Pence pick, RNC

Trump attack on Khans

Manafort quits

Debate, Access Hollywood

Debate,
Machado
controversy   Debates

NY/NJ
bombings

Comey letter

Headline
stories
Cable
mentions

News
stories

Bernie
endorses

WikiLeaks dump
Kaine pick
DNC

FBI statement

Clinton
foundation
letter

FBI report

Clinton illness,
deplorables remark

June   July   Aug   Sept   Oct

Figure 7.1.

Hillary Clinton's and Donald Trump's share of news coverage.

Sources: Internet Archive and Global Database of Events, Language, and Tone; Crimson Hexagon; Data Face.

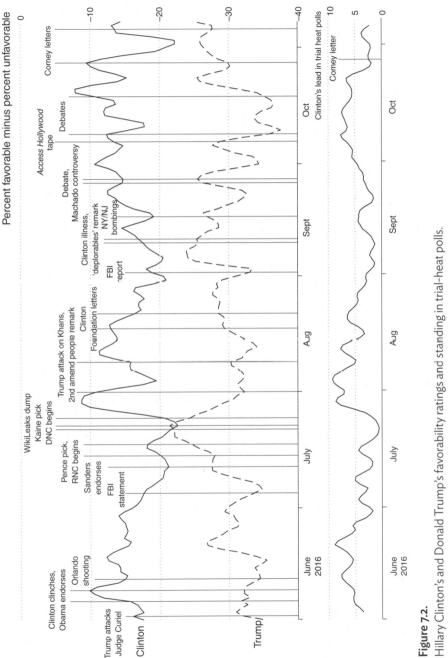

Percent favorable minus percent unfavorable

Clinton's lead in trial heat polls

Figure 7.2.

Hillary Clinton's and Donald Trump's favorability ratings and standing in trial-heat polls.

Trial-heat polls are located at the midpoint of their field dates.

Sources: The net favorable ratings are smoothed averages from daily Gallup surveys (bandwidth = 0.05). Clinton's lead in trial-heat polls is based on a smoothed average of all national polls compiled by the *Huffington Post's* Pollster (bandwidth = 0.08).

But Trump's ability to generate headlines made it worse for him, not better. Apart from the period around the party conventions, the correlation between Trump's advantage in news coverage and his standing in the polls was negative: the more Trump dominated the news, the worse he did in the polls. For example, the correlation between Trump's percentage of solo-headlined stories and his net favorability was −0.22.[19] This is the opposite of what happened in the primaries, when more coverage of Trump helped give him better poll numbers. At that point, news coverage played a different role, helping Trump to stand out in a large field of candidates. Now, with the field narrowed to two candidates, it was less important simply to get news coverage and more important to get positive news coverage. Positive coverage was often in short supply for Trump.

In June, the controversies included not only Trump's attacks on Judge Curiel but also his response to the mass shooting in Orlando. Trump insinuated that Obama was sympathetic to terrorism, saying, "People cannot, they cannot believe that President Obama is acting the way he acts and can't even mention the words 'radical Islamic terrorism.' There's something going on." Trump's charitable giving was also under scrutiny, and especially whether Trump's personal foundation functioned to benefit Trump and his family more than charitable causes. Meanwhile, Trump's campaign staff was in upheaval. Trump fired his campaign manager, Corey Lewandowski, and brought on Paul Manafort—a longtime Republican operative thought to have the experience to manage a potentially fractious Republican National Convention in Cleveland and steer Trump toward a more traditional campaign. Trump's selection of Indiana governor Mike Pence as his running mate brought on board another figure respected in the party.[20]

The potential rebellion at the convention proved unsuccessful, but even still Trump struggled. Party conventions are usually an extended infomercial for the candidate, and Trump certainly dominated the news during this period, receiving an average of 85 percent of solo-headlined stories. But the news was often bad. Some prominent Republicans, such as Mitt Romney and George W. Bush, did not even attend, and the roster of speakers included D-list celebrities like Scott Baio. Melania Trump's speech included passages lifted from Michelle Obama's speech at the 2008 Democratic National Convention. Ted Cruz refused to endorse Trump, telling delegates to "vote your conscience" and then leaving the stage as boos rained down. Trump's speech was called a "dystopian portrait of a country riven by division and grievances." Trump himself was unfazed, saying that his wife's speech "got more publicity than any in the history of politics especially if you believe that all press is good press!"[21]

The press was not good. A study by Harvard University's Shorenstein Center on Media, Politics, and Public Policy—which had trained coders evaluate news coverage—found that the month around the conventions was distinctively bad for Trump: 47 percent of coverage was negative, 38 percent was neutral, and 15 percent was positive. Coverage of Trump was more negative than positive even in stalwart conservative outlets like Fox News and the *Washington Times*. Although Trump received a modest positive bump in his favorability ratings, as is often true during party conventions, it was quickly eclipsed by the much larger bump that Clinton received after the Democratic National Convention. This seemed to confirm portrayals of the Republican convention as the "mistake by the lake."[22]

After the Democratic National Convention, Trump dominated news coverage for most of August. He attacked Khizr and Ghazala Khan, the parents of a Muslim American soldier who was killed in the Iraq War. They had criticized Trump in a speech at the Democratic convention for disrespecting minorities and especially Muslims. Trump also suggested that Obama was the "founder" of ISIS and that immigrants needed "extreme vetting" and an "ideological test." Trump even appeared to advocate violence against Clinton herself. At a campaign rally on August 9, he alluded to the Supreme Court and said, "If she gets to pick her judges, nothing you can do, folks. Although the Second Amendment people—maybe there is, I don't know." Upheaval in Trump's campaign staff continued. Manafort departed under scrutiny for his previous work as an adviser to the Ukrainian president Viktor Yanukovych, who had long had ties to Russian president Vladimir Putin.[23]

Manafort's replacement, Steve Bannon, the head of *Breitbart*, created even more controversy because of *Breitbart*'s incendiary coverage and Bannon's own views on issues like immigration and Islam. Bannon's arrival seemingly signaled Trump's desire to double down on the things that were hurting him in the first place. By this point in time, 65 percent of Americans said that the word "racist" described Donald Trump at least slightly well, 61 percent thought "the way Donald Trump talks appeals to bigotry," and 52 percent said that he was biased against women and minorities. The tenor of the headlines for Trump was often dire—"Inside the Failing Mission to Tame Donald Trump's Tongue" and "Has Donald Trump Hit Bottom?"[24]

But Trump had not hit bottom. Again, he appeared to threaten or condone violence against Clinton, criticizing her view of gun control by saying at a September 16 rally, "I think that her bodyguards should drop all weapons. I think they should disarm. Immediately. Let's see what happens to her. Take their guns away, O.K. It'll be very dangerous." After another terrorist attack in Manhattan and New Jersey by a man named Ahmad Khan Ramani that did not result in any casualties, Trump said that Hillary Clinton wanted to let into the country "hundreds of thousands of these same people" with "hatred and sickness in their heart," and he lamented the fact that Ramani, who was shot by police, would receive medical care and legal representation. A *New York Times* headline summed up another tumultuous period: "Donald Trump's Anything-Goes Campaign Sets an Alarming Political Precedent."[25]

During the first presidential debate, on September 26, Clinton attacked Trump for his "long record of engaging in racist behavior," including the "racist lie" that Obama was not born in the United States—a claim that Trump had finally admitted was false ten days prior after years of promoting it (although he then falsely blamed Clinton for starting the rumor). Clinton also attacked his treatment of women, citing the experience of Alicia Machado, a Venezuelan woman who had won the 1996 Miss Universe pageant, which was owned by Trump. Machado accused Trump of belittling her as "Miss Housekeeping" for her Latina ethnicity and "Miss Piggy" when she gained weight after the pageant. In the face of Clinton's attacks, Trump had no good reply, and polls showed that more Americans thought Clinton had won the debate. Afterward, Trump was unrepentant, saying that Machado had "gained a massive amount of weight and it was a real problem" and later calling her "disgusting" and accusing her of appearing in a sex tape.[26] The debate and the Machado controversy created a large spike in coverage of Trump and a sharp drop in the percentage of voters who rated him favorably (figures 7.1 and 7.2).

Then came perhaps the biggest controversy to affect Trump. It began when the *Washington Post* obtained and published a 2005 recording of Trump speaking with Billy Bush, the host of the NBC television show *Access Hollywood*. The recording captured a very vulgar and sexually explicit conversation that occurred as Bush and Trump rode to the set of the NBC soap opera *Days of Our Lives* to tape a segment about Trump's cameo on the show. Trump regaled Bush with a story about trying and failing to have sex with a married woman, saying, "I did try and fuck her. She was married. . . . I moved on her like a bitch, but I couldn't get there. Then all of a sudden I see her, she's got the big phony tits and everything. She's totally changed her look." When Bush and Trump saw Arianne Zucker, the actress who would be taking them onto the set, Bush called her "hot as shit," which led Trump to say, "I've got to use some Tic Tacs, just in case I start kissing her," and also, "When you're a star, they let you do it. You can do anything." After Bush replied, "Whatever you want," Trump said what would become the most infamous part of the tape: "Grab them by the pussy. You can do anything."[27] On the day that story broke, 90 percent of solo-headlined stories were about Trump. The first debate and this controversy produced a 12-point drop in Trump's net favorable rating between September 26 and October 9, while Clinton opened her largest lead in trial-heat polls of the entire campaign. More than ever, Trump's own behavior was turning what should have been a close race into an apparent blowout.

In the second debate, on October 9, Trump tried to turn the issue of sexual harassment and assault against Clinton. He held a press conference beforehand with three women who had accused Bill Clinton of sexual assault or harassment and then had those women sit in the debate audience. During the debate, he said that Hillary Clinton had attacked these women "viciously" and had "tremendous hate in her heart." Clinton responded by criticizing Trump not only for his comments on the *Access Hollywood* tape but also for birtherism and his attacks on Curiel and the Khan family. Polls again declared Clinton the victor, but Trump's performance was judged "sure-footed enough that no more Republican officials disavowed him" afterward. Consequently, the debate's apparent impact on voters was muted: Clinton's favorability dropped slightly and Trump's increased, but these changes were small and temporary.[28]

After the debate, the controversy over Trump's treatment of women continued, leading to more fighting within the party. Several women came forward to accuse Trump of doing exactly what he described to Billy Bush: forcibly touching or kissing them. In a *Washington Post*/ABC News poll, 68 percent said that Trump had probably "made unwanted sexual advances toward women." Behind the scenes, the Republican National Committee began to investigate whether it could replace Trump as nominee. Several Republicans later reported that Mike Pence himself was willing to take Trump's place. John McCain pulled his endorsement of Trump, and Paul Ryan said that he would no longer defend or campaign with Trump. Trump then attacked them both, calling McCain "foul-mouthed" and Ryan "weak and ineffective." It appeared that the GOP was in a state of "anarchy" and that Trump was "pulling Republicans . . . into a self-destructive feud that could imperil dozens of lawmakers in Congress and potentially throw conservative-leaning states into Hillary Clinton's column."[29]

There was thus a lot of pressure on Trump heading into the third and final debate on October 19. It was not a debate that many observers thought Trump had won.[30] But afterward, something very important happened: Republican voters who had soured on Trump after the first debate and release of the *Access Hollywood* tape returned to him (figure 7.3).

Republicans had always disliked Hillary Clinton: 90 percent or more viewed her unfavorably for most of the general election campaign. But Republicans' views of Trump himself were more varied. In general, Republicans warmed to Trump from June into September—his net favorable rating increased about 10 points during this time—but all his gains disappeared in late September and early October. Not until after this third debate did Trump's

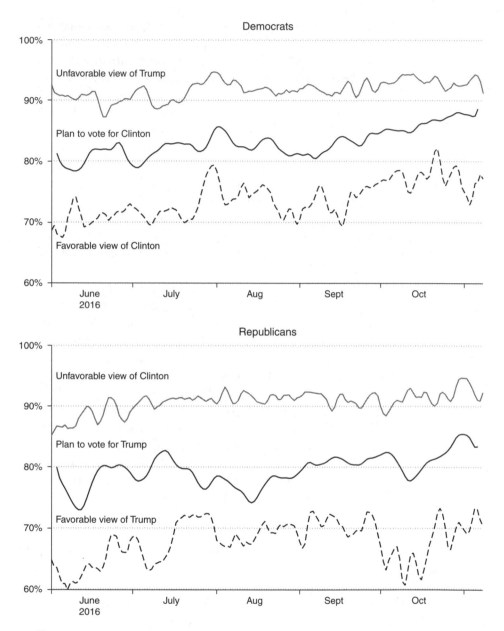

Figure 7.3.
Trends in candidate favorability ratings and standing in trial-heat polls among Democrats and Republicans.
Source: The favorability ratings are smoothed averages from daily Gallup surveys (bandwidth = 0.05). Vote intention is based on a smoothed average of all national polls compiled by the *Huffington Post*'s Pollster (bandwidth = 0.08).

standing began to increase in earnest. More Republicans expressed a favorable opinion of him and said that they planned to vote for him. It is unusual for the partisan rally to happen so late in the campaign. But eventually Trump's standing among Republicans nearly reached Clinton's standing among Democrats. This is the reason that Trump's net favorable ratings were higher at the end of the campaign than on June 1.

There are three important implications of these trends among Republicans. First, this Republican rally was arguably the most important reason that the polls tightened at the end of the campaign—and it is one reason why they tightened even before the release of James Comey's letter on October 28 (figure 7.2).

Second, almost all the impact of events like the *Access Hollywood* tape was concentrated among people who were otherwise predisposed to support Republican candidates. Democrats did not change their already very negative view of Trump (figure 7.3), and any trends among independents were less consequential in the aggregate because true independents are a small fraction of the electorate. In one sense, the impact of the *Access Hollywood* tape resembled the impact of Mitt Romney's infamous comments about "the 47%" in the 2012 campaign: most of the impact of Romney's remarks was among Republicans who also ended up supporting Romney.[31] This may explain why Trump's controversies tended to depress his poll numbers for only a few days before they bounced back. Only because the controversies came so often did the "Trump Tax" become a chronic feature of the campaign.

The third implication of the Republican rally to Trump is that any push against Trump by Republican leaders had a modest impact, at best. There were certainly some Republicans who said that they would not vote for Trump because of his political views or personal behavior. One tabulation counted seventy-eight Republican politicians, donors, and officials who were supporting Clinton, including General Colin Powell and Representative Richard Hanna of New York. At least some others, notably Senator Susan Collins, did not promise to vote for Clinton but did say that they would not vote for Trump.[32]

But these "never Trump" Republicans were relatively few and not very powerful within the party. The Berkman Klein Center report found that the conservative news outlets that housed prominent opponents of Trump—like the *National Review* and the *Weekly Standard*—became less central within the conservative media ecosystem in 2016 compared to 2012. Moreover, few of the seventy-eight Republicans voting for Clinton were current officeholders, household names, or power brokers within the party. More prominent Republicans tended to criticize Trump when necessary but ultimately stuck with him. Barely two weeks after the *Access Hollywood* tape, a *New York*

Times headline summed it up: "Some in G.O.P. Who Deserted Trump over Lewd Tape Are Returning." Meanwhile, others never deserted Trump in the first place. Reince Priebus, the head of the Republican National Committee, continued to support him. So did Marco Rubio, who said, "I disagree with him on many things, but I disagree with his opponent on virtually everything." Even Paul Ryan voted for Trump. And Ted Cruz, who had told Republican convention delegates to "vote their conscience," decided by October that his conscience was telling him to make phone calls in support of Trump.[33]

Although it was extraordinary for party leaders to criticize their presidential nominee at all, opposition to Trump among Republican Party leaders was never widespread or sustained enough to lead many Republican voters to defect, especially in the absence of any viable alternative. Clinton was extremely unpopular among Republicans, and third-party candidates are rarely an attractive option in an American system that favors the two major parties. Of course, it is hard to know whether more sustained opposition to Trump among Republican leaders would have made any difference. Trump had been defying those leaders since his campaign began but nevertheless spoke to the concerns of enough Republican voters to secure the nomination. And even among Republican voters who may have disagreed with Trump's unorthodox political views, party trumped ideology in the end.

Her Emails

Even though Trump confronted many controversies, Clinton had her own. Throughout the campaign, spikes in news coverage of her generally signified bad news, just as for Trump. Clinton was dogged by continued coverage of her private email server, alleged corruption at the Clinton Foundation, and emails from the Democratic National Committee (DNC) and her adviser, John Podesta, that were hacked by Russian operatives and publicly released by WikiLeaks. These scandals produced large spikes in news coverage of Clinton (figure 7.1), and most of this news was negative in tone. In fact, news coverage of her was not much more positive than coverage of Trump—and coverage of her scandals exceeded coverage of his.

The FBI investigation into Clinton's email server initially ended on July 5, when FBI director James Comey announced that no criminal charges would be filed but did say that Clinton and her staff "were extremely careless in their handling of very sensitive, highly classified information."[34] (Details of the FBI's report were later released on September 2, causing another spike in news coverage of Clinton.)

The unauthorized release of the DNC emails came on July 23, just after Clinton picked Virginia senator Tim Kaine as her running mate and just before the Democratic National Convention in Philadelphia began. The hack was attributed to actors working for the Russian government as part of a broader effort to influence the American election. The emails were given to and then distributed by the group WikiLeaks. They showed that DNC staffers had derided Bernie Sanders's campaign, and the ensuing controversy cost DNC chairwoman Debbie Wasserman Schultz her position. Trump sought to link the DNC emails to Clinton's email server by declaring that Russia should hack the emails that had been deleted before the server was turned over to the government.[35] Trump's ability to insert himself into the news even during the Democratic convention helps explain why Clinton's share of the news during the convention was smaller than Trump's share during the Republican convention.

The hacked DNC emails only stoked the ire of Sanders supporters who were delegates to the convention. On the convention's first night, some Sanders supporters booed when Clinton's name was mentioned and even during Sanders's speech endorsing her. Despite Sanders's endorsement and coordination between Clinton's staff and Sanders's staff to manage convention delegates on the floor, there would be other moments of conflict and rebellion that week. The combination of this strife and the email leak meant that the convention was hardly undiluted positive press for Clinton. During the convention period, the Shorenstein Center's data found that 37 percent of coverage of Clinton was neutral, 35 percent was negative, and 28 percent was positive. Even during the week of the convention itself, there was roughly an equal amount of positive and negative coverage. This was more positive than coverage of Trump during the Republican convention but still more negative than is typical for the convention period. In 2012, for example, both Romney and Obama received a higher ratio of positive to negative coverage during their respective conventions than did Trump or Clinton.[36]

Nevertheless, Clinton still received the traditional bump in the polls, which was most visible among Democrats, demonstrating the usual ability of the party conventions to rally partisans. Some of this bump dissipated after the convention, but Clinton's poll numbers rebounded, especially after Trump's remark about "Second Amendment people."

Then there was renewed attention to the Clinton Foundation. The story had been largely dormant, except on right-wing sites, since the spring of 2015. But the story entered mainstream news again after *Breitbart* and other news outlets claimed, erroneously, that the Clinton Foundation was being investigated by the IRS. News coverage on mainstream outlets peaked later in

August as Bill Clinton issued two separate letters promising that the Clinton Foundation would cease accepting foreign donations (see figure 7.1). Even though most of the Clinton Foundation's spending was for charitable activities, a poll showed that about half of Americans said that they did not know what the Clinton Foundation did, and among those who said they did know, many said the Clinton Foundation worked to benefit the Clintons. At the same time as the Clinton Foundation reentered the news, there was a slide in Clinton's poll numbers. By the end of August, her favorability and trial-heat poll lead had declined almost to where they were before the convention.[37]

In September, Clinton received a large spike in news coverage but, again, not for reasons she wanted. On September 10, it was revealed that she had said in a speech that half of Trump's supporters fit into a "basket of deplorables" ("The racist, sexist, homophobic, xenophobic, Islamophobic—you name it"). The statement played into Trump's argument that Clinton was an elitist who disdained "real Americans," and many of his supporters proudly embraced the term "deplorable." The very next day, Clinton collapsed after an appearance to commemorate the anniversary of the September 11 terrorist attacks. This fed speculation in right-wing media and by Trump himself that Clinton was concealing poor health. Clinton's illness produced a lot of news coverage (a sample headline: "Hillary Clinton's Health Just Became a Real Issue in the Presidential Campaign"), although she was diagnosed with only walking pneumonia. Neither of these incidents, however, had much short-term impact on her favorability.[38]

Then came Comey's letter to Congress on October 28. Comey announced that the FBI was investigating additional emails that had been discovered as part of a separate investigation into former representative Anthony Weiner, who was at that point the husband of Clinton's longtime aide Huma Abedin. (Weiner would plead guilty to sending sexually explicit messages to a minor.) Typically, the FBI does not announce investigations, but Comey expected Clinton to win and did not want the FBI to be perceived as helping her. The Trump campaign then did something remarkable: it realized that it should not step on the story and disarmed Trump by taking away his Twitter account. The result was the most media coverage that Clinton would receive during the entire general election campaign. The day after Comey's announcement, 71 percent of solo-headlined stories and 59 percent of cable network mentions were about Clinton. The story dominated the news for the rest of the campaign. For example, between October 29 and November 4, there would be thirty-seven articles about Clinton's emails in the *New York Times* alone, compared to only thirteen Trump stories that were not also about Clinton's emails.[39]

Overall, Clinton may have received less coverage than Trump, but the coverage that she did receive was almost as negative as his. The Shorenstein Center's analysis found that between August and Election Day, 43 percent of Clinton's coverage was negative, compared to 52 percent of Trump's.[40] The same pattern emerged in the data on news stories and solo-headlined stories, in which the tone of coverage was estimated by comparing the words in each story to dictionaries that measure the positive or negative valence of words. In both datasets, the overall tone of Clinton's coverage was nearly identical to the tone of Trump's coverage.

Some of this negative coverage was driven by scandals like the email server and Clinton Foundation. In fact, there was *more* coverage of her scandals than there was of Trump's. In the Shorenstein Center's analysis, 19 percent of her coverage was focused on these subjects, which included coverage of her health, the email server, and the like. By contrast, 15 percent of coverage of Trump was focused on his controversies. Thanks to the Comey letter, coverage of Clinton's controversies increased as the campaign ended—to 23 percent of her coverage in the penultimate week and 37 percent in the last week.[41]

The Berkman Center analysis, which examined dozens of national and regional news outlets, found the same thing: coverage of Clinton's scandals vastly exceeded coverage of Trump's scandals. From May 2015 until Election Day, there were approximately 100,000 sentences about Clinton's scandals, including the Clinton Foundation, her email server, the hack of the DNC and Podesta emails, and the attack on the American consulate in Benghazi. By contrast, there were just over 40,000 sentences devoted to Trump's scandals, including his refusal to release his tax returns, his treatment of women, Trump University, the Trump Foundation, and possible ties to Russia. Indeed, as coverage of Clinton's email server scandal was spiking, coverage of potential ties between the Trump campaign and Russia was more muted. An October 31 *New York Times* headline said, "Investigating Donald Trump, F.B.I. Sees No Clear Link to Russia."[42]

This attention to Clinton's scandals was largely not because shadowy outlets or Twitter bots pushed false stories about her on social media. Perhaps most famously, many false stories were traced to a single Macedonian teenager who was earning thousands of dollars every month. But very few of these false stories were among the most shared stories on Twitter and Facebook. Instead, Clinton's bigger challenge came from mainstream news coverage, for which the norms of objectivity and balance required attention to Clinton's controversies as well as Trump's. Clinton's problem was real news much more than fake news.[43]

The relationship of news coverage to Clinton's poll standing differed from what transpired with Trump. The trend in the volume of news coverage (figure 7.1) was not strongly associated with the trend in how favorably voters saw Clinton (figure 7.2). Although Trump's controversies often led to immediate declines in his favorability rating, that was less clear for Clinton. One reason may be that opinions of Clinton were less malleable, whereas opinions of Trump—especially among Republicans who had not embraced his candidacy from the start—were often in flux.

But media coverage did appear to affect Clinton's poll standing in one important case: the Comey letter. It catalyzed not only an increase in negative news coverage of Clinton but also a decline in her poll standing. Gallup's daily data showed Clinton's favorability declining sharply—by approximately 13 points between October 28 and November 3. This decline was evident among both Democrats (see figure 7.3) and independents. Other data also showed an apparent impact of the Comey letter. The Presidential Election Panel Survey was in the field when the letter was released, with almost 2,000 respondents interviewed between October 20 and October 27 and almost 500 respondents interviewed on or after October 28, when the Comey letter was released. These respondents had also been interviewed between September 12 and September 25, enabling us to see whether the Comey letter may have changed people's attitudes from the previous month. Compared to people interviewed before the letter's release, people interviewed afterward experienced a small decrease in how favorably they viewed Clinton and how favorably they evaluated her honesty and morality. The decreases were roughly equivalent to a 2-point shift on a 100-point scale.[44]

In other respects, however, the Comey letter's impact was more ambiguous. For one, in Gallup's data, the decrease in Clinton's favorability rating was temporary (see figure 7.2). Her rating improved substantially—even before Comey declared on November 6 that the investigation had turned up no new emails of consequence. Her net favorable ratings at the end of the campaign were about 4 points lower than before the Comey letter. A net 4-point shift is not necessarily inconsequential, but it is small in the aggregate.

Moreover, there is no clear evidence that the Comey letter affected people's intention to vote for Clinton. In trial-heat polls, there was some tightening of the race before the Comey letter was released, but less change afterward (figure 7.2). One challenge with the trial-heat polls, however, is that they are often conducted at irregular intervals by pollsters using different methodologies. Trial-heat readings can thus change from day to day, depending not only on genuine changes in opinions but also on differences in which pollsters happened to have polls in the field. Attempts to account for these complications generated equivocal answers. Some—notably *FiveThirtyEight*'s Nate Silver— saw a consequential shift against Clinton. Others were less certain. A comprehensive report on 2016 polling by a committee of the American Association of Public Opinion Research found that there was a 2-point shift away from Clinton after the letter's release, but that her poll numbers rebounded, suggesting only "mixed evidence" of the letter's ultimate impact. Similarly, in the Presidential Election Panel Survey data there was no significant shift in vote intentions after the Comey letter, even if evaluations of Clinton did change.[45]

Of course, it is impossible to know for sure whether the election would have turned out differently without Comey's letter. It is simply important to acknowledge the uncertainty underlying any such hypothetical.

But focusing on the Comey letter may have the unintended consequence of underestimating the effect of Clinton's controversies. The coverage of Clinton's scandals not only was more extensive than coverage of Trump's scandals but arguably created a more coherent narrative, with ongoing news coverage and revelations that emerged regularly over time. By contrast, Trump's scandals tended to come and go quickly and concerned many different topics, including his business practices, controversial positions on issues, and behavior toward women and minorities. Thus, the overall impact of Clinton's scandals and news coverage of them was bigger than the impact of the Comey letter itself.

As scholars of political communication have observed, news coverage often constructs a simplified portrait of political figures—George H. W. Bush's mildness and modesty meant that he was a "wimp," John Kerry's and Mitt Romney's formality meant that they were "stiff," George W. Bush's average grades and folksy manner meant that he was "dumb," and so on. Actions and statements by politicians will get more attention when they fit this portrait. In 2000, for example, Republican attacks and news coverage worsened voters' perceptions of Al Gore's honesty and made Gore's honesty a factor in how Americans voted.[46] This coverage perpetuated an existing narrative about Gore as ethically compromised and prone to exaggeration.

In 2016, the email server and the Clinton Foundation contributed to a similar narrative about Hillary Clinton. This narrative, which dated to Bill Clinton's presidency, portrayed the Clintons as dishonest, secretive, and unethical. After the 2008 election, one of Hillary Clinton's advisers, Howard Wolfson, said that the campaign had been concerned about "the unflattering residue of the nineties." Eight years later, Trump epitomized this narrative with a Twitter hashtag—#crookedhillary—and encouraged people attending his rallies to chant, "Lock her up!"[47]

Clinton's long and often hostile relationship with the news media made it harder for her to change this narrative. She acknowledged as much, saying later that she wanted to "avoid repeating past problems with the press corps" and "establish a more constructive give-and-take."[48] This never happened. For one, there was her own handling of the email server issue. Although some advisers wanted her to issue a quick apology, she instead made misleading statements in March 2015 that she had never sent or received classified information through her private server. Clinton thought this was enough, telling Podesta afterward, "I don't know how the story progresses." The story, of course, picked up steam in the summer of 2015 when the State Department's inspector general revealed that a small number of Clinton's emails contained classified information. Yet both Bill and Hillary Clinton were reportedly against issuing a contrite apology. Hillary Clinton even flippantly dismissed the issue: when reporters asked her in August 2015 about whether the email server was wiped before it was given to the FBI, Clinton said, "What? Like with a cloth or something?"[49] This hardly put to rest questions about the 32,000 deleted emails.

Throughout the campaign, Clinton was rarely available for press conferences or other on-the-record briefings with reporters, which may have also contributed to negative press coverage. As the political scientist John Zaller has written, the news media often respond with more critical coverage when politicians limit their access. Podesta appeared to realize this. In an April 2015 email that was subsequently hacked and leaked, he wrote, "If she thinks we can get to Labor Day without taking press questions, I think that's suicidal. We have to find some mechanism to let the steam out of the pressure cooker." Clinton later acknowledged, "The more they went after me, the more guarded I became, which only made them criticize me more."[50]

The power of this narrative about Clinton was visible in what voters reported hearing about her. In an early October YouGov poll, almost 80 percent of respondents said that they had "heard a lot" about the Clinton email story—more than any other story about Clinton or Trump. (For example, only 51% said they had heard a lot about Trump's calling Alicia Machado "Miss Piggy.") Throughout the campaign, the Gallup organization was also asking Americans what they had read, heard, or seen about Clinton. In August 2015, the most common word in people's responses was "emails." In the fall of 2016, the most common word was, again, "emails." Meanwhile, no single idea or theme dominated perceptions of Trump. This was the natural consequence of Clinton's having one continuous scandal that attracted extensive news coverage, compared to Trump's many scandals that each attracted less coverage.[51]

The impact of this narrative was also visible in how voters perceived Clinton and especially her honesty (figure 7.4). In the years leading up to her presidential campaigns (2005–6, 2014), a slender majority of Americans said that "honest" described Clinton. During her first presidential campaign, the percentage fell to an average of 46 percent in March 2008 and 39 percent in April. During the 2016 campaign, there was a deeper decline. By the fall of 2015, only about one-third of Americans believed that Clinton was honest. During the general election campaign—including after Comey's October 28 letter—perceptions of Clinton on this dimension did not worsen, but neither did they improve. Meanwhile, the percentage of people who described Trump

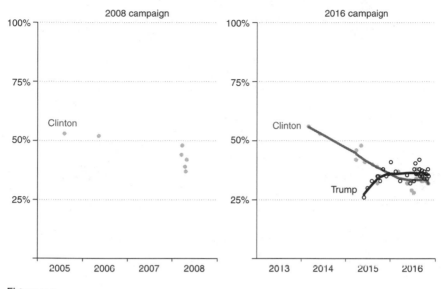

Figure 7.4.
Trends in the percentage saying Hillary Clinton or Donald Trump is honest (2005–8 and 2013–16).
ABC and CBS asked whether "honest and trustworthy" described Clinton. Gallup asked whether "honest and trustworthy" applied to Clinton. Pew asked whether "honest" described Clinton. There was only one archived poll question about Trump in 2009–13, in which 34 percent described Trump as honest in May 2011.
Sources: ABC, CBS, Gallup, and Pew polls archived at the Roper Center.

as honest actually improved as the campaign went on and, by the end of the campaign, slightly outnumbered the percentage who described Clinton as such. Clinton's scandals and news coverage appeared to reinforce a perception of her as dishonest and untrustworthy.

In the American National Election Studies, Clinton was also perceived as less honest than Obama was in 2012 and as less honest than Trump (figure 7.5).[52] Clinton's disadvantage in terms of honesty was even more striking because Trump was so prone to dishonesty himself. The *Guardian* documented 100 separate Trump falsehoods in the last 150 days of the campaign alone.[53] Trump was even viewed as slightly more honest than Romney. Trump also lagged Clinton only slightly in terms of leadership, despite Clinton's attempts to portray him as fundamentally unfit to lead the country. This is not to say that Trump had no disadvantages. Voters may have believed that he "spoke his mind," but they rated Clinton as more knowledgeable and even-tempered—a natural consequence of Trump's demonstrating a greater talent for provocation than policy expertise.

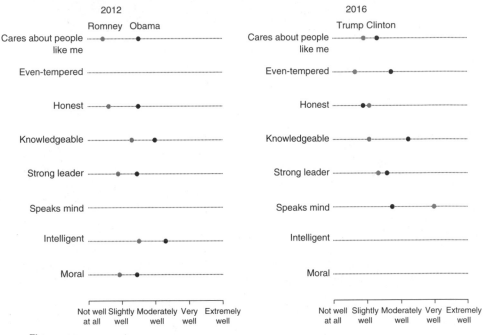

Figure 7.5.
Trait evaluations of the presidential candidates in 2012–16.
Source: American National Election Studies preelection survey.

But Clinton's scandals and the resulting news coverage constituted a fundamental challenge for her campaign. She wanted the election to be about Trump's character—his lack of preparedness, his weaknesses as a leader, his tendency to lie and insult others, his mistreatment of minorities and women. But the election was as much, if not more, about her own character. This shows how hard it is for candidates to raise and highlight an issue about their opponent without then being evaluated on that very same issue.

Endgame

Hillary Clinton and Donald Trump started the campaign as historically unpopular presidential candidates. At the campaign's end, they still were. And yet, a campaign that seemed unusual and unpredictable in so many ways had produced some predictability.

In particular, the 2016 campaign, like many presidential campaigns, made voters more predictable. One classic study of an American presidential election said this about voters: "Knowing a few of their personal characteristics, we can tell with fair certainty how they will finally vote: they join the fold to which they belong. What the campaign does is to activate their political predispositions." A central predisposition is partisanship. Presidential campaigns exert centripetal pressure within political parties, rallying the base and inducing party loyalty. This had happened in 2012, 2008, and many prior elections. In 2016, it happened again, as Democrats rallied to Clinton and Republicans belatedly, but clearly, rallied to Trump. It takes a significant force to split a party, and that force did not materialize in 2016.[54]

The 2016 campaign also revealed another facet of partisanship: the prevalence of dislike for the opposition, or "negative partisanship." For most of the summer and fall, 90 percent or more of Democrats viewed Trump unfavorably and 90 percent or more of Republicans viewed Clinton unfavorably (figure 7.3). More Democrats and Republican disliked the opposite candidate than liked their own. This mirrored a broader trend in which Democratic and Republican views of the opposite party have been growing less favorable.[55] There was no easy way to determine whether support for one's own party's candidate or dislike for the other party's candidate was more potent. Polls sometimes asked whether people were voting "for" one candidate or "against" the other, but people cannot reliably report on the reasons for their choices, including their vote intentions. Regardless, the "for" and "against" consequences of partisanship are mutually reinforcing. Both were operating in 2016.[56]

As partisans came back to the fold, the race tightened. This too was predictable. The polls in presidential elections typically move toward the outcome that the underlying political and economic fundamentals would predict.[57] Those fundamentals predicted a toss-up race, not the 8-point Clinton victory that polls suggested in mid-October. The closer race in early November was more in line with this prediction.

And yet a closer race did not necessarily mean a close race. This points to what was most unpredictable: Trump himself. Many of the dynamics of the campaign, including trends in news coverage and polls, revolved around him. Trump's penchant for controversy, as well as revelations about his past behavior, pulled voters' attitudes away from what the fundamentals predicted. By the end of the race, Trump finally seemed to believe that he was in trouble. Although he continued to insist that he would win, he was not sleeping much and needed his advisers to tell him repeatedly that his campaign was on track. *Vox*'s Trump Tax calculation showed that Trump was nearly 4 points behind where he "should" have been.[58]

A Clinton victory seemed all but assured.

CHAPTER 8

What Happened?

At 7:22 on the night of the election, the campaign of Donald Trump was not optimistic. One Trump staffer told CNN's Jim Acosta, "It will take a miracle for us to win." Hillary Clinton's campaign, by contrast, was wearing "the biggest smiles" when a *Boston Globe* reporter arrived at the scene of their anticipated victory party at 5:00 p.m.

As the night went on, this would all change. The early returns in Florida—where Clinton had a narrow lead in the polls and her campaign believed a surge in Latino turnout would propel her to victory—did not favor Clinton. Then the same thing happened in North Carolina and other battleground states, including Ohio, Michigan, Pennsylvania, and Wisconsin. By late that evening, the outcome was clear: Donald Trump was the next president of the United States. Sopan Deb of CBS News described the reaction at the Trump campaign's election night party: "It was a room full of gob smacked people. Not just reporters. Campaign staffers. Trump supporters. A lot of people." Clinton conceded around 2:30 a.m.[1]

Trump won a solid 304–227 majority in the Electoral College, even though Clinton led in the popular vote, which she ultimately won by 2.1 percentage points—larger than the margin for Richard Nixon in 1968 or John F. Kennedy in 1960. The divergence between Clinton's popular-vote victory and Electoral College defeat was extraordinary. In 2000, Al Gore narrowly won the popular vote by about half a point but lost the Electoral College by five votes. Trump, who had called the Electoral College a "disaster for a democracy" after the 2012 election, now called it "actually genius."[2]

Trump's victory flew in the face of a durable, but always dubious, piece of political commentary: that Democrats had an Electoral College advantage thanks to a phalanx of states known as the "blue wall," which included states that Trump ultimately won, such as Michigan, Pennsylvania, and Wisconsin. In reality, academic research suggested that the Democrats had a modest advantage at most, which made it less surprising that the blue wall crumbled on election night.[3]

The extraordinary divergence between the popular vote and Electoral College vote means that there is no simple way to explain or interpret the election outcome. Of course, Trump was the clear victor, given the rules of American presidential elections. At the same time, he also received many fewer votes than Clinton. Any explanation must be able to account for both facts. Any explanation must also improve on the notion that "anything" or "everything" could have mattered in such a close race. This was a popular refrain after the election, given that a shift of just over 77,000 votes in Michigan, Pennsylvania, and Wisconsin would have delivered victories in those states and thus in the Electoral College to Clinton. In fact, it is possible to evaluate the relative contribution of various factors. "Everything" did not "matter" equally.

The explanation of the election begins with fundamental political and economic conditions in the country. Two of these fundamentals—the state of the economy and evaluations of Barack Obama—forecasted Clinton's popular-vote victory. Indeed, her victory in the popular vote called into question the trope that 2016 was about voter "anger" or desire for "change." The identification of 2016 as a "change election" is hard to square with the fact that the same party won more votes for the third election in a row. A third fundamental—voters' party identification—also had a predictable impact, inducing loyalty among both Democrats and Republicans and helping Trump avoid the blowout that seemed imminent only a few weeks before Election Day.

But other aspects of the election were less predictable—and these helped provide Trump a path to victory in the Electoral College. For one, white voters shifted in different directions based on their level of formal education. Clinton's strength among white voters with more education helped her in some states, such as California and Texas, but these were not swing states in 2016. More important was Trump's strength among white voters with less formal education—the very voters that Clinton said "you have to win" back in 2008. These voters helped Trump win important battleground states—including Michigan, Pennsylvania, and Ohio—where they constituted a larger part of the population. Trump's strength among white voters without college degrees also helped explain why a relatively small but important fraction of Obama voters ended up voting for him. Ultimately, Clinton may have won more votes, but they were not in the right places or among the right groups. The "diploma divide" gave Trump votes exactly where he needed them.

The motivations of white voters were hotly debated during and after the election. The debate centered on whether white voters were motivated more by attitudes related to identity—race, religion, gender, and ethnicity—or by their concerns about their economic circumstances. Of these two factors, attitudes related to identity were more important. For one, views of racial inequality, Muslims, and immigration, as well as a more politicized white identity, not only were strongly related to whether Americans voted for Clinton or Trump but were also *more* strongly related to how people voted in 2016 than in other recent presidential elections. Economic concerns—such as fears of not being able to make a mortgage payment or pay a doctor's bill—were only weakly related to how people voted. For another, racial attitudes were the lens through which economic concerns became more politically actionable. This "racialized economics" meant that economic insecurity was connected to partisan choices when it was refracted through racial grievances.

Thus, no other factor appeared as distinctively powerful in 2016, compared to prior elections, as attitudes about racial issues and immigration, and no other factor explained the diploma divide among whites as fully. Of course, these attitudes were not the only factor that mattered in 2016. But they were the factor whose apparent impact was most distinctive, compared to recent elections. They were, unsurprisingly, the factor most strongly activated by a racialized campaign.

The increased salience of attitudes about race and immigration also helped Trump more than Clinton. For example, even in 2012, a substantial fraction of Obama voters expressed less favorable views of African Americans and immigration. Once those issues came to the fore in the campaign, they helped persuade some of these voters to support Trump.

Meanwhile, Clinton's supposed advantages—turnout among African Americans and other racial minorities, a surge in support among Latinos and women, the advantages of a well-funded and professionalized campaign—could not compensate. African American turnout dropped. The Latino surge was modest at best. Clinton's support among women was typical compared to earlier elections, while her losses among men were extraordinary. And although Clinton benefited from her advantages in televised advertising and field organization, their apparent impact was not large enough to tip the election in her favor.

Trump's victory thus reflected a blend of the usual and unusual. But what stands out as crucial to his victory was the unusually large role of identity-inflected anxieties.

The Predictable Impact of the Fundamentals

Clinton's popular-vote victory margin was surprisingly large for a candidate who lost the Electoral College, but it was entirely consistent with fundamental political and economic conditions in the country in 2016. The election's outcome was accurately predicted by economic growth in the first part of 2016 (figure 8.1). The data point for 2016 is almost exactly on the diagonal line that summarizes the relationship for the elections from 1948 to 2012. The election's outcome was also very close to a prediction based on both economic growth and presidential approval. As of June 2016, a statistical model including these two factors predicted that Clinton would win 51.8 percent of the major-party vote (chapter 2). She won 51.1 percent.

Although the election's outcome was quite in line with those two forecasts, Clinton's popular-vote margin actually *exceeded* some other forecasts. For example, the Democratic candidate was expected to lose in forecasting models that accounted for the lack of incumbent on the ballot or the Democrats' having held the White House for two terms. The most comprehensive average of forecasting models—by the website PollyVote—suggested a popular-vote split very close to 50–50. Clinton's popular-vote margin beat that by 2 points.

Election-year trends in consumer confidence and approval of Barack Obama (see chapter 2), combined with Clinton's popular-vote victory, contradict the popular idea that 2016 was a "change election" predicated on "voter anger" or economic anxiety. At a minimum, it seemed strange that, during the election year, "anxious" Americans demanding "change" remained quite positive about the economy, became *more* supportive of the incumbent president, and then on Election Day gave his successor a 3-million-vote margin. Clinton's popular-vote victory was not in line with casual punditry about voter anger, but it was in line with the state of the economy and approval of Barack Obama.

Another fundamental factor also powerfully, and predictably, shaped the election's outcome: partisanship. During the general election campaign, both Democrats and Republicans gravitated toward their party's nominee (chapter 7). On November 8, partisan intentions became a partisan reality. In the Election Day exit poll, 89 percent of Democrats voted for Clinton and 88 percent of Republicans voted for Trump—a level of partisan loyalty only

Incumbent party's percentage of major-party vote

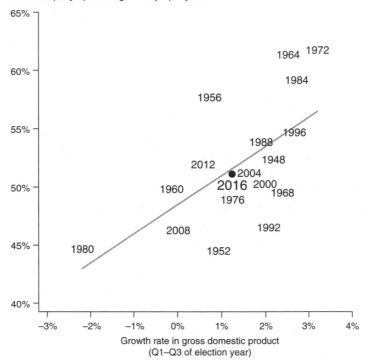

Figure 8.1.
Economic growth and presidential election outcomes, 1948–2016.
The relationship between change in GDP and the vote—the diagonal line—is a least squares regression line and is estimated without the 2016 election included.

slightly lower than in the 2012 exit poll, where 92 percent of Democrats reported voting for Obama and 93 percent of Republicans for Romney.

Another way to show the power of partisanship is to compare how the same group of Americans voted in 2012 and 2016, drawing again on the Views of the Electorate Research (VOTER) Survey (panel A of table 8.1). Barack Obama and Mitt Romney were quite different from Hillary Clinton and Donald Trump, but most voters picked the candidate from the same party in both years: 86 percent of Obama voters reported voting for Clinton, and 88 percent of Romney voters reported voting for Trump. About 83 percent of voters were "consistent partisans" who voted for the same major party's candidate in both years.

The extent of partisan loyalty was almost identical in the 2008 and 2012 elections: 80 percent were consistent partisans, as 87 percent of John McCain supporters voted for Romney and 89 percent of Obama supporters in 2008 voted for him again in 2012. In earlier surveys by the American National Election Studies (ANES), which also interviewed the same respondents four years apart, the percentage of voters who were consistent partisans was 85 percent from 2000 to 2004, 77 percent from 1992 to 1996 (including the independent candidate Ross Perot as a choice in both years), 72 percent from 1972 to 1976, and 76 percent from 1956 to 1960. In short, the stability from 2012 to 2016 matched that in recent elections and was higher than in elections from the 1990s and earlier.[4]

The power of partisanship was also visible in the willingness of primary voters to support their party's nominee—regardless of whether they had supported that person in the primary (panel B of table 8.1). Among Democratic primary voters who were interviewed about their primary preference in July 2016 and interviewed again after the general election, 79 percent of Bernie Sanders supporters reported voting for Clinton.[5] This level of partisan loyalty was higher than in 2008, when about 70 percent of Clinton primary voters reported voting for Barack Obama. Indeed, even the Sanders supporters that Clinton did not win over—notably the estimated 12 percent of Sanders voters who supported Trump in the general election—were probably not going to support her no matter what. When these Sanders-Trump voters had been interviewed four years prior, after the 2012 election, only 35 percent reported voting for Obama. Most of these voters were not really Democrats to begin with.[6]

Among Republicans who did not support Trump in the primary, nearly seven in ten (69%) voted for him in the general election. This was somewhat lower than in the 2008 Republican primary, when 87 percent of those who did not vote for McCain supported him in the general, and the 2012 Republican primary, when 79 percent of Republican primary voters who did not vote for Romney supported him in the general.[7] The divisions evident in the 2016 primaries were thus more difficult for Republicans than Democrats to overcome—a telling indicator of the factionalism that preceded the primary. Nevertheless, Trump still managed to win over most of the Republicans who did not vote for him in the primary.

Partisanship also helped to create stability across the campaign itself (panel C of table 8.1). In December 2015, survey respondents were asked whether they supported or leaned toward Clinton or Trump in a hypothetical matchup. In November 2016, when these respondents were asked whom they had voted for, most gave the same answer: 88 percent of initial Clinton supporters ended up voting for her, and 89 percent of initial Trump supporters voted for him. Of course, in the months between these two interviews, there was instability—particularly as some Republicans wavered on Trump. But the campaign's ability to activate partisanship helped ensure that people

Table 8.1.

Trends in Candidate Preferences

Panel A. 2012 to 2016 (cell entries are row percentages)

	2016 vote					
2012 vote	Hillary Clinton	Donald Trump	Gary Johnson	Jill Stein	Other candidate	No vote for president
Obama	86%	9%	2%	2%	1%	0.1%
Romney	5%	88%	3%	0.1%	3%	1%
Other candidate	26%	39%	22%	8%	6%	0.1%

Panel B. 2016 primary to 2016 general

	2016 vote					
2016 primary vote	Hillary Clinton	Donald Trump	Gary Johnson	Jill Stein	Other candidate	No vote for president
Democratic primary						
Clinton	96%	3%	0.4%	0.3%	0.3%	0.1%
Sanders	79%	12%	2%	4%	2.1%	0.2%
Republican primary						
Trump	1%	98%	0.4%	0.1%	0.1%	0%
Not Trump	14%	69%	7%	1%	7%	2%
Rubio	10%	67%	10%	0.2%	9%	4%
Cruz	3%	77%	9%	1%	6%	3%
Kasich	32%	57%	4%	0%	5%	1%
Someone else	17%	70%	3%	0.2%	10%	0%

Panel C. December 2015 to November 2016

	2016 vote				
December 2015 vote intention	Hillary Clinton	Donald Trump	Gary Johnson	Other candidate	No vote for president
Clinton	88%	6%	3%	3%	1%
Trump	5%	89%	3%	2%	1%
Other or not sure	20%	41%	20%	16%	2%

Note: Percentages are row percentages and may not add to 100 percent because of rounding. Panel A data are 7,180 self-reported voters interviewed in November 2012 and again between November 29 and December 29, 2016, as part of the VOTER Survey. Panel B data are 2,912 self-reported Democratic primary voters and 2,849 Republican primary voters from the December 2016 VOTER Survey. Primary vote choice was measured in an earlier July 2016 interview. Panel C data are 2,398 self-reported voters from the Presidential Election Panel Survey interviewed between December 14, 2015, and January 6, 2016, and then between November 9 and December 21, 2016.

ended up with the same preference that they had indicated almost a year before. This level of stability was only slightly lower than between December 2011 and November 2012.[8]

A further manifestation of partisanship involved the unusually large number of voters who had unfavorable views of both Clinton and Trump—a group that can be called "double negative" voters. In the exit poll, 18 percent of voters fit this pattern, and more of them voted for Trump (47%) than Clinton (30%). Why would Trump do better than Clinton among this group? It was not because they secretly liked Trump more. Other survey data showed that double negative voters had equally unfavorable views of both candidates.[9] But double negative voters were nevertheless disproportionately Republican. In Gallup's polling in the two weeks before Election Day, 45 percent of double negative voters were Republicans and 35 percent were Democrats. Among voters who did not have negative views of both candidates, 45 percent were Republicans and 50 percent were Democrats. It is no surprise, then, that Trump did better among those with unfavorable views of both candidates. They appeared to be holding their nose and voting their partisanship.

These patterns all show how 2016 was an ordinary election in certain respects. Partisan identities remained potent, despite lengthy and divisive primaries in both parties that many believed would create unusual disloyalty in the general election.

Surprising Shifts

But if this election was predictable in some ways, in other ways it was not. And these less predictable shifts pointed to the sources of Donald Trump's victory in the Electoral College.

First, there were the shifts in individual states (figure 8.2). An increasingly typical pattern in U.S. presidential elections is for most every state to shift, or "swing," in the same direction from one election to the next, depending on how much the fundamentals favor one party or the other. This tendency toward a more "uniform swing" has become more pronounced. For example, from 2008 to 2012, almost every state shifted in the direction of the Republican candidate because national conditions were less favorable for Democrats in 2012 than in 2008, when the Republicans were hamstrung by an unpopular incumbent and a worsening recession. One of the most accurate forecasts of the 2012 election simply added a uniform swing to the 2008 margins in the states.[10]

But between 2012 and 2016, the swing was less uniform. Based on the statistical forecasts, Clinton should have done a little worse than Obama did in

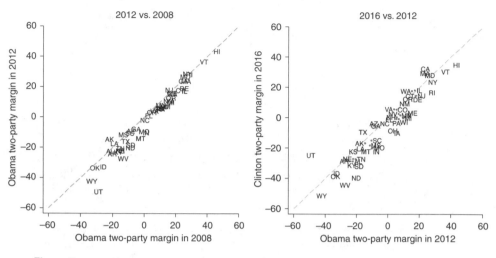

Figure 8.2.
Shifts in presidential vote margin in the states, 2008–16 (percentage points).
Source: U.S. Election Atlas, https://uselectionatlas.org/.

2012. But the state-level shifts were variable. In several states, Clinton did better than Obama, including in Arizona, California, Georgia, Massachusetts, and Texas. In some states, she essentially equaled his vote margin, including in battleground states such as North Carolina, Florida, and Colorado. But in other states, she did substantially worse. In states such as West Virginia, Democratic fortunes had been declining for some time. The shifts in other states, however, were more surprising and costly for Clinton in the Electoral College. In 2012, Obama beat Romney in Ohio by 3 points; Clinton lost it by more than 8 points. Obama won Iowa by 6 points; Clinton lost it by 10 points. Obama won Michigan by almost 10 points, Pennsylvania by almost 6 points, and Wisconsin by 7 points. Clinton lost each of these states by a slender margin. In fact, Clinton did better in the traditionally uncompetitive red states of Georgia (where she lost by about 5 points) and Texas (where she lost by 9.4 points) than she did in the traditionally competitive state of Iowa. She lost Texas by only slightly more than she lost Ohio.[11]

The contrasting shifts in the states between 2008 and 2012 and between 2012 and 2016 were mirrored in prominent demographic groups. In 2012, Obama's margin in almost every demographic narrowed somewhat, which was another manifestation of a nearly uniform swing. But in 2016, different demographics moved in different directions (figure 8.3). The most dramatic polarization was among whites with different levels of formal education. Before 2016, whites with and without college degrees had always shifted in the same direction from election to election.[12] But in 2016, Clinton's margin among

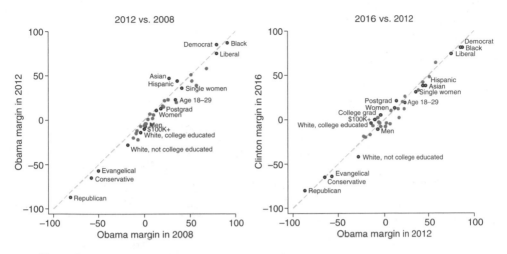

Figure 8.3.

Shifts in presidential vote margin in demographic groups, 2008–16 (percentage points). Sources: 2012 and 2016 national exit polls.

whites with a college degree was 10 points better than Obama's, while her margin among whites without a college degree was 14 points worse.

This polarization among whites helped Trump more than Clinton. White voters without a college degree are more prevalent: 47 percent of eligible voters are whites with no college degree, whereas 22 percent are whites with a college degree. (The remainder are nonwhite.) And among those who reported voting in 2016, the comparable percentages were 42 percent and 31 percent, according to the Census Bureau's Current Population Survey.[13] Trump's success among whites without a college degree was a key reason that voters who voted for Obama in 2012 but Trump in 2016 were more numerous than voters who went in the opposite direction, from Romney to Clinton (table 8.1). Among white Obama voters with at least some college education who reported voting in 2016, almost 90 percent voted for Clinton. Among those with a high school degree or less, only 74 percent voted for Clinton, whereas 22 percent voted for Trump.

The consequences for the Electoral College were dramatic. Although Clinton gained vote share relative to Obama in large states with a smaller fraction of voters who were white and did not have a college degree—thereby expanding her margin of victory in the popular vote—she lost vote share in key battleground states with a larger fraction of these voters, especially Michigan, Ohio, Pennsylvania, and Wisconsin (figure 8.4). The presence of many white, non-college-educated voters also helps explain why she did surprisingly poorly in states such as Minnesota, which Obama won by almost 8 points and Clinton by only 1.5. Excluding the two states where the shifts were due more

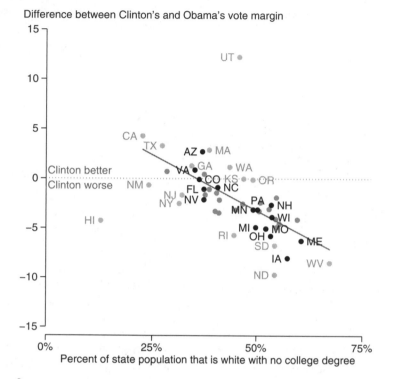

Difference between Clinton's and Obama's vote margin

Figure 8.4.
The relationship between 2012–16 vote shifts and the size of the white, non-college-educated population.
Battleground and other key states are highlighted in black. The diagonal line is a least squares regression line estimated for all states except Hawaii and Utah.
Sources: U.S. Election Atlas; American Community Survey.

to the absence of Obama and Romney—they had personal ties to Hawaii and Utah, respectively—a 10-point shift in the percentage of a state's population that was white with no college degree was associated with a 2.3-point decrease in Clinton's vote margin, relative to Obama's in 2012. In these forty-eight states, the percentage of a state's population that was white with no college degree explained 58 percent of the variation in the 2012–16 shifts.[14]

This polarization of whites along educational lines had been under way since Obama's election, with college-educated whites moving toward the Democratic Party and whites without a college degree moving to the Republican Party (see chapter 2). The 2016 election continued—and perhaps exacerbated—this trend.

The Activation of Identity among White Voters

Why did whites become more polarized based on education, and why did this help Donald Trump win the White House? There were five key parts of the story, all of which centered on identities and attitudes tied to race, ethnicity, and religion.

1. There were a substantial number of cross-pressured white Obama voters whose attitudes on race and immigration were out of step with the trajectory of the Democratic Party.
2. The campaign's focus on identity-inflected issues—and Clinton's and Trump's sharply divergent positions—led voters to perceive Clinton and Trump as farther apart on these issues than any major-party presidential candidates in over forty years.
3. In turn, voters' attitudes on these issues became more strongly related to how they voted in 2016 than in recent presidential elections. Other types of attitudes—including economic anxiety—did not show this pattern.
4. Racial attitudes shaped the way voters understood economic outcomes—a "racialized economics" rather than a purely "economic" anxiety.
5. Voters' attitudes on racial issues accounted for the "diploma divide" between less and better educated whites. Economic anxiety did not.

Cross-Pressured Obama Voters

The growing alignment of racial attitudes and partisanship was not so complete that all white Obama voters had favorable views of racial and ethnic minorities or supported liberal policies on issues like immigration. Polling from 2011 to 2012 showed that substantial numbers of white Obama voters were not sympathetic to the idea that blacks face systematic discrimination (table 8.2). Almost half (49%) did not think that "blacks have gotten less than they deserve," 39 percent did not believe that slavery and discrimination hindered the economic advancement of blacks, and 28 percent essentially blamed the economic disadvantages of blacks on their own lack of effort ("If blacks would only try harder they could be just as well off as whites").

Many white Obama voters also expressed conservative positions on other racially or ethnically inflected issues. Almost half (45%) favored the death penalty for persons convicted of murder. About a third wanted to make it slightly or much harder for foreigners to immigrate to the United States. Roughly a third believed that "illegal immigrants are mostly a drain on society" (as opposed to "making a contribution"). One in five (22%) opposed a path to

Table 8.2.

Political Beliefs among White Obama Voters (December 2011)

Survey question	Percentage with stated view
Disagreed that "over the past few years, blacks have gotten less than they deserve"	49
Agreed that blacks should "work their way up" without "any special favors"	46
Favored death penalty	45
Disagreed that "generations of slavery and discrimination have created conditions that make it difficult for blacks to work their way out of the lower class"	39
Believed abortion should be legal in some cases and illegal in other cases	35
Rated Muslims on the less favorable side of a 0–100 scale	35
Favored making it harder to immigrate to the United States	34
Believed illegal immigrants are mostly a drain on society	32
Agreed with the statement, "It's really a matter of some people not trying hard enough. If blacks would only try harder they could be just as well off as whites."	28
Opposed path to citizenship for illegal immigrants	22
Opposed increasing trade with other nations	19
Opposed government providing universal health care	13
Opposed gay marriage	12
Believed there was too much government regulation on business	10
Favored repealing the Affordable Care Act	9
Identified exclusively as pro-life	8
Doubted existence of global warming	8
Believed abortion should be illegal in all cases	4
Opposed increasing taxes on wealthy	3

Note: All opinions were measured in December 2011, and 2012 vote choice was measured in November 2012. "Don't know" was included as a valid response in all tabulations.
Source: VOTER Survey ($N = 2{,}717$ white Obama voters).

citizenship. And 35 percent rated Muslims unfavorably (between 0 and 49 on a 0–100 scale). These voters were "cross-pressured"—with their partisanship and views on racial issues increasingly in tension—and prior scholarship has shown that these are exactly the voters that a campaign can push into the opposite party's camp.[15]

Indeed, identity-inflected issues stand out for the sheer number of white Obama voters who seemed at odds with Obama's own positions and those of the Democratic Party. Excepting the 35 percent who had an ambivalent view of abortion—thinking it should be legal in some cases and illegal in others—there were fewer white Obama voters who opposed increasing trade or took conservative positions on health care, government regulation, gay marriage, and taxing the wealthy.

Many observers dismissed the role of race in 2016 by arguing that Obama voters could not have had unfavorable views of racial minorities. The liberal filmmaker Michael Moore said this about voters who had supported Obama and then Trump: "They're not racist. . . . They twice voted for a man whose middle name is Hussein." But this is just as inaccurate as saying everyone who voted against Obama was racially prejudiced. In fact, Obama even garnered support from whites with explicitly prejudiced views. About one-quarter of whites who opposed interracial dating—this is around 15 percent to 20 percent of whites—still voted for Obama in 2008 and 2012. Many whites with less favorable views of blacks wound up supporting Obama because of partisanship or some other factor.[16] Although many of those voters then left the Democratic Party during Obama's presidency (see chapter 2), there were still plenty of white Obama voters who could end up voting for Trump, specifically because of a campaign centered on issues like race and immigration.

Even more problematic for Clinton was this fact: there were many fewer Republicans who held views akin to hers. For example, only 6 percent of white Romney voters thought that illegal immigrants contributed to American society; nearly 80 percent thought that these immigrants were a drain. Thus, in a racialized campaign, the Republican Party stood to pick up more white voters than Democrats could.

Changing Voters' Perceptions

The campaign's focus on race—and the contrasting positions of Trump and Clinton—clearly registered with voters: there was a record gap in where voters perceived Trump and Clinton on racial issues. On its face this may seem impossible, given that an African American himself had been the Democratic nominee in the previous two elections. But Obama talked about race less than recent Democratic presidents and, when he did, often emphasized black personal responsibility.[17] He was even criticized by black leaders for refusing to push policies targeted at helping blacks. Obama's candidacy and presidency helped activate racial attitudes more because of who he was than what he said or did.

There was reason, then, to expect voters to notice when Clinton moved to Obama's left in both her rhetoric and policies on race-related issues—by speaking early and often about the pernicious consequences of racism, meeting with Black Lives Matter activists, standing up for undocumented immigrants

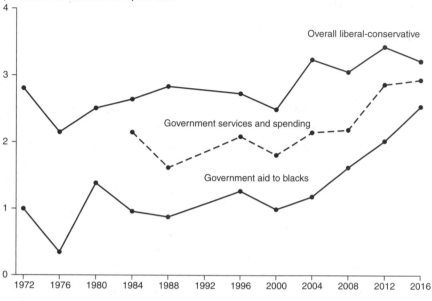

Figure 8.5.

Difference in whites' perceptions of the presidential candidates' positions.
Source: ANES.

who came to the United States as children, and generally contrasting her "Stronger Together" vision with Donald Trump's more restrictive conception of American identity. This reflected the Clinton campaign's focus on mobilizing the "Obama coalition" while largely ignoring white working-class voters and Republican-leaning states.[18] Meanwhile, it was clear to voters whose side Trump was on, given his opposition to immigration, racially charged rhetoric, and appeals to white grievances.

One long-standing survey has asked Americans to estimate where the presidential candidates stand on a seven-point scale ranging from "The government in Washington should make every effort to improve the social and economic position of blacks" to "The government should not make any special effort to help blacks because they should help themselves." Unsurprisingly, Americans have rated the Democratic presidential candidate as the more supportive of federal aid to blacks in every single survey since the question's inception in 1972 (figure 8.5). In 2008 and 2012, despite Barack Obama's relatively race-neutral rhetoric, whites saw a much greater disparity between Obama and both John McCain and Romney.

Then, in 2016, this disparity increased to record levels: whites rated Clinton about 2.5 points more supportive of aid to blacks than they did Trump.

Whites saw Clinton as more liberal than Obama in 2012 (a 0.13 shift on the scale) and Trump as significantly more conservative than Romney (a 0.37 shift). A key reason for these shifts was that more whites were coming to have opinions about where the candidates stood on this issue. Between 2012 and 2016, the percentage who could not place the Democratic candidate dropped from 13 percent to 7 percent, while the percentage who could not place the Republican dropped from 22 percent in 2012 to 7 percent in 2016. Because white respondents who could not place the candidates arguably saw little difference between them, this learning process helped create more racially polarized perceptions of the candidates.[19]

The same was true for immigration, according to research by the political scientist Daniel Hopkins. In a survey that interviewed the same respondents in 2012 and 2016, respondents saw the Republican Party as much more conservative on illegal immigration in 2016 than was Romney in 2012—specifically, closer to the policy option of returning illegal immigrants to their native countries. Similarly, they saw the Democratic Party as slightly more liberal than they did Obama in 2012—in this case, closer to the option of a path to citizenship. Although this comparison is complicated by the shift from asking about candidates in 2012 to parties in 2016, the results suggest the same pattern: polarizing perceptions of key electoral actors on a racially inflected issue.[20]

Notably, the shifts between 2012 and 2016 on the questions of aid to blacks and immigration were not mirrored in some other issues. There was only a small increase in where Americans perceived Trump and Clinton on the question of how much spending and services the government should provide (figure 8.5). There was a *decrease* in the perceived distance between Trump and Clinton on an overall spectrum from very liberal to very conservative. This was because Americans rated Trump as more liberal than Romney, which could have reflected Trump's somewhat muddled ideological message (see chapter 5).

In short, a campaign that emphasized race and immigration produced a distinctive polarization in perceptions of the candidates' positions on these issues. Because people saw such large differences between Clinton and Trump, these issues were then poised to matter more at the ballot box.

Identity and Vote Choice

In multiple surveys, attitudes about race and ethnicity were more strongly related to vote choice in 2016 than they were in 2008 and 2012—even after accounting for people's partisanship and their overall political ideology on the left-right scale, which themselves had become increasingly intertwined with attitudes about race, ethnicity, and religion. One attitude that manifested this pattern of "activation" was whether whites attributed racial inequality to structural factors like discrimination or to blacks' lack of effort (top panels of figure 8.6). Two different surveys, the ANES and the VOTER Survey, showed the same pattern. And in the VOTER Survey, views of African Americans were measured almost five years before the 2016 election, thereby guarding against the possibility that people changed their racial attitudes to "match" those that they perceived in Trump or Clinton. Even though racial attitudes had already become more strongly related to how people voted in presidential elections because of Barack Obama's candidacy, that relationship strengthened further in 2016, even without an African American candidate on the ballot. (The year-to-year differences in the slopes of the lines in figure 8.6 were statistically meaningful. See the appendix to this chapter for details.)

Voters' attitudes about immigration showed the same pattern of activation. This was true regardless of whether immigration attitudes were measured with a single question about people's feelings toward "illegal immigrants" (middle left panel of figure 8.6) or with a scale combining whether they believed illegal immigrants contributed to the United States, supported a path to citizenship for illegal immigrants, and believed immigration to the United States should be easier (middle right panel). After accounting for party and ideology, whites who rated illegal immigrants most unfavorably were about 25 points more likely to support John McCain than Barack Obama in 2008, compared to those who rated illegal immigrants most favorably. That difference was 65 points in 2016.

Voters' feelings about Muslims and their perception of discrimination against whites—a measure of a more politicized white identity—also became more strongly related to voter choices in 2016. The logic is the same: after a campaign that frequently centered on Muslims and how much of a threat they allegedly posed to Americans' security, it became easier for Americans to "use" their own feelings toward Muslims (here, measured five years before) to determine whether to support Trump or Clinton. Those with less favorable feelings were more likely to support Trump, and those with more favorable feelings to support Clinton. Similarly, after a campaign in which "white identity" was headline news time and time again, the connection between whites' perceptions of how much discrimination they faced and how they voted became tighter, compared both to 2004 and 2012.

Other surveys and scholarship showed the same pattern. Views of African Americans were more strongly linked to vote choice in 2016 than 2012 in surveys conducted by YouGov and the Public Religion Research Institute. The same was true among whites who were interviewed in both 2012 and 2016 as part of the Presidential Election Panel Survey. In this survey, racial attitudes were also more strongly related to whites' preferences for Trump over Clinton than they were in hypothetical matchups between Clinton and Ted Cruz

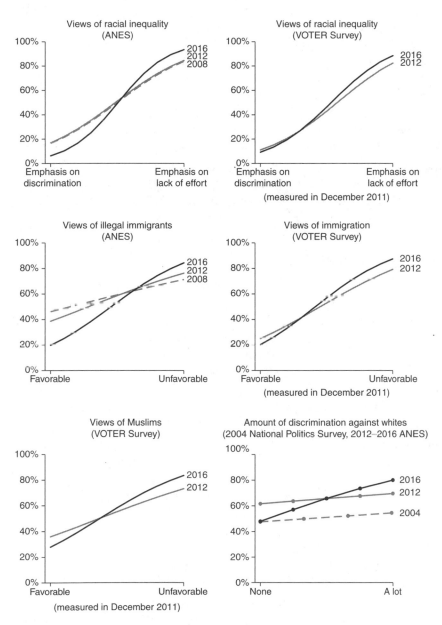

Figure 8.6.

Whites' racial attitudes and likelihood of voting for the Republican presidential candidate.

Findings based on statistical models that also account for party identification and self-reported ideology.

Sources: 2008–16 ANES; December 2016 VOTER Survey (with racial attitudes measured in December 2011); and 2004 National Politics Survey.

or Marco Rubio. This suggests that Trump's rhetoric made views about race more potent than they would have been had Clinton faced a different Republican opponent. Finally, Daniel Hopkins, drawing on a survey that interviewed the same people in both 2008 and 2016, found that stereotypes of blacks that were measured in 2008 were more strongly related to vote choice in 2016 than in 2008, when Obama first ran for president.[21]

There is no easy way to determine whether attitudes toward blacks, immigrants, or Muslims or a more politicized white identity was the "most important" factor. These factors are themselves strongly correlated with each other, making it difficult to disentangle their separate impacts. But the overall pattern is clear: whites' attitudes about race, ethnicity, and religion came to play a larger role in 2016 than other recent elections.[22]

Economic Anxiety and Vote Choice

The stronger relationships involving racial attitudes in 2016 would be less noteworthy if many other kinds of attitudes showed the same pattern. In particular, commentators frequently argued that the key to understanding white voters in 2016—especially why some voted for Trump after supporting Obama in 2012—was their economic anxieties.

After the election, many analysts and political leaders, including prominent Democrats like Bernie Sanders and Joe Biden, argued that Trump's appeal originated in the economic plight of white Americans and the social conditions that were tied to their economic plight. One widely discussed finding often linked to Trump support showed that mortality was increasing among middle-aged whites, especially those with less formal education, even as it decreased among whites with a college education, blacks, and Hispanics.[23] Counties where Trump had outperformed Mitt Romney had experienced slower gains in life expectancy. Moreover, these same counties had more "deaths of despair" from drug overdoses, alcohol abuse, and suicides. Another analysis of election returns found that counties where Trump outperformed George W. Bush in the 2000 presidential election had lost more jobs to competition from Chinese imports. At the same time, however, other analyses suggested that Trump did better in counties where there was a larger *drop* in unemployment and *more* social mobility. And a large study of county-level support for Trump concluded, "Trump's popularity cannot be neatly linked to economic hardship." The relationship between economic outcomes in counties and voting in 2016 was murky.[24]

But there was a bigger problem with these analyses: counties do not vote. People do. A rigorous test of the "economic anxiety" theory would need to show that white voters' economic anxieties became "activated" in

2016 compared to earlier elections—just as attitudes about race, immigration, or Islam did. For example, whether white voters were concerned about their finances, about losing their job, about not making their rent or mortgage payment, or about not being able to pay for health care should have more strongly influenced their choice between Trump and Clinton, compared to the choice between, say, Obama and Romney. If so, then economic anxiety would clearly be an important factor, alongside attitudes related to race and ethnicity.

This was not what the evidence suggested. In both 2012 and 2016, respondents to the ANES were asked this exact series of questions regarding their worries about finances, losing their job, and not making a housing or health care payment. In these two surveys, about 6–9 percent of respondents thought losing their job or not being able to make a housing payment was "very likely" or "extremely likely," 23–26 percent thought it was likely they would not be able to pay their health care costs, and about 23 percent were very or extremely worried about their financial situation (about 30–31% were "moderately" worried).[25]

But after accounting for partisanship, self-reported ideology, and views of racial inequality, there were generally weak relationships between these measures of economic anxiety and how people voted in 2012 or 2016 (figure 8.7). Moreover, these relationships were not consistently any stronger in 2016 than 2012. Even an omnibus measure of economic anxiety that included responses to all four questions was not much more strongly related to how people voted in 2016 versus 2012 (bottom left panel of figure 8.7). Any change in this relationship from 2012 to 2016 was not statistically significant. Meanwhile, even after accounting for economic anxiety, the relationship between racial attitudes and vote choice was large and clearly larger in 2016 than 2012 (bottom right panel). Similarly, research by political scientists Brian Schaffner, Matthew MacWilliams, and Tatishe Nteta found that changes in household income had little relationship to changes in people's votes between 2012 and 2016, but racial attitudes did.[26]

The same was true of other factors connected to economics. For example, if jobs lost to trade were a factor in county election returns, then people's feelings about whether to increase trade could plausibly be connected to how they voted. But in the VOTER Survey, there was no relationship between views of trade, measured in December 2011, and how people voted in either 2012 or 2016, once other factors were accounted for. Indeed, trade attitudes were more likely a consequence of people's vote intentions rather than a cause: Republicans became more opposed to free trade agreements during the campaign, suggesting that they changed their views of trade to match Trump's rather than drawing on their views of trade to choose a presidential candidate.[27]

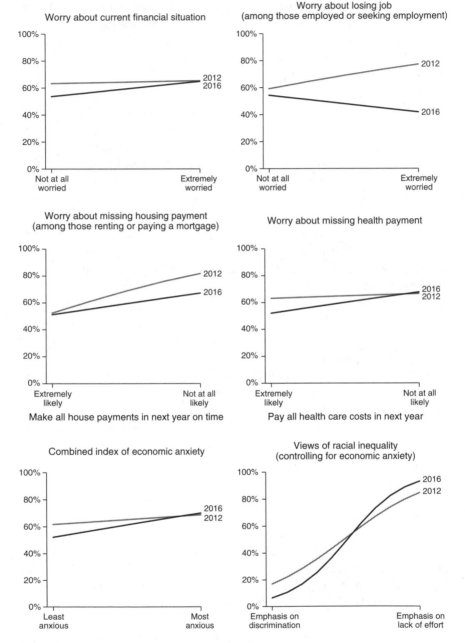

Figure 8.7.

Whites' economic anxiety and likelihood of voting for the Republican presidential candidate.

Findings based on statistical models that also account for party identification, self-reported ideology, and attitudes toward African Americans.

Source: 2012–16 ANES.

Similarly, if Trump's success was a reaction to "deaths of despair," then Trump voters should arguably have been more likely to know someone who abused alcohol or was addicted to illegal drugs or especially painkillers, like opioids, which had become such a scourge. But in the VOTER Survey, this was not the case. Almost equal numbers of Clinton and Trump voters—55 percent and 56 percent, respectively—said they knew someone who had been addicted to alcohol. Similarly, 40 percent of Clinton voters and 39 percent of Trump voters said they knew someone who had been addicted to illegal drugs, and 29 percent of Clinton voters and 31 percent of Trump voters said they knew someone who had been addicted to painkillers. Among whites, it was Clinton voters, not Trump voters, who were more likely to report knowing people in any of these circumstances.

The evidence for economic anxiety's influence in 2016 is thus much weaker than the evidence for the influence of attitudes related to race and ethnicity. Indeed, the influence of identity-based attitudes appears distinctive relative to many other attitudes as well. For example, views of government regulation of business, government involvement in health care, abortion, and same-sex marriage were not more strongly related to voters' choices in 2016 compared to 2012.[28] Of course, attitudes tied to race, ethnicity, and religion were not the only things related to people's choices in 2016. But they were *distinctively* related, compared to recent elections.

Racialized Economics

To downplay the role of economic anxiety is not to deny its existence. Many people face clear economic challenges, and their concerns and anxieties are real. But when economic concerns are politically potent, the prism of identity is often present. This is "racialized economics": the belief that undeserving groups are getting ahead while your group is left behind. And throughout American history, the groups considered undeserving have often been racial and ethnic minorities.[29]

Racialized economics was visible even before the election. Whites with less favorable views of blacks were most likely to think that the economy was in poor shape under Obama's stewardship (see chapter 2). Ethnographic research among whites in Youngstown, Ohio, and in rural communities also found that concerns about deservingness were common. In Youngstown, there were complaints about government assistance going to African Americans. One white man described recipients in racially coded terms, saying that they spent government payments on "gold chains and a Cadillac when I can barely afford a Cavalier." In one of the rural communities, a Catholic priest described a common complaint of whites: "Okay, you're Hispanic and we're Caucasian and you're getting all this help from government programs and nothing is happening for us and our kids."[30]

Trump repeatedly made similar arguments about deservingness. He regularly and misleadingly said that "illegal immigrants are treated better in America than many of our vets" and accused Clinton and Obama of caring more about illegal immigrants than veterans. He accused immigrants of draining public resources, saying (again falsely) that "illegal immigrant households receive far more in welfare benefits." He asserted that immigrants are "taking our jobs. They're taking our manufacturing jobs. They're taking our money. They're killing us." This scapegoating was so prominent in the campaign that Barack Obama explicitly warned about it in his farewell address: "If every economic issue is framed as a struggle between [the] hardworking white middle class and undeserving minorities, then workers of all shades will be left fighting for scraps while the wealthy withdraw further into their private enclaves."[31]

Racialized perceptions of economic deservingness were thus strongly related to support for Donald Trump. In the Republican primary, economic perceptions mattered most when refracted through group identities (see chapter 5). White voters' preference for Donald Trump as the Republican nominee was weakly related to their own job security but strongly related to concerns that minorities were taking jobs away from whites.

The same appeared to be true in the general election. In December 2016, we embedded a simple experiment in a national survey. Half of the respondents were asked whether they agreed or disagreed with a racially loaded statement: "Over the past few years, blacks have gotten less than they deserve." The other half was give the same statement, except that instead of "blacks," it said "average Americans"—a group that research has shown is implicitly synonymous with being white.[32]

A majority of respondents (57%) said that average Americans had gotten less than they deserved, whereas only 32 percent said this about African Americans (figure 8.8). Blacks were equally likely to agree with this statement regardless of whom it referenced, but whites were 30 points more likely to say that average Americans had gotten less than they deserved (58% versus 28% who thought African Americans had gotten less than they deserved). The disparity was even bigger among Trump voters. Almost two-thirds of Trump voters said that average Americans were not getting what they deserve, but only 12 percent said this about blacks. Among Clinton voters, there was no such disparity. In other words, the dividing line between Clinton and Trump voters was not the widespread belief that average Americans are being left behind. Rather, the divide was whether a racial minority deserved help.

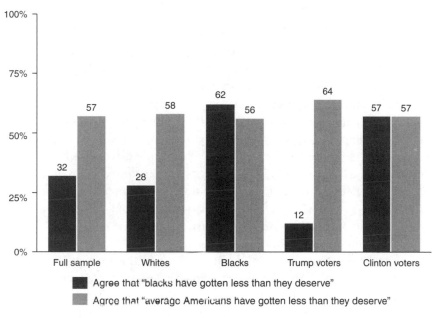

Figure 8.8.
Perceptions of racial deservingness.
Source: December 2016 HuffPost/YouGov Poll.

The same finding emerged in another experiment. The political scientists Matthew Luttig, Christopher Federico, and Howard Lavine found that Trump supporters were more opposed to a federal mortgage relief program when they were shown a picture of a black man standing next to a foreclosure sign than when shown the exact same picture but featuring a white man. Clinton supporters were not affected by the picture.[33]

These two experiments show how economics entered into white voters' choices in 2016: not through concern about their individual financial situations but through racialized perceptions of economic deservingness. These perceptions were in turn linked to white grievances. In one postelection survey, more Trump voters said that whites faced a lot of discrimination than said this of African Americans, Latinos, and Jews.[34] Thus, voters' choices in 2016 were not necessarily about how much prejudice they felt toward minorities, although there were certainly voters who expressed explicitly prejudiced views. Instead, the divide had more to do with how people explained economic outcomes in the first place—and especially whether they believed that hardworking white Americans were losing ground to less deserving minorities.

Explaining the "Diploma Divide"

The final part of the story entails explaining the growing educational divide among whites that helped Trump win votes in important battleground states. Here again, racial attitudes—more than economic anxiety—were key.

The relationship between education and support for Donald Trump is plain: Trump did worse—and Clinton better—among whites with college degrees or some postgraduate education than among whites who did not have college degrees (figure 8.9). However, this relationship disappeared once views of racial inequality and illegal immigrants were accounted for in the statistical analysis. Because whites with more formal education have long had more positive views of racial and ethnic minorities, and because these views were themselves strongly related to how Americans voted in 2016, the education gap was largely a racial attitudes gap.

Notably, economic factors did not much affect the correlation between education and voters' preference for Clinton or Trump. For example, voters' household incomes did not explain the educational divide. Trump voters who did not attend college were actually relatively affluent, and, moreover, the educational divide among whites was present among voters at all income levels. Similarly, economic anxiety did not explain much of the educational divide. The correlation between education and voters' choices was virtually unchanged when economic anxiety—the composite index in figure 8.7—was included as a factor.[35] In fact, one study of white voters without a college education or salaried job found that those who reported being in fair or poor financial shape were actually more likely to support Clinton, not Trump, compared to those who were in better financial shape.[36] Ultimately, no other factor in these surveys explained the education gap as well as racial attitudes—not partisanship, not ideology, not authoritarianism, not sexism, not income, not economic anxiety.

When combined, these threads tell a straightforward story. In 2016, the presidential campaign focused on issues tied to racial, ethnic, and religious identities and attitudes. The two candidates took very different positions on those issues, and voters perceived those differences. People's attitudes on these issues were then "activated" as decision-making criteria and became even more strongly associated with white voters' preference for Clinton or Trump than they were with their preferences in 2012 or other recent elections. This pattern emerged even when attitudes were measured years before the election—thereby guarding against the possibility that people changed their attitudes to match what their preferred candidate was saying. Thus, the origins of Trump's unique appeal in the general election were similar to the origins of his appeal in the primary: in both cases, his candidacy helped to

Percent support for Trump

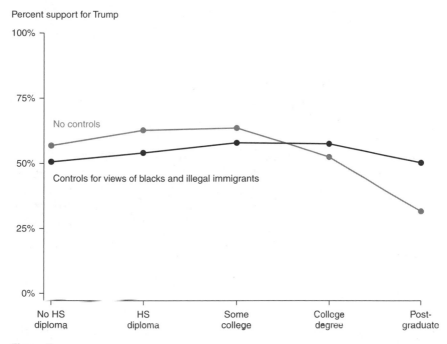

Figure 8.9.
Relationship between education and whites' support for Donald Trump.
Graph depicts the average percentage of whites who supported Trump at each
education level, with and without accounting for attitudes toward African Americans
and illegal immigrants.
Source: 2016 ANES.

make identity-inflected issues central to voters' choices. And it was these issues that largely explained the most notable demographic divide in the electorate: between voters with more or less formal education.

The activation of these issues helped Trump win because there were so
many Obama voters whose views on these issues were arguably closer to
Trump's than to Obama's or Clinton's—and these voters were especially prevalent in battleground states. Their shift to Trump helped him prevail in the
Electoral College, even while losing the popular vote.

The Drop in Black Turnout

Despite her losses among white voters, it was still possible for Hillary Clinton to win an Electoral College majority. She just needed the "Obama
coalition"—the voters she had always banked on—to turn out and vote. One

key part of the Obama coalition was African American voters. Of course, African Americans have been a crucial Democratic constituency since the civil rights era. But with Obama on the ticket, blacks developed not only a stronger Democratic identity (see chapter 2) but also turned out to vote in record numbers. Clinton needed black turnout to remain as high.

It did not. According to the Census Bureau's Current Population Survey, the percentage of blacks who turned out declined from 66 percent of eligible voters in 2012 to 59 percent in 2016. According to an analysis of voter file data by the political scientist Bernard Fraga and colleagues, black turnout declined by 5 points nationally and by even more in certain swing states. Black turnout decreased by over 12 percentage points in Michigan and Wisconsin, for example.[37]

Many, including Clinton herself, attributed this decrease to strict voter identification laws. "In short," Clinton wrote in her campaign memoir, "voting laws matter. A lot." But although there are good reasons to suspect that voter identification laws could depress African American turnout, the best-designed studies have thus far uncovered modest, if any, effects.[38] To be sure, black turnout dropped in some states with strict identification laws, such as Wisconsin and Mississippi. But in other states with restrictive laws, such as Texas and Virginia, black turnout dropped much less—in fact, less than it did nationally. Black turnout also dropped in places without strict identification laws, such as Michigan and Washington, DC.

A more important explanation for the drop in African American turnout had to do with Obama and Clinton themselves. When Obama ran in 2008 and 2012, black turnout was over 5 percentage points higher than it had been in any election on record. Obama's two campaigns confirmed research showing that African Americans' in-group identity—their identification with blacks as a group—impacts how they think and act in politics. Indeed, Barack Obama's extraordinary black support was concentrated among African Americans who expressed the most solidarity with other blacks.[39]

It was arguably unrealistic to expect similarly high levels of black turnout for a white Democratic candidate in 2016. That does not mean that Clinton was unpopular among African Americans. They were crucial to her victory in the Democratic primary, and throughout 2016, an average of 73 percent rated her favorably in both Gallup and YouGov polls. But despite that support and her campaign's outreach to black voters, Hillary Clinton still faced hurdles within the African American community.

For one, several prominent African Americans criticized her previous rhetoric and positions on criminal justice. Some black celebrities and public intellectuals even refused to vote for Clinton, whom they considered the lesser of two evils. Colin Kaepernick, the San Francisco 49ers quarterback who made headlines for protesting racial injustice by refusing to stand up during the pre-

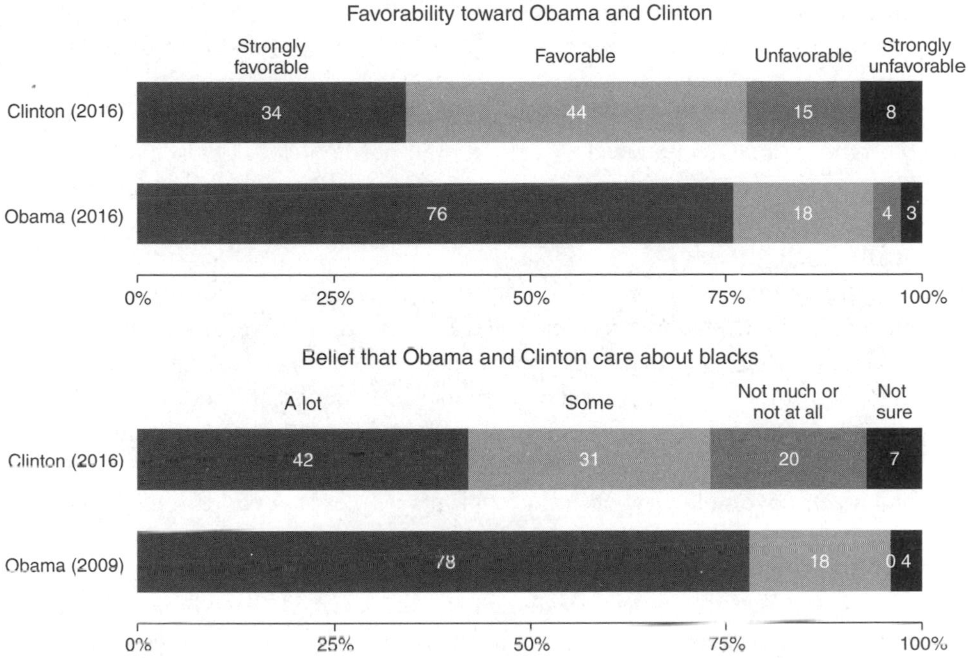

Favorability toward Obama and Clinton

Belief that Obama and Clinton care about blacks

Figure 8.10.
African American views of Barack Obama and Hillary Clinton.
Source for the top graph: African American respondents in the 2016 Collaborative Multiracial Post-election Survey. Sources for the bottom graph: African American respondents in an April 2009 CBS/*New York Times* poll and in four combined June–September 2016 YouGov/*Economist* polls.

game national anthem, did not vote and said that "it almost seems like [the candidates] are trying to debate who's less racist." The Trump campaign sought to capitalize on this controversy by repeatedly calling Clinton "a bigot," reminding black voters that Clinton had once implied that black youths were "super-predators," claiming that Democratic politicians had let down the African American community, and accusing Clinton of treating Barack Obama with "terrible disrespect" in their 2008 presidential debates. This was all in addition to falsely accusing Clinton's 2008 presidential campaign of starting the lie that Obama was not born in the United States.[40]

Unsurprisingly, then, Hillary Clinton was less popular with black voters than Barack Obama was in 2016 (figure 8.10). Although both Clinton and Obama were rated favorably by most African Americans, many fewer rated Clinton "very favorably"—a sentiment that may capture the enthusiasm that motivates voters to turn out. In the 2016 Collaborative Multiracial Post-election Survey, which included interviews with over 3,000 African Americans, only 34 percent rated Clinton very favorably, whereas 76 percent rated Obama very favorably. About one in five blacks actually rated Clinton unfavorably. African Americans were also much less likely to believe that Clinton "cares about the needs and problems of black people." In 2009, 78 percent of blacks said that Obama cared a lot about their needs. In four polls conducted between June and September 2016, only 42 percent of blacks said Clinton cared a lot about their needs; the majority said that she cared "some" (31%) or "not at all" (20%).

Unlike Obama, Clinton did not benefit from racial solidarity among blacks. In the Collaborative Multiracial Post-election Survey, most African Americans (62%) said that what happened to blacks as a group affected them "a lot" or "some," and 79 percent of them had a very favorable view of Obama, compared to 72 percent of blacks who expressed less solidarity. But support for Clinton was lower among both blacks who expressed racial solidarity (33% had a very favorable view of her) and blacks who expressed less racial solidarity (36%). Racial solidarity did little to help improve blacks' views of Clinton.

Clinton was also far less popular among blacks who believed that she did not care about their interests. About 85 percent of African Americans who thought that Hillary Clinton cared "a lot" about black people viewed both her and Obama very favorably. But among those who thought that Clinton did not care a lot about blacks, only 20 percent viewed her very favorably, even though 50 percent of this group viewed Obama very favorably.

In short, Hillary Clinton faced major challenges in sustaining the record black turnout that Barack Obama had inspired. She was not fully able to overcome those challenges, even though she faced an opponent whom 75 percent of African Americans described as "racist" in 2016 YouGov/*Economist* polls. Blacks were less confident that Clinton cared about their interests and arguably therefore less enthusiastic about her candidacy. The resulting drop in black turnout was a crucial factor in important battleground states.

The Sleeping Giant?

The focus on the "Obama coalition" concerned not only blacks but also Latinos. Sometimes called the "sleeping giant" of American politics, Latinos were portrayed as a group that could deliver the election to Hillary Clinton. There were headlines like "Trump, Waking a 'Sleeping Giant,' Helps Clinton Build an Unlikely Firewall" and "The Hispanic Sleeping Giant Has Awakened."[41] The argument was certainly plausible: Donald Trump's hostile rhetoric about immigrants would mobilize Latinos to vote for Clinton. This argument was so prominent that it was spoofed on the postelection episode of *Saturday Night Live*. In the sketch, a group of unsuspecting white Clinton supporters early on election night thinks that shifting demographics will give the Democrats the White House forever, leading them to make a toast: "To Latinos!"

So when the numbers came in on election night, many observers were stunned. According to the exit poll, Clinton won only 69 percent of the major-party vote among Latinos, which was down 3 points from Obama's share in 2012. That estimate immediately came in for criticism, with scholars arguing that the exit poll was skewed toward Latinos who did not live in high-density Latino precincts and who had higher incomes and greater English proficiency—thereby underestimating Latino support for Clinton. However, these biases in exit poll estimates of the Latino vote have been documented for years. Unless these biases were somehow worse in 2016, it is not clear that Clinton significantly outperformed Obama among Latinos.[42]

Moreover, other data do not consistently show an upsurge in Latino support for the Democrats. The Pew Hispanic Center's preelection survey of Latinos showed that the group preferred Clinton over Trump by a 58 percent to 19 percent margin, giving her 75 percent of the major-party vote in that survey. This was slightly less than the 77 percent that Obama received in Pew's preelection survey of Latinos in 2012. In the Latino Decisions 2016 Election Eve poll, 79 percent of Latinos supported Clinton, which was only slightly higher than the 75 percent that had supported Obama in their 2012 election eve poll. Moreover, results in some heavily Latino counties suggested that Clinton's average margin of victory was smaller than Obama's margin in 2012. In short, while Clinton certainly did well among Latinos, she did not clearly do any better than Obama, and she may have done worse.[43]

There was also little evidence of a large Latino surge in turnout. Census Bureau surveys, which rely on respondents' own reports of turnout, suggested a very modest increase in the percentage of eligible Latinos who voted: from 43.1 percent in 2012 to 44.9 percent in 2016. Voter file data avoid the issue of relying on people to report accurately whether they voted, but they do not record ethnicity for most voters. An analysis that imputed ethnicity for voters—based on factors such as voters' surnames and the demography of where they lived—suggested a 4-point increase in Latino turnout in 2016 compared to 2012. But even if Latino turnout increased, it was not enough to ensure Clinton's victory.[44]

How could it be that Donald Trump did not provoke a stronger backlash from Latinos? After all, Trump was certainly unpopular among Latinos and, by the end of the general election campaign, less popular than Mitt Romney was in 2012. According to the final Latino Decisions tracking polls in 2012 and 2016, Romney and Trump were rated unfavorably by 63 percent and 77 percent of Latinos, respectively.[45]

But Clinton was less popular among Latinos than was Barack Obama in 2012. According to the Latino Decisions polls, 81 percent of Latinos rated Obama favorably in 2012, but 71 percent rated Clinton favorably in 2016. Latinos, like African Americans, manifested less enthusiasm for Clinton as well: 60 percent of Latinos rated Obama very favorably in 2012, but only 41 percent rated Clinton very favorably in 2016. In fact, Latinos' net favorable ratings of the Democratic and Republican presidential candidates in 2012 and 2016— the percentage with a favorable view minus the percentage with an unfavorable view—showed that Clinton had no greater advantage over Trump than Obama had over Romney.[46] Trump's unpopularity among Latinos was less of a liability because Clinton herself was less popular than Obama had been.

Moreover, to improve on Obama's support among Latinos, Clinton had to reach out to a subset of Latinos that is harder to mobilize: those with weaker identities as Latinos. Although Latino group identity has grown stronger over time, Latinos still vary in how much they identify with other Latinos, which depends on factors such as their country of origin, generation, immigration experiences, socioeconomic status, and English proficiency. Moreover, Latinos who identify less strongly with other Latinos are less likely to respond to appeals to ethnic identity, which are often the go-to tactic for Democratic candidates who want to mobilize Latinos. Similarly, Latinos with a weaker identity are harder to mobilize in response to xenophobic rhetoric.[47]

Before 2016, Democrats had built considerable support among Latinos with a stronger group identity. In 2012, the ANES showed that Obama won the support of nearly 90 percent of Latinos who said that being Hispanic was an "extremely important" part of their identity, as well as about 90 percent of Latinos with a strong sense of linked fate with other Latinos. But about 19 percent of Latinos said that being Hispanic was "not at all" or only "a little" important to their identity, and fewer than 50 percent of them voted for Obama. Support for Obama also dropped to 70 percent among those with a weaker sense of linked fate.

In 2016, the same patterns held. Latinos with weaker group identities did not rally to Clinton, despite Trump's rhetoric and Clinton's argument that Trump was hostile to Latinos. In the ANES, Latinos with a weak group identity were still much less likely to support Clinton—about 40 points less likely— than were Latinos with the strongest identity. This relationship was essentially the same as in 2012.[48] Similarly, in the 2016 Collaborative Multiracial Post-election Survey, a sizable minority of Latino voters (23%) said that their decision to turn out was not motivated much or at all by "wanting to show solidarity and support for the Latino community," and only about half of them supported Clinton. By comparison, 53 percent said solidarity with the Latino community was a major factor, and 90 percent of them supported Clinton. A last piece of evidence comes from comparing Latinos who primarily speak Spanish—and tend to have a stronger Latino identity—with those who speak English.[49] In the Pew Hispanic Center survey, Clinton led Trump by 72 points among Latinos who primarily speak Spanish but by only 23 points among English-dominant Latinos.

Of course, Latinos are strongly Democratic leaning, and the 2016 election did little to change this. Given Trump's unpopularity among Latinos, it is not hard to imagine that a more popular Democratic candidate might have earned more Latino support. But Clinton's relative unpopularity and the challenge of mobilizing Latinos who do not strongly identify as such made it difficult for her to be that candidate.

The Highest and Hardest Glass Ceiling

Even if Clinton struggled to mobilize black and Latino voters, there was another possible source of support for her: women. Throughout the campaign, people speculated that Clinton's historic bid to become the first female president would mobilize unprecedented support from women. As Clinton herself wrote after the election, "Even before I ran, political commentators wondered whether I'd inspire an unbeatable wave of women to come out and vote for me, in the same way President Obama inspired record-breaking black turnout." But she had always had doubts, noting, "Gender hasn't proven to be the motivating force for women that some hope it might be."[50] That proved true in 2016: women did not rally to Clinton's candidacy, but men shifted to Trump—especially men with more sexist attitudes.

Clinton's skepticism about gender as a motivating force was based on personal experience. Her 2008 run for the Democratic presidential nomination had not mobilized women in the same way that Barack Obama's campaign had mobilized African Americans and racially liberal whites.[51] Despite playing the "woman card" in 2016, the song remained the same: in the primaries, Clinton did not draw disproportionate support from self-identified feminists, women with strong gender identities, or Democratic voters with the most progressive views about gender (see chapter 6).

But perhaps things would be different in the general election, where the salience of gender was magnified by Donald Trump's history of explicitly sexist comments; campaign controversies involving his remarks about Megyn Kelly, Alicia Machado, and others; and the accusations of sexual misconduct leveled against him—behavior that he explicitly acknowledged in the *Access*

Hollywood tape. In fact, Trump predicted back in 1998 that his record with "the women" would be a lightning rod for controversy if he ever ran for president.[52]

Certainly Trump's opponents, including Clinton, tried to ensure that his history of sexism would cost him on Election Day. Initially, this seemed to be working. In a poll shortly after the *Access Hollywood* tape surfaced, 63 percent of Americans said that they were paying close attention to "the recent news about allegations that Donald Trump made unwanted advances on different women."[53] Among those who were paying attention, most thought that the allegations were probably or definitely true. Unsurprisingly, then, four different surveys in late October showed that majorities of Americans thought that Trump was "biased against women" or that "sexist" described him somewhat or very well.[54] At that point, polling data suggested that, although Trump was winning men by margins typical of Republican presidential candidates, he was losing a historic share of the vote among women.[55] It seemed that the 2016 election was headed for a record gender gap, driven by women's aversion to Donald Trump.

There was indeed a historic gender gap in 2016—but not because the behavior of women changed. The exit polls showed Clinton winning women by 12 percentage points, which was similar to Obama's 13- and 11-point margins of victory among women in 2008 and 2012, respectively. Instead, it was men whose voting behavior changed. Trump won men by 12 points in 2016—compared to John McCain's 1-point margin in 2008 and Mitt Romney's 7-point margin in 2012. This was a wider margin among men than any candidate since George H. W. Bush won the 1988 election in a landslide.

Why did Clinton fail to perform better among women voters? One reason is the weaker gender solidarity among women. For example, in the September 2016 wave of the Presidential Election Panel Study, only about a third of women said that being a woman was "extremely important" to their identity, while 61 percent of blacks said their race was "extremely important." That lack of gender solidarity was politically consequential too. Hillary Clinton was significantly less popular than Obama was among the majority of women who did not see gender as extremely important to their identities. Thus, Clinton's performance among women in both the Democratic primary and the general election confirmed past research showing that race and partisanship are more important than gender in how people vote. The salience of race and partisanship helps explain why Clinton lost white women by 9 points—a deficit larger than Barack Obama's in 2008 and Al Gore's in 2000.[56]

If Clinton did not benefit from gender solidarity, was she penalized because of sexism? Democrats and Republicans have long been more divided

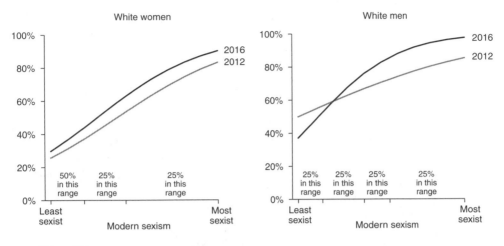

Figure 8.11.
Whites' sexism and likelihood of voting for the Republican presidential candidate. Findings based on statistical models that also account for party identification, self-reported ideology, and attitudes toward African Americans.
Source: 2012–16 VOTER Survey.

by gender attitudes—such as attitudes about feminism and women's roles in society—than by gender per se. Moreover, attitudes about gender roles tend to be strongly held and relatively stable at the individual level, which can help a political campaign "activate" those views much as a racialized campaign can activate views of racial and ethnic groups.[57]

That is what happened in 2016. Among men, the measure of "modern sexism" introduced in chapter 6 was more strongly correlated with vote choice in 2016 than it was in 2012 (figure 8.11). One caveat is that sexism was measured in surveys conducted during and after the 2016 campaign, and some people may have changed their answers to questions about sexual harassment based on their views of Trump and his accusers. If so, gender attitudes may be both a cause and a consequence of how people voted.

Still, the 2016 campaign appeared to activate modern sexism, especially among white men and even after accounting for party identification, self-reported ideology on the liberal-conservative spectrum, and attitudes toward African Americans. (Attitudes about gender were not significantly related to the vote choices of nonwhites.) Among white women interviewed in the December 2016 VOTER Survey (left panel of figure 8.11), the relationship between modern sexism and vote choice was similar, with both Obama and Clinton doing worse among white women with higher modern sexism scores. But in the aggregate, this did not cost Clinton many votes because relatively few women have higher scores on this scale. However, Clinton also failed to generate additional support, compared to Obama, among women who expressed less sexism.[58]

But there was unusually strong opposition to Clinton among more sexist men (right panel of figure 8.11). Although Clinton appeared to do somewhat better than Obama among white men who scored low in modern sexism, white men with higher scores were more likely to vote for Trump than they had been to vote for Romney. And this was a substantial number of white men: nearly a third scored above the midpoint on this measure. Thus, the increasing correlation between this measure of sexism and vote choice appeared to hurt Clinton overall. In the exit poll, Clinton lost white men by a whopping 31 points—a wider margin than any candidate since Walter Mondale lost forty-nine states to Ronald Reagan in 1984.

Gender may have also mattered in subtle ways that are more difficult to quantify. There are at least three possibilities, although the evidence is necessarily speculative. For one, the well-documented double bind that women in leadership roles often face—whereby women who show they are tough enough for the job risk being disliked—may have contributed to Hillary Clinton's low favorable ratings. Clinton certainly thought it did, referencing the double bind in her memoir and citing data that show "the more successful a man is, the more people like him. With women it's the exact opposite."[59]

Clinton may also have faced a double standard in which women are held to a higher ethical standard than men. Female candidates are generally perceived as more honest and ethical than male candidates. Because voters expect women to be honest, the penalty for appearing dishonest may be greater for women than for men. For example, one study found that the American Bar Association punished female attorneys more severely than male attorneys for similar ethical violations.[60] This double standard may help explain why the media and public focused so much on Clinton's honesty (or lack thereof) and why she was rated as less honest and trustworthy than Trump (see chapter 7).

Finally, there is the question of gender bias in media coverage of Clinton. In 2014, Clinton told an audience that there was a "double standard" for women leaders and that "the media is the principal propagator of its existence." Clinton's impression may have stemmed from her experience in the 2008 campaign. Although overall media coverage of Clinton in 2008 was not necessarily more negative than coverage of candidates like Obama, there were many examples of gendered language and even overt sexism in the broader media, especially in editorials and on cable news networks (for example, Tucker Carlson, then at MSNBC: "When she [Clinton] comes on television, I involuntarily cross my legs").[61]

Nothing about Clinton's experience in 2015–16 changed this. She saw a double standard in terms of personal appearance: in her mind, if she did not spend an hour or more each day on her hair, makeup, and clothes, she would not look as good and this would become a media story. Clinton also saw a double standard in how the media covered her speeches. "I suspect that for many of us," she wrote in her memoir, "it's discordant to tune into a political rally and hear a woman's voice booming ('screaming,' 'screeching') forth."[62]

She had a point. Media commentators made complaints about Clinton that were rarely if ever made of male candidates—for example, telling her to "lower her voice." One difference, however, was that sexist comments were called out more frequently. In 2008, one study found that news outlets did little to point out instances of sexist speech and portray Clinton as a victim of this speech, especially compared to their attention to racially insensitive remarks about Barack Obama. In 2016, however, the backlash was swifter. For example, after MSNBC's Joe Scarborough told Clinton to "smile" more, the comedian Samantha Bee mocked him with a Twitter campaign and viral hashtag, tweeting, "Ladies, it's very important that you #SmileforJoe."[63]

But hashtags may not have been enough. Despite the continual controversy that Trump generated, despite comments that both parties condemned, despite a comment that suggested he had sexually assaulted women by grabbing their genitals, it was Clinton's scandals, mainly the email server, that got more attention from the news media (see chapter 7). This helped make news coverage overall only slightly less negative for Clinton than it was for Trump.

Of course, the total impact of Clinton's gender is impossible to measure— short of replaying the 2016 campaign with a Democratic nominee who was identical to Clinton in every respect except gender. Nevertheless, it appears that she was hurt more by her gender than she was helped. Clinton did not draw much additional support from women, showing again the limited power of gender solidarity in U.S. elections. And she lost support among men, especially men with more sexist views. The combination helped keep Clinton from shattering what she often referred to as the "highest and hardest glass ceiling."

An "Arrogant" Campaign

When a candidate loses—especially one that most people thought was going to win—the verdict is usually harsh. This was certainly true for Clinton. News accounts cited an "arrogant" Clinton campaign that "made a series of strategic mistakes" because she "mastered the science of politics but forgot the art."[64]

Some of this criticism was ironic, to say the least. After all, the "science of politics"—the use of data to target voters and determine the most effective ways of reaching them—was widely credited for Obama's victories, much more so than the evidence would really support.[65] That the tenor of commentary would change so quickly shows that the postmortem evaluations of campaign strategy are mostly based on circular logic: winning campaigns were good because they won, and losing campaigns were bad because they lost.

To be sure, the Clinton campaign's polling underestimated Trump's strength. The campaign's data—which was fed into an algorithm named Ada for a famous nineteenth-century mathematician, Ada Lovelace—did recognize the importance of certain battleground states, such as Pennsylvania. But it did not see, at least until too late, Clinton's vulnerabilities in states like Michigan and Wisconsin. Of course, few people did. Publicly available polls suggested that she was likely to win an Electoral College majority. The Trump campaign's own data, as well as that of the Republican National Committee, gave him at best a 20 percent chance of winning. Thus, the shortcomings of horse race polling were systemic and not only an error of the Clinton campaign. Later analyses would suggest that state polling errors stemmed in part from late shifts to Trump and a failure to correct for the overrepresentation of college-educated voters in poll samples.[66]

But the critiques of the Clinton campaign were not just about data. They centered on what critics argued were two bigger failures: first, a failure of messaging, and second, a failure of resource allocation.

The question of Clinton's message was hotly debated within her own campaign as far back as the primary. After her narrow loss to Bernie Sanders in the Michigan primary, Clinton "complained to her communications team that her economic messaging sucked." After the November election, critics said the same thing and argued that she had focused too much on criticizing Trump. As a *Washington Post* story put it, "One error was to stick with a long-standing, one-dimensional campaign strategy: attacking Donald Trump. That strategy had been devised despite overwhelming evidence, not only in Trump's rise but also in Clinton's struggles during the Democratic primary against Bernie Sanders, that the electorate was looking for political and economic change." Of course, the electorate was not clearly "looking for change" at all, but many commentators said she focused too much on attacking Trump and did not offer a positive case for her candidacy.[67]

This criticism, however, must confront the evidence that Clinton's messaging seemed to work. In collaboration with the political scientist John Geer, we conducted experimental tests throughout the summer and fall of 2016 in which participants saw ads aired by or on behalf of Clinton and Trump during the week that the ads were initially aired.[68] In each experiment, a representative sample of American adults was randomly assigned to watch a Trump ad, a Clinton ad, or a nonpolitical ad (a Nationwide Insurance ad starring Peyton Manning). These experiments provided a clean test of causation: Did a specific ad change people's attitudes about the candidates? Of course, respondents could not easily avoid watching the ad, which meant that the experiments could have exaggerated the impacts of ads. On the other hand, respondents only saw the ad once, which could have mitigated its impact compared to what might have been happening in battleground states saturated with thousands of campaign advertisements.

Although not every ad was tested and their impacts varied, on average Clinton ads attacking Trump helped her. Compared to watching the nonpolitical ad, watching a Clinton ad attacking Trump lowered people's favorability rating of him by 2 points and increased her vote share by 1.6 points. In fact, Clinton's attacks were arguably more effective than Trump's attacks on her: watching a Trump ad attacking Clinton did increase his favorability rating by 2.7 points, on average, but did not affect her favorability rating or people's vote intentions. (See the appendix to this chapter for more details.) Clinton's attacks on Trump appeared most effective among respondents who identified as independents and thus were potential swing voters, or who had at least some college education, a group that was increasingly key to the Democratic coalition. Trump's attacks on her mainly polarized people along party lines—helping him among Republicans but hurting him among Democrats—which is one reason why their overall effect was more limited. In short, if attacking Trump was a failure of messaging, these tests do not show it—although of course these tests do not show what impact a different message might have had.

Was the impact of advertising in these experiments manifest in the real world? There, Clinton had a significant advantage. Clinton raised far more money than Trump did—$955 million to $546 million, including both candidate campaigns and outside groups. Her advantage was similar to Obama's in 2008, when John McCain was hamstrung by the cap on spending imposed by the public financing system, and much different from the parity between Obama and Romney in 2012. This exemplified Trump's struggle to build a professional campaign, including not only a fund-raising apparatus but also a policy shop and data and analytics team. The Trump campaign depended more than a typical Republican candidate on the Republican Party for a variety of important tasks.[69]

With less money to spend, Trump consistently trailed Clinton in television advertising in most media markets (figure 8.12). Clinton opened an early advantage in June, whereas Trump did not ramp up until August. Then, in

Clinton advantage in ad airings

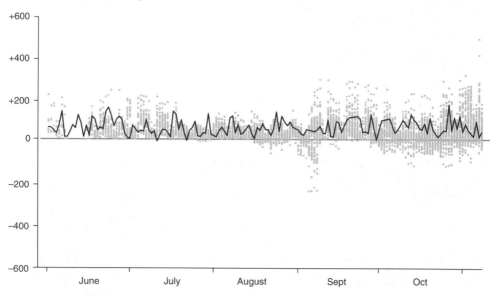

Figure 8.12.
Balance of Clinton and Trump advertising in media markets.
The dots represent the balance of ad airings in media markets on each day. Positive
numbers indicate an advantage for Hillary Clinton. Ads by the candidates and groups
advertising on their behalf are included. Markets with no advertising are clustered at
zero, although we do not show that clustering visually. The black line is the
population-adjusted average balance of ad airings in battleground states (Arizona,
Colorado, Florida, Ohio, Michigan, New Hampshire, Nevada, North Carolina,
Pennsylvania, and Wisconsin).
Source: Kantar Media/Campaign Media Analysis Group.

September, Trump's advertising all but vanished; a late surge in October and
early November could not begin to close the gap. Altogether, nearly three-
fourths (72%) of the television ads supported Clinton—a far greater imbalance than in recent presidential elections. In 2012, for example, Obama,
Romney, and their allies were evenly split (49.6% for Obama versus 50.4%
for Romney).[70]

Clinton's televised advertising appeared to help her. Her vote share at the
county level was higher in places where she advertised more heavily—even
after accounting for how well Obama had done in those counties in 2012, as
well as demographic characteristics of these counties and changes in demographics between 2012 and 2016. If Clinton's advertising is measured simply
by summing up the ads aired between June 1, 2016, and Election Day in each
county, each additional 1,000 ads that she ran in a given county was associ-

ated with an increase of 0.1 points of vote share in that county on Election Day. The relationship of vote share to Trump's advertising was much less precisely estimated, meaning that there is more uncertainty about whether that impact was real (see the appendix to this chapter).

But because the impact of televised campaign advertising is often short-lived, it may be more appropriate to focus on advertising closer to Election Day.[71] Here again, the same story emerges, but with an even larger apparent impact of Clinton's advertising. In the last week of the campaign, a 1,000-ad increase in Clinton's advertising in a given county was associated with an additional 0.7 points of vote share in that county, averaging across all counties. This is after accounting not only for both the 2012 presidential election results and the demographics in these counties but also for how many ads Obama and Romney themselves ran in these places. Accounting for Obama's and Romney's ads helps guard against the possibility that Clinton and Trump were simply advertising in places where presidential candidates always advertise and helps capture the unique impact of Clinton's ads on her vote share. Meanwhile, the apparent impact of Trump's advertising in this last week—when he ramped up his advertising—was smaller and imprecisely estimated, so much so that it is difficult to say with any confidence that his advertising was associated with his vote share.

Thus, both experimental tests and real-world advertising data suggest that Clinton's message and her large advantage on the airwaves helped her gain voters. The overall impact was small—likely measured in the tenths of a percentage point in the places where she ran thousands of advertisements—but that is typical for television advertising in a presidential general election.[72] Indeed, the impact of ads was small enough that Clinton would have had to run thousands more ads to have a chance of prevailing in key states. For example, to win Wisconsin or Pennsylvania, Clinton needed an additional 0.8 points of vote share across the state. Hypothetically, this would have meant running 1,000 more ads in the last week of the campaign in every media market in these states—or 11,000 more ads in Pennsylvania and 8,000 in Wisconsin. This would have been a massive increase: two and a half times what the Clinton campaign actually ran in Pennsylvania in the last week, and two times what they ran in Wisconsin. Of course, this assumes that the Clinton campaign had the financial resources to buy airtime for these ads, that there was enough available airtime on local networks to buy this many ads, and that additional ads would have had the same impact even though they might have needed to air during programs that fewer targeted voters were even watching. Just as was true for Mitt Romney in 2012, it appears unlikely that advertising alone could have given Clinton victories in these states—even though her advertising advantage helped her win votes.[73]

But perhaps the Clinton campaign made a different mistake: spending too much money on television ads and not enough in other mediums. After the election, the much-maligned Trump campaign was suddenly discovered to have been smart all along because it focused on digital advertising and especially advertising on Facebook. According to this account, the Trump campaign "saturated" the Facebook feeds of "millions of Americans" with "eye-catching ads." The Trump campaign's digital director, Brad Parscale, said, "If you imagine the country as the haystack, Facebook is the needle finder." One particularly breathless story was headlined "Here's How Facebook *Actually* Won Trump the Presidency."[74]

In fact, there is little evidence yet that digital advertising has much impact on voters or consumers. Experiments that have examined large digital ad campaigns by U.S. retailers have found it very difficult to identify any impact on consumer behavior. The same is true in politics. In one experiment, some participants saw an online ad about the Black Lives Matter movement an average of twenty-seven times, but it produced no changes in their attitudes about policing, racial bias, and the like. Two other experiments in electoral campaigns found that an even larger number of Facebook ads supporting either a state legislative or congressional candidate—a typical voter was exposed to the ads thirty-eight times—did not change views of them. And, of course, Facebook ads would likely matter *less* in a presidential election than in down-ballot races because opinions about presidential candidates are more difficult to change. Experiments measuring the impact of online ads or Facebook ads on voter turnout in presidential elections have found either very small effects or no effects at all. To be sure, the study of digital campaign advertising is in its infancy, and these ads may yield some benefits, such as donations. But there is no evidence that digital ads "won Trump the presidency" and little reason to believe that those ads persuaded many voters to choose Trump or Clinton.[75]

The critique of Clinton's campaign went beyond advertising, however. It faulted her for not investing enough in a field organization, particularly in midwestern states like Michigan and Wisconsin that she ended up losing. This criticism was ironic, too: before the election, her "extensive field organization" was thought to have given her a "big advantage" over Trump, since his campaign lacked such an organization and had to depend on the Republican Party for this as well. The Trump campaign's limitations were encapsulated in a report that one of its Colorado field offices was run by a twelve-year-old.[76]

But after the election, the prevailing view of Clinton's field organization quickly changed. Postmortem accounts reported that there were concerns about her campaign's field organization dating back to the primaries. Before the Michigan primary, Representative Debbie Dingell—a Democrat from one of the most venerable political families in the state—reportedly warned Clinton that she "didn't have enough of a presence on the ground." According to one account of the Michigan primary, the Clinton campaign was "relying on polling and analytics, instead of a robust organization in the state, to dictate strategy." The lengthy primary delayed Clinton's ability to build this robust organization. Then, in the general election, the campaign designated Michigan and Wisconsin only as "watch" states—ones the campaign "should keep its eye on"—but not as crucial battleground states. After the election, Democratic operatives in Michigan complained bitterly that the Brooklyn-based campaign headquarters ignored them and gave volunteers little to do. A Democratic organizer said of the campaign's Wisconsin operation, "What is the point of having a hundred people on the ground if you're not giving them any of the tools to do the work?" Of course, Wisconsin and Michigan alone would not have given Clinton an Electoral College victory, but these states became symbols of the Clinton campaign's mistakes.[77]

There is no question that Clinton's overall field organization was smaller than Obama's in 2012. The political scientist Joshua Darr estimated that Clinton had 537 field offices, compared to 789 for Obama in 2012. Clinton did not lag Obama everywhere, to be sure. According to our tabulation, she had more offices in Pennsylvania (57 versus 53) and almost the same number in Michigan (27 versus 28). But in Florida, Clinton had 59 offices to Obama's 102. In Ohio, it was 91 versus 130. In Wisconsin, it was 40 versus 67. For the most part, these differences arose because Clinton's offices were located more in areas with high concentrations of Democrats, whereas Obama's offices were spread more throughout these states.[78]

Could Clinton's smaller field organization have cost her the election? In fact, this is not at all clear. For one, the percentage of Democrats who said that they had been contacted by a campaign was almost the same as in 2012 (the percentage of Republicans who reported being contacted, however, dropped sharply). For another, the apparent impact of Clinton's field organization was not large enough that a bigger organization would necessarily have won her the election. As in other recent presidential elections, there was a positive correlation between the number of Clinton's field offices in a county and her vote share (see the chapter appendix for details).[79] After accounting for other factors in these counties—including demographics, Obama's vote share in 2012, and the number of offices that Obama had opened—each additional Clinton field office was associated with an additional 0.3 points of major-party vote share. Thus, the presence of Clinton field offices appeared to help her, over and above what was done in 2012.

But what does this add up to in terms of votes? Imagine that Clinton had emulated Obama's 2012 strategy and opened the same number of offices in each state, thereby increasing her total number of offices. Based on the 0.3-point increase in vote share per field office and the number of votes cast in each county, increasing the number of offices to mimic the Obama campaign would have netted Clinton about 195,000 more votes nationwide. What about the states that could have swung the election—and in which Clinton volunteers were reportedly begging for more to do? In Wisconsin, setting up the same number of offices as Obama did in 2012 would have netted Clinton about 10,300 additional votes—a measurable increase but not enough to overcome her margin of defeat (22,748 votes). Even doubling what Obama did in 2012 would not have been enough. The same was true in other battleground states where her field organization was smaller than Obama's. All of this is, again, a hypothetical based on a statistical model and a variety of assumptions. But these estimates are similar to what other research has found. It is difficult for the ground game alone to turn most election defeats into victories.[80]

Perhaps, however, the issue was not so much the sheer size of Clinton's field organization but rather how and where its efforts—and hers—were deployed within states. One critique on this score came from none other than Bill Clinton himself. He wanted Hillary Clinton to campaign to a broader coalition outside Democratic strongholds, including to the white voters integral to his own presidential win. This critique implied that Clinton needed to spend less time in places like Detroit and more time in places like Macomb County, a county north of central Detroit where 85 percent of the voters are white, according to the 2010 Census. One Clinton campaign official said, "If you're a white voter in Macomb County, [it] means something" for Hillary Clinton to come there.[81]

But this, too, was unclear. Candidate appearances in towns or counties often have small and temporary effects on poll numbers—and thus an uncertain impact on vote share. One person who knows campaigns from the inside and outside, former Mitt Romney staffer and political scientist Thomas Wood, captured this uncertainty in an article titled "What the Heck Are We Doing in Ottumwa, Anyway?" Setting aside time on Hillary Clinton's itinerary for speeches or glad-handing in Macomb County was arguably unlikely to make much difference.[82]

Perhaps the issue was different still. Many critics of the Clinton campaign focused on how her field organization was being used: to register and mobilize the core groups in the coalition she was targeting—a "focus on turning out supporters rather than trying to persuade fence-sitters." As one operative put it, "The undecided voters were being left to their own devices." To these critics, the Clinton campaign needed to be sending volunteers door to door to persuade people face to face. Critics faulted Clinton for eschewing tactics that her campaign's senior staff believed would be ineffective and inefficient.[83]

But these tactics really are often ineffective and inefficient. Multiple experiments show that face-to-face contact has little persuasive effect in presidential general elections. This buttresses the view of at least one Clinton campaign aide, who said, "Imagine you're on the ground and you're sent to suburban white voters to persuade them to support Hillary Clinton. Imagine what that experience would have been like and how many households you could really change." Indeed, attempts at face-to-face persuasion can even backfire. One study of the 2008 Obama campaign—which was routinely praised for the efficacy of its field organization—found that a face-to-face persuasion experiment in Wisconsin may have *reduced* support for Obama.[84] For these reasons, Clinton may have won more votes by focusing on mobilizing core Democratic voters, perhaps in black communities near Detroit, than on persuading white voters in Macomb County.

Of course, this analysis and earlier academic studies cannot conclusively determine what would have happened if the Clinton campaign had made different decisions. If the hypothetical involves a wholesale remaking of the campaign's strategy—message, field operation, coalition, and so on—then no analysis can credibly speak to that hypothetical. What can be said is this: the Clinton campaign's advantages in advertising and field organization appeared to help her win votes at levels typical of recent presidential elections. At the same time, the Clinton campaign was surely culpable for underestimating how close the campaign would be, and no doubt it would have allocated resources differently if it had known this. But as is often the case in presidential general elections, the impact of those resources would likely not have overcome the other forces at work.

The KKK, the FBI, and the KGB

On a phone call with a friend after the election, Hillary Clinton reportedly blamed three factors for her defeat: the KKK, the FBI, and the KGB. "The KKK" was shorthand for the role of white identity in building support for Trump. There was something to this. Although few whites support the KKK, more have a politicized white identity, and this became more strongly related to voters' choices in 2016.[85]

By "FBI," Clinton meant the investigation of her private email server and especially the brief reopening of the investigation in late October. Within days of the election, she and others in her campaign claimed that FBI director

James Comey's October 28 letter "stopped our momentum." Months later, Clinton said, "If the election had been on October 27, I would be your president." This is plausible but far from certain, given that the Comey letter's impact on Clinton's favorability rating was mostly temporary and public polling did not clearly show a decrease in her lead over Trump (see chapter 7). But we cannot know what might have happened absent the letter's release.[86]

By "KGB," Clinton meant Russian interference in the presidential election. This intervention took several forms. One was hacking emails from the Democratic National Committee and Clinton adviser John Podesta and releasing them via WikiLeaks, which then became the subject of multiple news stories. The Clinton campaign believed that the release of these hacked emails hurt their campaign, and Clinton would write that the combination of the email hack and the Comey letter was "devastating." Another form of Russian interference was purchasing advertisements on Facebook that focused on divisive issues such as race and immigration. Russian actors were also linked to Facebook and Twitter accounts that disseminated false stories. U.S. intelligence agencies concluded that these efforts were ordered by the Russian government and reflected an explicit attempt to hurt Clinton's candidacy and help Trump's. The investigation into Russian interference was criticized by Trump, who believed it cast doubt on the legitimacy of his victory. Trump ultimately fired Comey, leading to the appointment of a special prosecutor, former FBI director Robert Mueller, who sought to determine whether there had been contacts between the Trump campaign and Russian actors. Mueller brought indictments against several former members of the Trump campaign for offenses ranging from lying to federal officials to conspiracy to launder money. In February 2018, Mueller brought indictments against thirteen Russian individuals and three organizations for violating federal law by attempting to influence the U.S. election, largely through the information they had promulgated on social media. When these indictments came down, more breathless headlines followed: "Did Russia Affect the 2016 Election? It's Now Undeniable."[87]

In reality, it was deniable. Although Russian interference was and is deeply concerning, there are many reasons to doubt that it changed the outcome of the election. For one, although the hack of the Democratic National Committee and Podesta emails created unfavorable headlines for the Clinton campaign—anything that put "emails" in the headlines was a reminder of the investigation into Clinton's own email server—the release of these emails in late July and in October did not clearly affect her favorability, perceptions of her honesty, or her lead over Trump. Indeed, any impact was swamped by other events that helped Clinton, including the Democratic National Convention in July and the debates and release of the *Access Hollywood* tape in

October. Clinton's email problem was more the FBI investigation of her than the hacked emails from her campaign—and the case for the Comey letter's impact on the election is stronger than the case for the hacked emails.[88]

Similarly, Russian-sponsored content on social media likely did not decide the election. The money reportedly spent on specific Facebook ads was not targeted effectively at battleground states and was dwarfed by the estimated $81 million spent by the Trump and Clinton campaigns on digital ads. Moreover, although many news reports cited social media metrics that appeared large on their face—1,108 Russian-sponsored videos on YouTube, 2,752 Twitter accounts and 36,000 Twitter bots that had tweeted 1.4 million times during the election, and 126 million people who may have been exposed to Russian-sponsored content on Facebook—these reports typically suffered from a "denominator problem": they rarely calculated the total amount of content on various social media and thus what *fraction* of that content might have been Russian-sponsored propaganda. Given the billions if not trillions of tweets and posts on these media during the election campaign, Russian-sponsored content was an infinitesimal fraction.[89]

Moreover, even if people did happen to see and engage with Russian-sponsored content amid the blizzard of posts and tweets in their social media feeds, there is still the question of whether or how it affected their voting behavior. It is not that this content had no impact on anything. For example, Russian actors used Facebook ads to convince some people to show up for staged pro- or anti-Trump rallies. But it is far less clear whether it changed voters' minds about Trump or Clinton or encouraged them to turn out and vote. Studies of the false information propagated on social media showed not only that it was far from the most shared content (see chapter 7) but also that it was viewed mostly by a small number of diehard conservative news consumers. Moreover, another study estimated that for this false information to have changed the outcome of the election, a single false story would have needed to have massive impact—equal to seeing a television ad thirty-seven times.[90]

In short, the best way to think about how much Russian interference affected the outcome of the 2016 election is with something between agnosticism and skepticism—and probably leaning toward skepticism.[91] Evidence from this election and previous presidential elections shows that most voters are predictable partisans whose minds are hard to change, and thus very large and expensive efforts to change minds or mobilize voters, including the efforts of the presidential candidates' campaigns, have modest effects at best. Given that it would have taken very large shifts in televised advertising or field organizations to tip the election in Clinton's favor, it is not likely that the small fraction of online content attributed to Russian actors tipped the election in

Trump's favor—especially given the equivocal impact of digital ads and false stories, period.

Moreover, although the Russian content was misleading and polarizing in its intent—leading to headlines like "How Russia Harvested American Rage to Reshape U.S. Politics"—U.S. politics and the 2016 campaign were *already* full of misleading and polarizing information, and more than a little rage. And most of that information and emotion came not from Twitter bots but rather from the mouths of the candidates, especially Trump, and their surrogates. The real polarizers in politics are humans, not robots. For these reasons, Russian interference is best seen as a real cause for concern—but not because it threw the election to Trump.[92]

Conclusion

After the election, Clinton acknowledged that her campaign "likely contributed to [2016's] heightened racial consciousness." "As a result," she wrote, "some white voters may have decided I wasn't on their side."[93] This is a tidy summary of what happened. Of course, it was not only the result of her campaign. Trump's racially charged rhetoric and views set him apart from Clinton as well as past Republican nominees. And even before the 2016 election, the Democratic and Republican parties were already becoming more polarized in their beliefs about racial inequality, immigration, Muslims, and many related issues. The campaign magnified this polarization. Thus, the presidential election was not only remarkable for putting an unlikely candidate, Donald Trump, in the White House. It was also remarkable for how it crystallized the country's identity crisis: sharp divisions on what America has become, and what it should be.

CHAPTER 9

The Soul of a Nation

America is an idea, not a race.

—Senator Lindsey Graham (R-SC)

Donald Trump was angry.

It was not quite six months into his presidency, and he was looking at a list of how many immigrants had received visas to enter the United States in 2017. He had campaigned on limiting immigration, and now he thought the United States was still letting in too many immigrants—and from the wrong places. Trump called Afghanistan, which had sent 2,500 immigrants, a terrorist haven. He said that the 15,000 immigrants from Haiti "all have AIDS." He said that once the 40,000 Nigerian immigrants had lived in the United States, they would never "go back to their huts." Trump's staff proceeded to argue about who was to blame for admitting these immigrants.[1]

The White House denied that Trump had made those remarks, but seven months later, in January 2018, similar remarks surfaced. This time Trump was meeting with members of Congress in the Oval Office to discuss a possible immigration reform deal. When the topic of protecting immigrants from Haiti, El Salvador, and Africa came up, Trump said, "Why are we having all of these people from shithole countries come here?" The White House did not dispute the facts initially, but later two Republican senators who were at the meeting said that they had heard Trump say "shithouse" not "shithole." Of course, the distinction between "house" and "hole" was not exactly the source of the controversy. In a Quinnipiac poll conducted right after the meeting, 58 percent of Americans said that Trump's comments were racist.[2]

Issues like immigration, race, and Islam were central not only to Trump's election but also to his presidency. This brought the American identity crisis— the debate over who is and can be an American—from the campaign trail to the White House. After taking office, Trump vigorously pursued his campaign promises to limit immigration from Muslim-majority countries, build a border wall with Mexico, and impose limits on legal immigration generally. He ended the Obama-era protections for undocumented immigrants who had been brought to the United States as children. He pardoned Joe Arpaio, the former sheriff of Maricopa County, Arizona, who had been convicted for refusing to comply with a court order to end his office's racial profiling of Latinos. Meanwhile, the Department of Justice sought to challenge affirmative action policies at colleges and universities. Attorney General Jeff Sessions also vowed to crack down on crime and signaled his willingness to reconsider the agreements that the Obama administration had reached with local police forces accused of misconduct and potential violations of civil rights.[3]

Trump himself continued to make racially charged comments. He repeatedly criticized the mostly black National Football League players who knelt during the playing of the national anthem to protest police treatment of African Americans in America. In one rally in Alabama, he said, "Wouldn't you love to see one of these NFL owners, when somebody disrespects our flag, to say, 'Get that son of a bitch off the field right now?'" Perhaps most controversial was Trump's reaction to a white nationalist rally in Charlottesville, Virginia, to oppose the removal of a Confederate monument. A participant drove a car into a crowd of counterprotesters and killed a young woman. Trump's refusal to single out the white nationalists—he condemned the "hatred, bigotry, and violence on many sides, on many sides" and even expressed sympathy with the protesters, whom he said were defending their "heritage"— elicited widespread criticism from Democrats and Republicans alike. Joe Biden said, "We are living through a battle for the soul of this nation." Colorado Republican senator Cory Gardner said, "Mr. President—we must call evil by its name. These were white supremacists and this was domestic terrorism."[4]

Statements like Biden's and Gardner's were part of a broader backlash. There were ongoing demonstrations and protests targeting Trump and his agenda. There were extraordinary Democratic gains in the elections held in 2017 and early 2018. And Americans had historically low opinions of Trump— despite favorable conditions in the country, including continued economic growth.

Even more notable was the fact that public opinion on the issues central to Trump's presidency shifted *against* his policies. During the campaign, people had worried that Trump would inaugurate an era of increasing hostility to racial and ethnic minorities and women. In June 2016, Mitt Romney said, "I don't want to see a president of the United States saying things which change the character of the generations of Americans that are following. Presidents have an impact on the nature of our nation, and trickle-down racism, trickle-down bigotry, trickle-down misogyny, all these things are extraordinarily dangerous to the heart and character of America."[5] But instead of "trickle-down racism," the campaign and the Trump presidency brought about the opposite: "trickle-down tolerance." Trump's victory was never predicated on a wave of growing hostility or prejudice; rather, it relied on activating people's preexisting views of racial, ethnic, and religious minorities. Views of these groups actually became more favorable as Trump rose to power.

The problem, however, was that "trickle-down tolerance" arose largely because Democrats reacted against Trump's agenda. Thus, the alignment between partisanship and attitudes about issues like race and immigration only increased, and with it the likelihood of even more divisive politics. The resulting partisan polarization is the linchpin of America's identity crisis. This crisis helped make the 2016 presidential campaign so vitriolic, and it only intensified during Trump's presidency.

"This Shit Is Hard"

Trump and the Republicans came to power with grand ambitions. It is typical for the president and his loyalists, as well as some analysts, to assert that the election portends a mandate for the winner's policies or a "realignment" of the electorate that will keep the president and his party in power for years to come. The months after the 2016 election were no exception. Steve Bannon declared that if Trump delivered on his campaign promises, then "we'll govern for 50 years." There would be a "Trump dynasty," wrote one analyst. Others wrote that the Democratic Party had "lost the country," was "stuck in a profound identity crisis," had a "brand in crisis," and would "need to survive an unsettling reckoning with itself" to govern again. Similar claims are made after every presidential election. Obama's 2012 reelection was said to foretell a "clear mandate," an "emerging liberal majority," and "a Democratic realignment that dates back almost two decades." But that these claims proved dubious did not stop people from saying similar things after the 2016 election.[6]

Only a hundred days into Trump's presidency, however, the reality already belied any bullishness for the GOP. Trump himself said, "I thought it would be easier." One of his staff said, "I kind of pooh-poohed the experience stuff when I first got here. But this shit is hard." Trump's problems started right after the election. He and his team did not expect to win, and they were not prepared to occupy the White House. Indeed, at least some of them did not even know that they had to staff the entire West Wing. The work that had been done to prepare for the transition—an effort led by Chris Christie—was jettisoned after the election as Christie fell victim to factional rivalries among Trump's advisers.[7]

When Trump did take office, his presidency was full of what Tennessee Republican senator Bob Corker called "constant chaos." In his first year in office, 34 percent of Trump's higher-level staff left, compared to 9 percent in Obama's first year and 6 percent in George W. Bush's first year.[8] Chief of Staff Reince Priebus lasted six months. Steve Bannon lasted seven. There were four different communication directors between January 2017 and April 2018—one of whom, Anthony Scaramucci, lasted less than a week. There were three different national security advisers. The first of these, Michael Flynn, served only twenty-four days before resigning and eventually pleading guilty to lying to the FBI about his contacts with the Russian government during the presidential transition. Secretary of Health and Human Services Tom Price resigned under a cloud after eight months, having spent extraordinary amounts of taxpayer funds on travel by charter jet and military aircraft. Secretary of State Rex Tillerson—who had reportedly called Trump a "moron" in a Pentagon meeting—lasted fourteen months. Scott Pruitt at the Environmental Protection Agency also resigned after multiple scandals related to his spending and personal use of government resources.

Meanwhile, the investigations into the Trump campaign grew broader and deeper. Two others—George Papadopoulos and Rick Gates—pleaded guilty to making false statements, and Gates also pleaded guilty to conspiracy against the United States. Papadopoulos had been a member of the Trump campaign's foreign policy advisory panel, and Gates was an associate of Paul Manafort, Trump's former campaign manager, who pleaded not guilty to an extensive list of alleged crimes. Longtime Trump consigliere Michael Cohen saw his office raided by federal law enforcement. Cohen had helped Trump by, for one, overseeing payments in 2016 to two women, the porn star Stormy Daniels and Playboy playmate Karen McDougal, to obtain their silence about what they alleged were extramarital affairs with Trump.

These investigations enraged Trump. He repeatedly condemned Attorney General Jeff Sessions, who had recused himself from the Russia investigation because of his own contacts with Russian officials during the presidential campaign and transition. Trump reportedly contemplated firing Rod Rosenstein, the deputy attorney general who oversaw Robert Mueller's investigation and also authorized the raid on Cohen. And when James Comey published a book in 2018 that criticized Trump's conduct, Trump called Comey a "slimeball" and a "liar" and said that he should be in jail. At that point, Trump's reelection campaign was spending 20 percent of its funds on legal fees.[9]

Trump also struggled to get his legislative agenda enacted. Although Republicans controlled the White House and majorities in both the House and Senate, they failed to pass legislation that they had long promised, such as a wholesale repeal of the Affordable Care Act. Their main success was the Tax Cuts and Jobs Act of 2017, which reduced tax rates for businesses and individuals, with benefits flowing primarily to upper-income groups.[10] In a January 2018 ABC/*Washington Post* poll, 60 percent of Americans thought that the new tax plan favored the rich, compared to just 11 percent who thought it favored the middle class. In a January 2018 YouGov poll, 81 percent said Trump cared "a lot" or "some" about "the wealthy" but far fewer said he cared about "the working class" (45%), "the middle class" (44%), or "people like you" (40%).[11]

There was not a little irony in the fact that the Trump administration's signature legislative achievement was a tax cut benefiting corporations and the wealthy. During the primary campaign, Trump had talked about raising taxes on the wealthy, including himself. At that point, many conservative leaders were despondent. As one reporter put it in August 2016, "The vast apparatus of right-wing policy, built up over decades and seeded with millions of dollars to promote a conservative vision, has never seemed more quaintly irrelevant than it does today." After the election, a Trump adviser declared that Trump was "post-ideological," and it seemed that the Republican Party was still having an identity crisis.[12]

But as the tax law showed, Trump shifted toward traditional Republican thinking in important respects, just as he had done on issues like abortion before his presidential campaign began. This was not unexpected. The history of political parties shows that their ideas tend to change more readily as a response to organized groups and social movements. Within the GOP, the organized groups pushing conservative economic positions are well established, and their agenda is not easily dislodged—even by a president whose unusual willingness to endorse liberal economic policies on the campaign trail earned him support among Republican primary voters (see chapter 5).[13]

There were exceptions, of course. Trump ordered tariffs on products from China, Mexico, Canada, and the European Union and sparked fears of a trade war, including among many Republicans in Congress. Trump's stray tweets and comments sometimes suggested a willingness to compromise conservative ideals. Nevertheless, many Republicans came to believe that the tax bill,

Trump's proposed cuts to discretionary spending, and his attempts to roll back federal regulations made him ideologically acceptable after all. The *National Review*, which had published an entire issue opposing Trump in the Republican primary, called his first year in office "a year of achievement."[14]

But any achievements did not seem enough. As the midterm election approached, the tax bill was not popular—52 percent opposed it in an April 2018 Gallup poll, while only 39 percent supported it—and the continued chaos of the Trump White House made Republicans nervous and frustrated. Trump did not seem to be getting better at the job as time went on. Instead, he experienced, as the political scientist Michael Nelson wrote, a "cycle of decreasing influence and decreasing effectiveness." One Republican member of Congress, who had publicly defended Trump, nevertheless told the conservative writer Erick Erikson, "It's like Forrest Gump won the presidency, but an evil, really fucking stupid Forrest Gump."[15]

The Trump Tax, Continued

Another thing also carried over from the campaign into the White House: Trump's historic unpopularity. Majorities of Americans had an unfavorable view of Trump as a candidate, and majorities disapproved of the job he was doing as president—virtually from the time he took office. At the one-year mark, Trump's 40 percent approval rating was lower than the previous twelve presidents' ratings at the same point in their first terms.[16]

Trump's historically low approval ratings were even more remarkable because conditions in the country were so favorable. The country's economic expansion continued and consumer sentiment became more positive. But Trump's approval ratings did not reflect these trends (figure 9.1). His ratings were mired around 40 percent, whereas a president presiding over similarly favorable consumer sentiment would typically be polling near 60 percent, based on the historical relationship between consumer sentiment and approval for presidents between John F. Kennedy and George W. Bush. Of course, it would be unusual for voters to fully credit or blame the president for the economy so early in his term. Nevertheless, that Trump polled so poorly amid a growing economy suggests that his struggles were more about him than about fundamental conditions in the country.

If Trump were headed for a presidency in which his public standing was weakly connected to the public's views of the economy, he would have one other president for company: Barack Obama (see chapter 2 and figure 9.1). One reason for this weak connection was polarization in how partisans see both the economy and the president. In his first year in office, an average of

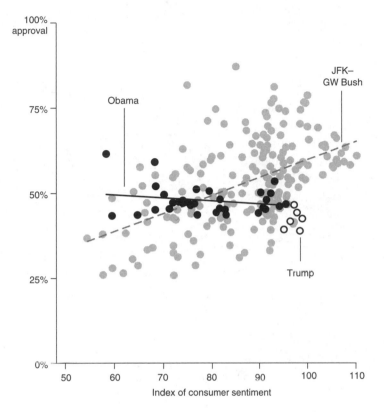

Figure 9.1.
The relationship between consumer sentiment and presidential approval.
The figure includes quarterly data from 1961–2018Q2.

8 percent Democrats and 83 percent of Republicans approved of Trump—a gap of 75 points. This exceeded the gap between Democrats and Republicans for every other president since Dwight D. Eisenhower, including Obama.

Democrats and Republican also had starkly different views of the economy—but which side they were on changed rapidly after Trump was elected. Gallup polls showed a steep drop in the percentage of Democrats who thought that the economy was getting better, whereas the percentage of Republicans who said the economy was getting better increased from 15 percent in October 2016 to 80 percent in February 2017 (figure 9.2). Most of these shifts occurred even before Trump took office. The same shifts were evident in Pew Research Center surveys, as well as the Views of the American Electorate Research (VOTER) Survey, which interviewed the same respondents in December 2016 and July 2017. In that survey, the percentage of Republicans who thought that the country was going in the right direction increased from

Percent saying that economic conditions are getting better

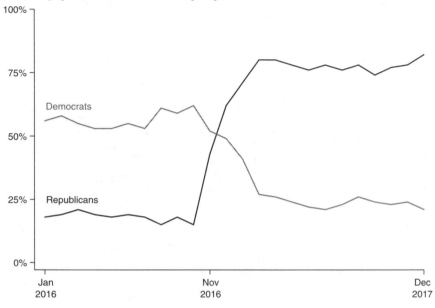

Figure 9.2.
Postelection changes in partisan views of the economy.
Source: Gallup polls, aggregated to monthly intervals.

24 percent in December 2016 to 70 percent in July 2017, whereas the percentage of Democrats who said this decreased from 37 percent to 13 percent. Republicans also quickly shifted to more positive views of the economy, their personal finances, and "life in America today for people like you," compared to "fifty years ago." Democrats became less positive about these things.[17]

This partisan flip-flop on the economy and direction of the country showed that much of the "voter anger" and dissatisfaction with the economy was about partisanship, not the actual economy (see chapter 2). The most angry and disaffected voters—Republicans—quickly became the most optimistic once Trump was elected, even as the economic fundamentals themselves did not change dramatically. This is another reason to downplay the role of subjective economic dissatisfaction in the election: it was largely a consequence of partisan politics, not a cause of partisans' choices.

These same partisan gaps emerged in other domains. Indeed, one reason that Trump's approval rating, although historically low, did not drop much below 40 percent was that Republicans tended to discount controversies like the Russia investigation. Trump's defenders in Congress and on conservative news outlets repeatedly criticized this investigation. Unsurprisingly, then, most Republicans in the public were skeptical of any improper relationships between Russia and the Trump campaign, and many Republicans increasingly distrusted the FBI as well. Approximately half said that they had little or no confidence that Robert Mueller would conduct a fair investigation, whereas nearly 75 percent of Democrats said they were confident. Similarly, most Republicans said that the Trump campaign probably or definitely did not have improper contact with Russia during the campaign.[18]

The challenge for Republicans, however, was that Democrats appeared more motivated by their opposition to Trump than Republicans did by their support for him. In polls, far more people strongly disapproved of Trump than strongly approved of him. And in elections conducted throughout 2017 and early 2018—including statewide elections in Virginia and New Jersey, as well as special elections in many other states—Democratic voters appeared more energized. Across ninety special elections, Democratic candidates outperformed Hillary Clinton by an average of 13 points.[19] This gave them victories in states and legislative districts that Trump had carried handily. Perhaps the most surprising was Democrats' triumph in Alabama's special election for the Senate seat previously occupied by Jeff Sessions, where the Democrat, Doug Jones, narrowly beat Roy Moore, the former chief justice of Alabama's Supreme Court. Moore faced a major scandal when several women accused him of pursuing a romantic relationship or even sexually assaulting them when they were teenagers and he was in his thirties. But even without such scandals, Republicans lost prominent races. In the Virginia governor's race, for example, the Democrat Ralph Northam beat Republican Ed Gillespie by almost 9 points— even though Gillespie essentially adopted Trump's platform on immigration.

In short, the aftermath of the 2016 election illustrated a predictable pattern in U.S. elections: winning does not beget winning, it begets losing. It was the same pattern that turned an "emerging liberal majority" into massive gains for the Republicans in Congress and state legislatures after Obama's election. Now, rather than "ruling for 50 years," Republicans found themselves losing races that should have been easy victories. And Democrats found themselves winning, even though there had not been any grand "reckoning" or "rebranding" within the party.

Trickle-Down Tolerance

On July 30, 2017, the lead story on the site *Breitbart* was "Seven Ways Trump Is Taking Back America's Culture."[20] The author suggested that Trump was winning the battle for the meaning of America: "In just six months, Trump has set the tone for a culture shift in America—back to the values of life,

210   Chapter 9

religious liberty, common sense civic order, and respect for the law of the land." But in fact, Trump was actually having the exact opposite effect on public opinion.

It is common for public opinion to shift against the president in what the political scientist Christopher Wlezien has called a "thermostatic" fashion. For example, in 2017 the percentage of Americans favoring government involvement in health care and the Affordable Care Act increased, even as Trump and other Republicans were seeking to repeal the ACA. As Trump took aim at free trade agreements and imposed tariffs, an increasing percentage of Americans said that foreign trade was "an opportunity for economic growth," not a "threat to the economy." Support for free trade agreements increased as well.[21]

Even more tellingly, the same thermostatic trends characterized attitudes about the identity-inflected issues central to Trump's agenda as a candidate and president (figure 9.3).[22] From late 2015 through 2017, more Americans rated Muslims favorably, thought that discrimination was a major cause of racial inequality, supported athletes' kneeling for the national anthem to protest racial injustice, and thought that gender discrimination and the sexual harassment of women were serious problems. (The shift in views of gender discrimination occurred before the allegations of movie mogul Harvey Weinstein's sexual misconduct and the ensuing #metoo movement.) Meanwhile, fewer Americans supported Trump's signature border wall, perceived immigrants to be burdens, and wanted to decrease immigration.[23]

These trends run counter to a prevailing view of Trump himself. In June 2018, Jim VandeHei of Axios wrote, "In our lifetime, no president has matched Donald Trump's ability to summon the power of the pulpit, friendly media, and the tweet-by-tweet power of repetition and persuasion to move minds en masse."[24] This overstates the persuasive impact of presidential rhetoric generally. But in the case of Trump, it is precisely backward: if Trump has moved minds, it has been in the opposite direction from what he intended.

Of course, these trends do not suggest that Trump's rhetoric and policy proposals had no negative consequences. Trump's criticisms of immigrants and Muslims, as well as his equivocal statements about white nationalism, may have emboldened some people to act on their prejudice. Early research found that exposing people to his controversial quotes about minorities caused them to say more offensive things about Mexicans and African Americans—particularly when other elites tacitly condoned Trump's offensive comments. Hate crime statistics compiled by the FBI show a significant increase in assaults against Muslims. In 2016, there were 127 victims of assault, compared to 56 in 2014 and 91 in 2015.[25] Nevertheless, the more prevalent trend in

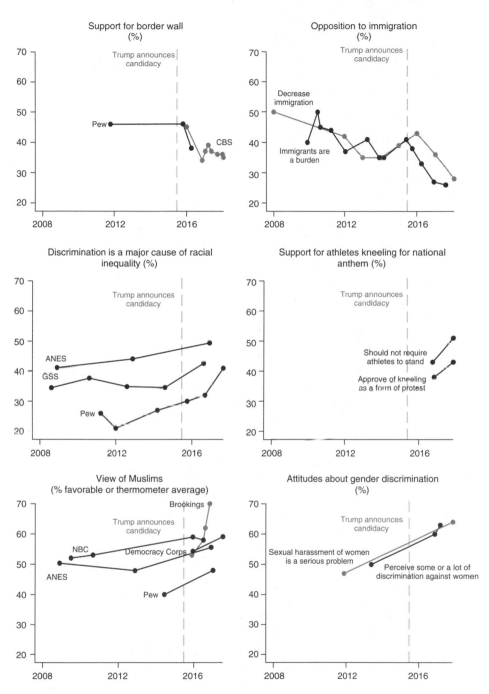

Figure 9.3.

Trends in attitudes about immigration, race, Muslims, and gender.

ANES = American National Election Studies; GSS = General Social Survey.

Sources: For the "opposition to immigration graph," the polls were conducted by Gallup ("decrease immigration") and the Pew Research Center ("immigrants are a burden"). For the NFL graph, the polls were conducted by Marist ("should not require athletes to stand") and Quinnipiac ("approve of kneeling"). For the gender discrimination graph, the polls were conducted by ABC/*Washington Post* ("sexual harassment") and the Pew Research Center ("discrimination against women").

American public opinion was toward more favorable views of racial, ethnic, and religious minorities.

Identity Politics Intensifies

But that shift has come at a cost. These changing attitudes on race, immigration, Islam, and gender were driven primarily by Democrats. The result has been accelerated partisan polarization over the same identity-inflected issues that helped make the 2016 election so divisive.

For one, views of racial inequality manifested this polarization (figure 9.4). In Pew Research Center polling, the percentage of Democrats who said that "racial discrimination is the main reason why many black people can't get ahead these days" had been trending upward between 2008 and 2014—illustrating the broader alignment of racial attitudes and partisanship (see chapter 2). But in the three polls conducted after Trump's entry in the presidential race, that percentage increased by 22 percentage points—from 44 percent in February 2014 to 66 percent in June 2017. The same pattern was evident in the American National Election Studies. Between 2012 and 2016, the percentage of Democrats who agreed that "blacks have gotten less than they deserve" increased by almost 20 points. Among respondents interviewed in both December 2011 and December 2016 as part of the VOTER Survey, Obama voters became significantly more supportive of affirmative action from 2011 to 2016, while the opinions of Romney voters were relatively stable.[26]

Democratic views of both immigrants and Muslims also became more favorable. The percentage of Democrats who said that "immigrants today strengthen the country" increased from 62 percent in May 2015, just before Trump entered the race, to 82 percent in June 2017. The percentage of Democrats with a favorable opinion of "illegal immigrants" increased by 13 points between 2012 and 2016. During the campaign itself, Democratic voters interviewed and reinterviewed in the Presidential Election Panel Survey turned against the border wall.[27]

These are dramatic shifts in opinion in a short time, and on issues of which many people hold strong views. An important source of these shifts is almost certainly the backlash to Donald Trump himself and to his rhetoric and behavior as president.[28] For example, after Trump defended the white nationalists protesting the removal of Confederate monuments, Trump voters were 60 points more likely than Clinton voters to oppose removing the statue of Robert E. Lee in Charlottesville (81% to 21%). After Trump pardoned Joe Arpaio, 70 percent of Trump voters supported the decision, compared to

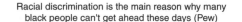

Racial discrimination is the main reason why many black people can't get ahead these days (Pew)

100% agree

Trump announces candidacy

75%

50%

25%

Democrats

Republicans

0%

2008 · 2012 · 2016

Over the past few years blacks have gotten less than they deserve (ANES)

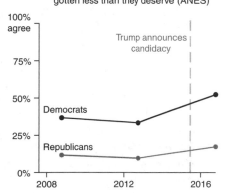

100% agree

Trump announces candidacy

75%

50%

Democrats

25%

Republicans

0%

2008 · 2012 · 2016

Immigrants today strengthen the country because of their hard work and talents (Pew)

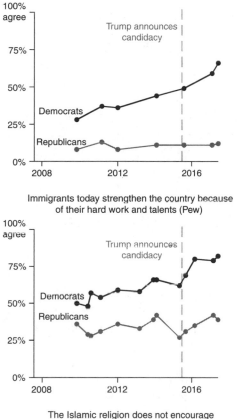

100% agree

Trump announces candidacy

75%

Democrats

50%

Republicans

25%

0%

2008 · 2012 · 2016

Favorable view of "illegal immigrants" (ANES)

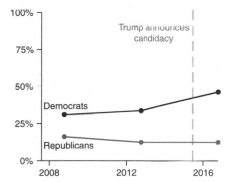
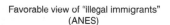

100%

Trump announces candidacy

75%

50%

Democrats

25%

Republicans

0%

2008 · 2012 · 2016

The Islamic religion does not encourage violence more than others (Pew)

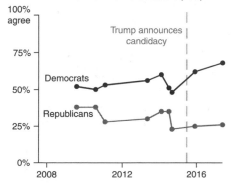

100% agree

Trump announces candidacy

75%

Democrats

50%

Republicans

25%

0%

2008 · 2012 · 2016

Favorable view of Muslims (ANES)

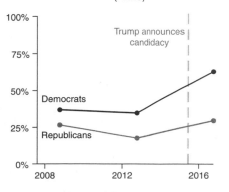

100%

Trump announces candidacy

75%

50%

Democrats

25%

Republicans

0%

2008 · 2012 · 2016

Figure 9.4.

Partisan polarization in views of racial inequality, immigrants, and Muslims.
Sources: Pew Research Center polls; American National Election Studies.

5 percent of Clinton voters. And when Trump criticized NFL players for kneeling during the national anthem, a whopping 92 percent of Trump voters said that these protests were inappropriate, compared to 17 percent of Clinton voters.[29]

These fraught politics have helped strengthen ethnic identities among minorities and further polarize whites based on their level of education. Trump's election immediately strengthened Latino and Asian American identity in particular, and Trump has been especially unpopular with young Latinos, who make up a disproportionate share of Latinos.[30] Meanwhile, the "diploma divide" among white voters has grown even larger than it was before the 2016 election. In Pew Research Center polls, the Democratic advantage in party identification among whites with a college degree increased from 1 point in 2014 (47% versus 46%) to 5 points in 2016 (50% versus 45%) and then again to 13 points in 2017 (54% versus 41%). The Republican advantage among whites with no college education increased by 5 points over this same period.

These changes in the party coalitions incentivize politicians in both parties to run on "identity politics." For Democrats, the divisions on issues related to race and immigration that have historically splintered their party are weakening, allowing Democratic politicians to advocate for racial and ethnic minorities with less risk of backlash. Moreover, this strategy may prove more successful at winning elections than would luring back those white voters who had previously supported Obama but voted for Trump. The views of Obama-Trump voters on many issues—but especially race and immigration— are very different from those of most Democrats today. In the 2020 election, Democrats may find it easier to mobilize or win back Obama supporters who did not vote in 2016 or voted for a third-party candidate.[31]

Meanwhile, Republican politicians have a similar incentive to run on issues connected to identity as opposed to a traditional platform of limited government. Trump's positions on immigration, Confederate monuments, and national anthem protests have proved more popular with Republican voters than have the GOP tax bill or Republican alternatives to the Affordable Care Act. Indeed, Trump's popularity with Republicans—even the economically liberal Republicans who supported him in the primary—has been quite impervious to his shift to a conservative economic agenda, suggesting that support for him hinges more on his identity agenda.

The effect of these incentives has already become visible in down-ballot races. The Virginia governor's race in 2017 was one example. Ed Gillespie had deep ties to the Republican establishment and was not an early Trump supporter by any means. Nevertheless, he ran a Trumpian campaign centered on Confederate monuments, immigration, restricting felon voting rights, and kneeling athletes. Another example was a March 2018 special election to the U.S. House in Pennsylvania, where Republicans abandoned a message focused on taxes to hammer the Democratic candidate on immigration and crime. In fact, Trump made his endorsement of some Republican congressional candidates contingent on their support for hawkish immigration politics. More and more, the party has rejected the Growth and Opportunity Project's 2013 recommendation to liberalize on immigration.[32]

Meanwhile, Democratic candidates and their allied interest groups have responded in kind. Gillespie's campaign was met with a controversial ad from the Latino Victory Fund that showed black, Latino, and Muslim children being chased down by a Gillespie supporter in a pickup truck displaying a Confederate flag. The ad ended by asking, "Is this what Donald Trump and Ed Gillespie mean by the American Dream?" Across the country, Democratic politicians were held to "an increasingly stringent standard on racial equity" in 2018 primaries.[33] Centrist Democrats often faced challenges in primaries from racial justice groups and Democratic candidates who supported such policies as defunding Immigration and Customs Enforcement. To be sure, Democratic leaders—to say nothing of a million op-eds—continue to debate the merits of emphasizing racial equality as opposed to pocketbook economics. But the party clearly faces rising pressure from its growing base of nonwhites and white progressives to double down on Hillary Clinton's rhetoric, oppose Trump's agenda, and explicitly support racial and ethnic minorities.

These growing divisions between the Democratic and Republican Parties threaten to make political conflict less about what the government should do and more about what it means to be an American. In turn, that is likely to make politics especially emotionally charged and divisive. In fact, a recent study by the political scientists Nicholas Valentino and Kirill Zhirkov found that Americans' growing dislike of the opposite party—the "negative partisanship"—is related precisely to the increasing overlap between race and party in their minds.[34] This is the American identity crisis, and it is getting worse.

The European Analogue

If the American party system continues to polarize along these lines, it will look more and more like the party systems of many European countries. In those systems, electoral rules facilitate the existence of multiple parties that are often distinguished by their platforms on issues like immigration. The rise of what are often called right-wing populist parties has depended in part on the political opportunities created by these rules. By contrast, American electoral rules favor two major parties with broader coalitions and agendas, which helps neutralize or at least moderate the sentiments that sustain right-wing populist parties in Europe. But that may change if the Democratic and Republican Parties are increasingly divided on issues like race and immigration.

Indeed, many analysts compare Trump's election in the United States to the increasing success of right-wing parties in Europe, as well as the unexpected vote in the United Kingdom to leave the European Union (a decision also known as Brexit). In both Europe and the United States, increasing racial, ethnic, and religious diversity, largely driven by immigration, challenges existing conceptions of national identity. This challenge is even more acute in Europe because Europeans are, on average, more concerned about increased diversity and less supportive of religious and cultural heterogeneity than are Americans. Moreover, many immigrants to Europe come from culturally and religiously distinctive Muslim nations, and Europe has suffered from a spate of terrorist attacks perpetrated by Islamist extremists. A great deal of research shows that support for both right-wing populist parties and Brexit was higher among those with less favorable views of immigration.[35]

Moreover, the role of "economic anxiety" in the success of right-wing populist parties is more modest, just as in the 2016 U.S. election and despite Europe's sluggish recovery from the Great Recession. In 2014–15, economic dissatisfaction was not related to support for right-wing populist parties in most European countries, especially compared to anti-immigrant sentiments. Moreover, actual economic conditions like unemployment have had no discernible impact on the prevalence of anti-immigrant sentiment in Europe—much the way that the Great Recession did not increase racial prejudice in the United States.[36]

Finally, economic anxiety's role in promoting far-right populist parties has been clearer when refracted through racial identity. Just as support for Donald Trump was associated with white Americans' concerns about losing ground to less deserving minority groups, support for Brexit was associated with how well whites thought they were doing compared to minorities—a sort of "status anxiety."[37] Perceptions of discrimination against whites were also strongly associated with support for Brexit (left panel of figure 9.5). Whites who thought there was a lot of discrimination against whites were over 60 percentage points more likely to support Brexit than whites who thought there was a lot of discrimination in favor of whites. The white identity politics that helped fuel Trump's victories seems potent in European politics as well.

Indeed, Trump may have become a symbol of white identity politics even in Europe. Most people in the United Kingdom were disappointed that Trump was elected: about 64 percent of those polled in a December 2016 British Election Study survey said they were unhappy with the result, compared

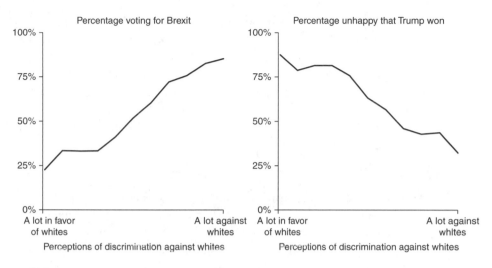

Figure 9.5.
Perceptions of discrimination and support for Brexit and Donald Trump among whites
in Britain.
Source: British Election Study.

to 17 percent who were happy about it and 19 percent who were neutral.
But whites who perceived a lot of discrimination against their group were
much less likely to be unhappy about Trump's election (right panel of
figure 9.5).[38]

Those results square with the affinity between Trump and far-right leaders in Europe. Geert Wilders of the Dutch Freedom Party attended a Trump
rally in 2016. Viktor Orban of Hungary also expressed support for Trump.
Trump himself has supported European leaders, such as Nigel Farage in the
United Kingdom and Marine Le Pen in France, who have emphasized threats
to native whites from immigration. During the campaign, Trump expressed
solidarity with Brexit supporters who were "angry over borders [and] angry
over people coming into their country and taking over." He praised them for
"taking back their country." Soon afterward, Trump was joined at a campaign
rally in Mississippi by Farage, who urged the crowd to "take back control of
their country, take back control of their borders and get back their pride and
self-respect." As president, Trump praised Le Pen during her unsuccessful bid
for president, saying that she was "the strongest on borders, and she's the
strongest on [the terrorism that's] been going on in France." Steve Bannon's
admiration of Le Pen was even more effusive: he told her supporters, "Let them
call you racist. Let them call you xenophobes. Let them call you nativists. Wear
it as a badge of honor."[39]

Of course, identifying the similarities and differences between Trump's rise and support for right-wing parties in Europe requires a more thorough analysis. But both cases appear to have some common origins—notably, the ability of political leaders like Trump, Le Pen, and others to activate pre-existing concerns that native whites are losing out to immigrants and minorities.

Choices

The American identity crisis cannot be undone easily. There are always going to be resentments percolating in the American electorate. For example, research on rural and working-class Americans found that resentments—about immigrants, welfare cheats, the government, and urban dwellers—surfaced again and again in conversations before the 2016 election. Social identities like race and ethnicity have been and will always be integral to party coalitions and to American politics.[40]

Could any of this change? To begin to answer that question, we can go back to Fayetteville.

Nine months after John McGraw sucker-punched Rakeem Jones at the Trump rally, he went to trial.[41] When McGraw entered his plea of no contest and was given the chance to speak, he said to Jones,

> I'm extremely sorry that this happened. This was between two men. You know what you did. And I know what I did. I'm not going to say you were wrong or I was wrong. You and I both know what occurred, and I hate it worse than anything else in the world. We got caught up in a political mess today. And you and me, we got to heal our country.

Jones said, "All right, man." He patted McGraw on the shoulder, McGraw put out his hand, Jones took it, and then the men embraced while observers applauded. As the men began to leave the courtroom, McGraw told Jones, "We've got to stick together. We can't let them come between us."

It was a partial reconciliation at best. Jones was frustrated that McGraw was not going to face jail time, whereas one of Jones's friends was facing five years in prison for a similar incident. Jones's friend Ronnie Rouse, who had taped McGraw's punch with his cell phone, said, "It was a slap in the face, man. What messed me up here was the guy didn't apologize." Jones agreed. Rouse continued, "If it was me? Ninety days, five-year probation, $1,000 fine. It's crazy." Rouse said, "He really believes in how he acted. He's just a stubborn old man." Jones replied, "It's real life. What you see is what you get."

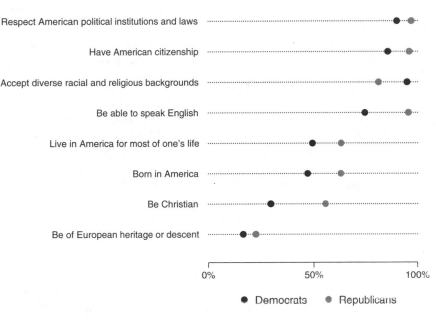

Figure 9.6.
Beliefs about American identity.
Source: December 2016 VOTER Survey.

Nevertheless, the next day, McGraw surprised Jones by calling to see how he was doing and to thank him for his decency. This was all very different from what he said about Jones the night of the rally: "We know he's not acting like an American."

In the American public writ large, there is also a definition of "acting like an American" that is inclusive. It defines American identity by values—such as believing in the country's ideals, working hard to achieve success, and contributing to your community—rather by race, nationality, religion, or partisanship. This is what Senator Lindsey Graham was describing when he challenged Donald Trump's remark about "shithole" nations by saying, "America is an idea, not a race."

Most Americans agree. In the December 2016 VOTER Survey, more Americans indicated that American identity is about beliefs, not race or religion (figure 9.6). Most Democrats and Republicans agreed that characteristics important to being American included respecting the country's institutions and laws and accepting people of diverse backgrounds. Most also endorsed American citizenship and speaking English—which are not purely matters of belief but are attainable nonetheless. By contrast, fewer Democrats or Republicans believed European heritage was important to being American. Other research has found a similar pattern. For example, in a 2004 survey, large majorities said that American identity involved things like "pursuing economic success via hard work" and "letting other people say what they want, no matter how much you disagree with them." Indeed, the 2016 survey results actually suggested less support for an exclusive conception of American identity than did earlier surveys.[42]

But the seeds of division about American identity were also apparent in this survey. Republicans and Democrats did not always agree—particularly regarding the importance of being Christian to being American. A majority of Republicans (56%) said that being Christian was very or fairly important, compared to 30 percent of Democrats. There has always been a strain of American identity that seeks sharp and often impermeable boundaries between who is American and who is not.[43] Critics accused Trump of drawing such boundaries when he said, "We should have more people from places like Norway."[44]

Public opinion thus contains reservoirs of sentiment that can serve both to unify and to divide. Take immigration. Places that experience rapid growth in the population of Latino immigrants do not necessarily become more anti-immigrant. A detailed study of two rural towns in Iowa by the political scientist J. Celeste Lay found that residents came to accept newly arrived immigrants—a process led by young people in these towns, to whom diversity was "no big deal." But the polarizing rhetoric of politicians "politicizes" the places where Americans live, and people who live in places with a recent influx of immigrants then become more concerned about immigration. This unfolded in 2016: white Democrats voted for Trump in the highest numbers where the Latino population had grown the most.[45]

What gave us the 2016 election, then, was not changes among voters. It was changes in the candidates. Only four years earlier, issues like race and immigration were not as central either to the candidates or to voters. The 2016 election was different because of what the candidates chose to do and say—and then, after the election, because of what Trump has chosen to do and say as president. Those choices have had consequences for voters.

Political leaders will always have those choices. They can call someone un-American or a "son of a bitch" or "deplorable." They can call someone's country a "shithole." They can tell us to "beat the crap" out of someone they disagree with. They can also ask us to welcome others, to find common ground, and even to heal the country. These choices are what helped build the identity crisis in American politics. They are also what can help take it apart.

Appendixes

APPENDIX TO CHAPTER 2

Figure A2.1 compares trends in consumer sentiment among different education groups, showing a similar pattern of parallel movement after the Great Recession. Attitudes toward the economy became more favorable in every group.

Forecasting Models of the Presidential Election

The statistical models of presidential election outcomes are based on the seventeen elections between 1948 and 2012. For each election, we calculated the incumbent party's percentage of the major-party vote—that is, the votes received by the Democratic and Republican candidates, leaving aside any third-party or independent candidates. The key factors in these models are the following:

- The change in gross domestic product between the first and third quarters of the election year. This is calculated as $\ln(\text{GDP}_t) - \ln(\text{GDP}_{t-2})$. The GDP data were obtained from the Saint Louis Federal Reserve's FRED database (the variable GDPC1).[1]
- The president's approval rating as of June of the election year. These data were originally collected by George Edwards and Gary Jacobson. We updated the data to include all polling on Barack Obama's approval rating, as compiled by the *Huffington Post*'s Pollster. If there were multiple polls in June, we took the average.
- A dichotomous variable for whether the incumbent president was running for reelection (1948, 1956, 1964, 1972, 1976, 1980, 1984, 1992, 1996, 2004, and 2012). This variable is important mainly in interaction with the change in GDP and presidential approval.
- A dichotomous variable for whether the incumbent party had held the White House for one term or two or more terms ("incumbent tenure").[2]

In calculating a forecast for 2016, we used the initial estimate of GDP growth (1.07 percentage points of nonannualized growth from the first to the third quarter of 2016) and Obama's observed approval rating of 50 percent. We estimated each model using the Clarify statistical package, generating one thousand simulated values of the coefficients, thereby

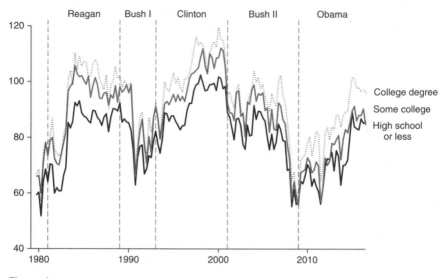

Figure A2.1.

The Index of Consumer Sentiment among education groups, 1980–2016.

taking into account their underlying uncertainty.[3] We also generated an estimate of the model's overall error, using the standard error of the regression multiplied by a random draw from a t-distribution with degrees of freedom equal to those in the model. Multiplying by this value from the t-distribution has the effect of adding uncertainty to the prediction because the t-distribution has greater dispersion than a standard normal distribution.

Using these values for the independent variables, coefficients, and errors, we generated one thousand predicted outcomes, the associated 95 percent confidence interval, and the likelihood that the incumbent party would win (that is, the percentage of the one thousand simulations in which the incumbent party received more than 50% of the vote). Table A2.1 shows the coefficients and standard errors from the models discussed in the text, as well as the associated forecast.

Model 1 shows the well-established impact of both GDP growth and presidential approval on election outcomes. The associated forecast favors the incumbent party (the Democrats), who are expected to win 51.8 percent of the major-party vote. Across the one thousand simulations, 72 percent resulted in the Democrats receiving more than half of the major-party vote.

Model 2 shows that the impact of presidential approval and GDP appear larger when the incumbent is running. To be sure, these effects are not estimated very precisely, given the small sample of elections here, and this lack of precision will of course add uncertainty to any forecast. But the magnitude of the coefficients—especially for presidential approval—suggests that these two factors matter more when the actual incumbent is on the ballot. As a result, this model predicts that ostensibly favorable economic and political conditions offer less benefit to the Democrats in 2016: their forecasted vote share is 49.7 percent, which translates into a 47 percent chance of winning.

Table A2.1.

Aggregate Models of 1948–2012 Presidential Election Outcomes and Associated Forecasts

	Model 1	Model 2	Model 3
Presidential approval rating (June)	0.27* [0.06]	0.16 [0.09]	0.20* [0.05]
Growth in GDP (Q1–Q3)	1.54* [0.56]	1.10 [1.11]	1.75* [0.45]
Approval × incumbent running		0.15 [0.11]	
GDP × incumbent running		0.31 [1.26]	
Incumbent running		−5.06 [5.27]	
Incumbent tenure			−3.77* [1 ?2]
Constant	36.63* [2.72]	40.78* [4.07]	45.66* [3.66]
Adjusted R-squared	0.76	0.77	0.83
Forecasted share for incumbent party	51.8%	49.7%	50.0%
95% confidence interval for forecast	[46.6, 56.8]	[44.5, 54.4]	[45.6, 54.4]
Chance of incumbent party victory	72%	47%	49.5%

Note: Coefficients and standard errors are from least squares regression models (N = 17). $p < 0.05$.

Finally, model 3 shows that incumbent tenure is associated with a lower vote share, as previous work has also found. This too operates as a penalty for the Democrats and creates a lower likelihood of a Democratic victory, compared to model 1 (49.5%).

APPENDIX TO CHAPTER 3

Figure A3.1 presents the percentage of Republican officeholders endorsing each individual Republican candidate before the Iowa caucus took place. This shows how none of the candidates in 2016 commanded a significant share of support from Republican Party leaders during the invisible primary.

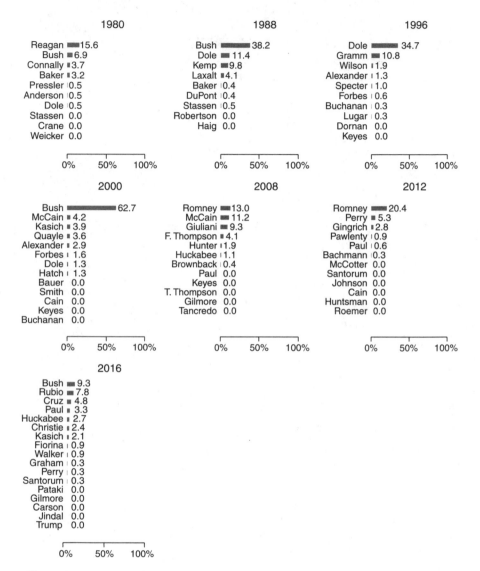

1980

Candidate	%
Reagan	15.6
Bush	6.9
Connally	3.7
Baker	3.2
Pressler	0.5
Anderson	0.5
Dole	0.5
Stassen	0.0
Crane	0.0
Weicker	0.0

0%   50%   100%

1988

Candidate	%
Bush	38.2
Dole	11.4
Kemp	9.8
Laxalt	4.1
Baker	0.4
DuPont	0.4
Stassen	0.5
Robertson	0.0
Haig	0.0

0%   50%   100%

1996

Candidate	%
Dole	34.7
Gramm	10.8
Wilson	1.9
Alexander	1.3
Specter	1.0
Forbes	0.6
Buchanan	0.3
Lugar	0.3
Dornan	0.0
Keyes	0.0

0%   50%   100%

2000

Candidate	%
Bush	62.7
McCain	4.2
Kasich	3.9
Quayle	3.6
Alexander	2.9
Forbes	1.6
Dole	1.3
Hatch	1.3
Bauer	0.0
Smith	0.0
Cain	0.0
Keyes	0.0
Buchanan	0.0

0%   50%   100%

2008

Candidate	%
Romney	13.0
McCain	11.2
Giuliani	9.3
F. Thompson	4.1
Hunter	1.9
Huckabee	1.1
Brownback	0.4
Paul	0.0
Keyes	0.0
T. Thompson	0.0
Gilmore	0.0
Tancredo	0.0

0%   50%   100%

2012

Candidate	%
Romney	20.4
Perry	5.3
Gingrich	2.8
Pawlenty	0.9
Paul	0.6
Bachmann	0.3
McCotter	0.0
Santorum	0.0
Johnson	0.0
Cain	0.0
Huntsman	0.0
Roemer	0.0

0%   50%   100%

2016

Candidate	%
Bush	9.3
Rubio	7.8
Cruz	4.8
Paul	3.3
Huckabee	2.7
Christie	2.4
Kasich	2.1
Fiorina	0.9
Walker	0.9
Graham	0.3
Perry	0.3
Santorum	0.3
Pataki	0.0
Gilmore	0.0
Carson	0.0
Jindal	0.0
Trump	0.0

0%   50%   100%

Figure A3.1.

Percentage of possible pre-Iowa endorsements won by Republican presidential candidates, 1980–2016.

The figure reflects endorsements by sitting Republican governors, senators, and members of the House.

APPENDIX TO CHAPTER 5

The main analyses in chapter 5 rely on three different surveys: the 2016 Views of the Electorate Research (VOTER) Survey, the Presidential Election Panel Survey (PEPS), and the 2016 American National Election Studies (ANES) Pilot Study. This appendix provides a brief summary of each survey, the variables used in the multivariate analyses, and the complete results of the statistical models that undergird figure 5.7.

The 2016 VOTER Survey

The VOTER Survey was conducted by the survey firm YouGov and designed and funded by the Democracy Fund Voter Study Group. In total, 8,000 adults (age eighteen and older) with internet access took the survey online between November 29 and December 29, 2016. The reported margin of error is plus or minus 2.2 percent. YouGov also supplied measures of primary voting behavior from the end of the primary period (July 2016), when these respondents had been contacted as part of a different survey project.

These respondents were originally interviewed by YouGov in 2011–12 as part of the 2012 Cooperative Campaign Analysis Project (CCAP). In that survey, 45,000 respondents were first interviewed in December 2011 and were interviewed a second time in one of the forty-five weekly surveys between January 1 and November 8, 2012. After the November election, 35,408 respondents were interviewed a third time. For this survey 11,168 panelists from the 2012 CCAP were invited to respond, and 8,637 of them (77%) completed the 2016 survey.

For more on this survey and to download the data, see https://www.voterstudygroup .org/.

The central measures for the analysis of voting behavior in the Republican primary follow. Unless indicated otherwise, all measures derive from the December 2011 interview and are rescaled to the 0–1 interval.

- Republican candidate preference as of July 2016 was asked to those who reported voting in a Republican primary. The responses were coded as 1 = Trump and 0 = Cruz, Kasich, Rubio, someone else, or do not recall.
- Opposition to immigration is a scale combining three questions: "Overall, do you think illegal immigrants make a contribution to American society or are a drain?" (coded 0 = contribution, .5 = neither or don't know, 1 = drain), "Do you favor or oppose providing a legal way for illegal immigrants already in the United States to become U.S. citizens?" (coded 0 = favor, .5 = don't know, 1 = oppose), and "Do you think it should be easier or harder for foreigners to immigrate to the US legally than it is currently?" (coded in five categories from 0 = much harder to 1 = much easier). The scale's reliability is 0.72.
- Coolness toward Muslims is measured with a feeling thermometer recoded so that 0 = warmest feelings and 1 = coolest feelings.
- Views of racial inequality are measured with four items with which respondents could agree or disagree on a four-point scale: (1) "Over the past few years, blacks have gotten less than they deserve"; (2) "Irish, Italian, Jewish, and many other minorities overcame prejudice and worked their way up. Blacks should do the same without any special favors"; (3) "It's really a matter of some people not trying hard

enough. If blacks would only try harder they could be just as well off as whites"; and (4) "Generations of slavery and discrimination have created conditions that make it difficult for blacks to work their way out of the lower class." Higher values on this scale indicate less agreement with (1) and (4) and more agreement with (2) and (3). The scale's reliability is 0.88.

- Economic anxiety is a scale combining two questions: "Overall, do you think the economy is getting better or worse?" (coded 0 = better, .5 = about the same, 1 = worse) and "Would you say that you and your family are better off financially, worse off financially, or about the same?" (coded in a similar fashion). The scale's reliability is 0.63.
- The importance of Medicare and Social Security is from a battery asking respondents how important various issues listed in random order were. The importance of each issue was coded 1 = very important, .5 = somewhat important, and 0 = not very or not at all important and then averaged.
- The importance of terrorism is from the same battery and is coded in four categories from 0 = not at all important to 1 = very important.
- Economic liberalism is a scale combining three questions: "Do you favor raising taxes on families with incomes over $200,000 per year?"; "Do you think it is the responsibility of the federal government to see to it that everyone has health care coverage?"; and "In general, do you think there is too much or too little regulation of business by the government?" The resulting scale has a reliability of 0.84 and is split near its median and coded 0 = less liberal and 1 = more liberal.
- "Do not identify as strong conservative" is based on a five-category measure of ideological self-identification, coded so that 0 = strong conservative and 1 = all other responses.
- Opposition to increasing trade is measured with this question: "Do you favor or oppose increasing trade with other nations?" (coded 0 = favor, .5 = don't know, and 1 = oppose).
- "Laid off or unemployed" is based on self-reported unemployment status, where 1 = temporarily laid off or unemployed and 0 = all other responses (employed, retired, student, and so on). This is measured in the December 2016 interview.
- Family income is measured in seventeen categories. Higher values equal higher incomes. The statistical model also includes a dummy variable to capture respondents who did not provide an income (about 13% of respondents). This is measured in the December 2016 interview.
- Education is measured in five categories. Higher values equal higher levels of formal education.
- Age is based on respondents' self-reported birth year, subtracted from 2016.

The Presidential Election Panel Survey

The PEPS was administered by the RAND Corporation to approximately 3,000 respondents drawn from its American Life Panel—a probability sample of U.S. adults who have been regularly interviewed since 2006. Surveys were completed online. There were six waves of interviewing in 2015–16. The analyses in chapter 5 rely on the initial wave, which was conducted between December 13, 2015, and January 6, 2016. More information about the PEPS is here: https://www.rand.org/labor/alp/projects/2016-election-panel-survey .html.

The measures in the analysis were from this initial wave and were also rescaled to the 0–1 interval:

- Republican candidate preference as of December 2015–January 2016 was asked of those who intended to vote in a Republican primary. The responses were coded as 1 = Trump and 0 = any other candidate or no preference.
- Opposition to immigration is measured with two items with which respondents could agree or disagree on a five-point scale: "The growing number of newcomers from other countries threatens traditional American customs and values" and "It bothers me when I come in contact with immigrants who speak little or no English" (alpha = 0.71).
- Coolness toward Muslims is measured with a four-category favorability measure coded so that 0 = very favorable and 1 = very unfavorable.
- Views of racial inequality are measured by combining two of the same items in the VOTER Survey. Respondents could agree or disagree on a four-point scale with the following statements: "It's really a matter of some people not trying hard enough. If blacks would only try harder they could be just as well off as whites" and "Generations of slavery and discrimination have created conditions that make it difficult for blacks to work their way out of the lower class" (alpha = 0.53).
- Economic anxiety is measured with one question: "Overall, do you think the economy is getting better or worse?" (coded 0 = better, .5 = about the same, 1 = worse).
- Economic liberalism is a scale combining these items: the difference in favorability of labor unions and "big business" (coded so that those with more favorable views of unions than of business are more liberal); and agreement or disagreement with three policies: "the government paying necessary medical costs for every American citizen"; "increasing taxes on individuals who make more than $200,000 a year"; and "raising the federal minimum wage." The scale's reliability is 0.80.
- "Do not identify as strong conservative" is based on a five-category measure of ideological self-identification, coded so that 0 = strong conservative and 1 = all other responses.
- A lack of political efficacy was measured as agreement with this item: "People like me don't have any say about what the government does."
- "Laid off or unemployed" is based on self-reported unemployment status, where 1 = temporarily laid off or unemployed and 0 = all other responses (employed, retired, student, and so on).
- Family income is measured in seventeen categories. Higher values equal higher incomes. There is no missing data for this measure.
- Education is measured in five categories. Higher values equal higher levels of formal education.

The 2016 American National Election Studies Pilot Study

The ANES Pilot Study was administered by the firm YouGov to a sample of N = 1,200 respondents between January 22 and January 28, 2016. More information about the survey is here: http://electionstudies.org/studypages/anes_pilot_2016/anes_pilot_2016.htm.

The measures in the analysis were again rescaled to the 0–1 interval:

- All respondents regardless of party were asked, "Regardless of whether you will vote in the Republican primary this year, which Republican candidate do you prefer?"

The sample is limited here to respondents who identified as Republican or identified as independent but said that they lean toward the Republican Party. Republican primary preference is coded as 1 = Trump and 0 = any other candidate or no preference.

- Strength of white identification is measured with four questions: "How important is it that whites work together to change laws that are unfair to whites?"; "How likely is it that many whites are unable to find a job because employers are hiring minorities instead?"; "How much discrimination is there in the United States today against each of the following groups: whites?"; and "How important is being white to your identity?" The combined scale has a reliability of 0.59.

- Opposition to immigration is measured with two questions: "When people from other countries legally move to the United States to live and work, is this generally good for the U.S., generally bad for the U.S., or neither good nor bad?" and "Should the number of people who are allowed to legally move to the United States to live and work be increased, decreased, or kept the same as it is now?" (alpha = 0.69). The ANES did include a separate question on birthright citizenship, but it was not strongly correlated with these other two items.

- Views of Muslims are measured with three items: a feeling thermometer recoded so that 0 = warmest feelings and 1 = coolest feelings and questions asking how well the terms *lazy* and *violent* described Muslims (coded in five categories from 0 = not at all well to 1 = very well). The reliability of this scale is 0.78.

- Views of racial inequality are measured by combining the same four items as in the VOTER Survey (alpha = 0.76).

- Economic anxiety is measured with five questions: "Would you say that as compared to one year ago, the nation's economy is now better, about the same, or worse? (coded in five categories from 0 = much better to 1 = much worse); "What about 12 months from now? Compared to now, do you think the nation's economy will be better, about the same, or worse in 12 months?" (coded in five categories from 0 = much better to 1 = much worse); "How much opportunity is there in America today for the average person to get ahead?" (coded in five categories from 0 = a great deal to 1 = none); "Compared to your parents, do you think it is easier, harder, or neither easier nor harder for you to move up the income ladder?" (coded in seven categories from 0 = a great deal easier to 1 = a great deal harder); and "Do you think people's ability to improve their financial well-being is now better, worse, or the same as it was 20 years ago?" (coded in seven categories from 0 = a great deal easier to 1 = a great deal harder). The scale's reliability is 0.66.

- Economic liberalism is a scale combining these questions: "Should the minimum wage be raised, kept the same, lowered but not eliminated, or eliminated altogether?" (coded from 0 = eliminated to 1 = raised); "Do you favor an increase, decrease, or no change in government spending to help people pay for health insurance when they can't pay for it all themselves?" (coded in seven categories from 0 = decrease a great deal to 1 = increase a great deal); and "Do you favor an increase, decrease, or no change in government spending to help working parents pay for child care when they can't pay for it all themselves?" (coded in seven categories from 0 = decrease a great deal to 1 = increase a great deal). The scale's reliability is 0.73.

- "Do not identify as strong conservative" is based on a five-category measure of ideological self-identification, coded so that 0 = strong conservative and 1 = all other responses.

Table A5.1
Models of Support for Donald Trump in the Republican Primary

	July 2016 VOTER Survey	December 2015 PEPS	January 2016 ANES Pilot Study	
Strength of white identity				3.21*
				(0.63)
Opposition to immigration	1.08*	1.66*	1.18*	0.63
	(0.20)	(0.36)	(0.53)	(0.56)
Coolness toward Muslims	0.35	0.67*	1.47*	0.90
	(0.19)	(0.27)	(0.51)	(0.54)
Views of racial inequality	1.12*	0.91*	2.39*	2.46*
	(0.27)	(0.35)	(0.70)	(0.75)
Economic anxiety	0.12	−0.05	−1.27	−0.95
	(0.19)	(0.24)	(0.74)	(0.77)
Importance of Social Security and Medicare	0.40*			
	(0.16)			
Importance of terrorism	−0.02			
	(0.15)			
Economic liberalism	0.29*	1.54*	1.89*	2.01*
	(0.10)	(0.34)	(0.56)	(0.60)
Do not identify as strong conservative	0.48*	−0.06	0.64*	0.71
	(0.12)	(0.20)	(0.29)	(0.38)
Opposed to increasing trade	0.08		0.29	0.28
	(0.13)		(0.47)	(0.48)
Lack of political efficacy		0.14		
		(0.24)		
Laid off or unemployed	1.14*	0.03	0.14	0.58
	(0.23)	(0.43)	(0.45)	(0.47)
Family income	−0.01	0.01	−0.09	−0.61
	(0.27)	(0.02)	(0.67)	(0.69)
Education	−1.14*	−1.86*	−0.51	−0.36
	(0.18)	(0.36)	(0.45)	(0.46)
Male	0.07	0.31*	0.09	0.20
	(0.10)	(0.16)	(0.24)	(0.25)
Age	0.58*	−0.11	0.40	0.09
	(0.22)	(0.43)	(0.54)	(0.56)
Constant	−2.59*	−2.76*	−4.48*	−5.67*
	(0.34)	(0.55)	(1.00)	(1.11)
N	2,633	1,044	371	371

Note: Cell entries are logit coefficients with standard errors in parentheses. The dependent variable is coded 1 for Trump and 0 for all other candidates (PEPS and ANES) or 0 for Kasich, Rubio, and Cruz (VOTER Survey). $p < .05$. For the VOTER Survey, all variables are measured in December 2011 except education, employment status, and income, which were measured in 2016. The VOTER Survey and ANES models also include a dummy variable for respondents who did not indicate their income. The sample is limited to self-reported Republican primary voters (VOTER Survey), likely Republican primary voters (PEPS), and self-identified Republicans (ANES).

- "Laid off or unemployed" is based on self-reported unemployment status, where 1 = temporarily laid off or unemployed and 0 = all other responses (employed, retired, student, and so on).
- Family income is measured in seventeen categories. Higher values equal higher incomes. The statistical model also includes a dummy variable to capture respondents who did not provide an income (about 9% of respondents).
- Education is measured in five categories. Higher values equal higher levels of formal education.
- Age is based on respondents' self-reported birth year, subtracted from 2016.

The models of voter choice in the Republican primary are presented in table A5.1.

Figure 5.7 is based on simultaneously shifting the indicated groups of variables from their minimum to maximum value. The resulting changes in predicted probabilities and associated confidence intervals were calculated using the SPost suite of commands for Stata.[1]

APPENDIX TO CHAPTER 6

Figure A6.1 presents the percentage of Democratic officeholders endorsing each individual Democratic candidate before the Iowa caucus took place. This shows, again, how much support Hillary Clinton locked up among Democratic Party leaders during the invisible primary.

Models of Preferences in the Democratic Primary

The appendix to chapter 5 described the three surveys and most of the variables used in the analysis in chapter 6. One important note about the American National Election Studies (ANES) Pilot Study is that all respondents were asked to state a preference in both the Democratic and Republican primaries, regardless of which primary they might participate in. Table A6.1 reports results for respondents who identified as Democrats, independents who leaned toward the Democratic Party, and independents who did not lean toward a party.

The models in table A6.1 present the relationship between support for Clinton or Sanders and, first, views of economic policy and trade (Model 1) and, second, the fuller range of factors (Model 2). Figure 6.12 in the text is based on the Views of the American Electorate Research (VOTER) Survey results in Model 2.

Additional models suggest that both sexism and attitudes toward racial, ethnic, and religious minorities were not strongly or consistently associated with preferences for Clinton or Sanders (table A6.2).

The measure of modern sexism is based on an index of agreement or disagreement with these statements:

- "When women demand equality these days, they are actually seeking special favors." (PEPS/VOTER Survey)

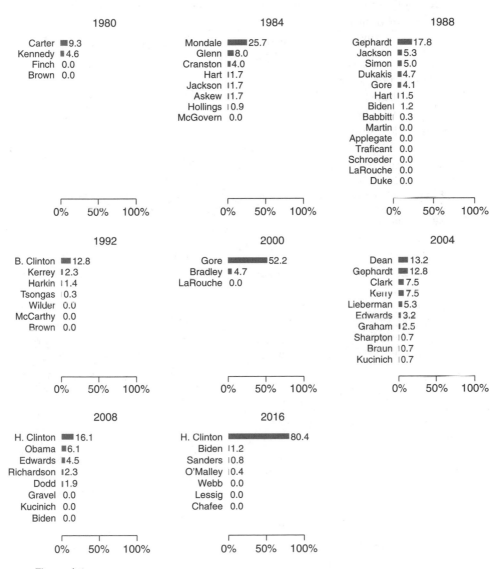

Figure A6.1.

Percent of possible pre-Iowa endorsements won by Democratic presidential candidates, 1980–2016.

The figure reflects endorsements by sitting Democratic governors, senators, and members of the House.

Table A6.1.

Models of Preferences for Hillary Clinton versus Bernie Sanders in the Democratic Primary

	July 2016 VOTER Survey	December 2015 PEPS	January 2016 ANES	
Model 1: Policy views only				
Economic policy liberalism	−0.25	1.63*	−0.87	
	(0.17)	(0.26)	(0.54)	
Opposed to increasing trade	−0.07			
	(0.11)			
Constant	0.52*	−1.12*	1.07*	
	(0.15)	(0.20)	(0.44)	
N	2,818	1,382	586	
Model 2: Multiple factors				
Economic policy liberalism	−0.23	−0.34	−1.28*	−0.57
	(0.20)	(0.34)	(0.62)	(0.63)
Opposed to increasing trade	−0.04			
	(0.12)			
Strength of Democratic partisanship	1.43*	1.77*	1.51*	1.40*
	(0.14)	(0.18)	(0.28)	(0.29)
Nonwhite	0.94*	0.86*	1.36*	1.05*
	(0.09)	(0.15)	(0.22)	(0.23)
Age	1.35*	2.16*	0.70	0.60
	(0.20)	(0.38)	(0.45)	(0.46)
Male	−0.05	−0.35*	0.05	−0.06
	(0.09)	(0.13)	(0.20)	(0.21)
View of economy	−0.63*	−0.68*	−0.78	−0.23
	(0.16)	(0.18)	(0.46)	(0.49)
Strength of liberal identification	−1.05*	−0.09	−1.61*	−1.58*
	(0.14)	(0.19)	(0.32)	(0.33)
Less trust in government	−0.35*			
	(0.12)			
Lack of political efficacy		−0.70*		
		(0.19)		
Views of economic mobility				−2.50*
				(0.50)
Constant	−0.35	−1.06	0.49	1.51*
	(0.24)	(0.33)	(0.58)	(0.63)
N	2,818	1,382	586	586

Note: Cell entries are logit coefficients with standard errors in parentheses. The dependent variable is coded 1 for Clinton and 0 for Sanders. For the VOTER Survey, candidate preferences were measured in July 2016, and all other variables were measured in December 2011. The sample is limited to self-reported Democratic primary voters (VOTER Survey), likely Democratic primary voters (Presidential Election Panel Survey [PEPS]), and self-identified Democrats, independents who lean toward the Democratic Party, and independents who do not lean toward a party (ANES). * $p < .05$.

Table A6.2.

Models of Preferences for Hillary Clinton versus Bernie Sanders in the Democratic Primary (with Additional Variables)

	July 2016 VOTER Survey	December 2015 PEPS	January 2016 ANES
Model 3: Including racial attitudes and modern sexism			
Economic policy liberalism	0.14	−0.55	0.21
	(0.22)	(0.37)	(0.69)
Opposed to increasing trade	−0.19		
	(0.13)		
Strength of Democratic partisanship	1.35*	1.74*	1.29*
	(0.14)	(0.18)	(0.30)
Nonwhite	1.06*	0.90*	1.08*
	(0.10)	(0.15)	(0.26)
Age	1.38*	2.13*	0.62
	(0.22)	(0.38)	(0.48)
Male	−0.02	−0.2	−0.01
	(0.14)	(0.19)	(0.22)
View of economy	−0.70*	−0.66*	−1.17*
	(0.17)	(0.18)	(0.56)
Strength of liberal identification	−1.00*	−0.1	−1.13*
	(0.15)	(0.20)	(0.35)
Less trust in government	−0.37*		
	(0.13)		
Lack of political efficacy		−0.71*	
		(0.20)	
Views of economic mobility			−2.67*
			(0.55)
Views of racial inequality	0.53*	−0.27	0.39
	(0.23)	(0.27)	(0.48)
Opposition to immigration	0.23	0.24	0.61
	(0.20)	(0.25)	(0.56)
Coolness toward Muslims	0.20	0.04	−1.73*
	(0.20)	(0.22)	(0.56)
Modern sexism	0.73	−0.27	
	(0.41)	(0.45)	
Modern sexism × male	−0.48	−0.46	
	(0.50)	(0.59)	
White identity			0.21
			(0.59)
Constant	−1.09*	−0.86*	0.25
	(0.33)	(0.42)	(0.74)
N	2,690	1,377	585

Note: Cell entries are logit coefficients with standard errors in parentheses. The dependent variable is coded 1 for Clinton and 0 for Sanders. For the VOTER Survey, candidate preferences were measured in July 2016 and all other variables were measured in December 2011 except modern sexism, which was measured after the election in December 2016. The sample is limited to self-reported Democratic primary voters (VOTER Survey), likely Democratic primary voters (PEPS), and self-identified Democrats, independents who lean toward the Democratic Party, and independents who do not lean toward a party (ANES). *$p < .05$.

- "Women often miss out on good jobs because of discrimination." (PEPS/VOTER Survey)
- "Women who complain about harassment cause more problems than they solve." (PEPS/VOTER Survey)
- "Sexual harassment against women in the workplace is no longer a problem in the United States." (VOTER Survey)
- "Increased opportunities for women have significantly improved the quality of life in the United States." (VOTER Survey)

The measures of views of racial inequality, immigration, and Muslims, as well as white identity, are described in the appendix to chapter 5. In both the VOTER Survey and the PEPS, there was no significant association between modern sexism and candidate preferences, including among men in particular. Similarly, views of minorities and white identity were not consistently associated with support for Clinton or Sanders. Views of racial inequality were associated with support for Clinton in the VOTER Survey but not in the PEPS or ANES. Coolness toward Muslims was associated with support for Clinton in the ANES but not the VOTER Survey or PEPS. In general, these attitudes appeared much less important in the Democratic primary than in the Republican primary.

APPENDIX TO CHAPTER 8

Part I: Activation of Identity-Related Attitudes

The analysis presented in figure 8.6 shows that white respondents' attitudes toward racial inequality, immigration, and Muslims were more strongly related to how people voted in the 2016 presidential election than in the 2012 election. This analysis relied on two surveys, the 2008–16 American National Election Studies (ANES) and the Views of the American Electorate Research (VOTER) Survey, which included interviews with 8,000 respondents in December 2011, November 2012, and December 2016.

Table A8.1 shows the statistical models using ANES data. A separate model was estimated for each election year. Each model included party identification (a seven-point scale ranging from strong Democrat to strong Republican) and self-reported ideology (a seven-point scale ranging from strong liberal to strong conservative). Views of racial inequality were measured by combining responses to four statements with which respondents could agree or disagree on a five-point scale:

- Over the past few years, Blacks have gotten less than they deserve.
- Irish, Italian, Jewish, and many other minorities overcame prejudice and worked their way up. Blacks should do the same without any special favors.
- It's really a matter of some people not trying hard enough; if Blacks would only try harder they could be just as well off as Whites.
- Generations of slavery and discrimination have created conditions that make it difficult for Blacks to work their way out of the lower class.

These four items scaled together reliably (alpha = 0.84 in the 2016 ANES). Views of "illegal immigrants" were measured with a 0–100 feeling thermometer.

The relationship between both views of racial inequality and illegal immigrants and vote choice was larger in 2016 than in 2008 or 2012 (table A8.1). This was apparent first

Table A8.1.
Models of Whites' Vote Choice, 2008–16 American National Election Studies

	2008	2012	2016	2008–16	2008	2012	2016	2008–16
Party identification	4.88* (0.36)	5.75* (0.26)	4.92* (0.32)	5.29* (0.18)	4.92* (0.35)	5.71* (0.26)	4.54* (0.29)	5.16* (0.17)
Ideology	4.28* (0.64)	4.37* (0.42)	3.45* (0.56)	4.09* (0.30)	4.45* (0.50)	4.70* (0.41)	4.37* (0.52)	4.52* (0.28)
Views of racial inequality	3.26* (0.46)	3.28* (0.32)	5.36* (0.41)	3.20* (0.30)				
Views of illegal immigrants					1.06* (0.41)	1.63* (0.28)	3.08* (0.34)	1.60* (0.27)
Racial inequality × 2008				0.11 (0.56)				
Racial inequality × 2016				2.37* (0.51)				
Illegal immigrants × 2008								−0.55 (0.50)
Illegal immigrants × 2016								1.57* (0.44)
Year 2008				−0.04 (0.39)				0.39 (0.34)
Year 2016				−1.02* (0.34)				−0.70* (0.30)
Constant	−6.65* (0.48)	−7.16* (0.33)	−7.13* (0.40)	−6.74* (0.27)	−5.30* (0.41)	−6.22* (0.30)	−6.12* (0.34)	−5.84* (0.24)
N	775	2,530	2,021	5,326	777	2,525	2,008	5,310

Note: Cell entries are logit coefficients with standard errors in parentheses. The dependent variable is coded 1 = Trump and 0 = Clinton. Party identification and ideology are coded such that higher values equal stronger Republican and conservative identification, respectively. Views of racial inequality and views of illegal immigrants are coded such that higher values equal more emphasis on blacks' lack of effort and less favorable views of illegal immigrants, respectively. $p < .05$.
Source: ANES 2008–16.

from estimating separate models in each of these years (which underlie figure 8.6). Pooling the data and estimating a single model that allowed the relationship of these two measures to vary by year showed that the differences between 2016 and earlier years were statistically significant.

Similar models using the 2016 VOTER Survey showed a similar pattern (table A8.2). The data were based on three waves of interviewing: December 2011 (when all independent variables were measured), November 2012 (when vote for Obama or Romney was measured), and December 2016 (when vote for Clinton or Trump was measured). Again, the use of measures from December 2011 guarded against the possibility that people changed their views of these issues to match the views of their preferred candidate.

Here, party identification, ideology, and views of racial inequality were measured in a similar fashion. Views of immigration were captured with a scale based on three items: support for or opposition to a path to citizenship for undocumented immigrants, beliefs about whether undocumented immigrants contribute to society or are a "drain," and beliefs about whether immigration should be increased or decreased. These items also scaled together reliably (alpha = 0.72). Views of Muslims were captured with a 0–100 feeling thermometer. All models included only whites who reported voting in both elections.

The results again showed that the relationship between vote choice and views of racial inequality, immigration, and Muslims was larger in 2016 than in 2012. Models that pooled the 2012 and 2016 waves of the survey showed that these differences across years are statistically significant.

Finally, models using surveys from 2004, 2012, and 2016 showed that whites' perceptions of how much discrimination they face became more strongly related to vote choice in 2016 (table A8.3). These models also account for party identification, ideology, and a two-item measure of views of racial inequality ("Blacks have gotten less than they deserve" and "Blacks should do the same without any special favors"), which were the only two items included in all three surveys. Again, models estimated separately by year showed this larger relationship. The difference between 2016 and the two earlier elections was statistically significant in a model that pooled all three surveys.

This pattern was confirmed in the 2016 VOTER Survey, with the important caveat that perceptions of discrimination against whites were measured in the December 2016 interview and could thus have been affected by the campaign itself. Nevertheless, the relationship between those perceptions and whites' choice of Clinton or Trump ($b = 2.05$; s.e. = 0.25) was larger than with those same whites' choice of Obama or Romney ($b = 1.14$; s.e. = 0.21), and this difference was statistically significant ($p = .02$). These models also accounted for party identification, ideology, and views of racial inequality as measured in the December 2016 wave.

Part II: Activation of Economic Anxiety

Similar models undergird the analysis of economic anxiety and whether its relationship to presidential vote choice increased in 2016 (see figure 8.7). This analysis draws on the 2012 and 2016 ANES, which asked a battery of questions about respondents' economic circumstances, including their level of worry about losing their job, whether they were likely to miss a housing payment, whether they were likely to miss a health care payment, and their overall level of worry about their financial situation. (Note: In the 2012 ANES, the question about missing a housing payment was asked only of respondents interviewed face to face, not respondents interviewed online. This explains the smaller sample in that statistical model.) Separate statistical models in 2012 and 2016 show no consistent

Table A8.2.
Models of Whites' Vote Choice, 2016 VOTER Survey

	2012	2016	2012–16	2012	2016	2012–16	2012	2016	2012–16
Party identification	5.30* (0.22)	3.96* (0.20)	4.50* (0.14)	5.38* (0.23)	4.00* (0.21)	4.62* (0.14)	5.07* (0.23)	4.03* (0.21)	4.50* (0.15)
Ideology	4.91* (0.35)	5.26* (0.34)	4.70* (0.22)	5.08* (0.35)	5.43* (0.35)	4.83* (0.22)	6.15* (0.39)	6.00* (0.37)	5.48* (0.23)
Views of racial inequality	3.63* (0.29)	4.33* (0.27)	3.65* (0.25)						
Views of immigration				2.44* (0.21)	3.31* (0.20)	1.95* (0.18)			
Views of Muslims							1.58* (0.24)	2.58* (0.23)	1.39* (0.21)
Racial inequality × 2016			0.75* (0.36)						
Immigration × 2016						1.53* (0.26)			
Muslims × 2016									1.19* (0.30)
Year 2016			−0.10 (0.26)			−0.53** (0.17)			−0.37* (0.18)
Constant	−7.44* (0.28)	−7.17* (0.26)	−7.01* (0.22)	−6.58* (0.24)	−6.41* (0.23)	−5.85* (0.17)	−6.42* (0.25)	−6.20* (0.24)	−5.71* (0.18)
N	5,152	5,152	11,167	5,111	5,111	11,088	4,743	4,743	10,269

Note: Cell entries are logit coefficients with standard errors in parentheses. The dependent variable is coded 1 = Trump and 0 = Clinton. Party identification and ideology are coded such that higher values equal stronger Republican and conservative identification, respectively. Racial resentment, views of immigration, and views of Muslims are coded such that higher values equal more emphasis on blacks' lack of effort or less favorable attitudes toward immigration and Muslims. All independent variables were measured in December 2011. * $p < .05$.
Source: VOTER Survey.

Table A8.3.

The Relationship between Whites' Perceptions of Discrimination against Whites and Vote for President

	2004	2012	2016	All 3 years
Perceived discrimination against whites	0.28 (0.40)	0.36 (0.33)	1.47* (0.39)	−0.24 (0.33)
Views of racial inequality	0.85* (0.41)	3.05* (0.32)	4.45* (0.38)	2.91* (0.20)
Party identification	8.88* (0.49)	5.48* (0.27)	4.81* (0.32)	5.94* (0.18)
Ideology	3.26* (0.41)	4.53* (0.45)	3.49* (0.56)	3.58* (0.25)
Perceived discrimination against whites × 2012				0.62 (0.46)
Perceived discrimination against whites × 2016				2.19* (0.52)
Year 2012				−0.18 (0.20)
Year 2016				−0.26 (0.22)
Constant	−6.68* (0.44)	−7.19* (0.35)	−7.19* (0.41)	−6.64* (0.26)
N	680	2,284	1,966	4,930

Note: Cell entries are logit coefficients with standard errors in parentheses. The dependent variable is coded 1 = Trump and 0 = Clinton. Party identification and ideology are coded such that higher values equal stronger Republican and conservative identification, respectively. The measure of ideology is a five-category scale in 2004 and a seven-category scale in 2012–16. Views of racial inequality and perceptions of discrimination against whites are coded such that higher values equal more emphasis on blacks' lack of effort and the perception of more discrimination against whites, respectively. The measure of perceived discrimination against whites is a four-category scale in 2004 and a five-category scale in 2012–16. $^*p<.05$. Sources: 2004 National Politics Survey; 2012–16 ANES.

statistically significant relationships between any of these items and white respondents' presidential vote choice in 2012 or 2016. Moreover, there was no consistent increase in the size of these relationships between 2012 and 2016 (table A8.4).

Combining these items into an omnibus measure of economic anxiety (alpha = 0.70 in the 2016 ANES) produced similar findings (table A8.5). Although the relationship between economic anxiety and presidential vote choice appeared larger in 2016 than 2012, this difference was not statistically significant. Moreover, the relationship between economic anxiety and vote choice was much smaller than the relationship between views of racial inequality and vote choice—and this latter relationship was larger in 2016 than 2012.

Several other findings support the conclusions of these models. For example, in the VOTER Survey, whites' subjective assessments of personal finances and the national economy (as measured in December 2011) were not more strongly related to voting in 2016 compared to 2012. (And even though these were measured in December 2011, they

Table A8.4.

The Relationship between Whites' Economic Anxiety and Vote for President

	2012	2016	2012	2016	2012	2016	2012	2016
Worry about losing job	0.85* (0.34)	−0.50 (0.38)						
Likelihood of missing housing payment			1.40* (0.52)	0.67 (0.40)				
Likelihood of missing health care payment					0.15 (0.20)	0.65* (0.26)		
Worry about financial situation							0.09 (0.23)	0.46 (0.29)
Views of racial inequality	2.90* (0.41)	6.06* (0.55)	2.35* (0.56)	5.22* (0.49)	3.31* (0.33)	5.29* (0.41)	3.32* (0.33)	5.28* (0.41)
Party identification	5.04* (0.36)	4.81* (0.42)	5.17* (0.52)	4.77* (0.39)	5.48* (0.27)	5.01* (0.33)	5.48* (0.27)	4.96* (0.32)
Ideology	4.89* (0.62)	3.68* (0.70)	3.69* (0.86)	4.02* (0.66)	4.58* (0.45)	3.46* (0.57)	4.57* (0.45)	3.50* (0.56)
Constant	−6.94* (0.43)	−7.59* (0.53)	−6.20* (0.58)	−7.48* (0.51)	−7.17* (0.35)	−7.40* (0.42)	−7.16* (0.35)	−7.33* (0.43)
N	1,266	1,324	403	1,395	2,282	2,014	2,285	2,019

Note: Cell entries are logit coefficients with standard errors in parentheses. The dependent variable is coded 1 = Trump and 0 = Clinton. Party identification and ideology are coded such that higher values equal stronger Republican and conservative identification, respectively. Views of racial inequality are coded such that higher values equal more emphasis on blacks' lack of effort. The economic measures are coded such that higher values indicate more concern or worry. * $p < .05$.

Source: 2012–16 ANES.

Table A8.5.
The Relationship between Whites' Economic Anxiety (Omnibus Index) and
Vote for President

	2012	2016	2012–16
Economic anxiety index	0.31	0.76*	0.44
	(0.28)	(0.37)	(0.27)
Economic anxiety index × 2016			0.13
			(0.44)
Views of racial inequality	3.29*	5.24*	3.84*
	(0.33)	(0.41)	(0.27)
Views of racial inequality × 2016			0.75**
			(0.28)
Party identification	5.49*	5.01*	5.25*
	(0.27)	(0.33)	(0.21)
Ideology	4.59*	3.45*	4.15*
	(0.45)	(0.56)	(0.35)
Constant	−7.21*	−7.36*	−7.31*
	(0.35)	(0.43)	(0.27)
N	2,287	2,021	4,308

Note: Cell entries are logit coefficients with standard errors in parentheses. The dependent variable is coded 1 = Trump and 0 = Clinton. Party identification and ideology are coded such that higher values equal stronger Republican and conservative identification, respectively. Views of racial inequality are coded such that higher values equal more emphasis on blacks' lack of effort. The economic measures are coded such that higher values indicate more concern or worry. * $p < .05$.
Source: 2012–16 ANES.

were still strongly affected by partisanship even then, making any correlation with voting behavior potentially spurious.)[1]

A stronger test is to compute changes in people's subjective assessments between December 2011 and December 2016 and see whether this was correlated with how people voted in 2016. People whose assessments worsened could have favored Trump, whereas those whose assessments improved could have favored Clinton. But there was no such correlation, once party identification, ideology, and views of racial inequality were taken into account. Similarly, in a model of 2016 vote choice that included only 2012 vote choice and changes in economic assessments, these assessments had no statistically significant impact.

Part III: Activation of Sexism

The analysis of gender attitudes relies on a measure described as "modern sexism." In the VOTER Survey, this was measured with five items, each of which asked respondents how much they agreed or disagreed with these statements:

- Women should return to their traditional roles in society.
- When women demand equality these days, they are actually seeking special favors.
- Women often miss out on good jobs because of discrimination.

Table A8.6.

The Relationship between Whites' Modern Sexism and Vote for President (VOTER Survey)

	White women			White men		
	2012	2016	2012–16	2016	2012	2012–16
Modern sexism	2.67*	3.09*	1.92*	1.76*	4.20*	1.41**
	(0.42)	(0.48)	(0.39)	(0.49)	(0.65)	(0.47)
Views of racial inequality	2.32*	3.59*	2.89*	2.56*	4.61*	3.31*
	(0.35)	(0.41)	(0.23)	(0.42)	(0.54)	(0.30)
Party identification	4.32*	4.72*	4.29*	5.17*	5.84*	5.50*
	(0.30)	(0.34)	(0.21)	(0.35)	(0.43)	(0.26)
Ideology	1.89*	3.36*	3.02*	6.10*	8.44*	6.76*
	(0.50)	(0.60)	(0.34)	(0.62)	(0.82)	(0.45)
Modern sexism × 2016			1.12*			1.61*
			(0.57)			(0.65)
Year 2016			0.18			−0.28
			(0.20)			(0.28)
Constant	−5.61*	−7.15*	−6.51*	−7.91*	−11.44*	−8.77*
	(0.32)	(0.41)	(0.26)	(0.43)	(0.72)	(0.36)
N	2,438	2,438	5,311	2,540	2,540	5,487

Note: Cell entries are logit coefficients with standard errors in parentheses. The dependent variable is coded 1 = Trump and 0 = Clinton. Party identification and ideology are coded such that higher values equal stronger Republican and conservative identification, respectively. Views of racial inequality are coded such that higher values equal more emphasis on blacks' lack of effort. Modern sexism is coded such that higher values equal higher levels of sexism. * $p < .05$.
Source: VOTER Survey.

- Women who complain about harassment often cause more problems than they solve.
- Sexual harassment against women in the workplace is no longer a problem in the United States.

In addition, the statistical models included views of racial inequality (measured as described earlier), party identification, and ideology (table A8.6). These models show the activation of sexism in 2016 compared to 2012.

The pattern in the VOTER Survey data emerges in the ANES as well (table A8.7), although only two of the items measuring modern sexism were included in these surveys ("special favors" and "complain about harassment").

Part IV: SpotCheck Advertising Analysis

The SpotCheck project was led by political scientists Lynn Vavreck and John Geer in collaboration with the survey firm YouGov, G2 Analytics, and SageEngage. Each week between February 2016 and Election Day, a representative sample of Americans was randomly assigned to three groups: two groups watched one of two political ads and a

Table A8.7.

The Relationship between Whites' Modern Sexism and Vote for President (ANES)

	White women			White men		
	2012	2016	2012–16	2012	2016	2012–16
Modern sexism	0.93	2.10*	0.74	1.64**	2.99*	1.47**
	(0.58)	(0.60)	(0.57)	(0.57)	(0.70)	(0.55)
Views of racial inequality	2.81*	5.23*	3.78*	3.27*	4.41*	3.76*
	(0.45)	(0.58)	(0.35)	(0.53)	(0.61)	(0.40)
Party identification	5.06*	4.82*	4.91*	5.98*	5.05*	5.59*
	(0.36)	(0.43)	(0.27)	(0.43)	(0.51)	(0.32)
Ideology	5.01*	2.81*	4.16*	4.18*	3.59*	3.88*
	(0.64)	(0.77)	(0.49)	(0.67)	(0.91)	(0.53)
Modern sexism × 2016			1.67*			1.89*
			(0.82)			(0.88)
Constant	−7.08*	−7.19*	−7.64*	−7.63*	−7.14*	−7.55*
	(0.49)	(0.57)	(0.54)	(0.64)	(0.40)	(0.42)
N	1,151	1,036	1,094	932	2,187	2,026

Note: Cell entries are logit coefficients with standard errors in parentheses. The dependent variable is coded 1 = Trump and 0 = Clinton. Party identification and ideology are coded such that higher values equal stronger Republican and conservative identification, respectively. Views of racial inequality are coded such that higher values equal more emphasis on blacks' lack of effort. Modern sexism is coded such that higher values equal higher levels of sexism. $*p<.05$.
Source: 2012–16 ANES.

third group watched a nonpolitical ad (for Nationwide Insurance, featuring Peyton Manning). Respondents rated the ads as they watched them and afterward answered questions about the ads and the candidates.

The analysis in this chapter uses the eighteen weeks of data from June 6—after Clinton and Trump had officially won enough delegates to become their parties' nominees—to Election Day ($N=23,000$). In most of these weeks, the ads tested were attack ads: seventeen waves between June 6 and Election Day tested an attack on Trump ($N=8,220$ saw one of these ads), and twelve waves tested an attack on Clinton ($N=4,240$).

We measured views of the candidates first with three-category favorability scales (−1 = somewhat or very unfavorable, 0 = neither favorable nor unfavorable, +1 = somewhat or very favorable). We also asked people their vote intentions, which we then measured two ways: as a binary variable capturing preference for Clinton or Trump (excluding those who were undecided or supported a third-party candidate) and as a three-category variable that placed undecided and third-party voters in the middle category. We modeled views of the candidates as a function of which ad respondents had seen (an anti-Clinton or an anti-Trump ad, with those who saw the Nationwide ad as the excluded category). The analysis also accounted for age, race, education, party identification, and gender. (Accounting for the amount of time until the election did not change these estimates.)

Table A8.8.

Treatment Effects of Campaign Ads in SpotCheck Experiments

	Vote intention (three categories)	Vote intention (two categories)	Trump favorability	Clinton favorability
Model 1:				
Saw attack on Trump	0.016	0.009	−0.020	0.014
	(0.009)	(0.005)	(0.012)	(0.011)
N	15,003	12,699	14,807	14,850
Model 2:				
Saw attack on Trump	0.01	0.01	0.01	0.01
	(0.02)	(0.01)	(0.02)	(0.02)
Saw attack × Democrat	0.01	0.002	−0.04	0.02
	(0.03)	(0.02)	(0.03)	(0.03)
Saw attack × independent	0.08	0.05	−0.10	0.04
	(0.03)	(0.02)	(0.03)	(0.03)
N	15,003	12,699	14,807	14,850
Model 3:				
Saw attack on Trump	−0.003	−0.01	−0.02	−0.02
	(0.02)	(0.01)	(0.02)	(0.02)
Saw attack × college grad	0.03	0.03	−0.01	0.06
	(0.02)	(0.01)	(0.02)	(0.02)
N	15,003	12,699	14,807	14,850
Model 4:				
Saw attack on Clinton	0.002	−0.01	0.03	−0.02
	(0.01)	(0.01)	(0.02)	(0.01)
N	8,650	7,423	8,563	8,572
Model 5:				
Saw attack on Clinton	−0.03	−0.03	0.04	−0.03
	(0.02)	(0.01)	(0.03)	(0.02)
Saw attack × college grad	0.04	0.03	−0.02	0.03
	(0.03)	(0.01)	(0.03)	(0.03)
N	8,650	7,423	8,563	8,572
Model 6:				
Saw attack on Clinton	−0.02	−0.01	0.05	−0.01
	(0.03)	(0.01)	(0.03)	(0.03)
Saw attack × Democrat	0.06	0.02	−0.09	0.03
	(0.04)	(0.02)	(0.04)	(0.04)
Saw attack × independent	0.04	0.02	−0.02	−0.03
	(0.04)	(0.02)	(0.04)	(0.04)
N	8,650	7,423	8,563	8,572

Note: Each model also includes these covariates: race/ethnicity, age, education, gender, and party identification. Models including interactions include all constituent terms of the interaction. Cell entries are least squares regression coefficients with standard errors in parentheses.
Source: SpotCheck.

Table A8.9.
The Relationship between Vote Share and Television Ads and Field Offices in U.S. Counties

	Cumulative ads (June 1–Election Day)		Ads in last week of campaign only		Number of field offices	
	Coefficient	Standard error	Coefficient	Standard error	Coefficient	Standard error
2012 Democratic vote share	0.856	0.016	0.857	0.016	0.855	0.016
Clinton ads (1,000s)	0.099	0.061	0.734	0.399		
Trump ads (1,000s)	−0.276	0.221	−0.152	0.578		
Obama 2012 ads			−0.524	0.362		
Romney 2012 ads			−0.091	0.311		
Clinton field offices					0.299	0.130
Obama 2012 field offices					0.046	0.099
No ads in media market	−0.264	0.203	−0.308	0.205		
Unemployment rate	0.071	0.077	0.075	0.079	0.067	0.078
Change in unemployment	−0.130	0.063	−0.126	0.062	−0.128	0.062
Median income ($1,000s)	−0.020	0.017	−0.021	0.017	−0.020	0.017
Change in income	−0.030	0.018	−0.030	0.018	−0.029	0.018
Population (millions)	0.513	0.370	0.501	0.362	0.295	0.308

	(1)		(2)		(3)	
Change in population (persons)	0.001	0.005	0.002	0.005	0.002	0.006
% college degree	0.454	0.026	0.454	0.027	0.448	0.026
Change in % college degree	−0.169	0.024	−0.169	0.024	−0.166	0.024
% no HS degree	0.101	0.028	0.099	0.028	0.098	0.027
Change in % no HS degree	−0.045	0.029	−0.044	0.029	−0.045	0.028
% Latino	0.104	0.014	0.103	0.014	0.105	0.014
Change in % Latino	−0.051	0.076	−0.054	0.077	−0.049	0.077
% black	0.162	0.014	0.162	0.014	0.161	0.014
Change in % black	−0.293	0.095	−0.290	0.094	−0.250	0.089
Median age	−0.073	0.016	−0.071	0.016	−0.071	0.016
Constant	−11.406	1.275	−11.457	1.293	−11.230	1.305
Fixed effects for states	Y		Y		Y	
N of counties	3,107		3,109		3,109	
N of states	49		49		49	
R-squared	0.97		0.97		0.97	

Note: Cell entries are least squares regression coefficients with estimated standard errors clustered by state. The dependent variable is Hillary Clinton's percentage of the major-party vote.

Table A8.8 presents the results of the models. First, neither Trump's attacks on Clinton nor her attacks on him affected her favorability ratings. Second, Trump's favorability ratings were 2 points lower among those who saw an ad attacking him and 2.7 points higher among those who saw an ad attacking Clinton. Third, in the model of three-category vote intentions, Clinton's vote share was 1.6 points higher among those who saw an attack on Trump, compared to those who saw the nonpolitical ad. (In the model of two-category vote intentions, it was about 1 point higher.) By contrast, there is little difference between those who saw an attack on Clinton and the control group.

The results also suggest that at least two groups were particularly affected by Clinton's attacks on Trump: political independents and those with college degrees. That political independents would respond more strongly is unsurprising, given that they have weaker preexisting loyalties to the parties and are thus more susceptible to the influence of campaign information. The larger reaction among college-educated voters suggests that Clinton's appeals were particularly effective among those predisposed to agree with her attacks on Trump's temperament and his treatment of women and racial and ethnic minorities. Trump's attacks on Clinton appeared to have a polarizing effect: increasing support for Trump among Republicans but increasing support for Clinton among Democrats.

Part V: Analysis of Television Advertising and Field Offices

The analyses of the relationship between vote share and both television advertising and field offices are based on statistical models of all counties in the United States (exclusive of boroughs in Alaska and Washington, DC), as shown in table A8.9. The dependent variable is Clinton's share of the major-party vote in each county. The television advertising data are from Kantar Media/Campaign Media Analysis Group under license to authors. Ads are measured in terms of thousands of ads aired (not gross ratings points) and include ads aired by the candidates' campaigns and by outside groups supporting each candidate. The field office data are from Clinton's campaign website and Obama's 2012 campaign website. Field offices are measured as the number of field offices in a county. The demographic variables are from the U.S. Census and the American Community Survey. Contemporaneous measures are from 2016, and changes in these measures are between 2012 and 2016. All statistical models also include fixed effects for states. The standard errors are clustered at the level of the state.

NOTES

Chapter 1: Fayetteville

1. For more on the Jones attack, see "Man Charged with Assaulting Protester during Trump Rally in Fayetteville," WRAL, March 10, 2016, http://www.wral.com/man -charged-with-assaulting-protesters-during-trump-rally-in-fayetteville/15513151/; Justin Wm. Moyer, Jenny Starrs, and Sarah Larimer, "Trump Supporter Charged after Sucker-Punching Protester in North Carolina Rally," *Washington Post*, March 11, 2016, https:// www.washingtonpost.com/news/morning-mix/wp/2016/03/10/trump-protester -sucker-punched-at-north-carolina-rally-videos-show/?utm_term=.f913a6b826c3.

2. See Kate Sommers-Dawes, "All the Times Trump Has Called for Violence at His Rallies," *Mashable*, March 12, 2016, http://mashable.com/2016/03/12/trump-rally-incite -violence/#vD4oqhHgdiqw.

3. An excellent overview of group identity and its role in politics is Leonie Huddy, "From Group Identity to Political Cohesion and Commitment," in *The Oxford Handbook of Political Psychology*, 2nd ed., ed. Leonie Huddy, David O. Sears, and Jack S. Levy (New York: Oxford University Press, 2013), 737–73.

4. On the conditions under which in-group identity and out-group hostility are activated, see Donald Kinder and Cindy Kam, *Us against Them: Ethnocentric Foundations of American Opinion* (Chicago: University of Chicago Press, 2009).

5. Pew Research Center, "On Views of Race and Inequality, Blacks and Whites Are Worlds Apart: 2. Views of Race Relations," June 27, 2016, http://www.pewsocialtrends .org/2016/06/27/2-views-of-race-relations/.

6. Michael Kranish and Robert O'Harrow Jr., "Inside the Government's Racial Bias Case against Donald Trump's Company, and How He Fought It," *Washington Post*, January 23, 2016, https://www.washingtonpost.com/politics/inside-the-governments-racial -bias-case-against-donald-trumps-company-and-how-he-fought-it/2016/01/23/fb90163e -bfbe-11e5-bcda-62a36b394160_story.html; Benjy Sarlin, "Donald Trump Says Central

Park Five Are Guilty, Despite DNA Evidence," NBC News, October 7, 2016, http://www
.nbcnews.com/politics/2016-election/donald-trump-says-central-park-five-are-guilty
-despite-dna-n661941.

7. Matt Grossmann, "Donald Trump Learned Overt Nativism from Losing His First
Campaign to Pat Buchanan," *Vox*, April 7, 2016, https://www.vox.com/polyarchy/2016/4
/7/11368658/trump-nativism-buchanan; Michael Tesler, "Birtherism Was Why So Many
Republicans Liked Trump in the First Place," *Monkey Cage* (blog), *Washington Post*,
September 19, 2016, https://www.washingtonpost.com/news/monkey-cage/wp/2016/09/19
/birtherism-was-why-so-many-republicans-liked-trump-in-the-first-place/?utm_term
=.cbc12291fadc; Michael Barbaro, "Donald Trump Clung to 'Birther' Lie for Years, and
Still Isn't Apologetic," *New York Times*, September 16, 2016, https://www.nytimes.com
/2016/09/17/us/politics/donald-trump-obama-birther.html.

8. We owe this distinction between waves and reservoirs to Larry Bartels, "The
'Wave' of Right-Wing Populist Sentiment Is a Myth," *Monkey Cage* (blog), *Washington
Post*, June 21, 2017, https://www.washingtonpost.com/news/monkey-cage/wp/2017/06
/21/the-wave-of-right-wing-populist-sentiment-is-a-myth/?utm_term=.89ae9a
42ab4f.

Chapter 2: "Whaddaya Got?"

1. Chuck Todd, "America: In Search of a Political Reset in 2016," NBC News, November 3, 2015, http://www.nbcnews.com/meet-the-press/america-search-political-reset-2016
-n456216.

2. Robert P. Jones, Daniel Cox, Betsy Cooper, and Rachel Lienesch, *Anxiety, Nostalgia,
and Mistrust: Findings from the 2015 American Value Survey* (Washington, DC: Public
Religion Research Institute, 2015), http://publicreligion.org/site/wp-content/uploads
/2015/11/PRRI-AVS-2015.pdf.

3. Carmen M. Reinhart and Kenneth Rogoff, *This Time Is Different: Eight Centuries
of Financial Folly* (Princeton: Princeton University Press, 2009).

4. The 1981–92 recession is dated to July 1981, when the unemployment rate was
7.2 percent. The unemployment rate reached 7.2 percent again in June 1984. At the beginning of the Great Recession, in December 2007, the unemployment rate was 5 percent.
It did not reach 5 percent again until October 2015.

5. Fred Dews, "'Misery Index' at Lowest Level," Brookings Institution, January 11,
2016, http://www.brookings.edu/blogs/brookings-now/posts/2016/01/misery-index-lowest
-level-since-1950s.

6. Thomas Piketty and Emmanuel Saez, "Income Inequality in the United States,
1913–1998," *Quarterly Journal of Economics* 118, no. 1 (2003): 1–39. Their updated data is
here: http://eml.berkeley.edu/~saez/TabFig2014prel.xls. See also Drew DeSilver, "For
Most Workers, Real Wages Have Barely Budged for Decades," Pew Research Center, October 9, 2014, http://www.pewresearch.org/fact-tank/2014/10/09/for-most-workers-real
-wages-have-barely-budged-for-decades/; and Chad Stone, Danilo Trisi, Arloc Sherman, and Roderick Taylor, "A Guide to Statistics on Historical Trends in Income Inequality," Center on Budget and Policy Priorities, 2015, http://www.cbpp.org/research
/poverty-and-inequality/a-guide-to-statistics-on-historical-trends-in-income
-inequality.

7. See the Census data here: http://www2.census.gov/programs-surveys/cps/tables
/time-series/historical-income-families/f03ar.xls. Income measures different from those

used by the Census Bureau showed even stronger growth between 2009 and 2015. See Gary Burtless, "Census Report of Big Jump in Income Is a Little Too Good to Be True," Brookings Institution, September 16, 2016, https://www.brookings.edu/blog/up-front /2016/09/16/census-report-of-big-jump-in-income-is-a-little-too-good-to-be-true/. The net worth of most groups—including racial minorities and whites without college degrees—also increased between 2013 and 2016. See Heather Long and Tracy Jan, "Minorities and Americans without College Degrees Showed Greatest Gains in Wealth since 2013, New Data Shows," *Washington Post*, September 27, 2017, https://www.washingtonpost .com/news/wonk/wp/2017/09/27/since-2013-minorities-and-americans-without-college -degrees-showed-greatest-gains-in-wealth-federal-reserve-report-shows/?noredirect =on&utm_term=.c8b7fa313248.

8. Pew Research Center, "The American Middle Class Is Losing Ground," December 9, 2015, http://www.pewsocialtrends.org/2015/12/09/the-american-middle-class-is -losing-ground/; Chris Arnade, "Working-Class Americans Feel Screwed. I Heard It across the Entire Country," *Guardian*, October 14, 2015, http://www.theguardian.com/us -news/2015/oct/14/donald-trump-working-class-americans-feel-screwed; Charlie Cook, "Economic Blues Define Campaign," *Cook Political Report*, April 22, 2016, http:// cookpolitical.com/story/9554.

9. The questions that make up the index are as follows: "We are interested in how people are getting along financially these days. Would you say that you (and your family living there) are better off or worse off financially than you were a year ago?"; "Now looking ahead—do you think that a year from now you (and your family living there) will be better off financially, or worse off, or just about the same as now?"; "Now turning to business conditions in the country as a whole—do you think that during the next twelve months we'll have good times financially, or bad times, or what?"; "Looking ahead, which would you say is more likely—that in the country as a whole we'll have continuous good times during the next five years or so, or that we will have periods of widespread unemployment or depression, or what?"; and "About the big things people buy for their homes—such as furniture, a refrigerator, stove, television, and things like that. Generally speaking, do you think now is a good or bad time for people to buy major household items?"

10. The average value over the first three quarters of 1984 was about 98. The average over the first three quarters of 2016 was 91.

11. During the Obama administration, the gap between the lowest and highest income terciles was 13.6 points. This was lower than during the administrations of George H. W. Bush (14.7), Bill Clinton (16.7), George W. Bush (18.4), and Ronald Reagan (21.3). And although the gap between those with a college degree and those with a high school degree or less was not distinctively low during the Obama administration, neither was it distinctively high compared to previous administrations.

12. On the debate about views of inequality and policy attitudes, see, for example, Nathan J. Kelley and Peter K. Enns, "Inequality and the Dynamics of Public Opinion: The Self-Reinforcing Link between Economic Inequality and Mass Preferences," *American Journal of Political Science* 54, no. 4 (2010): 855–70; Christopher D. Johnston and Benjamin J. Newman, "Economic Inequality and U.S. Public Policy Mood across Space and Time," *American Politics Review* 44, no. 1 (2016): 164–91; Graham Wright, "The Political Implications of American Concerns about Economic Inequality," *Political Behavior* (forthcoming); Larry M. Bartels, *Unequal Democracy: The Political Economy of the New Gilded Age*, 2nd ed. (Princeton: Princeton University Press, 2016); and Leslie McCall, *The*

Undeserving Rich: American Beliefs about Inequality, Opportunity, and Redistribution (New York: Cambridge University Press, 2013).

13. Christopher Achen and Larry M. Bartels, *Democracy for Realists* (Princeton: Princeton University Press, 2017); Christopher Wlezien, "The Myopic Voter? The Economy and US Presidential Elections," *Electoral Studies* 39 (2015): 195–204; Achen and Bartels, *Democracy for Realists*, 175. Their reference is to Donald A. Redelmeier, Joel Katz, and Daniel Kahneman, "Memories of Colonoscopy: A Randomized Trial," *Pain* 104 (2003): 187–94.

14. Charles Franklin (@PollsAndVotes), "Right direction/wrong track has been asked 2,770 times since 1/20/81. In that time wrong track has been larger in 88% of polls," Twitter, October 23, 2016, https://twitter.com/PollsAndVotes/status/790262467926646784. Scott Clement, "What's Wrong with the 'Right or Wrong Track' Polling Numbers," *Washington Post*, October 28, 2016, https://www.washingtonpost.com/opinions/whats -wrong-with-the-right-or-wrong-track-polling-numbers/2016/10/28/ccb0a14a-9c76-11e6 -b3c9-f662adaa0048_story.html?utm_term=.1f9331b56cd9; Nate Cohn, "Donald Trump vs. Hillary Clinton? Keep an Eye on Obama's Approval Rating," *New York Times*, July 29, 2016, http://www.nytimes.com/2016/07/30/upshot/how-unhappy-are-americans-and -what-does-it-mean-for-the-election.html?_r=1; Bradley Jones, "Presidential Approval a Stronger Indicator of Voter Choice than Satisfaction with the Country," Pew Research Center, September 21, 2016, http://www.nytimes.com/2016/07/30/upshot/how-unhappy -are-americans-and-what-does-it-mean-for-the-election.html?_r=1. On who people blamed, see William Jordan, "Does 'Right Direction/Wrong Track' Matter?," YouGov, August 12, 2016, https://today.yougov.com/news/2016/08/12/americans-are-unhappy -other-side/.

15. Pew Research Center, "Beyond Distrust: How Americans View Their Government," November 23, 2015, http://www.people-press.org/2015/11/23/beyond-distrust -how-americans-view-their-government/. Credit is due to the relatively few commentators who understood that there was no increase in anger. See, for example, Kevin Drum, "Charts of the Day: Americans Seem to Be About as Happy as Ever," *Mother Jones*, November 9, 2015, http://www.motherjones.com/kevin-drum/2015/11/charts-day-americans -seem-be-about-happy-ever; Aaron Blake, "Is 2016 the Anger Election? Not Quite," *Washington Post*, January 26, 2016, https://www.washingtonpost.com/news/the-fix/wp /2016/01/26/the-myth-of-the-angry-american-voter/; and Amy Walter, "Anger Management," *Cook Political Report*, May 19, 2016, http://cookpolitical.com/story/9625.

16. James A. Stimson, *Tides of Consent: How Public Opinion Shapes American Politics* (Cambridge: Cambridge University Press, 2014); Virginia A. Chanley, Thomas J. Rudolph, and Wendy M. Rahn, "The Origins and Consequences of Public Trust in Government: A Time Series Analysis," *Public Opinion Quarterly* 64, no. 3 (2000): 239–56; Luke Keele, "Social Capital and the Dynamics of Trust in Government," *American Journal of Political Science* 51, no. 2 (2007): 241–54.

17. In a least squares regression of approval on consumer sentiment, the coefficient for Obama (2009–16) is −0.14, with a standard error of 0.07. The results for the other presidents are as follows: Kennedy (b=0.52; s.e.=0.62), Johnson (b=2.08; s.e.=0.43), Nixon (b=0.86; s.e.=0.22), Ford (b=0.24; s.e.=0.10), Carter (b=0.86; s.e.=0.19), Reagan (b=0.25; s.e.=0.11), George H. W. Bush (b=0.45; s.e.=0.39), Clinton (b=0.62; s.e.=0.09), and George W. Bush (b=0.81; s.e.=0.26). The same finding emerges if approval is first regressed on the noneconomic factors in the model in John Sides and Lynn Vavreck, *The Gamble: Choice and Chance in the 2012 Presidential Election* (Princeton: Princeton Uni-

versity Press, 2013)—the Watergate scandal, Vietnam War deaths, positive and negative events, and the presence of divided government—and then the residuals from this regression are plotted in the same fashion. The unusual relationship between approval and consumer sentiment during the Obama years cannot be explained by these noneconomic factors.

18. To predict Obama's approval rating, we used the data in figure 2.5 and estimated a model of quarterly presidential approval from the years before the Obama presidency (1960–2008) that included consumer sentiment and fixed effects for each president. In the third quarter of 2016, the model predicted that 55 percent of Americans would approve of Obama, whereas his actual approval rating was 50 percent.

19. Sides and Vavreck, *The Gamble.*

20. Dan Balz, "The Republican Party's Uphill Path to 270 Electoral Votes in the 2016 Elections," *Washington Post*, January 18, 2014, https://www.washingtonpost.com/politics /the-gops-uphill-path-to-270-in-2016/2014/01/18/9404eb06-7fcf-11e3-93c1-0e888170b723 _story.html; Mark Halperin, "The Most Likely Next President Is Hillary Clinton," Bloomberg, October 26, 2015, http://www.bloomberg.com/politics/articles/2015-10-26/the-most -likely-next-president-is-hillary-clinton; Andreas Graefe, "Experts Still See Democrats in the Lead," Pollyvote, February 1, 2016, http://pollyvote.com/en/2016/02/01/experts-still -see-democrats-in-the-lead/.

21. Richard Nixon, *Six Crises* (New York: Doubleday, 1962), 311.

22. A similar model based on growth in real per capita disposable income in the first two quarters of 2016, rather than growth in GDP, forecasted a Democratic vote share of 51.5 percent and a 69 percent chance of winning. A forecast based only on an index of economic indicators—the Conference Board's Leading Economic Index—and not on presidential approval was also favorable to Democrats, giving them 51.8 percent of the major-party vote (personal communication with Christopher Wlezien, June 22, 2016).

23. David R. Mayhew, "Incumbency Advantage in U.S. Presidential Elections: The Historical Record," *Political Science Quarterly* 123, no. 2 (2008): 201–28; James E. Campbell, *The American Campaign: U.S. Presidential Elections and the National Vote*, 2nd ed. (College Station: Texas A&M University Press, 2008), 111.

24. James E. Campbell, Bryan J. Dettrey, and Hongxing Yin, "The Theory of Conditional Retrospective Voting: Does the Presidential Record Matter Less in Open-Seat Elections?," *Journal of Politics* 72, no. 4 (2010): 1083–95.

25. Donald E. Stokes and Gudmund R. Iverson, "On the Existence of Forces Restoring Party Competition," *Public Opinion Quarterly* 26, no. 2 (1962): 159–71; Alan I. Abramowitz, "Forecasting the 2008 Presidential Election with the Time-for-Change Model," *PS: Political Science and Politics* 41, no. 4 (2008): 691–95; Christopher Wlezien, "Policy (Mis)Representation and the Costs of Ruling: U.S. Presidential Elections in Comparative Perspective," *Comparative Political Studies* 50, no. 6 (2017): 711–38. See also Larry M. Bartels, "Electoral Continuity and Change, 1868–1996," *Electoral Studies* 17, no. 3 (1998): 301–26; and Mayhew, "Incumbency Advantage."

26. For an excellent critique and extension, see Benjamin E. Lauderdale and Drew Linzer, "Under-performing, Over-performing, or Just Performing? The Limitations of Fundamentals-Based Presidential Election Forecasting," *International Journal of Forecasting* 31, no. 3 (2015): 965–79.

27. The political scientists Jacob Montgomery and Florian Hollenbach averaged six different forecasting models and estimated that the Republican would win 50.9 percent of the major-party vote and the Democrat would win 49.1 percent of the vote. See Dylan

Matthews, "The Trump Tax," *Vox*, November 8, 2016, http://www.vox.com/a/trump-tax. An average of an even larger number of these models found a similarly close race, with the Democratic candidate winning 50.2 percent of the major-party vote. See Pollyvote, "Economic Models," accessed May 21, 2018, http://pollyvote.com/en/components/econo metric-models/. The betting market data are from PredictWise, which combines several different markets: PredictWise, "2016 President—Winner," accessed May 21, 2018, http://predictwise.com/politics/2016-president-winner.

28. Angus Campbell, Philip E. Converse, Warren E. Miller, and Donald E. Stokes, *The American Voter* (1960; Midway repr., Chicago: University of Chicago Press, 1976), 121. On the link between elite polarization and mass partisanship, see John Zaller, *The Nature and Origins of Mass Opinion* (New York: Cambridge University Press, 1992); and Marc Hetherington, "Resurgent Mass Partisanship: The Role of Elite Polarization," *American Journal of Political Science* 95 (2001): 619–31. On partisan hostility, see Marc Hetherington, Meri T. Long, and Thomas J. Rudolph, "Revisiting the Myth: New Evidence of a Polarized Electorate," *Public Opinion Quarterly* 80, no. S1 (2016): 321–50; Shanto Iyengar, Gaurav Sood, and Yphtach Lelkes, "Affect, Not Ideology: A Social Identity Perspective on Polarization," *Public Opinion Quarterly* 76, no. 3 (2012): 405–31; Shanto Iyengar and Sean J. Westwood, "Fear and Loathing across Party Lines: New Evidence on Group Polarization," *American Journal of Political Science* 59, no. 3 (2014): 690–707; Lilliana Mason, *Uncivil Agreement: How Politics Became Our Identity* (Chicago: University of Chicago Press, 2018); and Stephen P. Nicholson, Chelsea M. Coe, Jason Emory, and Anna V. Strong, "The Politics of Beauty: The Effects of Partisan Bias on Physical Attractiveness," *Political Behavior* 38, no. 4 (2016): 883–98. On sorting among activists and the electorate, see Geoffrey C. Layman, Thomas M. Carsey, John C. Green, Richard Herrera, and Rosalyn Cooperman, "Activists and Conflict Extension in American Party Politics," *American Political Science Review* 104, no. 2 (2010): 324–46; Matthew Levendusky, *The Partisan Sort: How Liberals Became Democrats and Conservatives Became Republicans* (Chicago: University of Chicago Press, 2009); Greg D. Adams, "Abortion: Evidence of an Issue Evolution," *American Journal of Political Science* 41 (1997): 718–37; and Delia Baldassarri and Andrew Gelman, "Partisans without Constraint: Political Polarization and Trends in American Public Opinion," *American Journal of Sociology* 114, no. 2 (2008): 408. On increasing ideological homogeneity, see Seth J. Hill and Chris Tausanovitch "A Disconnect in Representation? Comparison of Trends in Congressional and Public Polarization," *Journal of Politics* 77, no. 4 (2015): 1058–75. On perceptions of differences between the parties, see Corwin Smidt, "Polarization and the Decline of the American Swing Voter," *American Journal of Political Science* 61, no. 2 (2016): 365–81.

29. Angus Campbell et al., *The American Voter*, 133; Achen and Bartels, *Democracy for Realists*, ch. 10; Larry M. Bartels, "Beyond the Running Tally: Partisan Bias in Political Perceptions," *Political Behavior* 24 (2002): 117–50.

30. Peter K. Enns, Paul M. Kellstedt, and Gregory E. McAvoy, "The Consequences of Partisanship in Economic Perceptions," *Public Opinion Quarterly* 76, no. 2 (2012): 287–310. See also Alan S. Gerber and Gregory A. Huber, "Partisanship, Political Control, and Economic Assessments," *American Journal of Political Science* 54, no. 1 (2010): 153–73; Suzanna De Boef and Paul M. Kellstedt, "The Political (and Economic) Origins of Consumer Confidence," *American Journal of Political Science* 48, no. 4 (2004): 633–49; and Marc J. Hetherington and Thomas J. Rudolph, *Why Washington Won't Work: Polarization, Political Trust, and the Governing Crisis* (Chicago: University of Chicago Press, 2015).

31. Republicans were also more likely than Democrats to express distrust in government and dissatisfaction with the direction of the country. In these YouGov/*Economist* polls, a whopping 87 percent of Republicans said that the country was on the wrong track. Only 38 percent of Democrats thought so, while the plurality (48%) thought the country was headed in the right direction.

32. Ariel Edwards-Levy, "Opinions on Barack Obama's Legacy Don't Have Much to Do with the Economy," *Huffington Post*, May 10, 2016, http://www.huffingtonpost.com/entry/obama-economic-legacy_us_57325736e4b016f3789778f7.

33. Gary C. Jacobson, *A Divider, Not a Uniter* (New York: Pearson, 2007).

34. Larry Bartels, "Partisanship and Voting Behavior, 1952–1996," *American Journal of Political Science* 40 (2000): 194–230; Smidt, "Polarization."

35. The Obama quote is from a February 2008 speech, a transcript of which is here: "Barack Obama's Feb. 12 Speech," *New York Times*, February 12, 2008, http://www.nytimes.com/2008/02/12/us/politics/12text-obama.html?pagewanted=all&_r=1.

36. Ta-Nehisi Coates, "'The Filter . . . Is Powerful': Obama on Race, Media, and What It Took to Win," *Atlantic*, December 20, 2016, https://www.theatlantic.com/politics/archive/2016/12/ta-nehisi-coates-obama-transcript/510965/.

37. Eric Schickler, *Racial Realignment: The Transformation of American Liberalism, 1932–1965* (Princeton: Princeton University Press, 2016); Edward G. Carmines and James A. Stimson, *Issue Evolution: Race and the Transformation of American Politics* (Princeton: Princeton University Press, 1989); James A. Stimson, *Tides of Consent: How Public Opinion Shapes American Politics* (Cambridge: Cambridge University Press, 2004); Michael Tesler, *Post-racial or Most-Racial? Race and Politics in the Obama Era* (Chicago: University of Chicago Press, 2016); Nicholas A. Valentino and David O. Sears, "Old Times There Are Not Forgotten: Race and Partisan Realignment in the Contemporary South," *American Journal of Political Science* 49 (2005): 672–88; Adam M. Enders and Jamil S. Scott, "The Increasing Racialization of American Electoral Politics, 1988–2016," *American Politics Review*, published ahead of print, February 27, 2018.

38. The data in figure 2.6 are from Pew Research Center polls: Pew Research Center, "Party Identification Trends, 1992–2017," March 20, 2018, http://www.people-press.org/2016/09/13/party-identification-trends-1992-2016/#race; and Pew Research Center, "2. Party Affiliation among Voters: 1992–2016," September 13, 2016, http://www.people-press.org/2016/09/13/2-party-affiliation-among-voters-1992-2016/2_4-5/. We thank Jocelyn Kiley for providing yearly estimates for whites broken down by education. We supplemented the data for Hispanics with additional Pew surveys identified in the Roper Center polling archive. For similar evidence, see the trend in Gallup polls: Jeffrey M. Jones, "U.S. Whites More Solidly Republican in Recent Years," Gallup, March 24, 2014, http://www.gallup.com/poll/168059/whites-solidly-republican-recent-years.aspx. On the lack of party identification among nonwhites, see Zoltan L. Hajnal and Taeku Lee, *Why Americans Don't Join the Party: Race, Immigration, and the Failure (of Political Parties) to Engage the Electorate* (Princeton: Princeton University Press, 2011). On the voting behavior of Asian Americans, see Karthick Ramakrishnan, "Asian Americans Voted Democrat. We Should Not Be Surprised," *Monkey Cage* (blog), *Washington Post*, November 29, 2012, http://themonkeycage.org/2012/11/asian-americans-voted-democrat-we-should-not-be-surprised/. On Latinos, see Mark Hugo Lopez, Mark Hugo, Ana Gonzalez-Barrera, Jens Manuel Krogstad, and Gustavo López, "4. Latinos and the Political Parties," Pew Research Center, October 11, 2016, http://www.pewhispanic.org/2016/10/11/latinos-and-the-political-parties/.

39. On shifts in the party coalitions before Obama, see Larry M. Bartels, "What's the Matter with 'What's the Matter with Kansas'?," *Quarterly Journal of Political Science* 1 (2006): 201–16. For a related postelection argument about pro-Republican shifts in the Midwest before 2016, see Harry Enten, "It's Not All about Clinton—The Midwest Was Getting Redder before 2016," *FiveThirtyEight*, December 9, 2016, http://fivethirtyeight .com/features/its-not-all-about-clinton-the-midwest-was-getting-redder-before-2016 /?ex_cid=538twitter.

40. Tesler, *Post-racial or Most-Racial?*, figure 7.2.

41. The survey questions on which this measure is based asked respondents how much they agreed or disagreed with these statements: "Over the past few years, blacks have gotten less than they deserve"; "Irish, Italian, Jewish, and many other minorities overcame prejudice and worked their way up. Blacks should do the same without any special favors"; "It's really a matter of some people not trying hard enough; if blacks would only try harder they could be just as well off as whites"; and "Generations of slavery and discrimination have created conditions that make it difficult for blacks to work their way out of the lower class." The graph displays the one-third who attributed the most blame to blacks' lack of effort and the remaining two-thirds. On the origins of this measure, see Donald R. Kinder and Lynn M. Sanders, *Divided by Color: Racial Politics and Democratic Ideals* (Chicago: University of Chicago Press, 1996). On its meaning, see Cindy D. Kam and Camille D. Burge, "Uncovering Reactions to the Racial Resentment Scale across the Racial Divide," *Journal of Politics* 80, no. 1 (2018): 314–20.

42. Cornell Belcher, *A Black Man in the White House* (Healdsburg, CA: Water Street, 2016); Tesler, *Post-racial or Most-Racial?*

43. Cindy Kam and Donald R. Kinder, "Ethnocentrism as a Short-Term Influence in the 2008 Election," *American Journal of Political Science* 56, no. 2 (2012): 326–40; Michael Tesler and David O. Sears, *Obama's Race: The 2008 Election and the Dream of a Post-Racial America* (Chicago: University of Chicago Press, 2010); Tesler, *Post-racial or Most-Racial?*

44. Although the trend in the right-hand side of figure 2.8 is more pronounced among Democrats than Republicans, other survey questions show larger changes in the views of Republicans. For example, Republicans' feelings toward undocumented immigrants became less favorable in the Obama years. See also Marisa Abrajano and Zoltan L. Hajnal, *White Backlash: Immigration, Race, and American Politics* (Princeton: Princeton University Press, 2014).

45. John R. Wright, "Unemployment and the Democratic Electoral Advantage," *American Political Science Review* 106, no. 4 (2012): 685–702.

46. Tesler, *Post-racial or Most-Racial?*; Michael Tesler, "Economic Anxiety Isn't Driving Racial Resentment. Racial Resentment Is Driving Economic Anxiety," *Monkey Cage* (blog), *Washington Post*, August 22, 2016, https://www.washingtonpost.com/news/monkey -cage/wp/2016/08/22/economic-anxiety-isnt-driving-racial-resentment-racial-resent ment-is-driving-economic-anxiety/?utm_term=.362c8732a5d6.

47. David Maraniss and Robert Samuels, "The Great Unsettling," *Washington Post*, March 17, 2016, https://www.washingtonpost.com/politics/looking-for-america-the -great-unsettling/2016/03/17/e9cb3eaa-e544-11e5-bc08-3e03a5b41910_story.html?tid =a_inl.

48. Antoine J. Banks, *Anger and Racial Politics: The Emotional Foundation of Racial Attitudes in America* (New York: Cambridge University Press, 2014); Marc Hetherington

and Jonathan D. Weiler, *Authoritarianism and Polarization in American Politics* (New York: Cambridge University Press, 2009).

49. Ruy Teixeira, William H. Frey, and Robert Griffin, *States of Change: The Demographic Evolution of the American Electorate, 1974–2060* (Washington, DC: Center for American Progress, 2015), 6; Alan Rappeport, "Lindsey Graham Says Republicans Are 'in a Hole' with Hispanics," *New York Times*, July 8, 2015, http://www.nytimes.com /politics/first-draft/2015/07/08/lindsey-graham-says-republicans-are-in-a-hole-with -hispanics/?_r=0; Balz, "Republican Party's Uphill Path."

50. Sean Trende, "The Case of the Missing White Voters, Revisited," Real Clear Politics, June 21, 2013, https://www.realclearpolitics.com/articles/2013/06/21/the_case_of _the_missing_white_voters_revisited_118893.html; Thomas B. Edsall, "Should the Republican Party Just Focus on White Voters?," *New York Times*, July 3, 2013; Larry M. Bartels, "Can the Republican Party Thrive on White Identity?," *Monkey Cage* (blog), *Washington Post*, April 16, 2014, https://www.washingtonpost.com/news/monkey-cage /wp/2014/04/16/can-the-republican-party-thrive-on-white-identity/; Zoltan L. Hajnal, "Opposition to Immigration Reform Is a Winning Strategy for Republicans," *Monkey Cage* (blog), *Washington Post*, February 27, 2015, https://www.washingtonpost.com/news /monkey-cage/wp/2015/02/27/opposition-to-immigration-reform-is-a-winning-strategy -for-republicans/.

51. Maureen A. Craig and Jennifer A. Richeson, "On the Precipice of a 'Majority-Minority' America: Perceived Status Threat from the Racial Demographic Shift Affects White Americans' Political Ideology," *Psychological Science* 25, no. 6 (2014): 1189–97; Maureen A. Craig and Jennifer A. Richeson, "More Diverse yet Less Tolerant? How the Increasingly Diverse Racial Landscape Affects White Americans' Racial Attitudes," *Personality and Social Psychology Bulletin* 40, no. 6 (2014): 750–61; Ryan D. Enos, *The Space between Us: Social Geography and Politics* (New York: Cambridge University Press, 2017); Mara Cecilia Ostfeld, "The New White Flight? The Effects of Political Appeals to Latinos on White Democrats," *Political Behavior* (forthcoming). On House races under Obama's presidency, see Tesler, *Post-racial or Most-Racial?*; Matthew D. Luttig, "Obama, Race, and the Republican Landslide in 2010," *Politics, Groups, and Identities*, 5, no. 2 (2017): 197–219; Ronald Brownstein, "White-Out: Where Democrats Lost the House," *National Journal*, January 13, 2015.

Chapter 3: Indecision

1. Quoted in Peter Hamby, "Inside the GOP's Secret School," CNN, October 15, 2014, http://www.cnn.com/2014/10/15/politics/gop-secret-school/index.html?sr=twpoli101514 gopsecretschool11astorytoplink.

2. Marty Cohen, David Karol, Hans Noel, and John Zaller, *The Party Decides: Presidential Nominations before and after Reform* (Chicago: University of Chicago Press, 2008).

3. For a similar argument, see Marty Cohen, David Karol, Hans Noel, and John Zaller, "Party versus Faction in the Reformed Presidential Nominating System," *PS: Political Science and Politics* 49, no. 4 (2016): 701–8.

4. Andrew Dugan and Frank Newport, "Americans Still Give Obama Better Odds to Win Election," Gallup, October 31, 2008, http://www.gallup.com/poll/158444/americans -give-obama-better-odds-win-election.aspx; Phillip Rucker, "Romney's Belief in Himself

Never Wavered," *Washington Post*, November 7, 2012, https://www.washingtonpost.com /politics/decision2012/romneys-belief-in-himself-never-wavered/2012/11/07/50cd03fc -27b8-11e2-9972-71bf64ea091c_story.html; John Sides and Lynn Vavreck, *The Gamble: Choice and Chance in the 2012 Presidential Election* (Princeton: Princeton University Press, 2013), 172, 238.

5. Philip A. Klinkner, *The Losing Parties: Out-Party National Committees, 1956–1993* (New Haven: Yale University Press, 1994), 192, 199.

6. Henry Barbour, Sally Bradshaw, Ari Fleischer, Zori Fonalledas, and Glenn Mc-Call, *Growth and Opportunity Project* (Washington, DC: Republican National Committee, 2013), 25, http://goproject.gop.com/rnc_growth_opportunity_book_2013.pdf. On the Democratic advantage in campaign data and analytics, see Daniel Kreiss, *Prototype Politics: Technology-Intensive Campaigning and the Data of Democracy* (New York: Oxford University Press, 2016), 10.

7. The Priebus quote is from McKay Coppins, *The Wilderness: Deep inside the Republican Party's Combative, Contentious, Chaotic Quest to Take Back the White House* (New York: Little, Brown, 2016), 69. Joshua Putnam, "RNC Creates New Rules Dealing with Presidential Primary Debates," *Frontloading HQ* (blog), May 12, 2014, http://frontloading .blogspot.com/2014/05/rnc-creates-new-rule-dealing-with.html; Barbour et al., *Growth and Opportunity Project*, 71; Joshua Putnam, "Republican Proportionality Rules Changes for 2016, Part 1," *Frontloading HQ* (blog), April 15, 2015, http://frontloading.blogspot.com /2015/04/republican-proportionality-rules.html.

8. Barbour et al., *Growth and Opportunity Project*, 12, 76; Quoted in Coppins, *The Wilderness*, 69.

9. Jeff Zeleny, "Romney Campaign Manager Says He Regrets Immigration Stance," *New York Times*, December 3, 2012, http://thecaucus.blogs.nytimes.com/2012/12/03/romney -campaign-manager-says-he-regrets-immigration-stance/; Jennifer Steinhauer, "Speaker 'Confident' of Deal with White House on Immigration," *New York Times*, November 8, 2012, http://www.nytimes.com/2012/11/09/us/politics/boehner-confident-of-deal-with -white-house-on-immigration.html; James Rainey, "Fox News Star Sean Hannity Suddenly Likes Immigration Reform," *Los Angeles Times*, November 9, 2012, http://articles .latimes.com/2012/nov/09/nation/la-na-pn-sean-hannity-immigration-20121109.

10. The Domenech quote is in Sides and Vavreck, *The Gamble*, 174. The Limbaugh quote is in Coppins, *Wilderness*, 71. The Cruz quote is from Jeffrey Toobin, "The Absolutist," *New Yorker*, June 30, 2014, http://www.newyorker.com/magazine/2014/06/30/the -absolutist-2.

11. Michael A. Bailey, Jonathan Mummolo, and Hans Noel, "Tea Party Influence: A Story of Activists and Elites," *American Politics Research* 40, no. 5 (2012): 769–804; Theda Skocpol and Vanessa Williamson *The Tea Party and the Remaking of Republican Conservatism* (New York: Oxford University Press, 2013); Hans Noel, "Ideological Factions in the Republican and Democratic Parties," *ANNALS of the American Academy of Political and Social Science* 667 (2016): 166–88.

12. See Bailey et al., "Tea Party Influence," for evidence of the relationship between Tea Party activism and whether members of Congress voted to raise the debt ceiling.

13. The King quote is in Alec MacGillis, "How Republicans Lost Their Best Shot at the Hispanic Vote," *New York Times Magazine*, September 18, 2016, http://www.nytimes .com/2016/09/18/magazine/how-republicans-lost-their-best-shot-at-the-hispanic-vote .html?_r=0.

14. For a typical poll, see Dan Balz and Scott Clement, "Poll: Major Damage to GOP after Shutdown, and Broad Dissatisfaction with Government," *Washington Post*, October 22, 2013, https://www.washingtonpost.com/politics/poll-major-damage-to-gop-after -shutdown-and-broad-dissatisfaction-with-government/2013/10/21/dae5c062-3a84-11e3 -b7ba-503fb5822c3e_story.html. Michael C. Bender and Kathleen Hunter, "Republican Civil War Erupts: Business Groups v. Tea Party," Bloomberg, October 18, 2013, http:// www.bloomberg.com/news/articles/2013-10-18/republican-civil-war-erupts-business -groups-v-tea-party; Abby Phillip, "Republican Civil War over Shutdown Drama," ABC News, October 19, 2013, http://abcnews.go.com/Politics/republican-infighting -obamacare-raises-2014-concerns/story?id=20615308. On primary challenges, see Robert G. Boatright, *Getting Primaries: The Changing Politics of Congressional Primary Challenges* (Ann Arbor: University of Michigan Press, 2013); and Robert G. Boatright, "The 2014 Congressional Primaries in Context" (paper presented at "What the 2014 Primaries Foretell about the Future of American Politics," event cohosted by the Campaign Finance Institute and the Brookings Institution, Washington, DC, September 30, 2014).

15. Pew Research Center, "Majority Says Any Budget Deal Must Include Planned Parenthood Funding," September 15, 2015, http://www.people-press.org/2015/09/28/majority -says-any-budget-deal-must-include-planned-parenthood-funding/; Molly E. Reynolds, "Speaker Ryan Meets the Realities of Governing," Brookings Institution, June 10, 2016, https://www.brookings.edu/blog/fixgov/2016/06/10/speaker-ryan-meets-the-realities-of -governing/. The Boehner quotes were widely reported but can be found in MacGillis, "How Republicans Lost."

16. John H. Aldrich, *Why Parties? The Origin and Transformation of Political Parties in America* (Chicago: University of Chicago Press, 1995); Cohen et al., *The Party Decides*; Evan Andrews, "Boss Tweed's Flight from Justice," December 3, 2015, History.com, https://www.history.com/news/boss-tweeds-flight-from-justice.

17. Ironically, the shift to using primaries and caucuses was not the explicit goal of these reforms. See James W. Ceaser, *Presidential Selection: Theory and Development* (Princeton: Princeton University Press, 1979), 262–64. On the invisible primary, see Cohen et al., *The Party Decides*; Andrew J. Dowdle, Randall E. Adkins, and Wayne P. Steger, "The Viability Primary: Modeling Candidate Support before the Primaries," *Political Research Quarterly* 62, no. 1 (2009): 77–91; and Wayne P. Steger, "Who Wins Nominations and Why? An Updated Forecast of the Presidential Primary Vote," *Political Research Quarterly* 60, no. 1 (2007): 91–99. For a rigorous test of how state party endorsements can move voters, see Thad Kousser, Scott Lucas, Seth Masket, and Eric McGhee, "Kingmakers or Cheerleaders? Party Power and the Causal Effects of Endorsements," *Political Research Quarterly* 68, no. 3 (2015): 443–56.

18. Gary Jacobson and Samuel Kernell, *Strategy and Choice in Congressional Elections* (New Haven: Yale University Press, 1983).

19. See the various quotes in Catherine Rampell, "The GOP's 'Embarrassment of Riches' of Presidential Contenders, Down to Just One Rich Embarrassment," *Washington Post*, May 11, 2016, https://www.washingtonpost.com/news/rampage/wp/2016/05/11/the-gops -embarrassment-of-riches-of-presidential-contenders-down-to-just-one-rich-embar rassment/?utm_term=.102adf6f5a67.

20. Peter Hamby, Gloria Borger, and Alexandra Jaffe, "Why Mitt Romney Bowed Out," CNN, January 31, 2015, http://www.cnn.com/2015/01/30/politics/romney-exit-ticktock/.

21. Rachel Weiner, "McCain Calls Paul, Cruz, Amash 'Wacko Birds,'" *Washington Post*, March 8, 2013, https://www.washingtonpost.com/news/post-politics/wp/2013/03/08 /mccain-calls-paul-cruz-amash-wacko-birds/?utm_term=.36c1ccaf2329.

22. Ben White and Marc Caputo, "Inside Jeb's 'Shock and Awe' Launch," *Politico*, February 18, 2015, http://www.politico.com/story/2015/02/inside-jeb-bushs-shock-and-awe -launch-115272; Ed O'Keefe and Matea Gold, "Jeb Bush and His Allies Amass an Unprecedented $114 Million Haul," *Washington Post*, July 9, 2015, https://www.washingtonpost .com/news/post-politics/wp/2015/07/09/jeb-bush-raised-11-4-million-in-first-quarter-of -the-year/?utm_term=.0982d13cf702.

23. Andrew Dugan, "Among Republicans, GOP Candidates Better Known than Liked," Gallup, July 24, 2015, http://www.gallup.com/poll/184337/among-republicans -gop-candidates-better-known-liked.aspx.

24. Coppins, *The Wilderness*, 176.

25. Coppins, *The Wilderness*, 325, 35–36.

26. Coppins, *The Wilderness*, 223, 231.

27. Maggie Haberman and Alexander Burns, "Donald Trump's Presidential Run Began in an Effort to Gain Stature," *New York Times*, March 12, 2016, https://www .nytimes.com/2016/03/13/us/politics/donald-trump-campaign.html?_r=0.

28. Christopher L. Anderson, "Which Party Elites Choose to Lead the Nominations Process?," *Political Research Quarterly* 66, no. 1 (2013): 61–76; Wayne Steger, "Interparty Elite Differences in Elite Support for Presidential Nomination Candidates," *American Politics Research* 36, no. 5 (2008): 724–49.

29. David A. Graham, "Ben Carson's Risky Strategy," *Atlantic*, October 26, 2015, http://www.theatlantic.com/notes/2015/10/ben-carsons-risky-strategy/412483/; Sides and Vavreck, *The Gamble*, 37. For a similar conclusion about endorsements in the 2016 Republican primary, see also Noel, "Ideological Factions."

30. More formally, these are first- and second-dimension NOMINATE scores derived from the 114th Congress (2015–16). On the meaning of the second dimension, see Harry Enten, "Establishment v Insurgent: The New Political Dynamic," *Guardian*, January 8, 2013, https://www.theguardian.com/commentisfree/2013/jan/08/establishment-v -antiestablishment-capitol-political-dynamic; Noel, "Ideological Factions"; and Keith Poole, "House: Vote on Clean DHS Funding Bill," *Voteview Blog*, March 6, 2015, https:// voteviewblog.com/2015/03/06/hello-world/. To determine whether the groups of endorsers differed ideologically, we regressed both NOMINATE scores on dummy variables for each group of endorsers. On the first-dimension score, Bush endorsers were significantly less conservative than all other candidates' endorsers and those that did not endorse. Cruz endorsers were significantly more conservative than the other endorsers and those that did not endorse. Rubio and Paul endorsers were in between and not significantly different from each other or from nonendorsers. On the second-dimension score, Cruz and especially Paul supporters stand out as different, scoring closer to the "outsider" end of that scale. See also Harry Enten, "Why Aren't Republican Leaders Rallying behind Marco Rubio?," *FiveThirtyEight*, January 22, 2016, https://fivethirtyeight.com/features /why-arent-republican-leaders-rallying-behind-marco-rubio/; and Noel, "Ideological Factions."

31. The state legislative endorsement data were kindly provided by Boris Shor. Carrie Levine, Michael Beckel, Ben Wieder, Dave Levinthal, and Alexander Cohen, "Presidential Campaign Honors Hedge Bets," Center for Public Integrity, July 16, 2015, https:// www.publicintegrity.org/2015/07/16/17680/presidential-campaign-donors-hedge-bets.

32. On the increase in the availability of early money, see Cohen et al., "Party versus Faction." For fund-raising totals, see Center for Responsive Politics, "Also-Rans: 2016 Presidential Race," OpenSecrets.org, http://www.opensecrets.org/pres16/also-rans. On Cruz, see Katie Zezima and Matea Gold, "Cruz's Quiet Fundraising Strength: A Network of Wealthy Donors," *Washington Post*, October 26, 2015, https://www.washingtonpost .com/politics/cruzs-secret-fundraising-strength-a-network-of-wealthy-donors/2015/10 /26/d170532e-7c0b-11e5-beba-927fd8634498_story.html?postshare=56514459038 12366&utm_term=.46d63c9f80ad.

33. Mark Blumenthal, "Sarah Palin Can't Win, Shouldn't Run, HuffPost-Patch GOP Power Outsiders Say," *Huffington Post*, August 31, 2011, http://www.huffingtonpost .com/2011/08/31/sarah-palin-polls_n_943615.html; Mark Blumenthal, "Michele Bachmann Can't Win, HuffPost-Patch GOP Power Outsiders Say," *Huffington Post*, September 21, 2011, http://www.huffingtonpost.com/2011/09/21/michele-bachmann-polls_n_973995 .html; Mark Blumenthal, "Newt Gingrich, Intelligent but Unelectable? Power Outsiders Ponder," *Huffington Post*, November 16, 2011, http://www.huffingtonpost.com/2011/11 /16/newt-gingrich-polls-power-outsiders-intelligent-unelectable_n_1095847.html; Mark Blumenthal, "Mitt Romney Is Presidential, Electable, HuffPost-Patch GOP Power Outsiders Say," *Huffington Post*, September 14, 2011, http://www.huffingtonpost.com/2011/09 /14/mitt-romney-presidential-electable-power-outsiders_n_962167.html; Mark Blumenthal, "GOP Power Outsiders Souring on Perry, Warming to Romney," *Huffington Post*, November 27, 2011, http://www.huffingtonpost.com/2011/09/27/rick-perry-mitt romney -polls-huffpost-patch-gop-power-outsiders_n_983659.html.

34. Mark Blumenthal and Ariel Edwards-Levy, "We Polled True Activist Grassroots Republicans, and Here's Who They're Backing," *Huffington Post*, September 9, 2015, http://www.huffingtonpost.com/entry/republican-activists-primary-poll_us_55afd 500e4b0a9b9485352ad?mirrizfr=&.

35. Joseph Weber, "Walker's Moment? Wisconsin Governor Builds on 2016 Buzz, Staffs Up Political Operation," Fox News, February 3, 2015, http://www.foxnews.com/poli tics/2015/02/03/walker-appears-to-be-making-best-sudden-but-early-attention-in -potential-2016.html; Matea Gold, Jenna Johnson, and Dan Balz, "Inside the Collapse of Scott Walker's Presidential Bid," *Washington Post*, September 22, 2015, https://www .washingtonpost.com/politics/inside-the-collapse-of-scott-walkers-presidential -campaign/2015/09/22/6d1b8c9a-6144-11e5-8e9e-dce8a2a2a679_story.html.

Chapter 4: "The Daily Donald Show"

Epigraphs: Walter Shapiro, "'I Can Think of Nothing as Unfair' in 30 Years of Covering Presidential Politics," *Roll Call*, January 14, 2016, http://www.rollcall.com/news/walter -shapiro-i-can-think-of-nothing-as-unfair-in-30-years-of-covering-presidential -politics/?dcz; Paul Bond, "Leslie Moonves on Donald Trump: 'It May Not Be Good for America, but It's Damn Good for CBS," *Hollywood Reporter*, February 29, 2016, http:// www.hollywoodreporter.com/news/leslie-moonves-donald-trump-may-871464.

1. Josh Jordan (@NumbersMuncher), Twitter, March 19, 2016, 12:05 p.m., https:// twitter.com/NumbersMuncher/status/711267318630785024; Jonathan Martin (@jmart NYT), Twitter, March 19, 2016, 12:47 p.m., https://twitter.com/jmartNYT/status/7112779 24436025345. On CNN's focus on Trump to the exclusion of other candidates, see Jonathan Mahler, "'That Is Great Television': Inside the Strange Symbiosis between the CNN President Jeff Zucker and Donald Trump," *New York Times Magazine*, April 9, 2017.

2. Ryan Grim, "All Three Networks Ignored Bernie Sanders' Speech Tuesday Night, 'Standing by for Trump,'" *Huffington Post*, March 15, 2016, http://www.huffingtonpost .com/entry/all-three-networks-ignored-bernie-sanders-speech-tuesday-night -promising-trump-would-be-speaking-soon_us_56e8bad1e4b0860f99daec81;   Jennifer Bendery, "Networks Didn't Cut from Donald Trump's Speech Once to Air Hillary Clinton," *Huffington Post*, March 8, 2016, http://www.huffingtonpost.com/entry/hillary-clinton -donald-trump-networks_us_56df9346e4b0860f99d72720.

3. Nelson Polsby, *Consequences of Party Reform* (Oxford: Oxford University Press, 1983), 72. See also Wayne Steger, "Two Paradigms of Presidential Nominations," *Presidential Studies Quarterly* 43, no. 2 (2013): 377–87; Andrew J. Dowdle, Randall E. Adkins, and Wayne P. Steger, "The Viability Primary: Modeling Candidate Support before the Primaries," *Political Research Quarterly* 62, no. 1 (2009): 77–91. On the increase in news coverage of the invisible primary, see Marty Cohen, David Karol, Hans Noel, and John Zaller, "Party versus Faction in the Reformed Presidential Nominating System," *PS: Political Science and Politics* 49, no. 4 (2016): 701–8.

4. Paul Lazarsfeld and Robert Merton, "Mass Communication, Popular Taste, and Organized Social Action," in *The Communication of Ideas*, ed. Lyman Bryson (New York: Institute for Religious and Social Studies, 1948), 95–118.

5. The experience of Cain and the cycle of "discovery, scrutiny, and decline" is documented in John Sides and Lynn Vavreck, *The Gamble: Choice and Chance in the 2012 Presidential Election* (Princeton: Princeton University Press, 2013). The prevalence of horse race coverage in primaries and general elections is documented, for example, in Thomas E. Patterson, *The Mass Media Election: How Americans Choose Their President* (New York: Praeger, 1980); Michael J. Robinson and Margaret A. Sheehan, *Over the Wire and on TV* (New York: Russell Sage Foundation, 1983); Henry E. Brady and Richard Johnston, "What's the Primary Message: Horse Race or Issue Journalism," in *Media and Momentum*, ed. Gary R. Orren and Nelson W. Polsby (Chatham, NJ: Chatham House, 1987), 127–86; Thomas E. Patterson, *Out of Order* (New York: Knopf, 1993); Pew Research Center, "Winning the Media Campaign," October 22, 2008, http://www.journalism.org /2008/10/22/winning-media-campaign/; and Pew Research Center, "Winning the Media Campaign," November 2, 2012, http://www.journalism.org/2012/11/02/winning-media -campaign-2012/. The percentage of horse race coverage was somewhat lower in 2012 than in 2008, but it was still the largest category of coverage.

6. The newspapers were *USA Today*, the *Wall Street Journal*, the *New York Times*, the *Los Angeles Times*, the *Washington Post*, the *Chicago Tribune*, the *Houston Chronicle*, the *Arizona Republic*, the *Dallas Morning News*, the *San Francisco Chronicle*, the *Boston Globe*, and the *Atlanta Journal-Constitution*.

7. More information about the data is here: GDELT Project, "Presidential Campaign 2016: Candidate Television Tracker," accessed May 24, 2018, http://television.gdeltproject .org/cgi-bin/iatv_campaign2016/iatv_campaign2016.

8. Other data than the two sources described here also showed Trump's dominance. By November 2015, Trump had received more evening network news coverage (234 minutes) than the entire Democratic field. (By contrast, Ted Cruz had received 7 minutes.) Trump also received 54 percent of the coverage in newspapers between July and December 2015. See Nate Silver, "Trump Boom or Trump Bubble?," *FiveThirtyEight*, December 15, 2015, https://fivethirtyeight.com/features/trump-boom-or-trump-bubble/; Rich Noyes, "TV's Campaign '16 News: An Avalanche of Trump Coverage, Not Much for Others," Newsbusters, August 4, 2015, http://www.newsbusters.org/blogs/nb/rich-noyes

/2015/08/03/tvs-campaign-16-news-avalanche-trump-coverage-not-much-others; and Callum Borchers, "Donald Trump Has Gotten More Nightly Network News Coverage than the Entire Democratic Field Combined," *Washington Post*, December 7, 2015, https:// www.washingtonpost.com/news/the-fix/wp/2015/12/07/donald-trump-has-gotten-more -nightly-network-news-coverage-than-the-entire-democratic-field-combined/ ?postshare=5581449521770491&tid=ss_tw&utm_term=.ca1e7f48ca8c.

9. The correlations between the "unsmoothed" measures of Trump's poll standing and news coverage are also quite large (0.80 or above).

10. The reciprocal relationship between polls and news coverage is apparent when news coverage and polls on any given day are modeled as a function of news and polls on the preceding day. A more elaborate analysis of polls and cable news data from 2012 and 2016 finds that news coverage of Trump affected both his poll standing and voter interest in him, as measured with Google search data—but that poll numbers did not affect news coverage as strongly. See Kevin Reuning and Nick Dietrich, "Media, Public Interest, and Support in Primary Elections" (working paper, written August 11, 2016, last revised March 14, 2018), https://papers.ssrn.com/sol3/papers.cfm?abstract_id=2709208.

11. On economic incentives and news coverage, see James Hamilton, *All The News That's Fit to Sell: How the Market Transforms Information into News* (Princeton: Princeton University Press, 2006).

12. Donald Trump, *The Art of the Deal* (New York: Random House, 1987), 176.

13. William E. Geist, "The Expanding Empire of Donald Trump," *New York Times Magazine*, April 8, 1984, http://www.nytimes.com/1984/04/08/magazine/the-expanding empire-of-donald-trump.html?pagewanted=all; David Hopkins, "More on Donald Trump as Media Creature," *Honest Graft* (blog), June 27, 2016, http://www.honestgraft .com/2016/06/more-on-donald-trump-as-media-creature.html. There are many examples of the "The media didn't create Trump" argument: https://www.google.com/search ?q=%22the+media+didn%27t+create+trump%22&ie=utf-8&oe=utf-8. Susan Mulcahy, "Confessions of a Trump Tabloid Scribe," *Politico*, May/June 2016, http://www.politico .com/magazine/story/2016/04/2016-donald-trump-tabloids-new-york-post-daily-news -media-213842; Neil Barsky, "Trump, the Bad, Bad, Businessman," *New York Times*, August 5, 2016, https://www.nytimes.com/2016/08/07/opinion/sunday/trump-the-bad-bad-business man.html.

14. John Sides, "Why Is Trump Surging? Blame the Media," *Monkey Cage* (blog), *Washington Post*, July 20, 2015, https://www.washingtonpost.com/news/monkey-cage /wp/2015/07/20/why-is-trump-surging-blame-the-media/?utm_term=.428e0b382e6f.

15. Drew Harwell and Mary Jordan, "Trump Once Said TV Ruined Politics. Then It Made Him a Star," *Washington Post*, September 22, 2016, https://www.washingtonpost .com/politics/trump-once-said-tv-ruined-politics-then-it-made-him-a-star/2016/09/22 /30533596-7c51-11e6-bd86-b7bbd53d2b5d_story.html?utm_term=.c15c3cc64d04; Mark Lei-bovich, "Donald Trump Is Not Going Anywhere," *New York Times Magazine*, September 29, 2015, https://www.nytimes.com/2015/10/04/magazine/donald-trump-is-not-going -anywhere.html?_r=1. A similar story of Trump looking for himself on television after a January 2014 speech in New Hampshire is in McKay Coppins, *The Wilderness: Deep inside the Republican Party's Combative, Contentious, Chaotic Quest to Take Back the White House* (New York: Little, Brown, 2016), 227.

16. Kyle Blaine, "How Donald Trump Bent Television to His Will," *Buzzfeed*, March 18, 2016, https://www.buzzfeed.com/kyleblaine/how-donald-trump-bent-television-to-his-will ?utm_term=.vfB6GAVoa#.jaz3wM1eB.

17. Daniel Victor, "Donald Trump's Lousy Week (Except for the Polling)," *New York Times*, July 2, 2015, https://www.nytimes.com/2015/07/03/us/politics/donald-trumps-lousy-week-except-for-the-polling.html; Donald J. Trump (@realDonaldTrump), Twitter, July 2, 2015, 8:09 a.m., https://twitter.com/realdonaldtrump/status/616624797527764992.

18. Jonathan Martin and Alan Rappeport, "Donald Trump Says John McCain Is No War Hero, Setting Off Another Storm," *New York Times*, July 18, 2015, https://www.nytimes.com/2015/07/19/us/politics/trump-belittles-mccains-war-record.html.

19. Lauren Carroll, "In Context: Donald Trump's Comments on a Database of American Muslims," PolitiFact, November 24, 2015, http://www.politifact.com/truth-o-meter/article/2015/nov/24/donald-trumps-comments-database-american-muslims/; Jenna Johnson and David Weigel, "Donald Trump Calls for 'Total Ban' on Muslims Entering United States," *Washington Post*, December 8, 2015, https://www.washingtonpost.com/politics/2015/12/07/e56266f6-9d2b-11e5-8728-1af6af208198_story.html?utm_term=.9a153dba466b; Andrew Prokop, "One Tweet That Shows How Expertly Donald Trump Is Manipulating the Media," *Vox*, December 8, 2015, http://www.vox.com/2015/12/8/9871542/donald-trump-media.

20. The Baier quote is from Michael M. Grynbaum, "Television Networks Struggle to Provide Equal Airtime in the Era of Trump," *New York Times*, May 30, 2016, https://www.nytimes.com/2016/05/31/business/media/television-networks-struggle-to-provide-equal-airtime-in-the-era-of-trump.html?ref=politics&_r=0. The story about camera placement is from Blaine, "How Donald Trump Bent Television to His Will." John Sides and Kalev Leetaru, "A Deep Dive into the News Media's Role in the Rise of Donald J. Trump," *Monkey Cage* (blog), *Washington Post*, June 24, 2016, https://www.washingtonpost.com/news/monkey-cage/wp/2016/06/24/a-deep-dive-into-the-news-medias-role-in-the-rise-of-donald-j-trump/?utm_term=.f15cbc6cfc02. An analysis of Trump's tactics and the resulting news coverage finds that coverage increased after Trump's tweets got a larger number of retweets and after Trump's staged public events. See Chris Wells, Dhavan V. Shah, Jon C. Pevehouse, JungHwan Yang, Ayellet Pelled, Frederick Boehm, Josephine Lukito, Shreenita Ghosh, and Jessica L. Schmidt, "How Trump Drove Coverage to the Nomination: Hybrid Media Campaigning," *Political Communication* 33, no. 4 (2016): 669–76.

21. Alex Welprin, "2016 Election Coverage Keeps Shattering Cable News Ratings Records," *Politico*, March 29, 2016, http://www.politico.com/blogs/on-media/2016/03/cable-tv-news-ratings-2016-election-221346; Gabriel Sherman, "Don't Expect a Lasting Truce in the Trump-Fox News War," *New York*, September 24, http://nymag.com/daily/intelligencer/2015/09/dont-expect-a-truce-in-the-trumpfox-news-war.html. The VandeHei quote was from *Morning Joe* on May 26, 2016. See the Poynter roundup of media news here: James Warren, "Top Media News Stories This Morning," Poynter, May 26, 2016, http://us9.campaign-archive2.com/?u=79fa45ed20ff84851c3b9cd63&id=288340cc46&e=596f5af522. Jim Rutenberg, "The Mutual Dependence of Donald Trump and the News Media," *New York Times*, March 20, 2016, https://www.nytimes.com/2016/03/21/business/media/the-mutual-dependence-of-trump-and-the-news-media.html; Paul Bond, "Leslie Moonves on Donald Trump: 'It May Not Be Good for America, but It's Damn Good for CBS,'" *Hollywood Reporter*, February 29, 2016, http://www.hollywoodreporter.com/news/leslie-moonves-donald-trump-may-871464.

22. Jack Shafer, "Trump Isn't a Media Creation," *Politico*, September 21, 2015, http://www.politico.com/magazine/story/2015/09/trump-media-coverage-213170; Jack Shafer,

"Did the Media Create Trump?," *Politico*, March 2, 2016, http://www.politico.com/magazine/story/2016/03/donald-trump-2016-media-213695.

23. Coppins, *The Wilderness*, 368.

24. Carly Fiorina's rise and fall illustrates the same pattern. Her news coverage and poll numbers peaked after the September 16 debate. Just before the debate, Trump had criticized Fiorina's appearance, saying, "Look at that face! Would anyone vote for that? Can you imagine that, the face of our next president!" (Peter Solotaroff, "Trump Seriously: On the Trail with the GOP's Tough Guy," *Rolling Stone*, September 9, 2015, http://www.rollingstone.com/politics/news/trump-seriously-20150909?page=13.) When asked about this remark in the debate, Fiorina said, "I think women all over this country heard very clearly what Mr. Trump said." (David Catanese, "Donald Trump, Carly Fiorina Tangle in Scrappy Second GOP Debate," *US News and World Report*, September 17, 2015, http://www.usnews.com/news/blogs/run-2016/2015/09/17/donald-trump-carly-fiorina-tangle-in-scrappy-second-gop-debate.) Political observers judged her reaction favorably, and her national poll standing increased from about 5 percent to the double digits. But the scrutiny thereafter—of her biography, her record at Hewlett-Packard, and unpaid bills from her Senate campaign—catalyzed a decline in her poll numbers and later news coverage. Fiorina dropped out of the race on February 10, 2016, and only made news again when, late in the primary campaign, Ted Cruz named her as his running mate in a last-gasp move not long before he also exited the race.

25. Nia-Malika Henderson and Theodore Schleifer, "Inside Ben Carson's Quiet Surge," CNN, September 1, 2015, http://www.cnn.com/2015/09/01/politics/2016-election-ben-carson/.

26. Alan Rappeport, "Ben Carson's Comments Stir Anger among Muslims," *New York Times*, September 21, 2015, https://www.nytimes.com/politics/first-draft/2015/09/21/ben-carsons-comments-stir-anger-among-muslims/; Theodore Schleifer and Eugene Scott, "Ben Carson Says the Darndest Things," CNN, October 8, 2015, http://www.cnn.com/2015/10/07/politics/ben-carson-debt-ceiling-marketplace/; Trip Gabriel, "Ben Carson Is Struggling to Grasp Foreign Policy, Advisers Say," *New York Times*, November 17, 2015, https://www.nytimes.com/2015/11/18/us/politics/ben-carson-is-struggling-to-grasp-foreign-policy-advisers-say.html?_r=3; David Catanese, "In Search of a Revival," *US News and World Report*, December 8, 2015, http://www.usnews.com/news/articles/2015/12/08/hampered-by-foreign-policy-woes-ben-carson-looks-for-new-life; Scott Glover and Maeve Reston, "A Tale of Two Carsons," CNN, November 5, 2015, http://www.cnn.com/2015/11/05/politics/ben-carson-2016-childhood-violence/; Kyle Cheney, "Exclusive: Carson Claimed West Point 'Scholarship' but Never Applied," *Politico*, November 6, 2015, http://www.politico.com/story/2015/11/ben-carson-west-point-215598; Sara Murray, "Ben Carson Tries to Salvage Campaign," CNN, January 1, 2016, http://www.cnn.com/2016/01/01/politics/ben-carson-campaign-turnaround/.

27. Ben Jacobs, "On the Iraq War, Jeb Bush Had a Terrible, Horrible, No Good, Very Bad Week," *Guardian*, May 15, 2015, https://www.theguardian.com/us-news/2015/may/15/jeb-bush-iraq-war-ivy-zietrich-isis-george-w-bush. The quotes dated to Bush's announcement are in Coppins, *The Wilderness*, 360. The "stuck like glue" comment is from Jesse Byrnes, "Ten Moments That Doomed Jeb Bush's Presidential Campaign," *Hill*, February 20, 2016, http://thehill.com/homenews/campaign/270173-ten-moments-that-doomed-jeb-bushs-presidential-campaign. See also Ashley Parker, "Jeb Bush Sprints to Escape Donald Trump's 'Low Energy' Label," *New York Times*, December 29, 2015,

https://www.nytimes.com/2015/12/30/us/politics/jeb-bush-sprints-to-escape-donald
-trumps-low-energy-label.html. Sopan Deb, "Trump, Bush Spat Ramps Up over 9/11 Comments," CBS News, October 17, 2015, http://www.cbsnews.com/news/trump-bush-spat
-ramps-up-over-911-comments/; Philip Rucker and Matea Gold, "No More 'Shock and
Awe': Jeb Bush Now Just Another Presidential Aspirant," *Washington Post*, October 15, 2015,
https://www.washingtonpost.com/politics/jeb-bushs-fundraising-pace-dropped-sharply
-in-third-quarter/2015/10/15/b7eeaae8-7352-11e5-8d93-0af317ed58c9_story.html?utm_term=
.b939caa62288; Philip Rucker, Ed O'Keefe, and Sean Sullivan, "Bush Campaign Downsizes in the Face of Trump Strength," *Washington Post*, October 23, 2015, https://www
.washingtonpost.com/politics/bush-campaign-downsizes-in-the-face-of-trump-strength
/2015/10/23/4908181e-79a9-11e5-a958-d889faf561dc_story.html?utm_term=.feeda214c9f3.

28. Sasha Issenberg, "The Best-Laid Free Media Plan of Marco Rubio," Bloomberg,
March 3, 2016, https://www.bloomberg.com/politics/articles/2016-03-03/the-best-laid-free
-media-plan-of-marco-rubio.

29. Chris Cillizza, "This Is the Most Painful 180 Seconds of Marco Rubio's Presidential Campaign So Far," *Washington Post*, May 18, 2015, https://www.washingtonpost
.com/news/the-fix/wp/2015/05/18/this-is-the-most-painful-180-seconds-of-marco
-rubios-presidential-campaign-so-far/?utm_term=.5cf83a08eb40; Michael Barbaro and
Steve Eder, "Billionaire Lifts Marco Rubio, Politically and Personally," *New York Times*,
May 9, 2015, https://www.nytimes.com/2015/05/10/us/billionaire-lifts-marco-rubio-polit
ically-and-personally.html?_r=0; Alan Rappeport and Steve Elder, "Rubios on the Road
Have Drawn Unwanted Attention," *New York Times*, June 5, 2015, https://www.nytimes
.com/politics/first-draft/2015/06/05/marco-rubio-and-his-wife-cited-17-times-for-traffic
-infractions-2/; Kenneth T. Walsh, "Marco Rubio Hits Back at *New York Times*," *US News
and World Report*, June 11, 2015, http://www.usnews.com/news/blogs/ken-walshs-washing
ton/2015/06/11/marco-rubio-hits-back-at-new-york-times; Chris Cillizza, "Winners and
Losers from the CNN Debate," *Washington Post*, September 16, 2015, https://www.washington
post.com/news/the-fix/wp/2015/09/16/winners-and-losers-from-the-cnn-debate/?tid
=pm_politics_pop_b&utm_term=.ee89c191d173; Tom LoBianco, "Conservatives Boo
Trump after Rubio 'Clown' Insult," CNN, September 25, 2015, https://www.cnn.com/2015
/09/25/politics/donald-trump-marco-rubio-michael-cohen/index.html; Paul Waldman,
"Why Everyone Suddenly Decided Marco Rubio Will Be the GOP Nominee," *Washington
Post*, October 6, 2015, https://www.washingtonpost.com/blogs/plum-line/wp/2015/10/06
/why-everyone-suddenly-decided-marco-rubio-will-be-the-gop-nominee/?utm_term=
.b31f9bd3a837; John Cassidy, "Marco Rubio's Big Night at the Republican Debate," *New
Yorker*, October 29, 2015, http://www.newyorker.com/news/john-cassidy/marco-rubios
-big-night-at-the-republican-debate.

30. Amber Phillips, "Marco Rubio's Very Big Night in Iowa," *Washington Post*, February 2, 2016, https://www.washingtonpost.com/news/the-fix/wp/2016/02/02/marco-rubios
-very-big-night-in-iowa/?utm_term=.a9d5ef966f79; Nate Silver, "Marco Rubio Stole
Ted Cruz's Iowa Bounce," *FiveThirtyEight*, February 5, 2016, https://fivethirtyeight.com
/features/marco-rubio-stole-ted-cruzs-iowa-bounce/. The prediction market data is here:
David M. Rothschild, "State of Republican Primary after Three Primary Votes," PredictWise, February 21, 2016, http://predictwise.com/blog/2016/02/state-of-republican-primary
-after-three-primary-votes/.

31. Molly Ball, "Did Marco Rubio Squander His Big Moment?," *Atlantic*, February
7, 2016, https://www.theatlantic.com/politics/archive/2016/02/did-marco-rubio-squander
-his-big-moment/460362/.

32. David Sherfinski, "Ted Cruz on Donald Trump: A Lot of GOP Contenders 'Went out of Their Way to Beat Him with a Stick,'" *Washington Times*, July 16, 2015, http://www .washingtontimes.com/news/2015/jul/16/ted-cruz-donald-trump-lot-gop-contenders -went-out-/; Kelsey Snell, "Budget and Tax: House Passes a Highway Bill, Ted Cruz Threatens to Filibuster a Highway Bill, and the IRS Keeps Hanging Up on You," *Washington Post*, July 16, 2015, https://www.washingtonpost.com/news/powerpost/wp/2015 /07/16/budget-and-tax-house-passes-a-highway-bill-ted-cruz-threatens-to-filibuster-a -highway-bill-and-the-irs-keeps-hanging-up-on-you/?utm_term=.1e70718ef208; Katie Zezima, "Donald Trump, Ted Cruz Headline Capitol Rally against Iran Nuclear Deal," *Washington Post*, September 9, 2015, https://www.washingtonpost.com/news/post-politics /wp/2015/09/09/donald-trump-ted-cruz-to-headline-capitol-rally-against-iran-nuclear -deal/?utm_term=.d172282f2f1a.

33. On Cruz's debate performance, see Mark Halperin, "Report Card: Cruz and Rubio Shine at Battle of Boulder," Bloomberg, October 28, 2015, https://www.bloomberg .com/politics/articles/2015-10-29/cruz-and-rubio-shine-at-battle-of-boulder; and Dan Balz, "Why No One Is Dropping Out of the GOP Presidential Race," *Washington Post*, November 11, 2015, https://www.washingtonpost.com/politics/fourth-gop-presidential -debate-did-little-to-narrow-the-field/2015/11/11/13968642-888c-11e5-be39-0034bb576eee _story.html. Chris Cillizza, "It's Cruz, Not Trump, Who Looks More Like Favorite to Win GOP Nomination," *Washington Post*, December 13, 2015, https://www.washington post.com/politics/its-cruz-not-trump-who-looks-more-like-the-favorite-to-win-gop- primary/2015/12/13/bf8c57de-a1a9-11e5-b53d-972e2751f433_story.html?utm_term=.c8d 42cf92f1c. Examples of scrutiny of Cruz include Jennifer Steinhauer, "Ted Cruz, Shunned in the Senate, Play Unpopularity to His Advantage," *New York Times*, December 17, 2015, https://www.nytimes.com/2015/12/18/us/politics/ted-cruz-shunned-in-the-senate-plays -unpopularity-to-his-advantage.html?smid=tw-nytpolitics&smtyp=cur&_r=1; Callum Borchers, "How Bret Baier Just Made Ted Cruz Wilt," *Washington Post*, December 17, 2015, https://www.washingtonpost.com/news/the-fix/wp/2015/12/17/getting-front-runner -treatment-from-the-press-ted-cruz-shows-first-sign-of-wilting/?utm_term= .co5c7a5cee95&wpisrc=nl_most&wpmm=1; and David Fahrenthold, "The Five Times Ted Cruz Swears He Didn't Change His Mind," *Washington Post*, December 18, 2015, https://www.washingtonpost.com/politics/5-times-that-ted-cruz-swears-he-didnt -change-his-mind/2015/12/18/0065ef76-a46c-11e5-9c4e-be37f66848bb_story.html?utm _term=.281b153d8791&wpisrc=nl_most&wpmm=1. Stephanie Condon, "Donald Trump: Birther Questions about Ted Cruz Could Be a Problem," CBS News, January 5, 2016, http:// www.cbsnews.com/news/donald-trump-birther-questions-about-ted-cruz-could-be-a -problem/; Kenneth T. Walsh, "Donald Trump Hints at Going after Ted Cruz's Wife," *US News and World Report*, March 23, 2016, http://www.usnews.com/news/blogs/ken-walshs -washington/2016/03/23/donald-trump-hints-at-going-after-ted-cruzs-wife. It was unclear what Trump was referring to in threatening Heidi Cruz. She had had an episode of de- pression in 2005 that resulted in a police report when she was found sitting on the grass near a Houston expressway. But this was already well known.

34. Sean Sullivan and David Weigel, "Cruz-Kasich Alliance against Trump Appears to Falter Early," *Washington Post*, April 25, 2016, https://www.washingtonpost.com/politics /cruz-kasich-strike-tenuous-deal-in-attempt-to-slow-down-trump/2016/04/25/3ed573b0 -0afd-11e6-8ab8-9ad050f76d7d_story.html?utm_term=.fb216200f66b.

35. Ashley Parker, "Jeb Bush Takes Voter Questions, but Has No Answer for Donald Trump," *New York Times*, December 8, 2015, https://www.nytimes.com/politics/first-draft

/2015/12/08/jeb-bush-takes-voter-questions-but-has-no-answer-for-donald-trump/; Peter Weber, "John Kasich Says He'd Be Winning If Only the Media Would 'Drool' over Him like They Do Donald Trump," *The Week,* December 10, 2015, http://theweek .com/speedreads/593551/john-kasich-says-hed-winning-only-media-drool-over-like -donald-trump; Hadas Gold, "Ted Cruz: Media Executives 'Have Made a Decision to Get behind Donald Trump,'" *Politico,* May 3, 2016, http://www.politico.com/blogs/on -media/2016/05/ted-cruz-criticizes-rupert-murdoch-roger-ailes-222738; Michael M. Grynbaum, "Chris Wallace, In-House Moderate at Fox News, Has Less Predictable Targets," *New York Times,* April 28, 2016, https://www.nytimes.com/2016/04/29/business /media/chris-wallace-in-house-moderate-at-fox-has-less-predictable-targets.html?_r=1; Michael M. Grynbaum, "Television Networks Struggle to Provide Equal Airtime in the Era of Trump," *New York Times,* May 30, 2016, https://www.nytimes.com/2016/05/31 /business/media/television-networks-struggle-to-provide-equal-airtime-in-the-era-of -trump.html?ref=politics&_r=0.

36. Wayne Steger, "A Quarter Century of News Coverage of Candidates in Presidential Nomination Campaigns," *Journal of Political Marketing* 1, no. 1 (2002): 91–115; Sides and Vavreck, *The Gamble.*

37. Nate Silver, "Trump Boom or Trump Bust," *FiveThirtyEight,* December 15, 2015, https://fivethirtyeight.com/features/trump-boom-or-trump-bubble/.

38. Shafer supplied a list in "Trump Isn't a Media Creation." MSNBC's Steve Kornacki also assembled a collage of headlines: Steve Kornacki (@SteveKornacki), "The media totally failed to vet Trump and instead has been providing nothing but fawning, lapdog coverage like this," Twitter graphic, March 29, 2016, 7:42 a.m., https://twitter.com/Steve Kornacki/status/714825179872890880.

39. Marc Ambinder, "Has the Media Made Mistakes in How They've Covered Donald Trump?," Quora, March 9, 2016, https://www.quora.com/Has-the-media-made -mistakes-in-how-theyve-covered-Donald-Trump/answer/Marc-Ambinder?share =e3391daf; Ezra Klein, "Donald Trump Lies—Yes, Lies—about His Policies. And He Does It Constantly," *Vox,* March 8, 2016, http://www.vox.com/2016/3/8/11178872/donald -trump-policies; Ben Smith, "The Media Keeps Letting Trump Get Away with His Iraq Lie," *Buzzfeed,* May 3, 2016, https://www.buzzfeed.com/bensmith/trump-supported -iraq-war?utm_term=.dnWL3KebO#.dnWL3KebO; Greg Dworkin, "David Folkenflik on Complex Media Role in Donald Trump's Rise," Storify, March 27, 2016, https:// storify.com/DemFromCT/david-folkenflik-on-complex-media-role-in-donald-t (site discontinued).

40. Sides and Leetaru, "Deep Dive."

41. Nate Silver, "How Trump Hacked the Media," *FiveThirtyEight,* March 30, 2016, https://fivethirtyeight.com/features/how-donald-trump-hacked-the-media/?ex_cid =538twitter.

42. Thomas Patterson, "Pre-primary News Coverage of the 2016 Presidential Race: Trump's Rise, Sanders' Emergence, Clinton's Struggle," Shorenstein Center on Media, Politics and Public Policy, June 13, 2016, https://shorensteincenter.org/pre-primary-news -coverage-2016-trump-clinton-sanders/.

43. Dana Milbank, "Republicans Should Blame Themselves—Not the Media—for Trump," *Washington Post,* March 8, 2016, https://www.washingtonpost.com/opinions /republicans-should-blame-themselves—not-the-media—for-trump/2016/03/08 /58b8477e-e570-11e5-b0fd-073d5930a7b7_story.html?utm_term=.33a2b30bbb2b.

44. Barton Swaim, "Teflon Don (or, Why It's Near-Impossible to Attack the GOP Front-Runner)," *Washington Post*, December 15, 2015, https://www.washingtonpost .com/news/the-fix/wp/2015/12/15/the-unattackable-donald-trump/?postshare=49414 50196137196&tid=ss_tw&utm_term=.ea4fda5e7dbf.

45. Andrew Kaczynski, "Trump: I Don't Regret McCain Comments, My Poll Numbers Went Up," *Buzzfeed*, May 11, 2016, https://www.buzzfeed.com/andrewkaczynski /trump-i-dont-regret-mccain-comments-my-polls-numbers-went-up?utm_term =.lwvNwdJkP#.md8pjb9on; Kathy Frankovic, "Fiorina, Rubio Score Highly with Republicans in First Primary Debate," YouGov, August 11, 2015, https://today.yougov.com /news/2015/08/11/fiorina-rubio-score-well-first-gop-primary-debate-/; Kathy Frankovic, "Trump Still Leads as Rubio and Fiorina Rise," YouGov, October 1, 2015, https://today .yougov.com/news/2015/10/01/donald-trump-still-top-smaller-lead/; Patrick Healy and Jonathan Martin, "Ted Cruz and Marco Rubio Clash Harshly, Filling Void on G.O.P. Debate Stage," *New York Times*, January 28, 2016, https://www.nytimes.com/2016/01/29 /us/politics/republican-debate.html.

46. Some commentary also blamed other Republicans for failing to attack Trump enough. See, for example, Milbank, "Republicans Should Blame Themselves."

47. S. V. Dáte, "Donald Trump's Long, Easy Debate Ride," *National Journal*, February 26, 2016, https://www.nationaljournal.com/s/620311/donald-trumps-long-easy-debate -ride?mref=search-result; Coppins, *The Wilderness*, 14.

48. Tracy Jan and Annie Linskey, "Republican Groups Aim to Bring Down Donald Trump," *Boston Globe*, November 25, 2015, http://www.bostonglobe.com/news/politics /2015/11/24/gop-establishment-fears-donald trump-could-permanently-tarnish -republican-party-image/EbCIEyJlbD1xF74eXe1LfP/story.html?s_campaign=8315; Robert Costa and Philip Rucker, "Private Memo Lays Out How the GOP Would Deal with Trump as Its Nominee," *Washington Post*, December 2, 2015, https://www.washing tonpost.com/politics/private-memo-lays-out-how-the-gop-would-deal-with-trump-as -its-nominee/2015/12/02/78514cba-9909-11e5-94f0-9eeaff906ef3_story.html.

49. Philip Rucker and Robert Costa, "Time for Panic? Establishment Worried That Carson or Trump Might Win," *Washington Post*, November 13, 2015, https://www.washington post.com/politics/time-for-gop-panic-establishment-worried-carson-and-trump-might -win/2015/11/12/38ea88a6-895b-11e5-be8b-1ae2e4f50f76_story.html; Matea Gold and Robert Costa, "Plan A for GOP Donors: Wait for Trump to Fall. (There Is No Plan B.)," *Washington Post*, November 25, 2015, https://www.washingtonpost.com/politics/plan-a-for-gop-donors -wait-for-trump-to-fall-there-is-no-plan-b/2015/11/25/91436a00-92dd-11e5-8aa0 -5d094656oa97_story.html; Jonathan Martin, "Wary of Donald Trump, G.O.P. Leaders Are Caught in a Standoff," *New York Times*, December 1, 2015, https://www.nytimes.com/2015/12 /02/us/politics/wary-of-donald-trump-gop-leaders-are-caught-in-a-standoff.html?_r=1; Chris Cillizza, "Donald Trump Is a Disaster for Republicans. And They Can't Do a Thing about It," *Washington Post*, December 7, 2015, https://www.washingtonpost.com/news/the -fix/wp/2015/12/07/donald-trump-is-a-disaster-for-republicans-and-they-cant-do-a-thing -about-it/?utm_term=.eod980c371cd; McKay Coppins, "The Anti-Trump Cavalry That Never Came," *Buzzfeed*, January 14, 2016, https://www.buzzfeed.com/mckaycoppins/the -anti-trump-cavalry-that-never-came?utm_term=.ppB570NpP#.vlZYpoJPr.

50. Alex Isenstadt, "Trump and Cruz Send Shivers Down GOP Spines," *Politico*, January 5, 2016, http://www.politico.com/story/2016/01/donald-trump-ted-cruz-gop -fear-217345#ixzz3wOpwlCtl?NV:.gpdouw9:WGMx; Michael Gerson, "For the Sake of

the Republican Party, Both Trump and Cruz Must Lose," *Washington Post*, January 18, 2016, https://www.washingtonpost.com/opinions/giving-strength-and-momentum-to -prejudice/2016/01/18/2c35c596-be0b-11e5-bcda-62a36b394160_story.html?utm_term =.d1961b065e22&wpisrc=nl_most&wpmm=1; Tal Kopan, "Graham on Choosing between Trump and Cruz: 'It's like Being Shot or Poisoned,'" CNN, January 21, 2016, http://www .cnn.com/2016/01/21/politics/lindsey-graham-donald-trump-ted-cruz-poison-or-shot/; Robert Costa, "Palin's Endorsement the Latest Prize as Trump, Cruz Battle for Conserva- tives," *Washington Post*, January 19, 2016, https://www.washingtonpost.com/politics/palins -endorsement-the-latest-prize-as-trump-cruz-battle-for-conservatives/2016/01/19 /c243b326-bede-11e5-83d4-42e3bceea902_story.html?utm_term=.88fc8868c15b.

51. Sasha Issenberg, "Mike Murphy of Right to Rise Explains His Theory That Jeb Bush Is Still the Candidate to Beat," Bloomberg, October 20, 2015, https://www.bloom berg.com/politics/features/2015-10-20/mike-murphy-of-right-to-rise-explains-his -theory-that-jeb-bush-is-still-the-candidate-to-beat; Robert Costa and Philip Rucker, "Inside the GOP Field's New Strategy to Ride Out the Trump Tornado," *Washington Post*, August 20, 2015, https://www.washingtonpost.com/politics/inside-the-gop-fields-new -strategies-to-ride-out-the-trump-tornado/2015/08/20/0f0c9628-4761-11e5-846d -02792f854297_story.html?utm_term=.a836a9cc3ccc. The Homeland Security project is described in Coppins, *The Wilderness*, 328.

52. Alexandra Jaffe, "Donald Trump Has 'Small Hands,' Marco Rubio Says," NBC News, February 29, 2016, http://www.nbcnews.com/politics/2016-election/donald-trump -has-small-hands-marco-rubio-says-n527791; Gregory Krieg, "Donald Trump Defends Size of His Penis," CNN, March 4, 2016, https://www.cnn.com/2016/03/03/politics/donald -trump-small-hands-marco-rubio/index.html; Issenberg, "Best-Laid Free Media Plan"; Ben Kamisar, "Rubio Regrets Attacks: My Kids 'Embarrassed,'" *The Hill*, March 9, 2016, http://thehill.com/blogs/ballot-box/272451-rubio-regrets-attacks-my-kids-embar rassed; Jessie Hellman, "Rubio Apologized to Trump for 'Small Hands' Crack," *The Hill*, May 29, 2016, http://thehill.com/blogs/ballot-box/presidential-races/281636-rubio -apologized-to-trump-for-small-hands-comment.

53. Robert Costa and Philip Rucker, "Donald Trump Struggles to Turn Political Fling into Durable Campaign," *Washington Post*, August 9, 2015, https://www.washingtonpost .com/politics/inside-trumps-orbit-growing-pains-for-a-sudden-front-runner/2015/08 /09/7672a8be-3ec6-11e5-9443-3ef23099398b_story.html?utm_term=.71852dc066b2; Rob- ert Costa, Philip Rucker, and Dan Balz, "Donald Trump Plots His Second Act," *Washing- ton Post*, October 7, 2015, https://www.washingtonpost.com/politics/donald-trump-plots -his-second-act/2015/10/06/305790c2-6c68-11e5-9bfe-e59f5e244f92_story.html; Tim Fern- holz, "How Serious Is Donald Trump? His Campaign Lacks One Essential Tool," Quartz, October 20, 2015, https://qz.com/528543/is-donald-trump-really-running-hes-the-only -white-house-candidate-without-a-list-of-voters/; Trip Gabriel, "Donald Trump Cam- paign Lags in Mobilizing Iowa Caucus Voters," *New York Times*, December 19, 2015, https:// www.nytimes.com/2015/12/20/us/politics/donald-trump-campaign-lags-in-mobilizing -iowa-caucus-voters.html?_r=1.

Chapter 5: Hiding in Plain Sight

1. Philip Rucker, "It's Not Just Trump: Voter Anger Fuels Outsider Candidates," *Washington Post*, August 12, 2015, https://www.washingtonpost.com/politics/its-not-just -trump-voter-anger-fuels-outsider-candidates/2015/08/12/cd3fdb06-40f8-11e5-846d

-02792f854297_story.html?tid=pm_politics_pop_b&utm_term=.af5335a00775; Stuart Rothenberg, "Does Voter Anger Explain the Success of Presidential Outsiders?," *Roll Call*, September 28, 2015, http://www.rollcall.com/rothenblog/voter-anger-explain-success -presidential-outsiders/?dcz=lunchbreak.

2. Shanto Iyengar and Donald Kinder, *News That Matters: Television and American Opinion* (Chicago: University of Chicago Press, 1987); Michael Tesler, "Priming Predispositions and Changing Policy Positions: An Account of When Mass Opinion Is Primed or Changed," *American Journal of Political Science* 59, no. 4 (2015): 806–24.

3. Larry M. Bartels, *Presidential Primaries* (Princeton: Princeton University Press, 1988), 83.

4. Laura Stoker, "Judging Presidential Character: The Demise of Gary Hart," *Political Behavior* 15, no. 2 (1993): 193–223; Michael Tesler and David O. Sears, *Obama's Race: The 2008 Election and the Dream of a Post-Racial America* (Chicago: University of Chicago Press, 2010); Michael Tesler, "Moral Conservatives Spark the Santorum Surge," YouGov, February 21, 2012, https://today.yougov.com/news/2012/02/21/moral-conservatives-spark -santorum-surge/.

5. Gabriel Lenz, *Follow the Leader? How Voters Respond to Politicians' Policies and Performance* (Chicago: University of Chicago Press, 2012).

6. The 2011–12 interviews were part of the Cooperative Campaign Analysis Project, which is featured in John Sides and Lynn Vavreck, *The Gamble: Choice and Chance in the 2012 Presidential Election* (Princeton: Princeton University Press, 2013).

7. "Here's Donald Trump's Presidential Announcement Speech," *Time*, June 16, 2015, http://time.com/3923128/donald-trump-announcement-speech/.

8. Philip Converse, "The Nature of Belief Systems in Mass Publics," in *Ideology and Discontent*, ed. David E. Apter (New York: Free Press of Glencoe, 1964), 217; John Zaller, "Floating Voters in US Presidential Elections, 1948–2000," in *Studies in Public Opinion: Attitudes, Nonattitudes, Measurement Error, and Change*, ed. William Saris and Paul Sniderman (Princeton: Princeton University Press, 2004), 166–212.

9. The Pew Research Center polls are available here: Pew Research Center, "8. Perceptions of the Public's Voice in Government and Politics," November 23, 2015, http:// www.people-press.org/2015/11/23/8-perceptions-of-the-publics-voice-in-government -and-politics/; and "3. Views on Economy, Government Services, Trade," March 31, 2016, http://www.people-press.org/2016/03/31/3-views-on-economy-government-services -trade/.

10. For example, Trump tweeted the day after he lost the Iowa caucuses, "I don't believe I have been given any credit by the voters for self-funding my campaign, the only one. I will keep doing, but not worth it!" Donald J. Trump (@realDonaldTrump), Twitter, February 2, 2016, 8:39 a.m., https://twitter.com/realdonaldtrump/status/69456 0681090248704?lang=en.

11. For a similar conclusion, see Jeff Manza and Ned Crowley, "Working Class Hero? Interrogating the Social Bases of the Rise of Donald Trump," *Forum* 15, no. 1 (2017): 3–28.

12. In the RAND Presidential Election Panel Survey (PEPS), Trump also did about 30 points better among those who, in a prior January 2015 survey, were the most dissatisfied about their jobs, income, and lives, compared to those who were the most satisfied. See John Sides and Michael Tesler, "How Political Science Helps Explain the Rise of Trump (Part 3): It's the Economy Stupid," *Monkey Cage* (blog), *Washington Post*, March 4, 2016, https://www.washingtonpost.com/news/monkey-cage/wp/2016/03/04/how-political

-science-helps-explain-the-rise-of-trump-part-3-its-the-economy-stupid/?utm_term
=.94815de46552.

13. The statement about raising taxes on the wealthy is from an interview with the
Today Show's Savannah Guthrie. See Kyle Griffin (@kylegriffin1), "FLASHBACK:
April 2016. SAVANNAH GUTHRIE: 'Do you believe in raising taxes on the wealthy?'
TRUMP: 'I do. I do. Including myself. I do.'" Twitter video, April 26, 2017, 4:50 p.m., https://
twitter.com/kylegriffin1/status/857381320355454976. For an analysis of his tax plan, see
Alan Cole, "Details and Analysis of Donald Trump's Tax Plan, September 2016," Tax
Foundation, September 10, 2016, https://taxfoundation.org/details-analysis-donald-trump
-tax-plan-2016/; and Lynnley Browning, "Trump's Tough Talk on Hedge-Fund Taxes
Doesn't Match His Plan," Bloomberg, May 9, 2016, https://www.bloomberg.com/politics
/articles/2016-05-09/trump-s-tough-talk-on-hedge-fund-taxes-doesn-t-match-his-plan.

14. Philip Rucker and Dan Balz, "Trump's Growing List of Apostasies Puts Him at
Odds with Decades of Republican Belief," *Washington Post*, March 22, 2016, https://www
.washingtonpost.com/politics/trump-seeks-a-gop-platform-more-in-his-common
-sense-image/2016/03/22/0389d688-f046-11e5-89c3-a647fcce95e0_story.html?utm_term
=.d7155d49a946; *National Review* editors, "Against Trump," *National Review*, January
21, 2016, http://www.nationalreview.com/article/430137/donald-trump-conservative-move
ment-menace. On the growing conservatism of the Republican Party, see Nolan McCarty,
Keith T. Poole, and Howard Rosenthal, *Polarized America: The Dance of Ideology and Unequal Riches* (Cambridge, MA: Massachusetts Institute of Technology Press, 2006); and
Geoffrey Kabaservice, *Rule and Ruin: The Downfall of Moderation and the Destruction of
the Republican Party, from Eisenhower to the Tea Party* (New York: Oxford University
Press, 2013). On the Koch brothers' network, see Theda Skocpol and Alexander Hertel-
Fernandez, "The Koch Network and Republican Party Extremism," *Perspectives on Politics*
14, no. 3 (2016): 681–99.

15. Converse, "The Nature of Belief Systems."

16. Michael S. Lewis-Beck, William G. Jacoby, Helmut Norpoth, and Herbert F. Weis-
berg, *The American Voter Revisited* (Ann Arbor: University of Michigan Press, 2008);
Donald Kinder and Nathan Kalmoe, *Neither Liberal nor Conservative: Ideological
Innocence in the American Public* (Chicago: University of Chicago Press, 2017), 43;
D. Sunshine Hillygus and Todd G. Shields, *The Persuadable Voter: Wedge Issues in Presi-
dential Campaigns* (Princeton: Princeton University Press, 2009); Delia Baldassarri and
Andrew Gelman, "Partisans without Constraint: Political Polarization and Trends in
American Public Opinion," *American Journal of Sociology* 114, no. 2 (2008): 408–46.

17. Matt Grossmann and David A. Hopkins, *Asymmetric Politics: Ideological Repub-
licans and Group Interest Democrats* (New York: Oxford University Press, 2016); Yphtach
Lelkes and Paul M. Sniderman, "The Ideological Asymmetry of the American Party
System," *British Journal of Political Science* 46 (2014): 825–44; Christopher Ellis and
James A. Stimson, *Ideology in America* (New York: Cambridge University Press, 2012); John
Sides, "Republican Primary Voters Embrace Government. No, Really," YouGov, March 22,
2012, https://today.yougov.com/news/2012/03/22/republican-primary-voters-embrace-gov
ernment-no-re/; Henry Olsen and Dante J. Scala, *The Four Faces of the Republican Party*
(New York: Palgrave Macmillan, 2016).

18. Harry Enten, "Let's Be Serious about Ted Cruz from the Start: He's too Extreme
and too Disliked to Win," *FiveThirtyEight*, March 23, 2015, https://fivethirtyeight.com
/features/lets-be-serious-about-ted-cruz-from-the-start-hes-too-extreme-and-too
-disliked-to-win/.

19. Lynn Vavreck, "How Donald Trump Leverages America's Fault Lines," *New York Times*, November 3, 2015, https://www.nytimes.com/2015/11/03/upshot/how-donald-trump-leverages-americas-fault-lines.html. On partisan views of Black Lives Matter, see Pew Research Center, *On Views of Race and Inequality, Blacks and Whites Are Worlds Apart* (Washington, DC: Pew Research Center, 2016), http://assets.pewresearch.org/wp-content/uploads/sites/3/2016/06/ST_2016.06.27_Race-Inequality-Final.pdf. On the racialized nature of public opinion about criminal justice, see Mark Peffley and Jon Hurwitz, *Justice in America: The Separate Realities of Blacks and Whites* (Cambridge: Cambridge University Press, 2010); Joe Soss, Laura Langbein, and Alan R. Metelko, "Why Do White Americans Support the Death Penalty?," *Journal of Politics* 65, no. 2 (2003): 397–421; and Franklin D. Gilliam Jr. and Shanto Iyengar, "Prime Suspects: The Influence of Local Television News on the Viewing Public," *American Journal of Political Science* 44, no. 3 (2000): 560–73.

20. Martin Gilens, *Why Americans Hate Welfare: Race, Media, and the Politics of Antipoverty Policy* (Chicago: University of Chicago Press, 1999); Nicholas J. G. Winter, *Dangerous Frames: How Ideas about Race and Gender Shape Public Opinion* (Chicago: University of Chicago Press, 2008), 84. See also Donald R. Kinder and Cindy D. Kam, *Us against Them: Ethnocentric Foundations of American Opinion* (Chicago: University of Chicago Press, 2009).

21. "Here's Donald Trump's Presidential Announcement Speech."

22. Ronald Kessler, "Donald Trump: Mean-Spirited GOP Won't Win Elections," Newsmax, November 26, 2012, http://www.newsmax.com/Newsfront/Donald-Trump-Ronald-Kessler/2012/11/26/id/465363/.

23. Jonathan Martin and Patrick Healy, "In Republican Debate, Candidates Battle Sharply on Immigration," *New York Times*, November 10, 2015, https://www.nytimes.com/2015/11/11/us/republican-debate-fox-business.html.

24. On Rubio, see McKay Coppins, *The Wilderness: Deep inside the Republican Party's Combative, Contentious, Chaotic Quest to Take Back the White House* (New York: Little, Brown, 2016), 47, 73, 74. Patrick Healy, "In Republican Debate, Jeb Bush Attacks Donald Trump," *New York Times*, February 13, 2016, https://www.nytimes.com/2016/02/14/us/politics/republican-debate.html?_r=0.

25. Bradley Jones, "Americans' Views of Immigrants Marked by Widening Partisan, Generational Divides," Pew Research Center, April 15, 2016, http://www.pewresearch.org/fact-tank/2016/04/15/americans-views-of-immigrants-marked-by-widening-partisan-generational-divides/; Pew Research Center, "Partisan Polarization Surges in Bush, Obama Years," June 4, 2012, http://www.people-press.org/2012/06/04/partisan-polarization-surges-in-bush-obama-years/. The poll results regarding Trump's "rapists" statement are described in Dana Blanton, "Fox News Poll: Reshuffling of GOP Field, Many Agree with Trump on Immigration," Fox News, July 17, 2015, http://www.foxnews.com/politics/2015/07/17/fox-news-poll-reshuffling-gop-field-many-agree-with-trump-on-immigration.html.

26. Morris Levy, Matthew Wright, and Jack Citrin, "Mass Opinion and Immigration Policy in the United States: Re-assessing Clientelist and Elitist Perspectives," *Perspectives on Politics* 14, no. 3 (2016): 660–80. The quote is from 670. Emphasis added.

27. Theda Skocpol and Vanessa Williamson, *The Tea Party and the Remaking of Republican Conservatism* (New York: Oxford University Press, 2012), 57, 72. See also Christopher Parker and Matt Barreto, *Change They Can't Believe In: The Tea Party and Reactionary Politics in America* (Princeton: Princeton University Press, 2013), 165–72.

Gabriel Sherman, "Operation Trump: Inside the Most Unorthodox Campaign in Political History," *New York*, April 3, 2016, http://nymag.com/daily/intelligencer/2016/04 /inside-the-donald-trump-presidential-campaign.html/.

28. Theodore Schleifer, "Trump Doesn't Challenge Anti-Muslim Questioner at Event," CNN, September 18, 2015, http://www.cnn.com/2015/09/17/politics/donald-trump -obama-muslim-new-hampshire/; Glenn Kessler, "Trump's Outrageous Claim That 'Thousands' of New Jersey Muslims Celebrated the 9/11 Attacks," *Washington Post*, November 22, 2015, https://www.washingtonpost.com/news/fact-checker/wp/2015/11/22 /donald-trumps-outrageous-claim-that-thousands-of-new-jersey-muslims-celebrated -the-911-attacks/?utm_term=.3d5109bf30ed&wpisrc=nl_most&wpmm=1.

29. Maggie Haberman and Richard Pérez-Peña, "Donald Trump Sets Off a Furor with Call to Register Muslims in the U.S.," *New York Times*, November 20, 2015, https:// www.nytimes.com/2015/11/21/us/politics/donald-trump-sets-off-a-furor-with-call-to -register-muslims-in-the-us.html?_r=0; Sean Sullivan and Jenna Johnson, "Trump's Proposal to Keep Out Muslims Crosses a Line for Many in Both Parties," *Washington Post*, December 8, 2015, https://www.washingtonpost.com/politics/trumps-proposal-to -keep-out-muslims-crosses-a-line-for-many-in-both-parties/2015/12/08/bb887e64 -9dea-11e5-bce4-708fe33e3288_story.html?utm_term=.313ea9c9aeb3. Mike Pence (@Gov- PenceIN), Twitter, December 8, 2015, 7:30 a.m., https://twitter.com/govpencein/status /674249808610066433?lang=en.

30. John Sides and Kim Gross, "Stereotypes of Muslims and Attitudes toward the War on Terror," *Journal of Politics* 75, no. 1 (2013): 583–98; Kerem Ozan Kalkan, Geoffrey C. Layman, and Eric M. Uslaner, "'Band of Others'? Attitudes toward Muslims in Contemporary American Society," *Journal of Politics* 71, no. 4 (2009): 847–72; Pew Research Center, "Political Values: Government Regulation, Environment, Immigration, Race, Views of Islam," December 8, 2016, http://www.people-press.org/2016/12/08/3-political -values-government-regulation-environment-immigration-race-views-of-islam/; Tesler and Sears, *Obama's Race*.

31. Scott Clement, "Republicans Embrace Trump's Ban on Muslims While Most Others Reject It," *Washington Post*, December 14, 2015, https://www.washingtonpost .com/politics/americans-reject-trumps-muslim-ban-but-republicans-embrace-it/2015 /12/14/24f1c1a0-a285-11e5-9c4e-be37f66848bb_story.html?utm_term=.8e3941eddod7. Other polls with different question wordings generally showed majority support for the Muslim ban among Republicans. See Ariel Edwards-Levy, "Polls: American Support for Trump's Muslim Ban Is High—or Low," *Huffington Post*, December 11, 2015, http://www .huffingtonpost.com/entry/donald-trump-muslims-ban_us_566b5998e4b0e292150dfe86. For the exit poll results, see American Enterprise Institute, "Party Loyalty and Exit Polls: What Voters Are Saying," *AEI Political Report*, June 2016, https://www.aei.org/wp -content/uploads/2016/05/Political-Report-June-2016-1.pdf; Michael Tesler, "How Hostile Are Trump Supporters toward Muslims? This New Poll Will Tell You," *Monkey Cage* (blog), *Washington Post*, December 8, 2015, https://www.washingtonpost.com/news/monkey -cage/wp/2015/12/08/how-hostile-are-trump-supporters-toward-muslims-this-new-poll -will-tell-you/; and Nick Gass, "Poll: 67 Percent of Trump Voters Dislike Muslims," *Politico*, February 26, 2016, http://www.politico.com/blogs/2016-gop-primary-live-updates-and -results/2016/02/donald-trump-voters-dislike-american-muslims-219877.

32. For other analyses that reached a similar finding, see Lynn Vavreck, "Measuring Donald Trump's Supporters for Intolerance," *New York Times*, February 25, 2016, https:// www.nytimes.com/2016/02/25/upshot/measuring-donald-trumps-supporters-for -intolerance.html?_r=0; Emily Fitter and Chris Kahn, "Exclusive: Trump Voters More

Likely to View Blacks Negatively—Reuters/Ipsos Poll," Reuters, June 28, 2016, http://www
.reuters.com/article/us-usa-election-race-idUSKCN0ZE2SW; Public Policy Polling,
"Trump, Clinton Continue to Lead in SC," press release, February 16, 2016, http://www
.publicpolicypolling.com/pdf/2015/PPP_Release_SC_21616.pdf; and Sean McElwee and
Jason McDaniel, "Yes, Trump's Biggest Asset Is Racism," Salon, March 22, 2016, http://
www.salon.com/2016/03/22/yes_trumps_secret_weapon_is_racism_why_bigotry_not
_the_economy_is_the_biggest_factor_driving_his_rise/.

33. David O. Sears and Carolyn L. Funk, "Evidence of the Long-Term Persistence of
Adults' Political Predispositions," *Journal of Politics* 61 (1991): 1–28; P. J. Henry and
David O. Sears, "The Crystallization of Contemporary Racial Prejudice across the Lifes-
pan," *Political Psychology* 30, no. 4 (2009): 569–90; Tesler, "Priming Predispositions"; Tali
Mendelberg, *The Race Card: Campaign Strategy, Implicit Messages, and the Norm of
Racial Equality* (Princeton: Princeton University Press, 2001); Tali Mendelberg, "Racial
Priming Revived," *Perspectives on Politics* 6 (2008): 109–23.

34. For a review, see Donald R. Kinder, "Prejudice and Politics," in *Oxford Handbook
of Political Psychology*, 2nd ed., ed. Leonie Huddy, David O. Sears and Jack S. Levy
(New York: Oxford University Press, 2013), 812–51.

35. Cindy D. Kam and Camille D. Burge, "Uncovering Reactions to the Racial Resentment Scale across the Racial Divide," *Journal of Politics* 80, no. 1 (2018): 314–20.

36. Trump support was also related to whether people believed immigration was an
important issue. YouGov/*Economist* polls showed that by mid-July 2015, Trump was winning among nearly one-third of the 60 percent of Republicans who thought immigration
was very important. His support among Republicans who did not think immigration
was a very important issue was 30 points lower. Michael Tesler, "How Anti-immigrant
Attitudes Are Fueling Support for Donald Trump," *Monkey Cage* (blog), *Washington Post*,
November 24, 2015, https://www.washingtonpost.com/news/monkey-cage/wp/2015/11/24
/how-anti-immigrant-attitudes-are-fueling-support-for-donald-trump/. In the VOTER
Survey, nearly 60 percent of GOP voters who were deeply concerned about immigration
in 2011 supported Trump in the primaries, compared to just over 40 percent of those who
were less concerned about the issue.

37. On the cultural origins of immigration attitudes, see Jens Hainmueller and Dan
Hopkins, "Public Attitudes about Immigration," *Annual Review of Political Science* 17
(2014): 225–49.

38. Jesse Byrnes, "Kasich Hits Trump, Cruz on Muslim Rhetoric," *The Hill*,
March 28, 2016, http://thehill.com/blogs/ballot-box/presidential-races/274481-kasich-hits
-trump-cruz-on-muslim-rhetoric. During the campaign, several surveys showed that
Trump performed best among Republican voters who had unfavorable opinions of Mus-
lims, saw Islam as an immediate threat to the United States, or supported his proposed
Muslim ban. See Clement, "Republicans Embrace Trump's Ban."

39. Scott Bronstein and Drew Griffin, "Trump's Unwanted Support: White
Supremacists," CNN, February 5, 2016, http://www.cnn.com/2016/02/05/politics/donald
-trump-white-supremacists-new-hampshire/; Evan Osnos, "The Fearful and the Frustrated," *New Yorker*, August 31, 2015, http://www.newyorker.com/magazine/2015/08/31
/the-fearful-and-the-frustrated; Nick Confessore, "For Whites Sensing Decline, Donald
Trump Unleashes Words of Resistance," *New York Times*, July 13, 2016, https://www
.nytimes.com/2016/07/14/us/politics/donald-trump-white-identity.html?_r=1.

40. Ben Domenech, "Are Republicans for Freedom or White Identity Politics?," *Feder-
alist*, August 21, 2015, http://thefederalist.com/2015/08/21/are-republicans-for-freedom
-or-white-identity-politics/; Alan Rappeport, "Donald Trump Wavers on Disavowing

David Duke," *New York Times*, February 28, 2016, https://www.nytimes.com/politics /first-draft/2016/02/28/donald-trump-declines-to-disavow-david-duke/; Mitt Romney (@MittRomney), Twitter, February 29, 2016, 10:22 a.m., https://twitter.com/mittromney /status/704371093549805569?lang=en. Tucker Carlson's tweet is here: Noah Rothman (@NoahCRothman), "What is happening to us?," Twitter graphic, February 29, 2016, 7:05 p.m., https://twitter.com/NoahCRothman/status/704502767495290881.

41. One 2016 book on conservatism devoted a chapter to white nationalism but concluded that it "remains well outside the mainstream political discussion in America, and that is likely to remain the case for the foreseeable future." See George Hawley, *Right-Wing Critics of American Conservatism* (Lawrence: University Press of Kansas, 2016), 266. For an earlier account that anticipated white nationalism's significance, see Carol M. Swain, *The New White Nationalism in America: Its Challenge to Integration* (New York: Cambridge University Press, 2002).

42. Arlie Russell Hochschild, *Stranger in Their Own Land: Anger and Mourning on the American Right* (New York: New Press, 2016), 227–28. The 2016 survey is described in Democracy Fund Voice, "Stranger in My Own Country," January 25, 2017, http://democ racyfundvoice.org/stranger-in-my-own-country/. Ashley Jardina, "Demise of Dominance: Group Threat and The New Relevance of White identity for American Politics" (PhD diss., University of Michigan, 2014); Vincent L. Hutchings, Ashley A. Jardina, Robert Mickey, and Hanes Walton Jr., "The Politics of Race: How Threat Cues and Group Position Can Activate White Identity" (paper presented at the Annual Meeting of the American Political Science Association, Seattle, WA, September 2, 2011).

43. David O. Sears and Carolyn L. Funk, "The Role of Self-Interest in Social and Political Attitudes," *Advances in Experimental Social Psychology* 24 (1991): 1–91; David O. Sears, Jim Sidanius, and Lawrence Bobo, *Racialized Politics: The Debate about Racism in America* (Chicago: University of Chicago Press, 2000); Donald R. Kinder and Lynn M. Sanders, *Divided by Color: Racial Politics and Democratic Ideals* (Chicago: University of Chicago Press, 1996). Here is another, similar finding. In an October 2015 Public Religion Research Institute poll, Trump did better among Republicans who thought that the federal government does not look out for the needs and interests of whites. Meanwhile, Trump support was essentially unrelated to how well Republicans thought the government represents the needs and interests of "people like you."

44. John Sides, Michael Tesler, and Lynn Vavreck, "Donald Trump and the Rise of White Identity Politics" (paper presented at the Annual Meeting of the American Political Science Association, Philadelphia, PA, August 31, 2017).

45. In the VOTER Survey, there was a significant association between being unemployed or laid off and voting for Trump. However, only about 5 percent of the sample described themselves as unemployed or laid off, so any association with Trump support did not translate into many votes overall. Moreover, the PEPS and ANES surveys showed no such association.

46. Manza and Crowley, in "Working Class Hero?," also find that responses to the "income ladder" question were not strongly correlated with Trump support, even among those with less formal education or lower incomes.

47. One piece of research argues that support for both Trump and Bernie Sanders was related to distrust of government. See Joshua J. Dyck, Shanna Pearson-Merkowitz, and Michael Coates, "Primary Distrust: Political Distrust and Support for the Insurgent Candidacies of Donald Trump and Bernie Sanders in the 2016 Primary," *PS: Political Science and Politics* 51, no. 2 (2018): 351–57. However, that research does not account for

many other factors, including anything related to views of racial issues, immigration, and the like. In the VOTER Survey, there was only a very modest relationship between distrust of government and support for Trump after accounting for those factors. Moreover, in the PEPS and 2016 ANES Time Series Survey, there was no statistically significant relationship between support for Trump and political trust after accounting for other factors. If "distrust" was driving Trump support in some fashion, it may involve distrust of various elites (the rich, the powerful), not distrust of government per se. See J. Eric Oliver and Wendy M. Rahn, "Rise of the *Trumpenvolk*: Populism in the 2016 Election," *ANNALS of the American Academy of Political and Social Science* 667, no. 3 (2016): 189–206.

48. On the conflicting evidence about authoritarianism's apparent impact, see Amanda Taub, "The Rise of American Authoritarianism," *Vox*, March 1, 2016, https://www.vox.com/2016/3/1/11127424/trump-authoritarianism; Matthew C. MacWilliams, "Who Decides When the Party Doesn't? Authoritarian Voters and the Rise of Donald Trump," *PS: Political Science and Politics* 49, no. 4 (2016): 716–21; "Trump and the Academy," *Economist*, September 1, 2016, https://www.economist.com/united-states/2016/09/01/trump-and-the-academy; Eric Oliver and Wendy Rahn, "Trump's Voters Aren't Authoritarians, New Research Says. So What Are They?," *Monkey Cage* (blog), *Washington Post*, March 9, 2016, https://www.washingtonpost.com/news/monkey-cage/wp/2016/03/09/trumps-voters-arent-authoritarians-new-research-says-so-what-are-they/?utm_term=.85cc59566ia3. One potential reason for the inconsistent findings is that authoritarians were "cross-pressured" in the 2016 primaries. The standard measure of authoritarianism in political science research captures views about many issues—race, religion, morality, sexuality, and so on—and those constituent parts had mixed implications for voting in the Republican primary. Those with traditional views of morality or sexuality were more likely to support Cruz. But views related to race were more related to support for Trump. Thus, authoritarianism, at least as conventionally measured, is not best suited to identify Trump's supporters in the primaries.

49. On the racial divide among Democrats and Republicans, see Paul M. Sniderman and Edward G. Carmines, *Reaching beyond Race* (Cambridge, MA: Harvard University Press, 1997); and Paul M. Sniderman and Edward H. Stiglitz, "Race and the Moral Character of the Modern American Experience," *Forum* 6, no. 4 (2008): article 1. On the racial divide in Democratic presidential nominations, see Michael Dawson, *Behind the Mule: Race and Class in African-American Politics* (Princeton: Princeton University Press, 1994); and Donald Kinder and Allison Dale-Riddle, *The End of Race? Obama, 2008, and Racial Politics in America* (New Haven: Yale University Press, 2012). On the "color-blind policy alliance," see Desmond S. King and Rogers M. Smith, *Still a House Divided: Race and Politics in Obama's America* (Princeton: Princeton University Press, 2011).

50. On implicit racial appeals, see Mendelberg, *The Race Card*; and Charlton McIlwain and Stephen M. Caliendo, *Race Appeal: How Candidates Invoke Race in US Political Campaigns* (Philadelphia: Temple University Press, 2011). On the impact of racial appeals, see Mendelberg, *The Race Card*; Nicholas A. Valentino, Vincent L. Hutchings, and Ismail K. White, "Cues That Matter: How Political Ads Prime Racial Attitudes during Campaigns," *American Political Science Review* 96 (2002): 75–90; Ian Haney Lopez, *Dog Whistle Politics: How Coded Racial Appeals Have Reinvented Racism and Wrecked the Middle Class* (New York: Oxford University Press, 2014); and Tesler, "Priming Predispositions."

51. Attitudes toward blacks are measured with the four-item views of racial inequality scale and attitudes toward Muslims with either four- or five-category favorability scales

(2008 and 2016) or a 0–100 feeling thermometer (2012 and 2016). In 2008, attitudes toward a path to citizenship were measured with an item asking whether "illegal immigrants should be arrested and deported" or "current residents should be allowed to become citizens." In 2012, these attitudes were measured by asking whether respondents favored or opposed "providing a legal way for illegal immigrants already in the United States to become U.S. citizens." In 2016, these attitudes were measured with an item in which respondents could say that undocumented immigrants "should be allowed to stay in the U.S. and apply for citizenship," "should be allowed to stay in the U.S. but not become citizens," or "should be required to leave the U.S." The first two responses were combined into one category in figure 5.8.

52. For example, see Jim Geraghty, "Donald Trump: Pat Buchanan's Heir," *National Review*, August 31, 2015, http://www.nationalreview.com/article/423294/donald -trump-pat-buchanan-heir; and Eleanor Clift, "Pat Buchanan: Donald Trump Stole My Playbook," *Daily Beast*, June 1, 2016, http://www.thedailybeast.com/articles/2016/06 /01/pat-buchanan-donald-trump-is-running-as-me.html.

53. Nicholas Confessore, "How the G.O.P. Elite Lost Its Voters to Donald Trump," *New York Times*, March 28, 2016, https://www.nytimes.com/2016/03/28/us/politics/donald -trump-republican-voters.html?_r=0.

54. Alec MacGillis, "How Republicans Lost Their Best Shot at the Hispanic Vote," *New York Times Magazine*, September 18, 2016, http://www.nytimes.com/2016/09/18 /magazine/how-republicans-lost-their-best-shot-at-the-hispanic-vote.html?_r=0; Ken Vogel, "Behind the Retreat of the Koch Brothers' Operation," *Politico*, October 27, 2016, http://www.politico.com/story/2016/10/koch-brothers-campaign-struggles-230325.

Chapter 6: Cracks in the Ceiling

1. Patrick Healy, "Delegate Count Leaving Bernie Sanders with Steep Climb," *New York Times*, February 21, 2016, https://www.nytimes.com/2016/02/22/us/politics/delegate -count-leaving-bernie-sanders-with-steep-climb.html?mcubz=2. See the betting market data at Predictwise: PredictWise, "2016 President—Democratic Nomination," accessed May 30, 2018, http://predictwise.com/politics/2016-president-democratic-nomination.

2. Alan Rappeport, "Bernie Sanders, Long-Serving Independent, Enters Presidential Race as a Democrat," *New York Times*, April 29, 2015, https://www.nytimes.com/2015/04 /30/us/politics/bernie-sanders-campaign-for-president.html?mcubz=2.

3. John Judis, "The Bern Supremacy," *National Journal*, November 19, 2015, https:// www.nationaljournal.com/bernie-sanders-democratic-socialist-2016-election; Matthew Yglesias, "Bernie Sanders Is (Still) the Future of the Democratic Party," *Vox*, April 20, 2016, https://www.vox.com/2016/4/20/11466376/bernie-sanders-future-democrats.

4. For useful examples of "Democrats in disarray," see Hendrik Hertzberg, "Disarray This," *New Yorker*, March 26, 2006, http://www.newyorker.com/magazine/2006/03/27 /disarray-this. For a scholarly analysis of the parties in 1972 that shows a larger number of groups within the Democratic Party, see John Kessel, *Presidential Campaign Politics*, 3rd ed. (Chicago: Dorsey, 1988), chap. 3. On the Democrats' weaker track record of consensus in presidential primaries, see Christopher L. Anderson, "Which Party Elites Choose to Lead the Nominations Process?," *Political Research Quarterly* 66, no. 1 (2013): 61–76.

5. Zeke Miller, "When Donald Trump Praised Hillary Clinton," *Time*, July 17, 2015, http://time.com/3962799/donald-trump-hillary-clinton/.

6. Ken Rudin, "Joe Biden Has History on His Side, but Little Else If Hillary Clinton Decides to Run," *National Public Radio*, May 7, 2013, http://www.npr.org/sections /politicaljunkie/2013/05/07/181338426/joe-biden-has-history-on-his-side-but-little-else -if-hillary-clinton-runs; Philip Rucker, "Biden Ponders a 2016 Bid, but a Promotion to the Top Job Seems to Be a Long Shot," *Washington Post*, May 2, 2013, https://www .washingtonpost.com/politics/2013/05/02/445fa480-b278-11e2-9a98-4be1688d7d84_story .html?utm_term=.57c8f660a312.

7. Nick Gass, "Report: Joe Biden's Sons Urged Him to Run in 2016," *Politico*, June 29, 2015, http://www.politico.com/story/2015/06/beau-biden-push-joe-biden-running-2016 -presidential-election-119524; Maureen Dowd, "Joe Biden in 2016: What Would Beau Do?," *New York Times*, August 1, 2015, https://www.nytimes.com/2015/08/02/opinion/sunday /maureen-dowd-joe-biden-in-2016-what-would-beau-do.html?mcubz=2&_r=0; Paul Kane, "Biden, Warren Huddle amid 2016 Speculation," *Washington Post*, August 23, 2015, https:// www.washingtonpost.com/news/post-politics/wp/2015/08/22/biden-warren-huddle -amid-2016-speculation/?utm_term=.b915093ba54c.

8. Peter Baker and Maggie Haberman, "Joe Biden Concludes There's No Time for a 2016 Run," *New York Times*, October 21, 2015, https://www.nytimes.com/2015/10/22/us /joe-biden-concludes-theres-no-time-for-a-2016-run.html?mcubz=2. The Plouffe quote is from Glenn Thrush, "Party of Two," *Politico Magazine*, July/August, 2016 http://www .politico.com/magazine/story/2016/07/2016-barack-obama-hillary-clinton-democratic -establishment-campaign-primary-joe-biden-elizabeth-warren-214023.

9. Campaign Finance Institute, "Clinton Has Received 56% from Donors Who Have Maxed Out, Rubio 43%, and Cruz 16%," February 24, 2016, http://cfinst.org/Press /PReleases/16-02-24/2016_Presidential_Fundraising_Through_Jan_31st.aspx.

10. Jeffrey M. Jones, "Clinton Favorability, Familiarity Bests 2016 Contenders," Gallup, March 12, 2015, http://www.gallup.com/poll/181949/clinton-favorability-familiarity -bests-2016-contenders.aspx; Lydia Saad, "Sanders Surges, Clinton Sags in U.S. Favorability," Gallup, July 24, 2015, http://www.gallup.com/poll/184346/sanders-surges-clinton -sags-favorability.aspx. The July 2015 figure is from Gallup's daily polling between July 8 and July 12, 2015. In those Gallup polls, only 8 percent of Democrats did not have an opinion of Clinton.

11. The news data come from the set of twenty-four prominent news outlets monitored by the firm Crimson Hexagon; the dataset was made available May 16, 2015 (see also chapter 4 and figure 4.1). Using the cable network data we discussed in chapter 4 would tell a similar story. The relevant correlations between Sanders's polling average and different measures of his share of news coverage are 0.49 (raw news stories), 0.69 (smoothed news stories), 0.73 (raw cable network data), and 0.86 (smoothed cable network data). Models of Sanders's news coverage and poll numbers show that lagged values of news coverage were correlated with his poll numbers and vice versa—suggesting a reciprocal relationship similar to that observed in the GOP primary.

12. A list of rallies and the estimated sizes, including links to contemporary news accounts, is here: u/Khaloc, "Chart/Table of all the rally attendance for the various candidates that I will be updating," Reddit, post in r/SandersForPresident thread, August 12, 2015, https://www.reddit.com/r/SandersForPresident/comments/3gpzu6/chart table_of_all_the_rally_attendance_for_the/. Ed O'Keefe and John Wagner, "100,000 People Have Come to Recent Bernie Sanders Rallies. How Does He Do It?," *Washington Post*, August 11, 2015, https://www.washingtonpost.com/politics/how-does-bernie -sanders-draw-huge-crowds-to-see-him/2015/08/11/4ae018f8-3fde-11e5-8d45-d815146f81fa

_story.html?utm_term=.4082048dd361; Ben Schreckinger, "How Bernie Sanders Makes His Mega-rallies," *Politico*, August 19, 2015, http://www.politico.com/story/2015/08/bernie -sanders-rallies-2016-grassroots-support-121512.

13. Alex Seitz-Wald, "Can Bernie Sanders Take the 'Burlington Revolution' National?," MSNBC, May 26, 2015, http://www.msnbc.com/msnbc/can-bernie-sanders -take-the-burlington-revolution-national.

14. Paul Lazarsfeld and Robert Merton, "Mass Communication, Popular Taste, and Organized Social Action," in *The Communication of Ideas*, ed. Lyman Bryson (New York: Institute for Religious and Social Studies, 1948), 101.

15. Trip Gabriel and Patrick Healy, "Challenging Hillary Clinton, Bernie Sanders Gains Momentum in Iowa," *New York Times*, May 31, 2015, https://www.nytimes.com /2015/06/01/us/politics/challenging-hillary-clinton-bernie-sanders-gains-momentum -in-iowa.html?mcubz=2; Thomas Patterson, "Pre-primary News Coverage of the 2016 Presidential Race: Trump's Rise, Sanders' Emergence, Clinton's Struggle," Shorenstein Center on Media, Politics and Public Policy, June 13, 2016, https://shorensteincenter.org /pre-primary-news-coverage-2016-trump-clinton-sanders/.

16. To compare coverage of Trump and Sanders, we calculated each candidate's share of cable network mentions from April 1, 2015, to June 30, 2016—except using as the denominator the combined number of mentions of both Republican and Democratic candidates. Trump's share of the mentions of all candidates was positively correlated with Sanders's share ($r = 0.11$; $p = .02$) but negatively correlated with Clinton's ($r = -0.58$; $p < .001$), Bush's ($r = -0.63$; $p < .001$), Rubio's ($r = -0.31$; $p < .001$), and Carson's ($r = -0.17$; $p < .001$).

17. Michael S. Schmidt, "Hillary Clinton Used Personal Email Account at State Dept., Possibly Breaking Rules," *New York Times*, March 2, 2015, https://www.nytimes .com/2015/03/03/us/politics/hillary-clintons-use-of-private-email-at-state-department -raises-flags.html.

18. Dan Merica and Laura Koren, "Team Clinton: 'Nothing Nefarious' at State," CNN, March 3, 2015, http://www.cnn.com/2015/03/02/politics/hillary-clinton-2016-emails -secretary-of-state/.

19. Peter Schweizer, *Clinton Cash: The Untold Story of How and Why Foreign Governments and Businesses Helped Make Bill and Hillary Rich* (New York: Harper, 2015); Jo Becker and Mike McIntire, "Cash Flowed to Clinton Foundation amid Russian Uranium Deal," *New York Times*, April 23, 2015, https://www.nytimes.com/2015/04/24/us/cash -flowed-to-clinton-foundation-as-russians-pressed-for-control-of-uranium-company .html?_r=0.

20. A good sense of this can be seen in CNN's timeline of the email scandal: Casey Hicks, "Timeline of Hillary Clinton's Email Scandal," CNN, updated November 7, 2016, http://www.cnn.com/2016/10/28/politics/hillary-clinton-email-timeline/.

21. Patterson, "Pre-primary News Coverage." See also Nate Silver, "Hillary Clinton Is Stuck in a Poll-Deflating Feedback Loop," *FiveThirtyEight*, September 16, 2015, https:// fivethirtyeight.com/features/hillary-clinton-is-in-a-self-reinforcing-funk/.

22. Jeffrey M. Jones, "Clinton Favorability among Dems Better than Last Campaign," Gallup, March 27, 2015, http://news.gallup.com/poll/182177/clinton-favorability-among -dems-better-last-campaign.aspx.

23. Philip Rucker and John Wagner, "How Bernie Sanders Is Plotting His Path to the Democratic Nomination," *Washington Post*, September 11, 2015, https://www.washing

tonpost.com/politics/how-bernie-sanders-is-plotting-his-path-to-the-democratic
-nomination/2015/09/11/08ddb472-573c-11e5-8bb1-b488d231bba2_story.html?utm_term=
.9d91cf129fcb&wpisrc=nl_wemost&wpmm=1; Patrick Healy, "Big-Name Plan B's for
Democrats Concerned about Hillary Clinton," *New York Times*, September 9, 2015,
https://www.nytimes.com/2015/09/10/us/politics/big-name-plan-bs-for-democrats
-concerned-about-hillary-clinton.html?_r=1; Chris Cillizza, "It Might Be Time for Hillary Clinton to Start Panicking," *Washington Post*, September 10, 2015, https://www
.washingtonpost.com/news/the-fix/wp/2015/09/10/it-might-be-time-for-hillary-clinton
-to-start-panicking/?tid=pm_politics_pop_b&utm_term=.c44772fa5d20.

24. Mark Blumenthal and Ariel Edwards-Levy, "Sanders Gains with Democratic
Activists, but Clinton Still Leads," *Huffington Post*, October 12, 2015, http://www
.huffingtonpost.com/entry/democratic-activist-poll_us_561c1eace4b050c6c4a27c52.
Rucker and Wagner, "How Bernie Sanders Is Plotting His Path."

25. Katie Glueck, "Insiders: A Runaway Victory for Clinton," *Politico*, October 14, 2015,
http://www.politico.com/story/2015/10/the-politico-caucus-democratic-debate-winner
-loser-insider-214771; Karen Tumulty, "A Self-Assured Performance by Clinton in Democratic Presidential Debate," *Washington Post*, October 13, 2015, https://www.washingtonpost
.com/politics/2015/10/13/c7bd324c-71cb-11e5-8d93-0af317ed58c9_story.html?utm_term=
.21708b199hfe; Patrick Healy, "Democratic Debate Turns Hillary Clinton's Way after
Months of Difficulties," *New York Times*, October 14, 2015, https://www.nytimes.com/2015
/10/14/us/politics/hillary-clinton-moves-quickly-to-re-establish-trust-in-honesty-and
-competence.html; Mark Blumenthal, Natalie Jackson, Ariel Edwards-Levy, and Janie
Velencia, "Huffpollster: Bernie Sanders Wins Focus Groups and Social Media, but Hillary
Clinton Wins Post Debate Polls," *Huffington Post*, October 16, 2015, http://www.huffington
post.com/entry/post-democratic-debate-poll-clinton-wins_us_5620e1dbe4b06462a13b948b
?crtfbt9=; Jenna Johnson, "Donald Trump Says Hillary Clinton 'Came Out the Winner'
of Democratic Debate," *Washington Post*, October 14, 2015, https://www.washingtonpost
.com/news/post-politics/wp/2015/10/14/donald-trump-says-hillary-clinton-came-out
-the-winner-of-democratic-debate/?tid=sm_tw&utm_term=.e2b6d91e4023; Patterson, "Pre-
primary News Coverage."

26. Although Clinton's polling bump seems due mostly to Biden's withdrawal, she
may have been helped by her daylong testimony before a House select committee investigating the Benghazi attack. News accounts noted that the hearing "revealed little new
information" and that Clinton "appeared calm, compassionate, concerned and competent." See Michael D. Shear and Michael S. Schmidt, "Benghazi Panel Engages Clinton in
Tense Session," *New York Times*, October 22, 2015, https://www.nytimes.com/2015/10/23
/us/politics/hillary-clinton-benghazi-committee.html?mcubz=2; and Leigh Ann
Caldwell, "Five Takeaways from Clinton's Benghazi Testimony," NBC News, October 22,
2015, http://www.nbcnews.com/politics/2016-election/five-takeaways-clintons-benghazi
-testimony-n449506.

27. Maggie Haberman and Nick Corasaniti, "Democrats and Bernie Sanders Clash
over Data Breach," *New York Times*, December 18, 2015, https://www.nytimes.com
/politics/first-draft/2015/12/18/sanders-campaign-disciplined-for-breaching-clinton
-data/?mcubz=2&_r=1; Hannah Fraser-Chanpong, "Bernie Sanders Apologizes for
Data Breach in Democratic Debate," CBS News, December 19, 2015, http://www.cbsnews
.com/news/bernie-sanders-apologizes-for-data-breach/; Scott Clement, "Democrats
L-o-v-e Hillary Clinton in New WaPo-ABC Poll. Bernie Sanders? Not So Much,"

Washington Post, November 13, 2015, https://www.washingtonpost.com/news/the-fix/wp
/2015/11/13/poll-hillary-clintons-image-among-democrats-much-stronger-than-bernie
-sanderss/?utm_term=.67df5590b73c; Jennifer Agiesta, "CNN/ORC Poll: In Democratic
Race, Clinton Solidifies Lead," CNN, December 4, 2015, http://www.cnn.com/2015/12/04
/politics/cnn-orc-poll-democrats-hillary-clinton-2016-election-democratic-primary/;
John Lapinski, Stephanie Psyllos, and Hannah Hartig, "Clinton Maintains Lead over
Sanders Heading into Primaries," NBC News, January 5, 2016, http://www.nbcnews
.com/storyline/data-points/clinton-maintains-lead-over-sanders-heading-primaries
-n490131.

28. In the last week of December, Clinton aired 2,263 ads in Iowa media markets and
Sanders aired 2,063. From January 1 to January 7, Clinton aired 7,031 and Sanders aired
9,004. On reactions to the "America" ad, see Lynn Vavreck, "The Ad That Moved People
the Most: Bernie Sanders's 'America,'" *New York Times*, December 30, 2016, https://www
.nytimes.com/2016/12/30/upshot/the-campaign-ads-that-moved-people-the-most
.html?_r=1.

29. The two polls released at that time that showed a narrow Clinton lead were the
January 7–10 *Des Moines Register*/Bloomberg/Selzer poll (Clinton +2) and the January 8–10
PPP poll (Clinton +6). The two showing a narrow Sanders lead were the January 5–10
Quinnipiac poll (Clinton −5) and the January 6–10 ARG poll (Clinton −3). For news cov-
erage, see Mark Murray, "Poll: Neck-and-Neck 2016 Races in Iowa, New Hampshire,"
NBC News, January 10, 2016, http://www.nbcnews.com/meet-the-press/poll-neck-neck
-2016-races-iowa-new-hampshire-n493361; and Eric Bradner, "Poll: Democratic 2016 Race
Narrows," CNN, January 11, 2016, http://www.cnn.com/2016/01/10/politics/poll-hillary
-clinton-bernie-sanders-iowa/.

30. John Sides and Lynn Vavreck, *The Gamble: Choice and Chance in the 2012 Presidential Election* (Princeton: Princeton University Press, 2013), 69–70.

31. See also Thomas E. Patterson, "News Coverage of the 2016 Presidential Primaries:
Horse Race Reporting Has Consequences," Shorenstein Center of Media, Politics, and
Public Policy, July 11, 2016, https://shorensteincenter.org/news-coverage-2016-presidential
-primaries/. In cable news outlets, Sanders's share of mentions of the Democratic candidates increased from 25 percent in the first week of January to over 40 percent for the rest
of the month. The shift in Clinton's polling lead is calculated by estimating a smoothed
daily average of her and Sanders's standings in the national primary polls, subtracting
one from the other, and comparing their values on January 1 and January 31. Amy
Chozick, "Hillary Clinton Gets Set for a Long Slog against Bernie Sanders," *New York
Times*, January 18, 2016, https://www.nytimes.com/2016/01/19/us/politics/hillary-clinton
-readies-for-a-long-slog-against-bernie-sanders.html?_r=0.

32. Patterson, "News Coverage."

33. In a Gallup poll conducted from June 1 to June 3, 2007, 74 percent of Democrats
and independents leaning Democratic had a favorable opinion of Clinton, and 23 percent
had an unfavorable rating. Her ratings changed little in Gallup polling throughout 2007–
2008. In a poll conducted a year later (May 30–June 1, 2008), opinions were very similar:
73 percent to 25 percent.

34. The RAND analysis is based on tracking the views of those who declared their
support for Clinton ($N = 749$) or Sanders ($N = 247$) as of December 2015. William Jordan, "Clinton Still Struggles with Sanders Democrats," YouGov, September 2, 2016,
https://today.yougov.com/news/2016/09/02/clinton-still-struggles-sanders
-democrats/.

35. Seema Mehta, Anthony Pesce, Maloy Moore, and Christine Zhang, "Who Gives Money to Bernie Sanders?," *Los Angeles Times*, June 3, 2016, http://www.latimes.com /projects/la-na-pol-sanders-donors/.

36. Marty Cohen, David Karol, Hans Noel, and John Zaller, *The Party Decides: Presidential Nominations before and after Reform* (Chicago: University of Chicago Press, 2008).

37. The Sanders quote "No . . . I'm an independent" is from Jonathan Allen and Amie Parnes, *Shattered: Inside Hillary Clinton's Doomed Campaign* (New York: Crown, 2017), 48. Paul Waldman, "Bernie Sanders Is Attacking the Establishment. He's Only Half Right," *Washington Post*, January 20, 2016, https://www.washingtonpost.com/blogs /plum-line/wp/2016/01/20/bernie-sanders-is-attacking-the-establishment-hes-only-half -right/?utm_term=.f80483b712f8.

38. Glenn Thrush, "Hillary Clinton Has Had Enough of Bernie Sanders," *Politico*, April 6, 2016, http://www.politico.com/story/2016/04/hillary-clinton-has-had-enough -of-bernie-sanders-221495.

39. Michael Tesler and David O. Sears, *Obama's Race: The 2008 Election and the Dream of a Post-Racial America* (Chicago: University of Chicago Press, 2010), 71.

40. For a full transcript of the speech, see Andrew Prokop, "Read: Hillary Clinton's Huge New Speech on Criminal Justice Reform," *Vox*, April 29, 2015, https://www.vox .com/2015/4/29/8514831/hillary-clinton-criminal-justice-transcript.

41. Sean Sullivan, "Hillary Clinton on Ferguson: 'We Are Better Than That,'" *Washington Post*, August 28, 2014, https://www.washingtonpost.com/news/post-politics /wp/2014/08/28/hillary-clinton-on-ferguson-we-are-better-than-that/?utm_term =.95741d3c4305.

42. Fredrick C. Harris, *The Price of the Ticket: Barack Obama and the Rise and Decline of Black Politics* (Oxford: Oxford University Press, 2012); Daniel Q. Gillion, *Governing with Words: The Political Dialogue on Race, Public Policy, and Inequality in America* (Cambridge: Cambridge University Press, 2016); Michael Eric Dyson, "Yes She Can: Why Hillary Clinton Will Do More for Black People than Barack Obama," *New Republic*, November 29, 2015, https://newrepublic.com/article/124391/yes-she-can.

43. Michelle Garcia, "Hillary Clinton: White People Need to Listen When People of Color Talk About Racism," *Vox*, February 22, 2016, https://www.vox.com/2016/2/22 /11069158/hillary-clinton-in-harlem.

44. See Michelle Alexander, "Why Hillary Clinton Doesn't Deserve the Black Vote," *Nation*, February 10, 2016, https://www.thenation.com/article/hillary-clinton-does-not -deserve-black-peoples-votes/.

45. Dan Balz and Haynes Johnson, *The Battle for America 2008: The Story of an Extraordinary Election* (New York: Viking, 2009), 173.

46. Quoted in Kate Phillips, "Clinton Touts White Support," *Caucus* (blog), *New York Times*, May 8, 2008, https://thecaucus.blogs.nytimes.com/2008/05/08/clinton-touts -white-support/comment-page-61/.

47. Tesler and Sears, *Obama's Race*; Pew Research Center, "Hillary Clinton's Career of Comebacks," December 21, 2012, http://www.people-press.org/2012/12/21/hillary -clintons-career-of-comebacks; Michael Tesler, *Post-Racial or Most-Racial? Race and Politics in the Obama Era* (Chicago: University of Chicago Press, 2016), 218n14.

48. Michael Tesler, "Bernie Sanders's Surge Doesn't Mean the Democratic Race Is Wide Open. Here's Why," *Monkey Cage* (blog), *Washington Post*, September 17, 2015, https://www.washingtonpost.com/news/monkey-cage/wp/2015/09/17/bernie-sanderss -surge-doesnt-mean-the-democratic-race-is-wide-open-heres-why/.

49. On the Southern firewall, see Patrick Healy and Amy Chozick, "Hillary Clinton Relying on Southern Primaries to Fend Off Rivals," *New York Times*, September 5, 2015, https://www.nytimes.com/2015/09/06/us/politics/hillary-clinton-relying-on-southern -primaries-to-fend-off-rivals.html. On Clinton's strategy of tying herself to Obama, see Allen and Parnes, *Shattered*, 142.

50. See also Michael Tesler, "How the 'Obama Effect' Helps Hillary Clinton, and Hurts Bernie Sanders, with Black Voters," *Monkey Cage* (blog), *Washington Post*, February 16, 2016, https://www.washingtonpost.com/news/monkey-cage/wp/2016/02/16/how-the -obama-effect-helps-hillary-clinton-and-hurts-bernie-sanders-with-black-voters/. In 2008, Obama's name was not on the ballot in Michigan, but he was listed in the exit poll. We used the exit poll to estimate his vote share among whites and blacks. To calculate the total number of votes for Clinton and Obama, we combined votes for her with "uncommitted" votes.

51. On the role of racial attitudes in the 2008 Democratic primary, see Tesler and Sears, *Obama's Race*; and Donald Kinder and Allison Dale-Riddle, *The End of Race? Obama, 2008, and Racial Politics in America* (New Haven: Yale University Press, 2012). Other analysis also points to the importance of racial attitudes in both 2008 and 2016. In the Presidential Election Panel Study, which has been interviewing panelists since 2006, about 200 whites reported voting in both the 2008 and 2016 Democratic primaries. Among these respondents, racial attitudes were more strongly associated with changes in support for Clinton between 2008 and 2016 than any other factor.

52. Allen and Parnes, *Shattered*, 176.

53. On idealism and the young, see Kingsley Davis, "The Sociology of Parent-Youth Conflict," *American Sociological Review* 5, no. 4 (1940): 523–35; and Claudia Dalbert and Hedvig Sallay, *The Justice Motive in Adolescence and Young Adulthood: Origins and Consequences* (New York: Routledge, 2004). On young people and third parties, see Martin P. Wattenberg, *Is Voting for Young People?* (New York: Pearson, 2011). On 1984, see Larry M. Bartels, *Presidential Primaries and the Dynamics of Public Choice* (Princeton: Princeton University Press, 1988). On 2008, see Tesler and Sears, *Obama's Race*.

54. Nate Cohn, "Exit Polls and Why the Primary Was Not Stolen from Bernie Sanders," *Upshot* (blog), *New York Times*, June 27, 2016, https://www.nytimes.com/2016/06/28 /upshot/exit-polls-and-why-the-primary-was-not-stolen-from-bernie-sanders.html; Wattenberg, *Is Voting for Young People?*

55. Kathleen Hall Jamieson, *Beyond the Double Bind: Women and Leadership* (Oxford: Oxford University Press, 1995).

56. In fact, those reasons have been cited in research showing that men will penalize female candidates in presidential elections but not congressional elections. For more, see Yoshikuni Ono and Barry C. Burden, "The Contingent Effects of Candidate Sex on Voter Choice," *Political Behavior* (forthcoming).

57. Regina G. Lawrence and Melody Rose, *Hillary Clinton's Race for the White House: Gender Politics and the Media on the Campaign Trail* (Boulder, CO: Lynne Rienner, 2010), 110. See also Jennifer J. Jones, "Talk 'like a Man': The Linguistic Styles of Hillary Clinton, 1992–2013," *Perspectives on Politics* 14, no. 3 (2016): 625–42. A February 2008 ABC/*Washington Post* poll showed that 58 percent of Democrats thought that Clinton was a stronger leader, whereas only 31 percent said this of Obama.

58. Kinder and Dale-Riddle, *The End of Race?*, 50; Tesler and Sears, *Obama's Race*, chap. 6.

59. Mary McThomas and Michael Tesler, "The Growing Influence of Gender Attitudes on Public Support for Hillary Clinton, 2008–2012," *Politics and Gender* 12, no. 1 (2016): 28–49; Amy Chozick and Jonathan Martin, "Clinton '16 Would Give Gender More of a Role Than Clinton '08 Did," *New York Times*, February 24, 2015, https://www.nytimes.com/2015/02/25/us/politics/to-break-highest-glass-ceiling-clinton-gives-nod-to-gender.html?mcubz=2&_r=0.

60. Michael Tesler, "Parents of Daughters Support Hillary Clinton More Than Parents of Sons," *Monkey Cage* (blog), *Washington Post*, January 5, 2016, https://www.washingtonpost.com/news/monkey-cage/wp/2016/01/05/parents-of-daughters-support-hillary-clinton-more-than-parents-of-sons/?utm_term=.5a91d802e52d; Rebecca L. Warner and Brent S. Steel, "Child Rearing as a Mechanism for Social Change: The Relationship of Child Gender to Parents' Commitment to Gender Equity," *Gender and Society* 13, no. 4 (1999): 503–17; Ebonya Washington, "Female Socialization: How Daughters Affect Their Legislator Fathers' Voting on Women's Issues," *American Economic Review* 98, no. 1 (2008): 311–32; Adam N. Glynn and Maya Sen, "Identifying Judicial Empathy: Does Having Daughters Cause Judges to Rule for Women's Issues?," *American Journal of Political Science* 59, no. 1 (2015): 37–54.

61. Academic studies of modern sexism include Janet K. Swim, Kathryn J. Aikin, Wayne S. Hall, and Barbara A. Hunter, "Sexism and Racism: Old Fashioned and Modern Prejudices," *Journal of Personality and Social Psychology* 68 (1995): 199–214; and Janet K. Swim and Laurie Cohen, "Overt, Covert, and Subtle Sexism: A Comparison between the Attitude toward Women and Modern Sexism Scales," *Psychology of Women Quarterly* 21 (1997): 103–18.

62. The analysis in figure 6.11 is replicated in the VOTER Survey, which measured primary vote choice in July 2016 and included five items measuring modern sexism in a subsequent survey in December 2016. The VOTER Survey analysis is available on request.

63. Michael Tesler, "Why the Gender Gap Doomed Hillary Clinton," *Monkey Cage* (blog), *Washington Post*, November 9, 2016, https://www.washingtonpost.com/news/monkey-cage/wp/2016/11/09/why-the-gender-gap-doomed-hillary-clinton/?utm_term=.8ccf69d672e4. The relationship between feminism and support for Clinton is based on a measure of feminism in the December 2011 wave of the Cooperative Campaign Analysis Project, compared with preferences for Clinton or Sanders in the July 2016 VOTER Survey.

64. Nancy Burns and Donald Kinder, "Categorical Politics: Gender, Race and Public Opinion," in *New Directions in Public Opinion*, ed. Adam Berinsky (New York: Routledge, 2012), 159.

65. Susan Sarandon (@Susan Sarandon), Twitter, February 17 2016, 8:42 am, https://twitter.com/SusanSarandon/status/699997236500021248. Madeleine Albright, "Madeleine Albright: My Undiplomatic Moment," *New York Times*, February 13, 2016, https://www.nytimes.com/2016/02/13/opinion/madeleine-albright-my-undiplomatic-moment.html?_r=0.

66. The American National Election Studies Pilot Study asked all respondents to state a preference in both the Democratic and Republican primaries, regardless of which primary they might participate in. Table 6.1 reports results for respondents who identified as Democrats, independents who leaned toward the Democratic Party, and independents who did not lean toward a party. Other ways of identifying likely Democratic primary

voters produced similar conclusions. See Christopher H. Achen and Larry Bartels, "No, Sanders Supporters Are Not More Liberal Than Clinton's. Here's What Really Drives Elections," *Monkey Cage* (blog), *Washington Post*, June 7, 2016, https://www.washingtonpost.com/news/monkey-cage/wp/2016/06/07/no-sanders-supporters-are-not-more-liberal-than-clintons-heres-what-really-drives-elections/?utm_term=.b2fa97bb5b42.

67. Dan Hopkins, "Clinton Voters Like Obama More Than Sanders Voters Do," *FiveThirtyEight*, March 7, 2016, https://fivethirtyeight.com/features/voters-who-like-obama-like-clinton/; Dan Hopkins, "Does Bernie Sanders Represent the Future of the Democratic Party?," *FiveThirtyEight*, July 11, 2016, https://fivethirtyeight.com/features/does-bernie-sanders-represent-the-future-of-the-democratic-party/; Christopher Achen and Larry Bartels, "Do Sanders Supporters Favor His Policies?," Campaign Stops, *New York Times*, May 23, 2016, https://www.nytimes.com/2016/05/23/opinion/campaign-stops/do-sanders-supporters-favor-his-policies.html. For more evidence, see Pew Research Center, "Campaign Exposes Fissures over Issues, Values, and How Life Has Changed in the U.S.," March 31, 2016, http://www.people-press.org/2016/03/31/campaign-exposes-fissures-over-issues-values-and-how-life-has-changed-in-the-u-s/; and Michael Tesler, "Sorry Donald Trump. Trade Policy Won't Help You Win Sanders Voters," May 16, 2016, https://www.washingtonpost.com/news/monkey-cage/wp/2016/05/16/sorry-donald-trump-trade-policy-wont-help-you-win-sanders-voters/.

68. On the relationship between support for Sanders and trust in government, see also Joshua J. Dyck, Shanna Pearson-Merkowitz, and Michael Coates, "Primary Distrust: Political Distrust and Support for the Insurgent Candidacies of Donald Trump and Bernie Sanders in the 2016 Primary," *PS: Political Science and Politics* 51, no. 2 (2018): 351–57.

69. Rucker and Wagner, "How Bernie Sanders Is Plotting His Path." The 70 percent figure comes from a bivariate regression of Clinton's vote share on the percent of a state's population that is black (taking the square root of that percent so that the relationship visible in figure 6.13 is linear). In that regression, the adjusted r-squared is 0.69. Adding the percent of the primary electorate identifying as Democratic raises the adjusted r-squared to 0.79. Adding a dummy variable for Vermont (to capture a "home state" benefit for Sanders) raises it to 0.83.

Chapter 7: The Trump Tax

Epigraph: A screenshot of the Hannity tweet is here: Dan Murphy (@bungdan), "This is still the greatest Sean Hannity tweet ever," Twitter graphic, October 21, 2016, 3:39 p.m., https://twitter.com/bungdan/status/789597048051937280.

1. Anne Gearan and Dan Balz, "Even Supporters Agree: Clinton Has Weaknesses as a Candidate. What Can She Do?," *Washington Post*, May 15, 2016, https://www.washingtonpost.com/politics/even-supporters-agree-clinton-has-weaknesses-as-a-candidate-what-can-she-do/2016/05/15/132f4d7e-1874-11e6-924d-838753295f9a_story.html?utm_term=.b717f5e1fcf2&wpisrc=nl_most&wpmm=1; Amy Chozick, Alexander Burns, and Jonathan Martin, "Hillary Clinton Struggles to Find Footing in Unusual Race," *New York Times*, May 28, 2016, https://www.nytimes.com/2016/05/29/us/politics/hillary-clinton-donald-trump.html?_r=0.

2. Kristen East, "Trump Attacks 'Mexican' Judge in Trump University Lawsuit," *Politico*, May 28, 2016, http://www.politico.com/story/2016/05/donald-trump-university-judge-gonzalo-curiel-223684; Jennifer Steinhauer, Jonathan Martin, and David M.

Herszenhorn, "Paul Ryan Calls Donald Trump's Attack on Judge 'Racist,' but Still Backs Him," *New York Times*, June 7, 2016, https://www.nytimes.com/2016/06/08/us/politics /paul-ryan-donald-trump-gonzalo-curiel.html?_r=0; Kenneth P. Vogel, Eli Stokols, and Alex Isenstadt, "Trump's Relationship with RNC Sours," *Politico*, June 15, 2016, http:// www.politico.com/story/2016/06/donald-trump-republican-national-committee-224403; Ed O'Keefe, "Dozens of GOP Delegates Launch New Push to Halt Donald Trump," *Washington Post*, June 17, 2016, https://www.washingtonpost.com/politics/dozens-of-gop -delegates-launch-new-push-to-halt-donald-trump/2016/06/17/e8dcf74e-3491-11e6-8758 -d58e76e11b12_story.html?tid=pm_politics_pop_b&utm_term=.34f3e6099137; David Graham, "Trump Is on the Verge of Losing Even Republicans," *Atlantic*, June 21, 2016, https:// www.theatlantic.com/politics/archive/2016/06/dump-trump-again/488093/.

3. The early June favorability numbers are from Gallup's daily polling from June 1 to June 4, 2016. Alan Abramowitz and John Sides, "Do Most Americans Dislike Clinton and Trump? No, Not at All," *Washington Post*, June 14, 2016, https://www.washing tonpost.com/news/monkey-cage/wp/2016/06/14/do-most-americans-dislike-clinton -and-trump no-not-at-all/?utm_term=.ed9bf25a7121. See also Dan Balz and Scott Clement, "Poll: Election 2016 Shapes Up as a Contest of Negatives," *Washington Post*, May 22, 2016, https://www.washingtonpost.com/politics/poll-election-2016-shapes-up -as-a-contest-of-negatives/2016/05/21/8d4ccfd6-1ed3-11e6-b6e0-c53b7ef63b45_story .html?utm_term=.2893b5236476&wplsit.=nl womost&wpmm=1,

4. See Lynn Vavreck, *The Message Matters* (Princeton: Princeton University Press, 2009).

5. "Full Text: Hillary Clinton's DNC Speech," *Politico*, July 28, 2016, https://www .politico.com/story/2016/07/full-text-hillary-clintons dnc-speech 226410.

6. The text of Gore's speech is here: www.presidency.ucsb.edu/ws/index.php?pid =25963.

7. On the prominence of the economy in Clinton's speeches, see David Roberts, "The Most Common Words in Hillary Clinton's Speeches, in One Chart," *Vox*, December 16, 2016, https://www.vox.com/policy-and-politics/2016/12/16/13972394/most-common -words-hillary-clinton-speech. The advertising results are based on coding data from Kantar Media/CMAG, which tracked the ads made and aired by both candidates and the number of times they ran between June 1 and Election Day. In each ad, we coded each verbal mention of domestic policy, foreign policy, the economy, traits, and defense spending. Repeated appeals were coded each time they were mentioned. Ads were weighted by the number of times they ran. On Clinton's lack of embrace of the Obama administration's economic record, see also Neil Irwin, "Hillary Clinton's Message: Yes, the Economy Is Messed Up. But I Can Fix It," *New York Times*, June 22, 2016, https://www.nytimes .com/2016/11/01/us/politics/fbi-russia-election-donald-trump.html?mcubz=3&_r=0. On Gore's campaign, see Vavreck, *The Message Matters*. Clinton's quote is from Hillary Clinton, *What Happened* (New York: Simon and Schuster, 2017), 67.

8. "Full Text: Donald Trump 2016 RNC Draft Speech Transcript," *Politico*, July 21, 2016, https://www.politico.com/story/2016/07/full-transcript-donald-trump-nomination -acceptance-speech-at-rnc-225974. The two Trump television ads are available here: https://www.youtube.com/watch?v=odYHGAicJ7k and https://www.youtube.com/watch ?v=_5JJ_hC4y9s.

9. "Full Text: Hillary Clinton 2016 RNC Draft Speech Transcript."

10. Matt Flegenheimer, "Hillary Clinton Says 'Radical Fringe' Is Taking Over G.O.P. under Trump," *New York Times*, August 25, 2016, https://www.nytimes.com/2016/08/26 /us/politics/hillary-clinton-speech.html?mcubz=3.

11. See Vavreck, *The Message Matters*; and Erica Franklin Fowler, Travis N. Ridout, and Michael M. Franz, "Political Advertising in 2016: The Presidential Election as Outlier?," *Forum* 14, no. 4 (2016): 445–69.

12. On Trump and crime statistics, see D'Angelo Gore, "Trump Wrong on Murder Rate," FactCheck.org, October 28, 2016, http://www.factcheck.org/2016/10/trump-wrong -on-murder-rate/; Sean Sullivan and Mike DeBonis, "Top Republicans Join Obama in Condemning Trump's Words," *Washington Post*, June 14, 2016, https://www.washing tonpost.com/politics/top-republicans-join-obama-in-condemning-trumps-words/2016 /06/14/fb1619c0-325e-11e6-95c0-2a6873031302_story.html?tid=pm_politics_pop_b&utm _term=.8baf6c570ae0. On Nixon's campaign, see Vavreck, *The Message Matters*, 86–90.

13. Trump's quote about Clinton and the "rigged system" is from his convention speech ("Full Text: Donald Trump 2016 RNC Draft Speech Transcript"). The attack lines "pay to play politics" and "decades of lies and scandal" are from this Trump ad: https:// www.youtube.com/watch?v=epbmHco8sF0&feature=youtu.be. A Trump ad attacking Clinton on immigration is here: Ace Metrix, "Trump for President 'Two Americas: Immigration,'" YouTube video, 0:31, August 31, 2016, https://www.youtube.com/watch?v =XricTusWepQ. The accusation regarding the Clinton Foundation and Saudi Arabia is from a Facebook post: Donald J. Trump, Facebook, June 13, 2016, https://www.facebook .com/DonaldTrump/posts/10157164335365725#. Other conservative news outlets amplified this charge. See Robert M. Faris, Hal Roberts, Bruce Etling, Nikki Bourassa, Ethan Zuckerman, and Yochai Benkler, *Partisanship, Propaganda, and Disinformation: Online Media and the 2016 U.S. Presidential Election* (Cambridge, MA: Berkman Klein Center for Internet and Society, Harvard University, 2017), http://nrs.harvard.edu/urn-3:HUL .InstRepos:33759251, 116–24.

14. The CNN data come from a collaboration between the Global Database of Events, Language, and Tone and the Internet Archive: http://television.gdeltproject.org/cgi-bin /iatv_ftxtsearch/iatv_ftxtsearch?primary_keyword=campaign&context_keywords =&filter_network=CNN&filter_timespan=ALL&filter_displayas=PERCENT&filter _combineseparate=SEPARATE&filter_outputtype=DISPLAY. We first searched for all stories with the phrase "presidential campaign." We then searched for all stories with the terms "presidential campaign" and "immigration" or "immigrant." This returns the number of stories that included "immigration" or "immigrant" within four sentences of the phrase "presidential campaign." The percentage of campaign stories that also referred to immigration increased from 1.5 percent between June 2011 and October 2012 to 5 percent between June 2015 and October 2016. The percent of campaign stories that mentioned "Islam" or "Muslim" increased from 0.5 percent to 2.6 percent over the same periods. These data likely undercount attention to these issues because the database examines only sentences proximate to mentions of the presidential campaign, but it should capture the direction of these trends. The more systematic data is from Faris et al., *Partisanship, Propaganda, and Disinformation*.

15. On Trump versus a generic Republican, see Lynn Vavreck, "How Much Is Donald Trump Hurting the G.O.P.? Here's a Way to See," *New York Times*, August 30, 2016, https://www.nytimes.com/2016/08/31/upshot/theres-a-way-to-see-how-much-donald -trumps-nomination-has-cost-the-gop.html?_r=0; and Tobias Konitzer and David Rothschild, "There Is No 'Trump Bump' in the Polls—Just a Growing Lead for the Democrats," *Monkey Cage* (blog), *Washington Post*, June 7, 2016, https://www.washing tonpost.com/news/monkey-cage/wp/2016/06/07/the-trump-bump-is-misleading-public

-opinion-is-trending-steadily-toward-the-democratic-nominee-for-president/?utm
_term=.eecf3207ab44. On the "Trump Tax," see Dylan Matthews, "The Trump Tax: Donald Trump Is Polling 3.8 Points behind Where the Republican Nominee Should Be This Year," *Vox*, November 8, 2016, https://www.vox.com/a/trump-tax.

16. The eight outlets in the solo-headlined story data were the *New York Times*, the *Washington Post*, the *Chicago Tribune*, the *Wall Street Journal*, *Slate*, *Politico*, Fox News, and the *Weekly Standard*. These data came from the analytics site the Data Face, and we are grateful to Jack Beckwith for sharing them. Overall, these three measures are correlated between 0.75 and 0.80. For other evidence of basic patterns that we document—especially Trump's dominance of news coverage—see, for example, Faris et al., *Partisanship, Propaganda, and Disinformation*.

17. It is possible that some of the shifts in polling data were due not to attitude change but rather to changes in the willingness of Democrats or Republicans to answer polls—a phenomenon known as partisan nonresponse. See Andrew Gelman, Sharad Goel, Douglas Rivers, and David Rothschild, "The Mythical Swing Voter," *Quarterly Journal of Political Science* 11 (2016): 103–30. The theory is that partisans may be less likely to answer polls when events in the campaign are "bad" for their party, thereby creating the impression that their party's candidate is losing support in the electorate. Some analysts saw this pattern at work in 2016. See Benjamin Lauderdale and Douglas Rivers, "Beware the Phantom Swings: Why Dramatic Bounces in the Polls Aren't Always What They Seem," YouGov, November 1, 2016, https://today.yougov.com/news/2016/11/01/beware-phantom-swings-why-dramatic-swings-in-the-p/. We cannot adjudicate between partisan nonresponse and opinion change with these data, and it is possible that some of the fluctuations in figure 7.2 derive from partisan nonresponse. But even partisan nonresponse represents a tangible consequence of the flow of campaign information.

18. A meta-analysis of studies of media coverage of the 1948–96 presidential general elections found no consistent differences across candidates in the volume of coverage. See Dave D'Alessio and Mike Allen, "Media Bias in Presidential Elections: A Meta-analysis," *Journal of Communication* 50, no. 4 (2000): 133–56. Analyses of media coverage in the 2012 presidential general election found the same thing. See John Sides and Lynn Vavreck, *The Gamble: Choice and Chance in the 2012 Presidential Election* (Princeton: Princeton University Press, 2013); as well as Pew Research Center, "Winning the Media Campaign 2012," November 2, 2012, http://www.journalism.org/2012/11/02/winning-media-campaign-2012/.

19. This correlation includes all days between June 1 and Election Day, excluding the period from July 18 to July 28. Generally, there are negative correlations between the various news coverage measures and both Trump's net favorability and standing in trial-heat polls. These correlations are even larger for the postconvention period (August 1 to Election Day).

20. Sam Frizell, "Donald Trump Faces Backlash for Tweets about Orlando Shooting," *Time*, June 12, 2016, http://time.com/4365411/orlando-shooting-donald-trump-tweet-congrats/; Jenna Johnson, "Donald Trump Seems to Connect President Obama to Orlando Shooting," *Washington Post*, June 13, 2016, https://www.washingtonpost.com/news/post-politics/wp/2016/06/13/donald-trump-suggests-president-obama-was-involved-with-orlando-shooting/?tid=a_inl&utm_term=.2a0ac41b0c10; David Fahrenthold, "Trump Promised Millions to Charity. We Found Less than $10,000 over 7 Years," *Washington Post*, June 28, 2016, https://www.washingtonpost.com/politics/trump-promised-millions-to-charity-we-found-less-than-10000-over-7-years/2016/06/28/cbab5d1a-37dd-11e6-8f7c-d4c723a2becb_story.html?utm_term=.1278a8019c3a.

21. On the patterns of news coverage of conventions, see Thomas M. Holbrook, *Do Campaigns Matter?* (Thousand Oaks, CA: Sage, 1996). The description of Trump's speech is from Eli Stokols, "Trump's Four Dysfunctional Days in Cleveland," *Politico*, July 22, 2016, https://www.politico.com/story/2016/07/rnc-2016-donald-trump-dysfunction -226001. Trump's comment about Melania Trump's speech was, unsurprisingly, a tweet: Donald J. Trump (@realDonaldTrump), Twitter, July 20, 2016, 8:31 a.m., https://twitter .com/realDonaldTrump/status/755787159735570432.

22. Thomas E. Patterson, "News Coverage of the 2016 National Conventions: Negative News, Lacking Context," Shorenstein Center on Media, Politics, and Public Policy, September 21, 2016, https://shorensteincenter.org/news-coverage-2016-national-conven tions/. On convention bumps, see James E. Campbell, *The American Campaign: U.S. Presidential Elections and the National Vote*, 2nd ed. (College Station: Texas A&M University Press, 2008), 145–51; Holbrook, *Do Campaigns Matter?*; and Robert S. Erikson, and Christopher Wlezien, *The Timeline of Presidential Elections* (Chicago: University of Chicago Press, 2012). The "mistake by the lake" quote is from Matthew Yglesias, "This Week We Saw That the Republican Party—Not Just Trump—Is the Problem," *Vox*, July 22, 2016, https://www.vox.com/2016/7/22/12247432/republican-convention-trump.

23. Jose A. DelReal and Anne Gearan, "Trump Stirs Outrage after He Lashes Out at the Muslim Parents of a Dead U.S. Soldier," *Washington Post*, July 30, 2016, https://www .washingtonpost.com/politics/backlash-for-trump-after-he-lashes-out-at-the-muslim -parents-of-a-dead-us-soldier/2016/07/30/34b0aad4-5671-11e6-88eb-7dda4e2f2aec_story .html?utm_term=.569f6cf62d70; Katie Zezima, "Republicans Denounce Trump as Confrontation with Muslim Parents Escalates," *Washington Post*, August 1, 2016, https:// www.washingtonpost.com/politics/republicans-denounce-trump-as-confrontation -with-muslim-parents-escalates/2016/07/31/54397028-5722-11e6-9aee-8075993d73a2 _story.html; Sabrina Siddiqui, "Donald Trump Calls Obama the 'Founder of ISIS,'" *Guardian*, August 11, 2016, https://www.theguardian.com/us-news/2016/aug/11/donald-trump -calls-barack-obama-the-founder-of-isis; Dara Lind, "Donald Trump's Plan to Subject Immigrants to 'Ideological Tests,' Explained," *Vox*, August 16, 2016, https://www.vox.com /2016/8/16/12491000/trump-extreme-vetting-test-immigrant; Nick Corasaniti and Maggie Haberman, "Donald Trump Suggests 'Second Amendment People' Could Act against Hillary Clinton," *New York Times*, August 9, 2016, https://www.nytimes.com/2016/08/10 /us/politics/donald-trump hillary-clinton.html?action=click&contentCollection =Politics&module=RelatedCoverage&region=Marginalia&pgtype=article&_r=0.

24. Philip Rucker, Robert Costa, and Jenna Johnson, "Inside Donald Trump's New Strategy to Counter the View of Many That He Is 'Racist,'" *Washington Post*, August 23, 2016, https://www.washingtonpost.com/politics/inside-donald-trumps-new-strategy -to-shed-the-view-of-him-as-racist/2016/08/23/eedc4fd0-6945-11e6-99bf-f0cf3a6449a6 _story.html; Alexander Burns and Maggie Haberman, "Inside the Failing Mission to Tame Donald Trump's Tongue," *New York Times*, August 13, 2016, https://mobile.nytimes .com/2016/08/14/us/politics/donald-trump-campaign-gop.html?_r=0; Dan Balz, "Has Donald Trump Hit Bottom?," *Washington Post*, August 13, 2016, https://mobile.nytimes.com /2016/08/14/us/politics/donald-trump-campaign-gop.html?_r=0.

25. Nick Corasaniti, Nicholas Confessore, and Michael Barbaro, "Donald Trump Says Hillary Clinton's Bodyguards Should Disarm to 'See What Happens to Her,'" *New York Times*, September 16, 2016, https://www.nytimes.com/2016/09/17/us/politics/donald -trump-hillary-clinton.html; Alexander Burns and Nicholas Confessore, "After Bombings, Hillary Clinton and Donald Trump Clash over Terrorism," *New York Times*, September 19,

2016, https://www.nytimes.com/2016/09/20/us/politics/donald-trump-hillary-clinton
.html?mcubz=3; Michelle Ye Hee Lee, "Trump's Claim Linking New York Bombing to
an 'Extremely Open Immigration System,'" *Washington Post*, September 20, 2016, https://
www.washingtonpost.com/news/fact-checker/wp/2016/09/20/trumps-claim-linking
-new-york-bombing-to-an-extremely-open-immigration-system/?utm_term=
.57841f5a8fe0; Jessica Taylor, "Trump: 'Sad' N.Y. Bombing Suspect Gets Quality Medical
Care, Lawyer," NPR, September 19, 2016, http://www.npr.org/2016/09/19/494633030/trump
-calls-it-sad-that-n-y-bombing-suspect-gets-medical-care-lawyer; Jonathan Martin, "Donald Trump's Anything-Goes Campaign Sets an Alarming Political Precedent," *New York
Times*, September 17, 2016, https://www.nytimes.com/2016/09/18/us/politics/donald-trump
-presidential-race.html?mcubz=3&_r=0.

26. Michael Barbaro and Megan Twohey, "Shamed and Angry: Alicia Machado, a
Miss Universe Mocked by Trump," *New York Times*, September 27, 2016, https://www
.nytimes.com/2016/09/28/us/politics/alicia-machado-donald-trump.html?mcubz=3&_r
=0; Patrick Healy and Jonathan Martin, "Hillary Clinton and Donald Trump Press
Pointed Attacks in Debate," *New York Times*, September 26, 2016, https://www.nytimes
.com/2016/09/27/us/politics/presidential-debate.html?_r=0; Jenna Johnson, "Trump Ad-
mits Obama Was Born in U.S., but Falsely Blames Clinton for Starting Rumors," *Washington Post*, September 26, 2016, https://www.washingtonpost.com/news/post-politics/wp
/2016/09/16/trump-admits-obama-was-born-in-u-s-but-falsely-blames-clinton-for
-starting-rumors/?tid=pm_politics_pop_b&utm_term=.c00c598a6543; David Weigel,
"How Trump's Fortunes Turned South with a Rambling 'Birther' Answer," *Washington
Post*, September 27, 2016, https://www.washingtonpost.com/politics/how-trumps-fortunes
-turned-south-with-a-rambling-birther-answer/2016/09/27/09443292-8440-11e6-92c2
-14b64f3d453f_story.html?utm_term=.a90836ded88b; Natalie Jackson and Ariel Edwards-
Levy, "Post-debate Polls Show Hillary Clinton Won the Debate," *Huffington Post*, September 29, 2016, http://www.huffingtonpost.com/entry/polls-hillary-clinton-won-debate
_us_57ed0323e4b0c2407cdbe9c2?qw79pfttn4kne9udi.

27. David A. Fahrenthold, "Trump Recorded Having Extremely Lewd Conversation about Women in 2005," *Washington Post*, October 8, 2016, https://www.washing
tonpost.com/politics/trump-recorded-having-extremely-lewd-conversation-about
-women-in-2005/2016/10/07/3b9ce776-8cb4-11e6-bf8a-3d26847eeed4_story.html?utm
_term=.e620636928c9.

28. Patrick Healy and Jonathan Martin, "In Second Debate, Donald Trump and
Hillary Clinton Spar in Bitter, Personal Terms," *New York Times*, October 9, 2016,
https://www.nytimes.com/2016/10/10/us/politics/presidential-debate.html?_r=0.

29. Megan Twohey and Michael Barbaro, "Two Women Say Donald Trump
Touched Them Inappropriately," *New York Times*, October 12, 2016; Sean Sullivan, "Four
Women Accuse Trump of Forcibly Groping, Kissing Them," *Washington Post*, October 13, 2016; Scott Clement and Dan Balz, "Washington Post-ABC News Poll: Clinton
Holds Four-Point Lead in Aftermath of Trump Tape," *Washington Post*, October 16, 2016;
McKay Coppins, "God's Plan for Mike Pence," *Atlantic*, January/February 2018, https://
www.theatlantic.com/magazine/archive/2018/01/gods-plan-for-mike-pence/546569/
?wpmm=1&wpisrc=nl_daily202; Philip Rucker and Robert Costa, "The GOP Tumbles
toward Anarchy: 'It's Every Person for Himself or Herself,'" *Washington Post*, October 10,
2016, https://www.washingtonpost.com/politics/the-gop-tumbles-toward-anarchy-its
-every-person-for-himself-or-herself/2016/10/10/31bc6d24-8f13-11e6-a6a3-d50061aa9fae
_story.html; Sean Sullivan, Robert Costa, and Dan Balz, "Trump Declares War on GOP,

Says 'the Shackles Have Been Taken Off,'" *Washington Post*, October 11, 2016, https://www
.washingtonpost.com/politics/trump-declares-war-on-the-republican-party-four
-weeks-before-election-day/2016/10/11/93b21dc4-8fc9-11e6-9c52-0b10449e33c4_story
.html; Alexander Burns and Jonathan Martin, "Split over Donald Trump Threatens to
Tilt Republican States," *New York Times*, October 11, 2016.

30. See James Hohmann, "The Daily 202: Trump's Lack of Self-Control Allows Clinton to Sweep the Debates," *Washington Post*, October 20, 2016, https://www.washing
tonpost.com/news/powerpost/paloma/daily-202/2016/10/20/daily-202-trump-s-lack-of
-self-control-allows-clinton-to-sweep-the-debates/5807e456e9b69b640f54c6a9/?utm
_term=.2d932b3e8497&wpisrc=nl_most&wpmm=1.

31. Sides and Vavreck, *The Gamble*.

32. Aaron Blake, "78 Republican Politicians, Donors, and Officials Who Are Supporting Hillary Clinton," *Washington Post*, November 7, 2016, https://www.washing
tonpost.com/news/the-fix/wp/2016/06/30/heres-the-growing-list-of-big-name
-republicans-supporting-hillary-clinton/?postshare=3741467301467849&tid=ss
_tw&utm_term=.4492b8c8fb4a; Susan Collins, "GOP Senator Susan Collins: Why I Cannot Support Trump," *Washington Post*, August 8, 2016, https://www.washingtonpost
.com/opinions/gop-senator-why-i-cannot-support-trump/2016/08/08/821095be-5d7e
-11e6-9d2f-b1a3564181a1_story.html.

33. On conservative news outlets, see Faris et al., *Partisanship, Propaganda, and
Disinformation*; Jonathan Martin, "Some in G.O.P. Who Deserted Trump over Lewd
Tape Are Returning," *New York Times*, October 12, 2016, https://www.nytimes.com/2016
/10/13/us/politics/gop-reaction-donald-trump.html; Sullivan, Costa, and Balz, "Trump
Declares War on GOP"; Tom Kludt, "Paul Ryan on Voting for Trump: I Already Voted
'for Our Nominee,'" CNN, November 1, 2016; Aaron Blake, "Sad Ted Cruz Phone-
Banking for Donald Trump Is a Pretty Great Meme," *Washington Post*, October 6, 2016.

34. "Statement by FBI Director James B. Comey on the Investigation of Secretary
Hillary Clinton's Use of a Personal E-Mail System," Federal Bureau of Investigation,
July 5, 2016, https://www.fbi.gov/news/pressrel/press-releases/statement-by-fbi-director
-james-b-comey-on-the-investigation-of-secretary-hillary-clinton2019s-use-of-a
-personal-e-mail-system; Eric Lichtblau and Adam Goldman, "F.B.I. Papers Offer Closer
Look at Hillary Clinton Email Inquiry," *New York Times*, September 2, 2016, https://www
.nytimes.com/2016/09/03/us/politics/hillary-clinton-fbi.html?mcubz=3.

35. Michael Crowley and Tyler Pager, "Trump Urges Russia to Hack Clinton's Email,"
Politico, July 27, 2016, http://www.politico.com/story/2016/07/trump-putin-no-relationship
-226282.

36. Patrick Healy and Jonathan Martin, "Democrats Struggle for Unity on First Day
of Convention," *New York Times*, July 25, 2016, https://www.nytimes.com/2016/07/26/us
/politics/dnc-speakers-protests-sanders.html?_r=1; Annie Karni, Gabriel Debenedetti,
and Edward-Isaac Dovere, "How Clinton Quelled an Insurgency," *Politico*, July 29, 2016,
https://www.politico.com/story/2016/07/dnc-2016-hillary-clinton-bernie-sanders
-supporters-226415; Patterson, "News Coverage of the 2016 National Conventions." On
media coverage of the 2012 conventions, see Pew Research Center, "The Conventions to
the Debates: Set Piece Moments Still Matter," November 1, 2012, http://www.journalism
.org/2012/11/01/conventions-debates-set-piece-moments-still-matter/.

37. This account of news coverage is based on Faris et al., *Partisanship, Propaganda,
and Disinformation*, 103–15. On the expenditures of the Clinton Foundation, see Charity-
Watch's evaluation here: CharityWatch, "Clinton Foundation: Charity Ratings," Janu-

ary 2018, https://www.charitywatch.org/ratings-and-metrics/bill-hillary-chelsea-clinton
-foundation/478. On the poll results, see Lynn Vavreck, "What People Don't Know
about the Clinton Foundation Is Revealing in Itself," *New York Times*, September 16,
2016, https://www.nytimes.com/2016/09/17/upshot/what-people-dont-know-about-the
-clinton-foundation-is-revealing-in-itself.html.

38. Amy Chozick, "Hillary Clinton Calls Many Trump Backers 'Deplorables,' and
G.O.P. Pounces," *New York Times*, September 10, 2016, https://www.nytimes.com/2016
/09/11/us/politics/hillary-clinton-basket-of-deplorables.html?_r=0; Chris Cillizza, "Hillary Clinton's Health Just Became a Real Issue in the Presidential Campaign," *Washington Post*, September 11, 2016, https://www.washingtonpost.com/news/the-fix/wp/2016/09
/11/hillary-clintons-health-just-became-a-real-issue-in-the-presidential-campaign/?utm
_term=.97df4ff61017.

39. On Comey's decision, see Matt Apuzzo, Michael S. Schmidt, Adam Goldman,
and Eric Lichtblau, "Comey Tried to Shield the F.B.I. from Politics. Then He Shaped an
Election," *New York Times*, April 22, 2017, https://www.nytimes.com/2017/04/22/us/politics
/james-comey-election.html?_r=1. On the Trump campaign's decision, see Maggie
Haberman, Ashley Parker, Jeremy W. Peters, and Michael Barbaro, "Inside Donald
Trump's Last Stand: An Anxious Nominee Seeks Assurance," *New York Times*, November 6, 2016, https://www.nytimes.com/2016/11/07/us/politics/donald-trump-presidential
-race.html. On *New York Times* coverage, see Rob Savillo, "STUDY: Top Newspapers
Give Clinton Email Story More Coverage than All Other Trump Stories," Media Matters
for America, November 4, 2016, https://www.mediamatters.org/research/2016/11/04/study
-top-newspapers-give-clinton-email-story-more-coverage all-other-trump-stories
/214309. For additional data on the traction of stories related to the Comey letter, see
Nate Silver, "The Comey Letter Probably Cost Clinton the Election," *FiveThirtyEight*,
May 3, 2017, https://fivethirtyeight.com/features/the-comey-letter-probably-cost-clinton
-the-election/.

40. Thomas E. Patterson, "News Coverage of the 2016 General Election: How the
Press Failed Voters," Shorenstein Center on Media, Politics, and Public Policy, December 7, 2016, https://shorensteincenter.org/news-coverage-2016-general-election/.

41. Patterson, "News Coverage of the 2016 General Election."

42. Faris et al., *Partisanship, Propaganda, and Disinformation*, 87; Eric Lichtblau and
Steven Lee Meyers, "Investigating Donald Trump, F.B.I. Sees No Clear Link to Russia,"
New York Times, October 31, 2016, https://www.nytimes.com/2016/11/01/us/politics/fbi
-russia-election-donald-trump.html?mcubz=3&_r=0. Stories about Clinton's emails and
email hacking also dominated Twitter much more than any other story. See Echelon
Insights, "The Year in News 2016," December 28, 2016, https://medium.com/echelon
-indicators/the-year-in-news-2016-41f876d4c618.

43. Alexander Smith and Vladimir Banc, "Fake News: How a Partying Macedonian
Teen Earns Thousands Publishing Lies," NBC News, December 9, 2016, https://www
.nbcnews.com/news/world/fake-news-how-partying-macedonian-teen-earns
-thousands-publishing-lies-n692451. On profit-oriented Facebook content, see Faris et al.,
Partisanship, Propaganda, and Disinformation, 20.

44. In the Presidential Election Panel Survey data, respondents were asked how
favorably they viewed Clinton on a four-category scale and also whether the terms "honest" and "moral" described Clinton "extremely well," "somewhat well," or "not very well
at all." Each of these measures was recoded to the 0–1 scale and regressed on respondents' assessment of Clinton on that dimension on the prior survey in September, as well

as a variable capturing whether they were interviewed before or after the Comey letter's release. The coefficients and standard errors for the Comey variable were $b=-0.023$ (s.e. $=0.010$) for favorability, $b=-0.023$ (s.e. $=0.011$) for honesty, and $b=-0.028$ (s.e. $=0.014$) for morality. There were not comparable effects on how well people thought "strong leader" or "cares about people like me" described Clinton. There was no effect on Trump's favorability either.

45. Silver, "Comey Letter." See also Sean McElwee, Matt McDermott, and Will Jordan, "4 Pieces of Evidence Showing FBI Director James Comey Cost Clinton the Election," *Vox*, January 11, 2017, https://www.vox.com/the-big-idea/2017/1/11/14215930/comey-email-election-clinton-campaign; Courtney Kennedy et al., "An Evaluation of the 2016 Election Polls in the U.S.," American Association of Public Opinion Research, 2017, http://www.aapor.org/Education-Resources/Reports/An-Evaluation-of-2016-Election-Polls-in-the-U-S.aspx. Another analysis that showing no clear impact of the Comey letter is Aaron Weinschenk and Costas Panagopoulos, "Did Comey Give Trump the Presidency? We Don't Think So," *Washington Post*, September 18, 2017, https://www.washingtonpost.com/news/monkey-cage/wp/2017/09/18/did-comey-give-trump-the-presidency-we-dont-think-so/?utm_term=.99e70bd80930.

46. On the tendency for news coverage to create narratives of candidates, see Kathleen Hall Jamieson and Paul Waldman, *The Press Effect: Politicians, Journalists, and the Stories That Shape the Political World* (New York: Oxford University Press, 2003). For example, they write about the new media's "psychological profiling that seeks patterns . . . and from them draws inferences with a broad brush" (25). On the 2000 election, see Richard Johnston, Michael G. Hagen, and Kathleen Hall Jamieson, *The 2000 Presidential Election and the Foundations of Party Politics* (New York Cambridge University Press, 2000); and Gabriel Lenz, *Follow the Leader? How Voters Respond to Politicians' Policies and Performance* (Chicago: University of Chicago Press, 2012).

47. The Wolfson quote is from John F. Kennedy School of Government, Institute of Politics, *Campaign for President: The Managers Look at 2008* (Lanham, MD: Rowman and Littlefield, 2009), 125.

48. Clinton, *What Happened*, 68.

49. Jonathan Allen and Amie Parnes, *Shattered: Inside Hillary Clinton's Doomed Campaign* (New York: Crown, 2017), 56–65; Ryan Struyk and Liz Kreutz, "Hillary Clinton Jokes about Wiping Email Server 'with a Cloth or Something,'" ABC News, August 18, 2015, http://abcnews.go.com/Politics/hillary-clinton-jokes-wiping-email-server-cloth/story?id=33165517.

50. On Zaller's writing, see Jonathan Ladd, "Why Don't the Clintons and the Media Get Along?," *Mischiefs of Faction* (blog), March 16, 2016, http://www.mischiefsoffaction.com/2015/03/why-dont-clintons-and-press-get-along.html. The Podesta quote is from Abby Phillip and John Wagner, "Hacked WikiLeaks Emails Show Concerns about Clinton Candidacy, Email Server," *Washington Post*, October 12, 2016, https://www.washingtonpost.com/politics/hacked-wikileaks-emails-show-concerns-about-clinton-candidacy-email-server/2016/10/12/cdacbbd0-908f-11e6-a6a3-d50061aa9fae_story.html. Clinton, *What Happened*, 69.

51. On the YouGov poll, see Will Jordan (@williamjordann), "What voters hear a lot about and what bothers them a lot (there's some correlation)," Twitter graphic, October 4, 2016, 7:16 a.m., https://twitter.com/williamjordann/status/783309723332476928. On the Gallup data, see Lydia Saad and Frank Newport, "'Email' Defines Clinton; 'Immigration' Defines Trump." Gallup, September 16, 2015, http://news.gallup.com/poll/185486/email-defines-clinton-immigration-defines-trump.aspx; Frank Newport, Lisa Singh,

Stuart Soroka, Michael Traugott, and Andrew Dugan, "'Email' Dominates What Americans Have Heard about Clinton," Gallup, September 19, 2016, http://news.gallup.com/poll/195596/email-dominates-americans-heard-clinton.aspx; and Lisa Singh, Stuart Soroka, Michael Traugott, and Frank Newport, "Tracking the Themes of the 2016 Election," Election Dynamics, November 7, 2016, http://electiondynamics.org/index.php/2016/11/07/tracking-the-themes-of-the-2016-election/.

52. In 2012, the American National Election Studies changed the response categories for these trait questions to have five categories rather than four. Thus, we cannot make apples-to-apples comparisons to elections before 2012.

53. Alan Yuhas, "How Does Donald Trump Lie? A Fact Checker's Final Guide," *Guardian*, November 7, 2016, https://www.theguardian.com/us-news/2016/nov/07/how-does-donald-trump-lie-fact-checker.

54. Paul F. Lazarsfeld, Bernard Berelson, and Hazel Gaudet, *The People's Choice: How the Voter Makes Up His Mind in a Presidential Campaign* (New York: Columbia University Press, 1948), 73. See also Bernard R. Berelson, Paul F. Lazarsfeld, and William N. McPhee, *Voting: A Study of Opinion Formation in a Presidential Campaign* (Chicago: University of Chicago Press, 1954); Steven E. Finkel, "Reexamining the 'Minimal Effects' Model in Recent Presidential Campaigns," *Journal of Politics* 55 (1993): 1–31; and Andrew Gelman and Gary King, "Why Are American Presidential Election Campaign Polls So Variable When Votes Are So Predictable?," *British Journal of Political Science* 23, no. 4 (1993): 409–51. On partisan activation in the 1952–2008 presidential elections, see Erikson and Wlezien, *Timeline of Presidential Elections*, chap. 7. On partisan activation in the 2000 election, see D. Sunshine Hillygus and Simon Jackman, "Voter Decision Making in Election 2000: Campaign Effects, Partisan Activation, and the Clinton Legacy," *American Journal of Political Science* 47, no. 4 (2003): 583–96. On partisan activation in the 2008 election, see Michael Tesler and David O. Sears, *Obama's Race: The 2008 Election and the Dream of a Post-Racial America* (Chicago: University of Chicago Press, 2010), 70–73. On partisan activation in the 2012 election, see Sides and Vavreck, *The Gamble*.

55. On negative partisanship, see Alan I. Abramowitz and Steven Webster, "The Rise of Negative Partisanship and the Nationalization of U.S. Elections in the 21st Century," *Electoral Studies* 41, no. 1 (2016): 12–22. On the trend in views of the opposite party, see Shanto Iyengar, Gaurav Sood, and Yphtach Lelkes, "Affect, Not Ideology: A Social Identity Perspective on Polarization," *Public Opinion Quarterly* 76, no. 3 (2012): 405–31.

56. On the challenges of reporting on the reasons for choices, see Richard E. Nisbett and Timothy D. Wilson, "Telling More Than We Can Know: Verbal Reports on Mental Processes," *Psychological Review* 84 (1977): 231–59.

57. Holbrook, *Do Campaigns Matter?*

58. Haberman, Parker, Peters, and Barbaro, "Inside Donald Trump's Last Stand."

Chapter 8: What Happened?

1. These quotes and timeline are from Brian Stelter, "In Their Own Words: The Story of Election Night 2016," CNN, January 5, 2017, http://money.cnn.com/2017/01/05/media/election-night-news-coverage-oral-history/index.html. Elements of the argument in this chapter were initially published in John Sides, Michael Tesler, and Lynn Vavreck, "How Trump Lost and Won," *Journal of Democracy* 28, no. 2 (2017): 34–44.

2. Trump's tweets are here: Donald J. Trump (@realDonaldTrump), "The electoral college is a disaster for democracy," Twitter, November 6, 2012, 8:45 p.m., https://twitter.com/realdonaldtrump/status/266038556504494082?lang=en; Donald J. Trump (@realDonald

Trump), "The Electoral College is actually genius in that it brings all states, including the smaller ones, into play. Campaigning is much different!," Twitter, November 15, 2016, 5:40 a.m., https://twitter.com/realDonaldTrump/status/798521053551140864. The same pattern was visible in public opinion, too. See Carl Bialik, "The Electoral College Has Become Another Partisan Issue," *FiveThirtyEight*, December 19, 2016, http://fivethirty eight.com/features/the-electoral-college-has-become-another-partisan-issue/.

3. On "blue wall" punditry, see Nate Silver, "It Wasn't Clinton's Election to Lose," *FiveThirtyEight*, January 23, 2017, http://fivethirtyeight.com/features/it-wasnt-clintons -election-to-lose/. The academic research is Thomas M. Holbrook, *Altered States: Changing Populations, Changing Parties, and the Transformation of the American Political Landscape* (New York: Oxford University Press, 2016).

4. The 2008–12 party loyalty estimates were based on 2,046 respondents in the Study of Citizens and Politics and were provided by Dan Hopkins. On partisan stability in presidential elections, see also Robert S. Erikson, and Christopher Wlezien, *The Timeline of Presidential Elections* (Chicago: University of Chicago Press, 2012), chap. 7. Validating turnout by matching respondents to voter files for both the 2012 and 2016 general elections did not change the basic pattern of results. Approximately 8 percent of Obama voters and 7 percent of Romney voters did not vote in 2016. Including these nonvoters in the calculation, 80 percent of Obama voters voted for Clinton, and 83 percent of Romney voters voted for Trump. Obama-Trump voters outnumbered Romney-Clinton voters by a similar amount. Most nonvoters in 2012 did not vote in 2016 either (81%), while 9.5 percent voted for Clinton and 7.4 percent voted for Trump. Despite the speculation of some commentators, Trump did not appear to benefit from mobilizing "new" voters— although no strong conclusions should be drawn from just this one panel study.

5. Similar results obtain if we limit the sample to voters who could be successfully matched to state voter files for both a presidential primary and the general election. (Most self-reported voters who cannot be matched to the voter file likely did not vote.)

6. On the 2008 primary, see Michael Henderson, D. Sunshine Hillygus, and Trevor Thompson, "'Sour Grapes' or Rational Voting? Voter Decision Making among Thwarted Primary Voters in 2008," *Public Opinion Quarterly* 74, no. 3 (2010): 499–529. On Sanders-Trump voters, see John Sides, "Did Enough Bernie Sanders Supporters Vote for Trump to Cost Clinton the Election?," *Monkey Cage* (blog), *Washington Post*, August 24, 2017, https://www.washingtonpost.com/news/monkey-cage/wp/2017/08/24/did-enough -bernie-sanders-supporters-vote-for-trump-to-cost-clinton-the-election/?utm_term =.eba362ede956. That piece reports on two other surveys that estimated the fraction of Sanders supporters who voted for Trump at 12 percent and 6 percent, respectively.

7. The 2008 figure is from Henderson, Hillygus, and Thompson, "'Sour Grapes' or Rational Voting?" The 2012 figure is from the YouGov survey data analyzed in John Sides and Lynn Vavreck, *The Gamble: Choice and Chance in the 2012 Presidential Election* (Princeton: Princeton University Press, 2013).

8. Sides and Vavreck, *The Gamble*, 181.

9. In the preelection 2016 American National Election Studies, about 8 percent of respondents placed both Clinton and Trump between 0 and 49 on a 0–100 scale, indicating a less favorable view. Among these respondents, average assessments of Clinton and Trump were nearly identical (26.4 and 25.5, respectively). However, among this group, 51 percent identified as Republican, showing again that double negative voters leaned Republican.

10. Andrew Gelman and John Sides, "Can Trump Re-draw the Electoral Map? There's One Big Problem," *Monkey Cage* (blog), *Washington Post*, May 10, 2016, https://

www.washingtonpost.com/news/monkey-cage/wp/2016/05/10/can-trump-re-draw-the
-electoral-map-theres-one-big-problem/?utm_term=.a94dc5098300; Simon Jackman,
"The Predictive Power of Uniform Swing," *PS: Political Science and Politics* 47, no. 2
(2014): 317–21.

11. These calculations are based on each candidate's percentage of the votes for
Democratic and Republican candidates.

12. Alec Tyson and Shiva Maniam, "Behind Trump's Victory: Divisions by Race,
Gender, and Education," Pew Research Center, November 9, 2016, http://www.pewre
search.org/fact-tank/2016/11/09/behind-trumps-victory-divisions-by-race-gender
-education/; Brian F. Schaffner, Matthew MacWilliams, and Tatishe Nteta, "Understanding White Polarization in the 2016 Vote for President: The Sobering Role of Racism
and Sexism," *Political Science Quarterly* 133, no. 1 (2018): 9–34.

13. This is based on analysis of the Current Population Survey's November Voter
Supplement, reweighted to account for nonresponse and the overreporting of turnout.
See Michael McDonald's discussion and statistical code: Michael McDonald, "CPS
Vote Over-report and Non-response Bias Correction," United States Elections Proj-
ect, accessed June 6, 2018, http://www.electproject.org/home/voter-turnout/cps-method
ology. Other analysis, which relied instead on statistical modeling of turnout and
presidential vote choice, suggested that 45 percent of the electorate were non-college-
educated whites and 29 percent were whites with a college degree. See Rob Griffin, Ruy
Teixeira, and John Halpin, *Voter Trends in 2016* (Washington, DC: Center for American
Progress, 2017). Regardless, both these estimates and those based on the Current Population Survey suggest that the exit poll, which estimated that 34 percent of voters were whites
with no college degree and 37 percent were whites with a college degree, was wrong. Some
research has questioned exit poll estimates of the composition of the electorate. See Michael P. McDonald, "The True Electorate: A Cross-Validation of Voter Registration Files
and Election Survey Demographics," *Public Opinion Quarterly* 71, no. 4 (2007): 588–602.

14. The state estimates of the white, non-college-educated population are from the
2011–15 American Community Survey. See United States Census Bureau, "Table S1501:
Educational Attainment," American FactFinder, accessed June 6, 2018, https://fact
finder.census.gov/faces/tableservices/jsf/pages/productview.xhtml?pid=ACS_15_5YR
_S1501. The regression coefficient described is −0.23 with a standard error of 0.03; the *r*-
squared is 0.58. With Hawaii and Utah included, the coefficient is −0.17 (s.e. = 0.04) and
the *r*-squared is 0.28. The same pattern was visible within states at the county level. See
Jeff Guo, "Yes, Working Class Whites Really Did Make Trump Win. No, It Wasn't Simply
Economic Anxiety," *Washington Post*, November 11, 2016, https://www.washingtonpost
.com/news/wonk/wp/2016/11/11/yes-working-class-whites-really-did-make-trump-win
-no-it-wasnt-simply-economic-anxiety/?utm_term=.eb4e50689912.

15. D. Sunshine Hillygus and Todd D. Shields, *The Persuadable Voter: Wedge Issues
in Presidential Campaigns* (Princeton: Princeton University Press, 2009).

16. Jessica Chasmer, "Michael Moore Says Trump Voters Not Racist: 'They Twice
Voted for a Man' Named Hussein," *Washington Times*, November 11, 2016, https://www
.washingtontimes.com/news/2016/nov/11/michael-moore-says-trump-voters-not-racist
-they-tw/; Samuel Popkin and Douglas Rivers, "The Unmaking of President McCain,"
Pollster, November 4, 2008, http://www.pollster.com/blogs/Popkin%20Rivers%20Cam
paign%20Analysis%2011-04%20w%20graphs.pdf; Michael Tesler, "Obama Won Lots of
Votes from Racially Prejudiced Whites (and Some of Them Supported Trump)," *Monkey Cage* (blog), *Washington Post*, December 7, 2016, https://www.washingtonpost.com
/news/monkey-cage/wp/2016/12/07/obama-won-lots-of-votes-from-racially-prejudiced

-whites-and-some-of-them-supported-trump/?utm_term=.c4f716582568; Michael Tesler, *Post-Racial or Most-Racial? Race and Politics in the Obama Era* (Chicago: University of Chicago Press, 2016).

17. Kevin Coe and Michael Reitzes, "Obama on the Stump: Features and Determinants of a Rhetorical Approach," *Presidential Studies Quarterly* 40, no. 3 (2010): 391–413; Kevin Coe and Anthony Schmidt, "America in Black and White: Locating Race in the Modern Presidency, 1933–2011," *Journal of Communication* 62, no. 4 (2012): 609–27; Daniel Q. Gillion, *Governing with Words: The Political Dialogue on Race, Public Policy, and Inequality in America* (New York: Cambridge University Press, 2016); Fredrick Harris, *The Price of the Ticket: Barack Obama and Rise and Decline of Black Politics* (New York: Oxford University Press, 2012); Charlton McIlwain and Stephen M. Caliendo, *Race Appeal: How Candidates Invoke Race in US Political Campaigns* (Philadelphia: Temple University Press, 2011).

18. Jonathan Martin and Maggie Haberman, "Hillary Clinton Traces Friendly Path, Troubling Party," *New York Times*, June 6, 2015, https://www.nytimes.com/2015/06/07/us/politics/hillary-clinton-traces-friendly-path-troubling-party.html?nlid=3131863.

19. Respondents who did not place a candidate—either because they did not know or because (in surveys before 1996) they could not place themselves on this scale and were therefore not asked about the candidates—were placed at the midpoint of the scale. This had the effect of narrowing the average gap in perceptions of the candidates, as respondents who could not place the candidates arguably did not see a clear difference between them. Nevertheless, when these respondents were excluded altogether, there was still a similar trend in perceptions on the "aid to blacks" scale between 2008 and 2016, as well as an increase in the perceived distance between 2012 and 2016.

20. Dan Hopkins, "Trump's Election Doesn't Mean Americans Are More Opposed to Immigration," *FiveThirtyEight*, January 26, 2017, https://fivethirtyeight.com/features/while-trump-is-closing-the-borders-americans-are-warming-to-immigration/. See also Diana C. Mutz, "Status Threat, Not Economic Hardship, Explains the 2016 Presidential Vote," *Proceedings of the National Academy of Sciences* 115, no. 19 (2018): E4330–39, http://www.pnas.org/cgi/doi/10.1073/pnas.1718155115.

21. Michael Tesler, "Views about Race Mattered More in Electing Trump than in Electing Obama," *Monkey Cage* (blog), *Washington Post*, November 22, 2016, https://www.washingtonpost.com/news/monkey-cage/wp/2016/11/22/peoples-views-about-race-mattered-more-in-electing-trump-than-in-electing-obama/?utm_term=.50efa15801e0; Michael Tesler, "In a Clinton-Trump Matchup Racial Prejudice Makes a Striking Difference," *Monkey Cage* (blog), *Washington Post*, May 25, 2016, https://www.washingtonpost.com/news/monkey-cage/wp/2016/05/25/in-a-trump-clinton-match-up-theres-a-striking-effect-of-racial-prejudice/?utm_term=.ace2002cdde7; Schaffner, MacWilliams, and Nteta, "Understanding White Polarization"; Daniel J. Hopkins, "Prejudice, Priming, and Presidential Voting: Panel Evidence from the 2016 U.S. Election" (working paper, 2017), https://papers.ssrn.com/sol3/papers.cfm?abstract_id=3186800.

22. These findings echo other studies that link support for Trump to social dominance orientation and aversion to diversity and social change. See, respectively, Mutz, "Status Threat"; and Matt Grossman and Daniel Thaler, "Mass-Elite Divides in Aversion to Social Change and Support for Donald Trump," *American Politics Research*, published ahead of print, May 7, 2018, https://doi.org/10.1177/1532673X18772280.

23. Anne Case and Angus Deaton, "Mortality and Morbidity in the 21st Century," *Brookings Papers on Economic Activity*, March 23, 2017, https://www.brookings.edu/bpea-articles/mortality-and-morbidity-in-the-21st-century/.

24. Jacob Bor, "Diverging Life Expectancies and Voting Patterns in the 2016 US Presidential Election," *American Journal of Public Health* 107, no. 10 (2017): 1560–62; Shannon Monnat, "Deaths of Despair and Support for Trump in the 2016 Presidential Election" (research brief, Pennsylvania State University Department of Agricultural Economics, Sociology, and Education, December 4, 2016), http://aese.psu.edu/directory /smm67/Election16.pdf; David Autor, David Dorn, Gordon Hanson, and Kaveh Majlesi, "A Note on the Effect of Rising Trade Exposure on the 2016 Presidential Election" (unpublished paper, last revised March 2, 2017), https://economics.mit.edu/files/12418; Guo, "Yes, Working Class Whites"; Filipe Campante and David Yanagizawa-Drott, "Did Declining Social Mobility Cause Trump's Rise? In a Word, No," *Vox*, December 9, 2016, https://www.vox.com/the-big-idea/2016/12/9/13895184/social-mobility-economic -anxiety-trump-chetty; Jonathan T. Rothwell and Pablo Diego-Rosell, "Explaining Nationalist Political Views: The Case of Donald Trump" (working paper, posted August 15, 2016, last revised December 29, 2017), https://papers.ssrn.com/sol3/papers.cfm?abstract _id=2822059.

25. For similar findings, see Sean McElwee and Jason McDaniel, "Economic Anxiety Didn't Make People Vote Trump, Racism Did," *Nation*, May 8, 2017, https://www.thenation .com/article/economic-anxiety-didnt-make-people-vote-trump-racism-did/. The questions about health care payments and general financial situation were asked of all respondents. The question about housing payments was asked of those who pay a mortgage, rent, or pay some money for their housing. (In the 2012 ANES, the question was asked only of respondents interviewed face to face, not online.) The question about losing one's job in the future was asked of respondents who were employed, who were temporarily laid off, or who were students, homemakers, retired, or disabled but were also doing some work for money.

26. Schaffner, MacWilliams, and Nteta, "Understanding White Polarization." See also Mutz, "Status Threat."

27. John Sides, "Race, Religion, and Immigration in 2016," Democracy Fund Voter Study Group, 2017, https://www.voterstudygroup.org/publications/2016-elections/race -religion-immigration-2016. On growing Republican opposition to free trade agreements, see these Pew Research Center findings: Bradley Jones, "Support for Free Trade Agreements Rebounds Modestly, but Wide Partisan Differences Remain," Pew Research Center, April 25, 2017, http://www.pewresearch.org/fact-tank/2017/04/25/support-for-free -trade-agreements-rebounds-modestly-but-wide-partisan-differences-remain/.

28. Sides, "Race, Religion, and Immigration."

29. Michael B. Katz, *The Undeserving Poor: America's Enduring Confrontation with Poverty* (New York: Oxford University Press, 2013); Cybelle Fox, *Three Worlds of Relief: Race, Immigration, and the American Welfare State from the Progressive Era to the New Deal* (Princeton: Princeton University Press, 2012).

30. The research on Youngstown is Justin Gest, *The New Minority: White Working Class Politics in an Age of Immigration and Inequality* (New York: Oxford University Press, 2016), 95. The research on rural communities is Robert Wuthnow, *The Left Behind: Decline and Rage in Rural America* (Princeton: Princeton University Press, 2018), 147.

31. Michele Lee He Yee, "Trump's Ridiculous Claim That Veterans Are 'Treated Worse' Than Undocumented Immigrants," *Washington Post*, September 13, 2016; "Trump Still off on Immigration," FactCheck.org, September 1, 2016, https://www.factcheck .org/2016/09/trump-still-off-on-immigration/; Louis Jacobson and Mirian Vlaverde, "Donald Trump's False Claim Veterans Treated Worse Than Immigrants," PolitiFact, September 9, 2016, http://www.politifact.com/truth-o-meter/statements/2016/sep/09/don

ald-trump/trump-says-veterans-treated-worse-illegal-immigran/; Sally Cohn, "Nothing Donald Trump Says on Immigration Holds Up," *Time*, June 29, 2016, http://time.com /4386240/donald-trump-immigration-arguments/; Brennan Hoban, "Do Immigrants 'Steal' Jobs from American Workers?," Brookings Institution, August 24, 2017, https:// www.brookings.edu/blog/brookings-now/2017/08/24/do-immigrants-steal-jobs-from -american-workers/; "Read the Full Transcript of President Obama's Farewell Speech," *Los Angeles Times*, January 10, 2017, http://beta.latimes.com/politics/la-pol-obama -farewell-speech-transcript-20170110-story.html.

32. See Michael Tesler, "Trump Voters Think African Americans Are Much Less Deserving Than 'Average Americans,'" *Huffington Post*, December 19, 2016, https://www .huffingtonpost.com/michael-tesler/trump-voters-think-africa_b_13732500.html; and Thierry Devos and Mahzarin R. Banaji, "American = White?," *Journal of Personality and Social Psychology* 88, no. 3 (2016): 447–66.

33. Matthew D. Luttig, Christopher M. Federico, and Howard Lavine, "Supporters and Opponents of Donald Trump Respond Differently to Racial Cues: An Experimental Analysis," *Research & Politics*, November 1, 2017, https://doi.org/10.1177/205316801 7737411.

34. Ariel-Levy Edwards, "Nearly Half of Trump Voters Think Whites Face a Lot of Discrimination," *Huffington Post*, 2016, https://www.huffingtonpost.com/entry/discrim ination-race-religion_us_5833761ee4b099512f845bba.

35. The bivariate correlation between education and vote choice in the 2016 ANES was −0.19. Once the index of economic anxiety was accounted for, the (partial) correlation between education and vote choice was −0.17. The same finding emerged in the VOTER Survey. There, the correlation between education and people's preference for Trump over Clinton was again negative ($r = -0.13$). But once attitudes toward African Americans and immigration were accounted for, the correlation disappeared ($r = 0.01$).

36. Nicholas Carnes and Noam Lupu, "It's Time to Bust the Myth: Most Trump Voters Were Not Working Class," *Monkey Cage* (blog), *Washington Post*, June 5, 2017, https://www.washingtonpost.com/news/monkey-cage/wp/2017/06/05/its-time-to-bust -the-myth-most-trump-voters-were-not-working-class/?utm_term=.9a3fa2021084. See also Daniel Cox, Rachel Lienesch, and Robert P. Jones, "Beyond Economics: Fears of Cultural Displacement Pushed the White Working Class to Trump," Public Religion Research Institute, May 9, 2017, https://www.prri.org/research/white-working-class-attitudes -economy-trade-immigration-election-donald-trump/; and Schaffner, MacWilliams, and Nteta, "Understanding White Polarization."

37. See Bernard Fraga, *The Turnout Gap: Race, Ethnicity, and Political Inequality in a Diversifying America* (New York: Cambridge University Press, forthcoming); and Bernard Fraga, Sean McElwee, Jesse Rhodes, and Brian Schaffner, "Why Did Trump Win? More Whites—and Fewer Blacks—Actually Voted," *Monkey Cage* (blog), *Washington Post*, May 8, 2017, https://www.washingtonpost.com/news/monkey-cage/wp/2017/05/08 /why-did-trump-win-more-whites-and-fewer-blacks-than-normal-actually-voted/?utm _term=.8f1662ce7d7b.

38. Hillary Clinton, *What Happened* (New York: Simon and Schuster, 2017), 420. For a review of this literature, see Benjamin Highton, "Voter Identification Laws and Turnout in the United States," *Annual Review of Political Science* 20 (2017): 149–67. See also Fraga, *The Turnout Gap*; Fraga finds no consistent relationship between the establishment of voter identification and the turnout of racial and ethnic minorities.

39. On black in-group identity, see Patricia Gurin, Shirley Hatchett, and James Jackson, *Hope and Independence: Blacks' Response to Electoral and Party Politics* (New York: Russell Sage Foundation, 1989); Michael Dawson, *Behind the Mule: Race and Class in African American Politics* (Princeton: Princeton University Press, 1994); Melissa Harris-Lacewell, *Barbershops, Bibles, and BET: Everyday Talk and Black Political Thought* (Princeton: Princeton University Press, 2004); and Katherine Tate, *From Protest to Politics: The New Black Voters in American Elections* (Cambridge, MA: Harvard University Press, 1994). On Obama support and black solidarity, see Donald Kinder and Allison Dale-Riddle, *The End of Race? Obama, 2008, and Racial Politics in America* (New Haven: Yale University Press, 2012); and Tesler, *Post-Racial or Most-Racial?*

40. Prominent African Americans who spoke against Clinton included Cornel West, Marc Lamont Hill, and Eddie Glaude Jr. The Kaepernick quote is from Yamiche Alcindor, "Colin Kaepernick Says Presidential Candidates Were Trying to 'Debate Who's Less Racist,'" *New York Times*, September 28, 2016. Phillip Bump, "Donald Trump's Risky Plan to Use the Internet to Suppress Hillary Clinton's Turnout," *Washington Post*, October 27, 2016, https://www.washingtonpost.com/news/the-fix/wp/2016/10/27/donald-trumps-risky-plan-to-use-the-internet-to-suppress-hillary-clintons-turnout/?utm_term=.cb78a82cab05.

41. Jonathan Martin and Alexander Burns, "Trump, Waking a 'Sleeping Giant,' Helps Clinton Build an Unlikely Firewall," *New York Times*, November 2, 2016, https://www.nytimes.com/2016/11/03/us/politics/donald-trump-waking-a-sleeping-giant-helps-hillary-clinton-build-an-unlikely-firewall.html. Brent Budowsky, "The Hispanic Sleeping Giant Has Awakened," *The Hill*, November 6, 2016, http://thehill.com/blogs/pundits-blog/presidential-campaign/304543-the-hispanic-sleeping-giant-has-awakened.

42. Gary Segura and Matt Baretto, "Lies, Damn Lies, and Exit Polls . . . ," *Huffington Post*, November 10, 2016, https://www.huffingtonpost.com/latino-decisions/lies-damn-lies-and-exit-p_b_12903492.html; Matt A. Barreto, Fernando Guerra, Mara Marks, Stephen A. Nuño, and Nathan D. Woods, "Controversies in Exit Polling: Implementing a Racially Stratified Homogenous Precinct Approach," *PS: Political Science and Politics* 39, no. 3 (2006): 477–83.

43. Mark Hugo Lopez, Ana Gonzalez-Barrera, Jens Manuel Krogstad, and Gustavo López, *Democrats Maintain Edge as Party "More Concerned" about Latinos but Views Similar to 2012* (Washington, DC: Pew Research Center, 2016), http://assets.pewresearch.org/wp-content/uploads/sites/7/2016/10/PH_2016.10.11_Politics_FINAL4.pdf. For the Latino Decisions 2012 and 2016 polls, see Latino Decisions, "2012 Weekly Political Tracking Poll Week 11: Nov 5, 2012," accessed June 6, 2018, http://www.latinodecisions.com/files/5913/5204/1319/Tracker_-_toplines_week_11.pdf; and Latino Decisions, "NALEO Educational Fund/Noticias Telemundo/Latino Decisions Weekly Tracking Poll—September–November 2016," accessed June 6, 2018, http://www.latinodecisions.com/files/1514/7839/2130/Wk8_Full_Tracker.pdf. On the country-level data, see Harry Enten, "Trump Probably Did Better with Latino Voters Than Romney Did," *FiveThirtyEight*, November 18, 2016, https://fivethirtyeight.com/features/trump-probably-did-better-with-latino-voters-than-romney-did/.

44. For estimates of the Census Bureau data that correct for overreporting and nonresponse error, see Michael McDonald's estimates here: Michael McDonald, "Voter Turnout Demographics," United States Elections Project, accessed June 6, 2018, http://www.electproject.org/home/voter-turnout/demographics. For the analysis based on voter file data, see Fraga, *The Turnout Gap*.

45. Michael Tesler, "The Massive Gap between Whites and Latinos in How They Perceive Donald Trump," *Monkey Cage* (blog), *Washington Post*, January 21, 2016, https://www.washingtonpost.com/news/monkey-cage/wp/2016/01/21/the-massive-gap -between-whites-and-latinos-in-how-they-perceive-donald-trump/?utm_term= .28c3317a816f; Frank Newport, "Trump Has a Major Image Problem with Hispanics," Gallup, March 11, 2016, http://news.gallup.com/poll/189887/trump-major-image-problem -hispanics.aspx. For the 2012 Latino Decisions data, see Latino Decisions, "2012 Weekly Political Tracking." For 2016 polling, see Latino Decisions, "NALEO Educational Fund."

46. In Latino Decisions' final 2012 preelection tracking poll, Obama's and Romney's net favorable ratings were +64 and −38, respectively, yielding an absolute difference of 102. In Latino Decisions' final 2012 preelection tracking poll, Clinton's and Trump's net favorable ratings were +45 and −59, respectively, yielding an absolute difference of 104 between the candidates.

47. On the strengthening of Latino group identity, see Matt Barreto and Gary Segura, *Latino America: How America's Most Dynamic Population Is Poised to Transform the Politics of the Nation* (New York: PublicAffairs, 2014). On the diversity among Latinos, see Jack Citrin and David O. Sears, *American Identity and the Politics of Multiculturalism* (New York: Cambridge University Press, 2014); Deborah J. Schildkraut, *Americanism in the Twenty-First Century* (New York: Cambridge University Press, 2011); and Gabriel R. Sanchez and Natalie Masuoka, "Brown-Utility Heuristic? The Presence and Contributing Factors of Latino Linked Fate," *Hispanic Journal of Behavioral Sciences* 32, no. 4 (2010): 519–31. On the impact of appeals to Latino group identity, see Ali A. Valenzuela and Melissa R. Michelson, "Turnout, Status, and Identity: Mobilizing Latinos to Vote with Group Appeals," *American Political Science Review* 110, no. 4 (2016): 615–30. On appeals focused on xenophobic rhetoric, see Efrén O. Pérez, "Xenophobic Rhetoric and Its Political Effects on Immigrants and Their Co-ethnics," *American Journal of Political Science* 59, no. 3 (2015): 549–64.

48. In a least squares regression, the relationship between Hispanic group identity and support for Obama versus Romney was $b = 0.124$ (s.e. = 0.022). In 2016, the relationship was very similar $b = 0.123$ (s.e. = 0.025). Unfortunately, the samples of Latinos in the 2012 and 2016 ANES were not large enough to say conclusively that Clinton or Obama performed better or worse among subgroups of Latinos defined by the strength of their identity.

49. Natalie Masuoka, "Defining the Group: Latino Identity and Political Participation," *American Politics Research* 36, no. 1 (2008): 33–61; Valenzuela and Michelson, "Turnout, Status, and Identity"; Citrin and Sears, *American Identity*.

50. Clinton, *What Happened*, 128.

51. Kinder and Dale-Riddle, *The End of Race?*; Michael Tesler and David O. Sears, *Obama's Race: The 2008 Election and the Dream of a Post-Racial America* (Chicago: University of Chicago Press, 2010).

52. "Decades-Old Video Shows Trump Predict His Campaign Problems with Women," NBC News, October 10, 2016, https://www.nbcnews.com/nightly-news/video /decades-old-video-shows-trump-predict-his-campaign-problems-with-women -783048771685.

53. Monmouth University Polling Institute, "Trump Hurt by Misconduct Claims as Clinton Lead Widens," October 17, 2016, https://www.monmouth.edu/polling-institute /reports/monmouthpoll_us_101716/.

54. The surveys and their results were as follows: ABC/*Washington Post* (October 29–November 1), 55 percent said Trump is biased against women, compared to 40 percent not biased; Associated Press (October 20–24), 46 percent said "sexist" describes Trump "very well," 13 percent "somewhat well," 18 percent "slightly well," and 21 percent "not well at all"; CBS/*New York Times* (October 28–November 1), 20 percent said Trump respects women "a lot," 25 percent "some," 15 percent "not much," and 38 percent "not at all"; and Pew Research Center (October 20–25), 14 percent said Trump respects women "a great deal," 24 percent "a fair amount," 24 percent "not too much," and 36 percent "not at all." Results accessed from Roper Center's iPOLL archive.

55. Harry Enten, "Men Are Treating 2016 as a 'Normal' Election; Women Aren't," *FiveThirtyEight*, October 17, 2016, http://fivethirtyeight.com/features/men-are-treating -2016-as-a-normal-election-women-arent/.

56. On gender consciousness among women, see Patricia Gurin, "Women's Gender Consciousness," *Public Opinion Quarterly* 49, no. 2 (1985): 143–63; Nancy Burns and Donald Kinder, "Categorical Politics: Gender, Race and Public Opinion," in *New Directions in Public Opinion*, ed. Adam Berinsky (New York: Routledge, 2012), 139–67; Kinder and Dale-Riddle, *The End of Race?*; and Christopher T. Stout, Kelsy Kretschmer, and Leah Ruppanner, "Gender Linked Fate, Race/Ethnicity, and the Marriage Gap in American Politics," *Political Research Quarterly* 70, no. 3 (2017): 509–22. On gender identity and views of Clinton and Obama, see Michael Tesler, "Why the Gender Gap Doomed Hillary Clinton," *Monkey Cage* (blog), *Washington Post*, November 9, 2016, https://www .washingtonpost.com/news/monkey-cage/wp/2016/11/09/why-the-gender-gap-doomed -hillary-clinton/.

57. James A. Stimson, *Tides of Consent: How Opinion Movements Shape American Politics* (Cambridge: Cambridge University Press, 2004); Leonie Huddy and Johanna Willmann, "Partisan Sorting and the Feminist Gap in American Politics" (unpublished manuscript, Stony Brook University, 2017); Mary McThomas and Michael Tesler, "The Growing Influence of Gender Attitudes on Public Support for Hillary Clinton, 2008– 2012," *Politics and Gender* 12, no. 1 (2016): 28–49.

58. For similar findings regarding the activation of sexism, see Schaffner, Mac-Williams, and Nteta, "Understanding White Polarization"; Nicholas Valentino, Carly Wayne, and Marzia Oceno, "Mobilizing Sexism: The Interaction of Emotion and Gender Attitudes in the 2016 US Presidential Election," *Public Opinion Quarterly* 82 (special issue): 213–35; and results from the ANES described in the chapter appendix. On the correlation between attitudes toward gender and voting among nonwhites, see Lorrie Frasure, "Women Voters, Attitudes on Feminism, and Voting in 2016," *Journal of Race, Ethnicity, and Politics* (forthcoming).

59. Clinton, *What Happened*, 125. The data she cites are from Sheryl Sandberg's book *Lean In: Women, Work, and the Will to Lead* (New York: Knopf, 2013).

60. On the ethical standard, see Kelly Dittmar, *Navigating Gendered Terrain: Stereotypes and Strategy in Political Campaigns* (Philadelphia: Temple University Press, 2015). On the perception that female candidates are more honest than male candidates, at least in the abstract, see Kathleen Dolan, *When Does Gender Matter?* (New York: Oxford University Press, 2014). The study of the American Bar Association is Jessica Kennedy, Mary-Hunter McDonnell, and Nicole Stephens, "Does Gender Raise the Ethical Bar? Exploring the Punishment of Ethical Violations at Work," *Academy of Management Proceedings* 2016, no. 1 (2016): 11664, https://journals.aom.org/doi/10.5465/ambpp.2016 .11664abstract.

61. The 2014 quote from Clinton is reported in Glenn Thrush and Maggie Haberman, "What Is Hillary Clinton Afraid Of?," *Politico Magazine*, May/June 2014, https://www .politico.com/magazine/story/2014/05/hillary-clinton-media-105901. One study of coverage by Regina Lawrence and Melody Rose examined three major newspapers (the *Los Angeles Times*, *New York Times*, and *Washington Post*) and the nightly news broadcasts of ABC, NBC, and CBS and found that the overall tone of Clinton's coverage was more negative: 23 percent of stories had a negative comment about Clinton, compared to 16 percent of stories about Obama and 13 percent of stories about John McCain. See Regina G. Lawrence and Melody Rose, *Hillary Clinton's Race for the White House: Gender Politics and the Media on the Campaign Trail* (Boulder, CO: Lynne Rienner, 2010). But a Project for Excellence in Journalism study of a larger number of outlets did not find that the tone of Clinton's coverage was more negative than Obama's coverage. See Pew Research Center, "Character and the Primaries of 2008," May 29, 2008, http://www .journalism.org/2008/05/29/character-and-the-primaries-of-2008/. The Pew Research Center's finding comports with a recent in-depth study of newspaper coverage of male and female House candidates in the 2010 and 2014 elections. See Danny Hayes and Jennifer L. Lawless, *Women on the Run: Gender, Media, and Political Campaigns in a Polarized Era* (New York: Cambridge University Press, 2016). A source for the Tucker Carlson quote is Ryan Chiachiere, "Tucker Carlson on Clinton: '[W]hen She Comes on Television, I Involuntarily Cross My Legs,'" *Media Matters*, July 18, 2007, https://www.mediamatters .org/research/2007/07/18/tucker-carlson-on-clinton-when-she-comes-on-tel/139362.

62. Clinton, *What Happened*, 121.

63. The 2008 study is Lawrence and Rose, *Hillary Clinton's Race*. On the reaction to sexist comments in 2016, see Kelly Dittmar, *Finding Gender in Election 2016* (Cambridge, MA: Barbara Lee Family Foundation; New Brunswick, NJ: Center for American Women and Politics, 2017). Full Frontal (@FullFrontalSamB), March 16, 2016, 8:17 a.m., https:// twitter.com/fullfrontalsamb/status/710122782638661634?lang=en.

64. David Catanese, "DNC Staff: Arrogance Cost Clinton the Election," *U.S. News and World Report*, November 11, 2016, https://www.usnews.com/news/the-run-2016 /articles/2016-11-11/dnc-staff-arrogance-cost-hillary-clinton-the-election-vs-donald -trump; Abby Phillip, John Wagner, and Anne Gearan, "A Series of Strategic Mistakes Likely Sealed Clinton's Fate," *Washington Post*, November 12, 2016, https://www.washing tonpost.com/politics/a-series-of-strategic-mistakes-likely-sealed-clintons-fate/2016/11 /11/82f3fcc0-a840-11e6-ba59-a7d93165c6d4_story.html?utm_term=.0408f31e c21c&wpisrc=nl_wemost&wpmm=1; Sam Stein, "Clinton Camp Mastered the Science of Politics but Forgot the Art, Staffers Say," *Huffington Post*, November 21, 2016, https:// www.huffingtonpost.com/entry/clinton-campaign-politics_us_5833866de4b030 997bc10520.

65. See Sides and Vavreck, *The Gamble*.

66. On the Ada algorithm, see John Wagner, "Clinton's Data-Driven Campaign Relied Heavily on an Algorithm Named Ada. What Didn't She See?," *Washington Post*, November 9, 2016, https://www.washingtonpost.com/news/post-politics/wp/2016/11/09 /clintons-data-driven-campaign-relied-heavily-on-an-algorithm-named-ada-what -didnt-she-see/?utm_term=.d9c753bdc956. On forecasts based on the public polls, see the aggregation here: Josh Katz, "Who Will Be President?," *Upshot* (blog), *New York Times*, November 8, 2016, https://www.nytimes.com/interactive/2016/upshot/presidential -polls-forecast.html. On the Trump campaign and Republican National Committee forecast, see Jon Ward, "Trump's Victory Stunned Even GOP Digital Team," Yahoo,

November 9, 2016, https://www.yahoo.com/news/trumps-victory-stunned-even-gop
-digital-team-081014018.html. On polling error, see especially the report commissioned
by the American Association of Public Opinion Research: Courtney Kennedy et al., "An
Evaluation of the 2016 Election Polls in the U.S." American Association of Public Opinion Research, 2017, http://www.aapor.org/Education-Resources/Reports/An-Evaluation
-of-2016-Election-Polls-in-the-U-S.aspx. On the overrepresentation of college-educated
voters, see also Nate Silver, "Pollsters Probably Didn't Talk to Enough White Voters
without College Degrees," *FiveThirtyEight*, December 1, 2016, https://fivethirtyeight
.com/features/pollsters-probably-didnt-talk-to-enough-white-voters-without-college-de
grees/. Polling errors were strongly correlated with the share of the electorate that was
whites without college degrees. On last-minute shifts, see Dan Hopkins, "Voters Really
Did Switch to Trump at the Last Minute," *FiveThirtyEight*, December 20, 2016, http://
fivethirtyeight.com/features/voters-really-did-switch-to-trump-at-the-last-minute/.
There was less evidence that Trump supporters simply were less willing to reveal their
support for him in polls. See Harry Enten, "'Shy' Voters Probably Aren't Why the Polls
Missed Trump," *FiveThirtyEight*, November 18, 2016, https://fivethirtyeight.com/features
/shy-voters-probably-arent-why-the-polls-missed-trump/.

67. Jonathan Allen and Amie Parnes, *Shattered: Inside Hillary Clinton's Doomed
Campaign* (New York: Crown, 2017), 190; Philip, Wagner, and Gearan, "Series of Strategic Mistakes,"

68. More information about the Spotcheck ad project is here: SpotCheck, "What Is
SpotCheck?," accessed June 6, 2018, https://www.vanderbilt.edu/spotcheck/.

69. In the primary and general elections, Clinton's campaign committee raised $564
million, while Trump's raised $333 million. Among outside groups, $231 million was
spent to support Clinton and $75 million was spent to support Trump. Clinton also
raised more money via joint fund-raising committees: $160 million versus $138 million
for Trump's campaign. The figures reported in the text add up these numbers. The data
on 2016 fund-raising is from OpenSecrets: OpenSecrets, "2016 Presidential Race," accessed June 6, 2018, https://www.opensecrets.org/pres16/; and OpenSecrets, "Joint Fund-
raising Committees," accessed June 6, 2018, https://www.opensecrets.org/jfc/index.php.
Obama's fund-raising in the 2008 general election period is summarized here: Campaign
Finance Institute, "Table 1: Sources of Funds for the Presidential Candidates, 2007–
2008," accessed June 6, 2018, http://www.cfinst.org/pdf/federal/president/2010_0106
_Table1.pdf. See also Adam Nagourney and Jeff Zeleny, "Obama Forgoes Public Funds in
First for Major Candidate," *New York Times*, June 20, 2008, http://www.nytimes.com/2008
/06/20/us/politics/20obamacnd.html?mcubz=3. Fund-raising in 2012 is summarized here:
OpenSecrets, "2012 Presidential Race," accessed June 6, 2018, https://www.opensecrets.org
/pres12/. Jon Ward, "Trump's Lack of a Data Operation Is Hurting the GOP, Operatives
Say," Yahoo, August 25, 2016, https://www.yahoo.com/news/trumps-lack-of-a-data
-operation-is-hurting-the-gop-operatives-say-192334775.html?soc_src=mail&soc_trk
=ma; Josh Rogin, "Inside the Collapse of Trump's D.C. Policy Shop," *Washington Post*,
September 8, 2016, https://www.washingtonpost.com/news/josh-rogin/wp/2016/09/08
/inside-the-collapse-of-trumps-d-c-policy-shop/?utm_term=.b8913a5103fa; Nicholas Confessore and Rachel Shorey, "Donald Trump, with Bare-Bones Campaign, Relies on
G.O.P. for Vital Tasks," *New York Times*, August 21, 2016, https://www.nytimes.com/2016
/08/22/us/politics/donald-trump-fundraising.html?_r=0.

70. On patterns in the 2016 advertising, see also Erika Franklin Fowler, Travis Ridout,
and Michael Franz, "Political Advertising in 2016: The Presidential Election as Outlier?,"

The Forum 14, no. 4 (2017): 445–469. On Trump's advertising strategy, see Steven Shepard, "Trump's Bizarre Ad Strategy," *Politico*, September 22, 2016, http://www.politico.com /story/2016/09/donald-trump-ad-strategy-228505. The 2012 data are from Sides and Vavreck, *The Gamble*. The imbalance in 2016 advertising stands out compared to other elections as well. In 2000, George W. Bush and allied party and interest groups aired 55 percent of the major-party presidential campaign advertising during the fall campaign, compared to 45 percent for Gore. See Daron Shaw, *The Race to 270: The Electoral College and the Campaign Strategies of 2000 and 2004* (Chicago: University of Chicago Press, 2006), 84. In 2004, John Kerry led Bush with 56 percent of the fall advertising. In 2008, Obama aired 59 percent of the major-party ads. See Michael M. Franz and Travis N. Ridout, "Political Advertising and Persuasion in the 2004 and 2008 Presidential Elections," *American Politics Research* 38, no. 2 (2010): 310.

71. Larry M. Bartels, "Remembering to Forget: A Note on the Duration of Campaign Advertising Effects," *Political Communication* 31, no. 4 (2014): 532–44; Seth J. Hill, James Lo, Lynn Vavreck, and John Zaller, "How Quickly We Forget: The Duration of Persuasion Effects from Mass Communication," *Political Communication* 30, no. 4 (2013): 521–47; Sides and Vavreck, *The Gamble*.

72. See, for example, Jörg L. Spenkuch and David Toniatti, "Political Advertising and Election Results," *Quarterly Journal of Economics*, published ahead of print, May 5, 2018, https://doi.org/10.1093/qje/qjy010; Sides and Vavreck, *The Gamble*; and Franz and Ridout, "Political Advertising and Persuasion."

73. On Romney's advertising, see Sides and Vavreck, *The Gamble*, 221.

74. Matea Gold and Elizabeth Dwoskin, "Trump Campaign's Embrace of Facebook Shows Company's Growing Reach in Elections," *Washington Post*, October 8, 2017, https:// www.washingtonpost.com/politics/trump-campaigns-embrace-of-facebook-shows -companys-growing-reach-in-elections/2017/10/08/e5e5f156-a93b-11e7-b3aa -c0e2e1d41e38_story.html?utm_term=.70a26c0c6c5d&wpisrc=nl_daily202&wpmm=1; Issie Lapowsky, "Here's How Facebook *Actually* Won Trump the Presidency," *Wired*, November 15, 2016, https://www.wired.com/2016/11/facebook-won-trump-election-not-just -fake-news/.

75. The consumer experiments are described in Randall A. Lewis and Justin M. Rao, "The Unfavorable Economics of Measuring the Returns to Advertising," *Quarterly Journal of Economics* (2015): 1941–73. The Black Lives Matter experiment is described in Alexander Coppock and David Broockman, "Summary Report: The Effectiveness of Online Ads: A Field Experiment" (unpublished manuscript, September 16, 2015), http:// alexandercoppock.com/papers/CB_blacklivesmatter.pdf. The campaign experiments are described in David E. Broockman and Donald P. Green, "Do Online Advertisements Increase Political Candidates' Name Recognition or Favorability? Evidence from Randomized Field Experiments," *Political Behavior* 36, no. 2 (2014): 263–89. Three experiments involving voter turnout are Jason J. Jones, Robert M. Bond, Eytan Bakshy, Dean Eckles, and James H. Fowler, "Social Influence and Political Mobilization: Further Evidence from a Randomized Experiment in the 2012 U.S. Presidential Election," *PLoS ONE* 12, no. 4 (2017): 1–9; Kevin Collins, Joshua L. Kalla, and Lauren Keane, "Youth Voter Mobilization through Online Advertising: Evidence from Two GOTV Field Experiments" (undated, unpublished manuscript), https://www.dropbox.com/s/4pr2fos26 svesie/Collins-Keane-Kalla-APSA-2014%20sans%20Fig%204.pdf?dl=0; and Joshua Kalla's analysis of online ads by NextGen Climate in 2016, described in Joshua Kalla, "RE: Results from 2016 Online Ad Voter Turnout Experiment," memo, June 26, 2017, https://

www.dropbox.com/s/ssd1cqccopk2oqq/NGC%20Online%20 a.d.%20GOTV%20Results
.pdf?dl=0.

76. The "big advantage" quote is from Alexander Burns and Jonathan Martin, "Clinton Pushes Minority Turnout as Trump Tries to Rally His Base," *New York Times*, November 3, 2016, https://www.nytimes.com/2016/11/04/us/politics/campaign-trump -clinton.html. Philip Bump, "Donald Trump Still Hasn't Figured Out the Ground Game," *Washington Post*, August 9, 2016, https://www.washingtonpost.com/news/the -fix/wp/2016/08/09/donald-trump-still-hasnt-figured-out-how-to-run-a-field-campaign/ ?utm_term=.acae47005e68&wpisrc=nl_most&wpmm=1; Rosie Gray and Tarini Parti, "In Key States, the Trump Campaign Still Lags Badly," *Buzzfeed*, August 14, 2016, https:// www.buzzfeed.com/rosiegray/in-key-states-the-trump-campaign-still-lags-badly?utm _term=.vjlPmBbXk#.ooVOJQME4; Mark Hensch, "12-Year-Old Running Trump Campaign Office in Colorado," *The Hill*, August 22, 2016, http://thehill.com/blogs/ballot-box /presidential-races/292180-12-year-old-running-trump-campaign-office-in-colo.

77. Allen and Parnes, *Shattered*, 182–83, 234–35, 312; Edward-Isaac Dovere, "How Clinton Lost Michigan—and Blew the Election," *Politico*, December 14, 2016, https:// www.politico.com/story/2016/12/michigan-hillary-clinton-trump-232547; Allen and Parnes, *Shattered*, 368.

78. Joshua Darr, "The Incredible Shrinking Democratic Ground Game," *Vox*, November 16, 2017, https://www.vox.com/mischiefs-of-faction/2017/11/16/16665756/shrinking -democratic-ground-game. Our data differ slightly from Darr's, but these differences do not change the substantive conclusions about 2012 versus 2016.

79. On the trends in self-reported campaign contact, see this graph by political scientist Barry Burden: Barry Burden (@bcburden), "Mobilization efforts by Dems as prevalent in '16 as in '04–12. Overall drop in '16 is GOP falloff due to absence of Trump ground game," Twitter graphic, July 17, 2017, 2:14 p.m., https://twitter.com/bcburden /status/887057997926715393. For studies of the effect of field organizations on presidential vote share, see Joshua Darr and Matthew Levendusky, "Relying on the Ground Game: The Placement and Effect of Campaign Field Offices," *American Politics Research* 42, no. 3 (2014): 529–48; and Seth Masket, John Sides, and Lynn Vavreck, "The Ground Game in the 2012 Presidential Election," *Political Communication* 33 (2016): 169–87.

80. For a similar conclusion, see also Nate Silver, "Clinton's Ground Game Didn't Cost Her the Election," *FiveThirtyEight*, February 13, 2017, https://fivethirtyeight.com/features /clintons-ground-game-didnt-cost-her-the-election/.

81. Allen and Parnes, *Shattered*, 307–8.

82. Thomas Wood, "What the Heck Are We Doing in Ottumwa, Anyway? Presidential Candidate Visits and Their Political Consequences," *ANNALS of the American Academy of Political and Social Science* 667, no. 1 (2016): 110–25. For a similar conclusion based on data from the 2000 and 2004 presidential campaigns, see Shaw, *The Race to 270*.

83. The "fence-sitters" reference is from Allen and Parnes, *Shattered*, 308. The "own devices" quote is from Stein, "Clinton Camp." See also Dovere, "How Clinton Lost Michigan."

84. The "imagine you're on the ground" quote is from Allen and Parnes, *Shattered*, 398. The study of the multiple experiments is Joshua L. Kalla and David E. Broockman, "The Minimal Persuasive Effects of Campaign Content in General Elections: Evidence from 49 Field Experiments," *American Politics Science Review* 112, no. 1 (2018): 148–66. The study of the Obama Wisconsin experiment is Michael Bailey, Daniel J. Hopkins, and Todd Rogers, "Unresponsive and Unpersuaded: The Unintended Consequences of Voter Persuasion Efforts," *Political Behavior* 38, no. 3 (2016): 713–46.

85. The phone call is described in Allen and Parnes, *Shattered*, 394. On white identity versus support for the KKK, see Ashley Jardina, "White Identity Politics Isn't Just about White Supremacy. It's Much Bigger," *Monkey Cage* (blog), *Washington Post*, August 16, 2017, https://www.washingtonpost.com/news/monkey-cage/wp/2017/08/16/white-identity -politics-isnt-just-about-white-supremacy-its-much-bigger/?utm_term=.66a85078236a.

86. Amy Chozick, "Hillary Clinton Blames F.B.I. Director for Election Loss," *New York Times*, November 12, 2016, https://www.nytimes.com/2016/11/13/us/politics/hillary -clinton-james-comey.html; Philip Rucker, "'I Would Be Your President': Clinton Blames Russia, FBI Chief for 2016 Election Loss," *Washington Post*, May 3, 2017, https://www .washingtonpost.com/politics/hillary-clinton-blames-russian-hackers-and-comey-for -2016-election-loss/2017/05/02/e62fef72-2f60-11e7-8674-437ddb6e813e_story.html?utm _term=.bd57b020acc3.

87. The "devastating combination" quote is from Clinton, *What Happened*, 407. Molly McKew, "Did Russia Affect the 2016 Election? It's Now Undeniable," *Wired*, February 16, 2018, https://www.wired.com/story/did-russia-affect-the-2016-election-its-now -undeniable/.

88. See also Harry Enten, "How Much Did WikiLeaks Hurt Hillary Clinton?," *FiveThirtyEight*, December 23, 2016, https://fivethirtyeight.com/features/wikileaks-hillary -clinton/.

89. Patrick Ruffini, "Why Russia's Facebook Ad Campaign Wasn't Such a Success," *Washington Post*, November 3, 2017, https://www.washingtonpost.com/outlook/why -russias-facebook-ad-campaign-wasnt-such-a-success/2017/11/03/b8efacca-bffa-11e7 -8444-a0d4f04b89eb_story.html?utm_term=.87c799fc5d13. The apparently large numbers are from Craig Timbert and Elizabeth Dwoskin, "Russian Content on Facebook, Google, and Twitter Reached Far More Users Than Companies First Disclosed, Congressional Testimony Says," *Washington Post*, October 30, 2017, https://www.washingtonpost .com/business/technology/2017/10/30/4509587e-bd84-11e7-97d9-bdab5a0ab381_story .html?utm_term=.4683d135f7fe.

90. Robert M. Faris, Hal Roberts, Bruce Etling, Nikki Bourassa, Ethan Zuckerman, and Yochai Benkler, *Partisanship, Propaganda, and Disinformation: Online Media and the 2016 U.S. Presidential Election* (Cambridge, MA: Berkman Klein Center for Internet and Society, Harvard University, 2017), http://nrs.harvard.edu/urn-3:HUL .InstRepos:33759251; Andrew Guess, Brendan Nyhan, and Jason Reifler, "Selective Exposure to Misinformation: Evidence from the Consumption of Fake News during the 2016 U.S. Presidential Campaign" (working paper, 2018), http://www.dartmouth.edu/~nyhan /fake-news-2016.pdf; Hunt Allcott and Matthew Gentzkow, "Social Media and Fake News in the 2016 Election" (working paper, 2017), http://www.nber.org/papers/w23089. See also Brendan Nyhan, "Fake News and Bots May Be Worrisome, but Their Political Power Is Overblown," *New York Times*, February 13, 2018, https://www.nytimes.com/2018/02/13 /upshot/fake-news-and-bots-may-be-worrisome-but-their-political-power-is -overblown.html.

91. For an agnostic view, see Nate Silver, "How Much Did Russian Interference Affect the 2016 Election?," *FiveThirtyEight*, February 16, 2018, https://fivethirtyeight.com/features /how-much-did-russian-interference-affect-the-2016-election/. A journalistic account with an appropriately uncertain answer about the impact of Russian interference is Jonathan Martin and Maggie Haberman, "Indictment Leaves No Doubt: Russia Backed Trump. But Was It the Difference?," *New York Times*, February 18, 2018, https://www .nytimes.com/2018/02/18/us/politics/trump-election-russia.html.

92. Nicholas Confessore and Daisuke Wakabayashi, "How Russia Harvested American Rage to Reshape U.S. Politics," *New York Times*, October 9, 2017. On the spread of false information by people versus bots, see Soroush Vosoughi, Deb Roy, and Sinan Aral, "The Spread of True and False News Online," *Science* 359, no. 6380 (2018): 1146–51.

93. Clinton, *What Happened*, 415. See Mara Cecilia Ostfeld, "The New White Flight? The Effects of Political Appeals to Latinos on White Democrats," *Political Behavior* (forthcoming), for scholarly evidence supporting Clinton's claim.

Chapter 9: The Soul of a Nation

Epigraph: Julie Hirschfeld Davis, "A Senior Republican Senator Admonishes Trump: 'America Is an Idea, Not a Race,'" *New York Times*, January 12, 2018, https://www.nytimes.com/2018/01/12/us/politics/trump-immigration-congress.html?_r=0.

1. Michael D. Shear and Julie Hirschfeld Davis, "Stoking Fears, Trump Defied Bureaucracy to Advance Immigration Agenda," *New York Times*, December 23, 2017, https://www.nytimes.com/2017/12/23/us/politics/trump-immigration.html.

2. Josh Dawsey, "Trump Derides Protections for Immigrants from 'Shithole' Countries," *Washington Post*, January 12, 2018, https://www.washingtonpost.com/politics/trump-attacks-protections-for-immigrants-from-shithole-countries-in-oval-office-meeting/2018/01/11/bfc0725c-f711-11e7-91af-31ac729add94_story.html?utm_term=.6a539467b037; Josh Dawsey, Robert Costa, and Ashley Parker, "Inside the Tense, Profane White House Meeting on Immigration," *Washington Post*, January 15, 2018, https://www.washingtonpost.com/politics/inside-the-tense-profane-white-house-meeting-on-immigration/2018/01/15/13c79fa4-fa1c-11e7-8f66-2dfob94bb98a_story.html?utm_term=.24255b5abf14; "U.S. Voters Split on Whether Trump Is Stable, Quinnipiac University National Poll Finds; President Is Dividing the Nation, Voters Say 2–1," press release, Quinnipiac University Poll, January 17, 2018, https://poll.qu.edu/national/release-detail?ReleaseID=2513.

3. Susan Svrluga and Nick Anderson, "Justice Department Investigating Harvard's Affirmative-Action Policies," *Washington Post*, November 21, 2017, https://www.washingtonpost.com/news/grade-point/wp/2017/11/21/justice-department-investigating-harvards-affirmative-action-policies/?utm_term=.064a6214eb80; Matt Zapotosky and Sari Horwitz, "Sessions Vows Crackdown on Violent Crime in First Major Speech as Attorney General," *Washington Post*, February 28, 2017, https://www.washingtonpost.com/world/national-security/sessions-vows-crackdown-on-violent-crime-in-first-major-speech-as-attorney-general/2017/02/27/b18af654-fd42-11e6-8f41-ea6ed597e4ca_story.html?utm_term=.3b14d77fd500; Sari Horwitz, Mark Berman, and Wesley Lowrey, "Sessions Orders Justice Department to Review All Police Reform Agreements," *Washington Post*, April 3, 2017, https://www.washingtonpost.com/world/national-security/sessions-orders-justice-department-to-review-all-police-reform-agreements/2017/04/03/ba934058-18bd-11e7-9887-1a5314b56a08_story.html?utm_term=.8fcc6640b9b4.

4. Bryan Armen Graham, "Donald Trump Blasts NFL Anthem Protesters: 'Get That Son of a Bitch off the Field,'" *Guardian*, September 23, 2017, https://www.theguardian.com/sport/2017/sep/22/donald-trump-nfl-national-anthem-protests; Joe Biden, "'We Are Living through a Battle for the Soul of This Nation,'" *Atlantic*, August 27, 2017, https://www.theatlantic.com/politics/archive/2017/08/joe-biden-after-charlottesville/538128/;

Tara Golshan, "GOP Senators React to Trump's Charlottesville Comments: 'Mr. President—We Must Call Evil by Its Name,'" *Vox*, August 12, 2017, https://www.vox.com/2017/8/12/16139144/gop-senators-react-trump-charlottesville; Glen Thrush and Maggie Haberman, "Trump Gives White Supremacists an Unequivocal Boost," *New York Times*, August 15, 2017, https://www.nytimes.com/2017/08/15/us/politics/trump-charlottesville-white-nationalists.html.

5. Ali Breland, "Romney: Trump Will Cause 'Trickle-Down Racism,'" *Politico*, June 10, 2016, https://www.politico.com/story/2016/06/mitt-romney-donald-trump-trickle-down-racism-224209.

6. Gabby Morrongiello, "Bannon Predicts '50 Years' of GOP Rule If Trump Delivers," *Washington Examiner*, November 18, 2016, https://www.washingtonexaminer.com/bannon-predicts-50-years-of-gop-rule-if-trump-delivers; Edward N. Luttwak, "Why the Trump Dynasty Will Last Sixteen Years," *Times Literary Supplement*, July 25, 2017, https://www.the-tls.co.uk/articles/public/trump-dynasty-luttwak/; Clare Malone, "Barack Obama Lost the White House but Democrats Lost the Country," *FiveThirtyEight*, January 19, 2017, https://fivethirtyeight.com/features/barack-obama-won-the-white-house-but-democrats-lost-the-country/; Matt Taibbi, "Yikes! New Behind-the-Scenes Book Brutalizes the Clinton Campaign," *Rolling Stone*, April 20, 2017, https://www.rollingstone.com/politics/features/taibbi-on-the-new-book-that-brutalizes-the-clinton-campaign-w477978; Noah Rothman, "The Democratic Party: A Brand in Crisis," *Commentary*, April 20, 2017, https://www.commentarymagazine.com/politics-ideas/liberals-democrats/definition-brand-problem-bernie-sanders-democratic-party/; Franklin Foer, "What's Wrong with the Democrats?," *Atlantic*, July/August 2017, https://www.theatlantic.com/magazine/archive/2017/07/whats-wrong-with-the-democrats/528696/. The quotes from after the 2012 election are documented in John Sides and Lynn Vavreck, *The Gamble: Choice and Chance in the 2012 Presidential Election* (Princeton: Princeton University Press, 2013), 228, 231.

7. Stephen Adler, Jeff Mason, and Steve Holland, "Exclusive: Trump Says He Thought Being President Would Be Easier Than His Old Life," Reuters, April 27, 2017, https://www.reuters.com/article/us-usa-trump-100days/exclusive-trump-says-he-thought-being-president-would-be-easier-than-his-old-life-idUSKBN17U0CA?feedType=RSS&feedName=topNews; Josh Dawsey, Shane Goldmacher, and Alex Isenstadt, "The Education of Donald Trump," *Politico*, April 27, 2017, https://www.politico.com/story/2017/04/27/the-education-of-donald-trump-237669; Carol E. Lee and Michael C. Bender, "RNC Chair Reince Priebus Is Named Donald Trump's Chief of Staff," *Wall Street Journal*, November 13, 2016, https://www.wsj.com/articles/leading-contender-for-donald-trump-s-chief-of-staff-is-rnc-chairman-reince-priebus-1479069597; Kenneth P. Vogel, Nancy Cook, and Alex Isenstadt, "Trump Team Rivalries Spark Infighting," *Politico*, November 11, 2016, https://www.politico.com/story/2016/11/donald-trump-team-rivals-231277.

8. Philip Rucker, "Corker Decries Trump's 'Constant Chaos,' Denounces His Attacks on Media and FBI," *Washington Post*, April 18, 2018; Kathryn Dunn Tenpas, "Why Is Trump's Staff Turnover Higher Than the 5 Most Recent Presidents?," Brookings Institution, January 19, 2018, https://www.brookings.edu/research/why-is-trumps-staff-turnover-higher-than-the-5-most-recent-presidents/.

9. Josh Dawsey, "Trump Assails Comey in Tweetstorm, Suggests Ex-FBI Director Deserves 'Jail,'" *Washington Post*, April 15, 2018, https://www.washingtonpost.com/politics/trump-assails-comey-in-tweetstorm-calls-for-ex-fbi-director-to-be-imprisoned/2018/04/15/af00c178-40af-11e8-ad8f-27a8c409298b_story.html?utm_term=.244a5eddc814;

Michelle Ye Hee Lee and Anu Narayanswamy, "Trump's Reelection Committee Has Spent More Than $1 out of Every $5 on Legal Fees This Year," *Washington Post*, April 15, 2018, https://www.washingtonpost.com/politics/trumps-reelection-committee-has-spent-more-than-1-out-of-every-5-on-legal-fees-this-year/2018/04/15/2a9248e8-40f1-11e8-8569-26fda6b404c7_story.html?utm_term=.8ac98ec2857e.

10. See the analysis of the Tax Policy Center: Tax Policy Center Staff, "Distributional Analysis of the Conference Agreement for the Tax Cuts and Jobs Act," Tax Policy Center, December 18, 2017, http://www.taxpolicycenter.org/publications/distributional-analysis-conference-agreement-tax-cuts-and-jobs-act.

11. Gary Langer, "Amid Record Low One-Year Approval Rating, Half of Americans Question Trump's Mental Stability: Poll," ABC News, January 21, 2018, http://abcnews.go.com/Politics/amid-record-low-year-approval-half-question-trumps/story?id=52473639.

12. Molly Ball, "The Republican Party in Exile," *Atlantic*, August 18, 2016, https://www.theatlantic.com/politics/archive/2016/08/the-party-in-exile/496268/; James Hohmann, "The Daily 202: Trump's Pollster Says He Ran a 'Post-ideological' Campaign," *Washington Post*, December 5, 2016, https://www.washingtonpost.com/news/powerpost/paloma/daily-202/2016/12/05/daily-202-trump-s-pollster-says-he-ran-a-post-ideological-campaign/5844d166e9b69b7e58e45f2a/?utm_term=.aac785be4d80&wpisrc=nl_most&wpmm=1; McKay Coppins, "The Republican Identity Crisis," *Atlantic*, April 1, 2017, https://www.theatlantic.com/politics/archive/2017/04/the-gops-ideological-identity-crisis/521316/.

13. See, for example, Daniel Schlozman, *When Movements Anchor Parties* (Princeton: Princeton University Press, 2015); Christopher Baylor, *First to the Party: The Group Origins of Political Transformation* (Philadelphia: University of Pennsylvania Press, 2018); and Eric Schickler, *Racial Liberalism: The Transformation of American Liberalism, 1932–1965* (Princeton: Princeton University Press, 2016). For skeptical views of Trump's influence on the party, see Conor Friedersdorf, "The GOP's Problems Are Bigger Than Trump," *Atlantic*, April 19, 2018, https://www.theatlantic.com/politics/archive/2018/04/donald-trump-hasnt-taken-over-the-gop/558305/; and Matt Grossmann, "Sorry, but the Republican Party Is Not in Crisis," Niskanen Center, January 4, 2018, https://niskanen center.org/blog/sorry-republican-party-not-crisis/.

14. Victor Davis Hanson, "A Year of Achievement," *National Review*, February 7, 2018, https://www.nationalreview.com/2018/02/donald-trump-first-year-conservative-success-story/. See also Abby Phillip and John Wagner, "Trump as a 'Conventional Republican'? That's What Some in GOP Establishment Say They See," *Washington Post*, April 13, 2017, https://www.washingtonpost.com/politics/gop-establishment-sees-trumps-flip-flops-as-move-toward-a-conventional-republican/2017/04/13/f9ce03f6-205c-11e7-be2a-3a1fb24d4671_story.html?utm_term=.992ee955e932.

15. Michael Nelson, *Trump's First Year* (Charlottesville: University of Virginia Press, 2018); Erick Erickson, "A Congressman's Profanity Laced Tirade in a Safeway Grocery Store," *The Resurgent* (blog), April 11, 2018, https://www.themaven.net/theresurgent/erick-erickson/a-congressman-s-profanity-laced-tirade-in-a-safeway-grocery-store-SeHI2l5bIECGQn4gmnzGaw/?full=1.

16. Harry Enten, "How Trump Ranks in Popularity vs. Past Presidents," *FiveThirtyEight*, January 19, 2018, https://fivethirtyeight.com/features/the-year-in-trumps-approval-rating/.

17. Pew Research Center, "Positive Views of Economy Surge, Driven by Major Shifts among Republicans," March 22, 2018, http://www.people-press.org/2018/03/22/positive

-views-of-economy-surge-driven-by-major-shifts-among-republicans/; Robert Griffin, "The First Six Months: How Americans Are Reacting to the Trump Administration," Democracy Fund Voter Study Group, September 2017, https://www.voterstudygroup .org/publications/2017-voter-survey/first-six-months.

18. Kathy Frankovic, "Despite Mueller Indictments, Many Republicans Doubt Russian Meddling Happened," YouGov, February 22, 2018, https://today.yougov.com/topics /politics/articles-reports/2018/02/22/despite-mueller-indictments-many-republicans -doubt; Ariel Edwards-Levy, "Republican Confidence in the FBI Has Dropped since 2015," *Huffington Post*, January 31, 2018, https://www.huffingtonpost.com/entry/republican -confidence-in-the-fbi-has-dropped-since-2015_us_5a721bbbe4b09a544b5616a7; Philip Bump, "An Increasing Number of Americans See the FBI as Biased against Trump," *Washington Post*, April 17, 2018, https://www.washingtonpost.com/news/politics/wp/2018 /04/17/an-increasing-number-of-americans-see-the-fbi-as-biased-against-trump/?utm _term=.b7153d3277f3. On views of the Russia investigation, see Pew Research Center, "Public Confidence in Mueller's Investigation Remains Steady," March 15, 2018, http:// www.people-press.org/2018/03/15/public-confidence-in-muellers-investigation -remains-steady/.

19. John Sides, "The Pennsylvania Special Election Was Another Great Night for the Democratic Party," *Monkey Cage* (blog), *Washington Post*, March 14, 2018, https://www .washingtonpost.com/news/monkey-cage/wp/2018/03/14/the-pennsylvania-special -election-was-another-great-night-for-the-democratic-party/?utm_term=.f172d1f5a994.

20. Susan Berry, "Seven Ways Trump Is Taking Back America's Culture," *Breitbart*, July 30, 2017, http://www.breitbart.com/big-government/2017/07/30/seven-ways-trump -taking-back-americas-culture/.

21. Christopher Wlezien, "The Public as Thermostat: Dynamics of Preferences for Spending," *American Journal of Political Science* 39, no. 4 (1995): 981–1000; Kristen Bialik, "More Americans Say Government Should Ensure Health Care Coverage," Pew Research Center, January 13, 2017, http://www.pewresearch.org/fact-tank/2017/01/13/more-ameri cans-say-government-should-ensure-health-care-coverage/. For polling on the Affordable Care Act, see the Kaiser Family Foundation's data: Henry J. Kaiser Family Foundation, "Kaiser Health Tracking Poll: The Public's Views on the ACA," May 10, 2018, https:// www.kff.org/interactive/kaiser-health-tracking-poll-the-publics-views-on-the-aca/# ?response=Favorable—Unfavorable&aRange=twoYear. Art Swift, "In US, Record-High 72% See Foreign Trade as Opportunity," Gallup, February 16, 2017, http://news.gallup.com /poll/204044/record-high-foreign-trade-opportunity.aspx; Bradley Jones, "Americans Are Generally Positive about Free Trade Agreements, More Critical of Tariff Increases," Pew Research Center, May 10, 2018, http://www.pewresearch.org/fact-tank/2018/05/10 /americans-are-generally-positive-about-free-trade-agreements-more-critical-of-tariff -increases/; Diana Mutz, "Free Trade Is Becoming More Popular—Especially among Republicans," *Monkey Cage* (blog), *Washington Post*, November 17, 2017, https://www .washingtonpost.com/news/monkey-cage/wp/2017/11/17/free-trade-is-becoming-more -popular-especially-among-republicans/?utm_term=.2e8b8d432cae.

22. For prior evidence of thermostatic movement on racial issues, see Paul M. Kellstedt, *The Mass Media and the Dynamics of American Racial Attitudes* (Cambridge: Cambridge University Press, 2003).

23. The polls featured in the graph about discrimination and racial inequality employed somewhat different question wordings. The graph depicts the percentage who agreed with the statement, "Generations of slavery and discrimination have created con-

ditions that make it difficult for blacks to work their way out of the lower class" (American National Election Studies); the percentage who agreed that the fact that "on the average African-Americans have worse jobs, income, and housing than white people" is "mainly due to discrimination" (General Social Survey); and the percentage who agreed more with the statement, "Racial discrimination is the main reason why black people can't get ahead these days," than with the statement, "Blacks who can't get ahead in the country are mostly responsible for their own condition" (Pew). The question wording about NFL protests in the two Quinnipiac polls was slightly different: "As you may know, some athletes and sports teams have begun not standing during the national anthem in order to protest police violence against the black community in the United States. Do you approve or disapprove of this form of protest?" and "As you may know, some athletes and teams in the NFL (National Football League) are choosing to kneel during the national anthem as a form of protest. Do you approve or disapprove of this form of protest?"

24. Jim VandeHei, "Trump's Mind-Control Superpowers," Axios, June 6, 2018, https://www.axios.com/trump-persuasion-gop-republicans-mueller-investigation -e1f12159-3635-4134-bde9-d8cd4ee7a92e.html?utm_source=twitter&utm_medium =twsocialshare&utm_campaign=organic.

25. Brian Schaffner, "Follow the Racist: The Consequences of Expressions of Elite Prejudice for Mass Rhetoric" (paper presented at the annual meeting of the Midwest Political Science Association, Chicago, IL, April 5–8, 2018); Benjamin Newman, Jennifer Merolla, Sono Shah, Danielle Lemi, Loren Collingwood, and Karthick Ramakrishnan, "The Trump Effect: An Experimental Investigation of the Emboldening Effect of Racially Inflammatory Elite Communication" (working paper, University of California, Riverside, 2018); Katayoun Kishi, "Assaults against Muslims in U.S. Surpass 2001 Level," Pew Research Center, November 15, 2017, http://www.pewresearch.org/fact-tank/2017/11/15/assaults -against-muslims-in-u-s-surpass-2001-level/.

26. See also Sean McElwee, "The Rising Racial Liberalism of Democratic Voters," *New York Times*, May 23, 2018, https://www.nytimes.com/2018/05/23/opinion/democrats -race.html.

27. See also Pew Research Center, "The Partisan Divide on Political Values Grows Even Wider: Sharp Shifts among Democrats on Aid to the Needy, Race, Immigration," October 5, 2017, http://www.people-press.org/2017/10/05/the-partisan-divide-on-political -values-grows-even-wider/; Shibley Telhami, "How Trump Changed Americans' Views of Islam—for the Better," *Monkey Cage* (blog), *Washington Post*, January 25, 2017, https:// www.washingtonpost.com/news/monkey-cage/wp/2017/01/25/americans-dont -support-trumps-ban-on-muslim-immigration/?utm_term=.9b983d0078e9; and Michael Tesler, "Donald Trump Is Making the Border Wall Less Popular," *Monkey Cage* (blog), *Washington Post*, August 16, 2016, https://www.washingtonpost.com/news/monkey-cage /wp/2016/08/16/donald-trump-is-making-the-border-wall-less-popular/?utm_term =.fafe40624121.

28. On partisan shifts against the president, see Gabriel Lenz, *Follow the Leader? How Voters Respond to Politicians' Policies and Performance* (Chicago: University of Chicago Press, 2012); Adam J. Berinsky, *In Time of War: Understanding American Public Opinion from World War II to Iraq* (Chicago: University of Chicago Press, 2009); and Stephen P. Nicholson, "Polarizing Cues," *American Journal of Political Science* 56, no. 1 (2012): 52–66.

29. The results regarding the Lee statue are from an August 13–15, 2017, YouGov/ *Economist* poll: https://d25d2506sfb94s.cloudfront.net/cumulus_uploads/document/9h

2c1c3new/econTabReport.pdf. The results regarding the Arpaio pardon are from an August 27–29, 2017, YouGov/*Economist* poll: https://d25d2506sfb94s.cloudfront.net/cumulus _uploads/document/bk136ee11c/econTabReport.pdf. The results regarding the NFL protests are from Ariel Edwards-Levy, "Americans Are Split over the NFL's Decision on Anthem Protests," *Huffington Post*, May 29, 2018, https://www.huffingtonpost.com/entry /americans-split-over-nfl-anthem-protest-ruling_us_5b0dc5ade4b0568a880f7e9b. See also John Sides, "National Anthem Protests Are Becoming More Popular. You Can Thank Donald Trump," *Monkey Cage* (blog), *Washington Post*, October 25, 2017, https://www.wash ingtonpost.com/news/monkey-cage/wp/2017/10/25/national-anthem-protests-are -becoming-more-popular-you-can-thank-donald-trump/?utm_term=.4906b98a2820.

30. On Latino identity: the political scientist Brian Schaffner reported that 40 percent of Latinos whom he reinterviewed in 2017 reported higher levels of "linked fate" with other Latinos than they did in October 2016. See Brian Schaffner (@b_schaffner), Twitter, April 2, 2017, 1:32 p.m., https://twitter.com/b_schaffner/status/848634363789 049856. On the rise in Asian American identity, see Danvy Le, Maneesh Arora, and Christopher Stout, "Asian American Identity in the Trump Era" (paper presented at the annual meeting of the Midwest Political Science Association, Chicago, IL, April 5–8, 2018). The unpopularity of Trump among younger Latinos was reported in a September 2017 Latino Decisions Poll: Latino Decisions, "National Latino Survey Sept 2017," accessed June 11, 2018, http://www.latinodecisions.com/files/4615/0652/1630/LVP_LD _09.28_Release_Xtabs.pdf.

31. For the role of race in dividing the Democratic coalition, see Thomas Byrne Edsall with Mary D. Edsall, *Chain Reaction: The Impact of Race, Rights, and Taxes on American Politics* (New York: W. W. Norton, 1992); Donald R. Kinder and Lynn M. Sanders, *Divided by Color: Racial Politics and Democratic Ideals* (Chicago: University of Chicago Press, 1996); and Paul M. Sniderman and Edward G. Carmines, *Reaching beyond Race* (Cambridge, MA: Harvard University Press, 1997). On Obama-Trump voters, see Sean McElwee, Jesse H. Rhodes, Brian F. Schaffner, and Bernard L. Fraga, "The Missing Obama Millions," *New York Times*, March 10, 2018, https://mobile.nytimes.com/2018/03 /10/opinion/sunday/obama-trump-voters-democrats.html.

32. Kevin Robillard, "Ed Gillespie's Split Personality Campaign," *Politico*, November 6, 2017, https://www.politico.com/story/2017/11/06/ed-gillespie-virginia-governor -race-244605; Kevin Robillard, "Republicans Abandon Tax Cut Message in Pa. Special Election," *Politico*, March 13, 2018, https://www.politico.com/story/2018/03/13/pennsylvania -special-election-preview-tax-republicans-458276; Kevin Robillard, "Here's the White House Questionnaire for GOP Candidates Who Want Trump's Backing," *Huffington Post*, April 26, 2018, https://www.huffingtonpost.com/entry/trump-gop-questionnaire _us_5ae0f0f5e4b04aa23f1ee5f2; Sean Sullivan, "GOP Candidates Echo Trump on Immigration as President Transforms Party in His Image," *Washington Post*, June 3, 2018, https://www.washingtonpost.com/powerpost/gop-candidates-echo-trump-on -immigration-as-president-transforms-party-in-his-image/2018/06/03/efbfc3da-6517 -11e8-a69c-b944de66d9e7_story.html?utm_term=.3215eb1edbba.

33. McElwee, "Rising Racial Liberalism."

34. Nicholas Valentino and Kirill Zhirkov, "Blue Is Black and Red Is White? Affective Polarization and the Racialized Schemas of US Party Coalitions" (working paper, University of Michigan, 2018).

35. On the parallels between Trump and right-wing European parties, see Cas Mudde, "The Trump Phenomenon and the European Populist Radical Right," *Monkey Cage*

(blog), *Washington Post*, August 26, 2015, https://www.washingtonpost.com/news /monkey-cage/wp/2015/08/26/the-trump-phenomenon-and-the-european-populist -radical-right/?utm_term=.1a680642e669. On the rise of far-right parties, see Ronald Inglehart and Pippa Norris, "Trump and the Populist Authoritarian Parties: The Silent Revolution in Reverse," *Perspectives on Politics* 15, no. 2 (2017): 443–54; and Pippa Norris, "It's Not Just Trump. Authoritarian Populism Is Rising across the West. Here's Why," *Monkey Cage* (blog), *Washington Post*, March 11, 2016, https://www.washingtonpost.com /news/monkey-cage/wp/2016/03/11/its-not-just-trump-authoritarian-populism-is-rising -across-the-west-heres-why/?utm_term=.168d3d484343. On rising diversity, immigration, and the challenges to national identity, see Sara Wallace Goodman, *Immigration and Membership Politics in Western Europe* (New York: Cambridge University Press, 2014). On explanations for far-right party success, see, among others, Matt Golder, "Far Right Parties in Europe," *Annual Review of Political Science* 19 (2016): 477–97; and Cas Mudde, *Populist Radical Right Parties in Europe* (New York: Cambridge University Press, 2007). On the differences between European and American views of diversity, see Bruce Drake and Jacob Poushter, "In Views of Diversity, Many Europeans Are Less Positive Than Americans," Pew Research Center, July 12, 2016, http://www.pewresearch.org/fact-tank /2016/07/12/in-views-of-diversity-many-europeans-are-less-positive-than-americans/; and Jack Citrin and John Sides, "Immigration and the Imagined Community in Europe and the United States," *Political Studies* 56, no. 1 (2008): 33–56. On immigration and the success of far-right parties and Brexit, see Golder, "Far Right Parties in Europe," and the cites therein. On Brexit, see Harold D. Clarke, Matthew Goodwin, and Paul Whiteley, *Brexit: Why Britain Voted to Leave the European Union* (New York: Cambridge University Press, 2017).

36. On the sluggish economic recovery in Europe, see Marilyn Geewax, "U.S. Economic Recovery Looks Good Compared with Sluggish Europe, Asia," National Public Radio, June 17 2016, https://www.npr.org/sections/thetwo-way/2016/06/17/482328208/u -s-economic-recovery-looks-good-compared-with-sluggish-europe-asia. On economic anxiety and right-wing populism, see Larry Bartels, "The 'Wave' of Right-Wing Populist Sentiment Is a Myth," *Monkey Cage* (blog), *Washington Post*, June 21, 2017, https://www .washingtonpost.com/news/monkey-cage/wp/2017/06/21/the-wave-of-right-wing -populist-sentiment-is-a-myth/?utm_term=.bfa04c930805. On the equivocal impact of objective economic conditions, see also Golder, "Far Right Parties in Europe."

37. Studies that get at status anxiety or group resentments include Gidron Noam and Peter A. Hall, "The Politics of Social Status: Economic and Cultural Roots of the Populist Right," *British Journal of Sociology* 68, no. S1 (2017): S57–S84; Jane Green, Timothy Hellwig, and Edward Fieldhouse, "The Ingroup vs. Outgroup Economic Vote" (paper presented at the annual meeting of the Midwest Political Science Association, Chicago, IL, April 5–8, 2018); Justin Gest, Tyler Reny, and Jeremy Mayer, "Roots of the Radical Right: Nostalgic Deprivation in the United States and Britain," *Comparative Political Studies*, published ahead of print, July 20, 2017, https://doi.org/10.1177/0010414017720705; and Robert Ford and Matthew J. Goodwin, *Revolt on the Right: Explaining Support for the Radical Right in Britain* (New York: Routledge, 2014). On the interaction of economic conditions and racial or ethnic factors in fostering the success of far-right populist parties, see Golder, "Far Right Parties in Europe"; as well as Rafaela M. Dancygier, *Immigration and Conflict in Europe* (New York: Cambridge University Press, 2010).

38. The relationship between the perception of discrimination against whites and support for both Brexit and Trump remained intact after accounting for other factors.

Controlling for party and ideology, whites who perceived a lot of discrimination against whites were still around 60 percentage points more likely to support Brexit and Trump than whites who perceived a lot of discrimination in favor of whites.

39. Cynthia Kroet, "Geert Wilders Will Attend Pro–Donald Trump Gay Rally," *Politico*, July 14, 2016, https://www.politico.eu/article/geert-wilders-will-attend-pro-donald-trump-gay-rally/; Margit Feher, "Hungary's Viktor Orban Expresses Support for Donald Trump's Foreign Policy Plans," *Wall Street Journal*, July 26, 2016, https://www.wsj.com/articles/hungarys-viktor-orban-expresses-support-for-donald-trumps-foreign-policy-plans-1469546261; Aidan Quigley, "Trump Expresses Support for French Candidate Le Pen," *Politico*, April 21, 2017, https://www.politico.com/story/2017/04/21/trump-supports-marine-le-pen-237464; Adam Nossiter, "'Let Them Call You Racists': Bannon's Pep Talk to National Front," *New York Times*, March 10, 2018, https://www.nytimes.com/2018/03/10/world/europe/steve-bannon-france-national-front.html.

40. The studies of resentment include Katherine Jean Cramer, *The Politics of Resentment: Rural Consciousness in Wisconsin and the Rise of Scott Walker* (Chicago: University of Chicago Press, 2016); Justin Gest, *The New Minority: White Working Class Politics in an Age of Immigration and Inequality* (New York: Oxford University Press, 2016); Arlie Russell Hochschild, *Strangers in Their Own Land: Anger and Mourning on the American Right* (New York: New Press, 2016); and Robert Wuthnow, *The Left Behind: Decline and Rage in Rural America* (Princeton: Princeton University Press, 2018). On social identities and the party coalitions, see Liliana Mason, *Uncivil Agreement: How Politics Became Our Identity* (Chicago: University of Chicago Press, 2018). On the centrality of race and ethnicity to debates over American identity, see Rogers M. Smith, *Civic Ideals: Conflicting Visions of Citizenship in U.S. History* (New Haven: Yale University Press, 1999). On "us" and "them" in American political culture, see James A. Morone, *The Devils We Know: Us and Them in America's Raucous Political Culture* (Lawrence: University of Kansas Press, 2014).

41. This account of the trial is taken from Terence McCoy, "He Was Assaulted and Called Un-American at a Trump Rally. Can He Forgive the Man Who Did It?," *Washington Post*, December 31, 2016, https://www.washingtonpost.com/national/he-was-assaulted-and-called-un-american-at-a-trump-rally-can-he-forgive-the-man-who-did-it/2016/12/31/ba91e876-c88a-11e6-bf4b-2c064d32a4bf_story.html?utm_term=.0dbc8d209379.

42. Deborah J. Schildkraut, *Americanism in the Twenty-First Century: Public Opinion in the Age of Immigration* (New York: Cambridge University Press, 2011); Lynn Vavreck, "The Great Political Divide over American Identity," *New York Times*, August 2, 2017, https://www.nytimes.com/2017/08/02/upshot/the-great-political-divide-over-american-identity.html.

43. On the different strains of national identity, see, among others, Jack Citrin and David O. Sears, *American Identity and the Politics of Multiculturalism* (New York: Cambridge University Press, 2014); Thierry Devos and Mahzarin R. Banaji, "American = White?," *Journal of Personality and Social Psychology* 88, no. 3 (2016): 447–66; John Higham, *Strangers in the Land: Patterns of American Nativism, 1860–1925* (New York: Anthem, 1963); Schildkraut, *Americanism*; and Jim Sidanius, Seymour Feshbach, Shana Levin, and Felicia Pratto, "The Interface between Ethnic and National Attachment: Ethnic Pluralism or Ethnic Dominance?," *Public Opinion Quarterly* 61, no. 1 (1997): 102–33. Elizabeth Theiss-Morse, *Who Counts as an American? The Boundaries of National Identity* (New York: Cambridge University Press, 2009).

44. Jen Kirby, "Trump Wants Fewer Immigrants from 'Shithole Countries' and More from Places like Norway," *Vox*, January 11, 2018, https://www.vox.com/2018/1/11/16880750/trump-immigrants-shithole-countries-norway.

45. The study of the Iowa towns is J. Celeste Lay, *A Midwestern Mosaic: Immigration and Political Socialization in Rural America* (Philadelphia: Temple University Press, 2012). On "politicized places," see Daniel J. Hopkins, "Politicized Places: Explaining Where and When Immigrants Provoke Local Opposition," *American Political Science Review* 104, no. 1 (2010): 40–60. On the 2016 Trump vote, see Ryan Enos, *The Space between Us: Social Geography and Politics* (New York: Cambridge University Press, 2017), 138–41.

Appendix to Chapter 2

1. On this logarithmic transformation, see Achen and Bartels, *Democracy for Realists*, 150n4.

2. This follows Abramowitz, "Forecasting the 2008 Presidential Election."

3. The logic of the Clarify package is presented in Gary King, Michael Tomz, and Jason Wittenberg, "Making the Most of Statistical Analyses: Improving Interpretation and Presentation," *American Journal of Political Science* 44, no. 2 (2000): 341–55.

Appendix to Chapter 5

1. See J. Scott Long and Jeremy Freese, *Regression Models for Categorical Dependent Variables Using Stata*, 3rd ed. (College Station, TX: Stata, 2014).

Appendix to Chapter 8

1. See Sides, "Race, Religion, and Immigration."

ACKNOWLEDGMENTS

The 2016 election was unpredictable in many ways. Certainly, the three of us did not predict its outcome. We thought early on that the 2016 election could be close; economic and political conditions in the country told us so. But like many analysts, we ultimately thought that the election would not be all that close, thanks to Donald Trump's controversial rhetoric and lack of a traditional campaign.

When Trump ended up winning, we sought to understand how it happened. The process took us longer than we wanted, but we believe that political science theory and the data we analyze help to explain why this improbable candidate succeeded. Our reliance on quantitative data means that this book probably has too many graphs and too few scoops—which certainly makes our story less juicy. But we hope that our findings, alongside the valuable reporting and firsthand accounts of journalists, add to the understanding of this election and its implications for American politics.

We are grateful to all the people who helped us along the way.

First, we must thank newly minted UCLA political science PhD Shawn Patterson, who provided research assistance throughout the entire project, and to the Andrew F. Carnegie Corporation, which supported his work.

We are also grateful to the many, many people who provided us with data or allowed us to help design original datasets for this project. These people include: Doug Rivers, Joe Williams, Sam Luks, Carolyn Chu, and Ashley Grosse at YouGov; Michael Pollard and everyone at the RAND Corporation for the Presidential Election Panel Survey; Joshua Putnam for the data on delegate counts; Boris Shor for data on state legislative endorsements during the invisible primary; Kalev Leetaru for help with the media data produced by the Internet Archive and GDELT; Jack Beckwith of the Data Face for sharing their data on media coverage; Gary King, Stephanie Newby, and John Donnelly at Crimson Hexagon; John Geer of Vanderbilt University, the Andrew F. Carnegie Corporation, G2 Analytics, YouGov Special Projects, and Sage Engage for helping to design and implement the SpotCheck project; Kantar Media and the Campaign Media Analysis

Group for data on the candidates' advertising buys; Ariel Edwards-Levy and others at the *Huffington Post*'s Pollster for their invaluable collection of polling data; Jocelyn Kiley at the Pew Research Center for their data on party identification; Dina Smeltz at the Chicago Council for their polling data; Davin Phoenix for access to the Collaborative Multiracial Post-Election Survey; and the School of Social Science at the University of California, Irvine, for supporting the acquisition of the Gallup data. Finally, we thank the Democracy Fund, and especially Joe Goldman and Henry Olsen, for convening the Voter Study Group and supporting the development of the VOTER Survey.

We have benefited from the feedback of many friends, political reporters, and scholars who read and commented on chapter drafts or who helped us with analyses. This includes Larry Bartels, Mark Blyth, Sara Goodman, Brian Hamel, Danny Hayes, Marc Hetherington, Dan Hopkins, Sasha Issenberg, Jeff Lewis, Seth Masket, Mary Mc-Thomas, Debbie Schildkraut, David Sears, Paul Sniderman, and John Zaller.

We also benefited from presenting this research to various audiences, including at Arizona State University; the Aspen Ideas Festival; Bucknell University; the Canadian Political Science Association; Canisius College; Colorado College; Cornell University; the Democracy Fund National Advisory Committee; George Washington University's American politics workshop; the Hammer Museum; the MacArthur Foundation Board of Directors; Miami University of Ohio; the National Capital Area Political Science Association's American politics workshop; Northwestern University; Ohio State University; Pennsylvania State University; the Political Psychology Preconference at Temple University; the Princeton University workshop on "Rethinking Democracy"; Southern Illinois University; Stanford University; Tufts University; the University of California, Berkeley; the University of California, Irvine; UCLA; the University of California, Riverside; the University of California, Santa Barbara; the University of Chicago's Harris School of Public Policy; the University of Michigan; the University of Minnesota; the University of Texas at Austin; and Vanderbilt University.

We are especially grateful for invitations to conferences on the 2016 election at Harvard University; Ohio State University; Tufts University; the University of California, Berkeley; the University of California, Riverside; the University of Georgia; the University of Iowa; and the University of Southern California. We thank Ryan Enos; Herb Weisberg and Tom Wood; Dan Drezner; Gabe Lenz, Amy Lerman, and Laura Stoker; Shaun Bowler and Todd Donovan; Keith Poole and Jamie Monagan; Caroline Tolbert; and Dennis Chong and Bob Shrum, respectively, for organizing those conferences.

Early versions of our argument were published in the *ANNALS* of the American Academy of Social and Political Sciences, the *Journal of Elections, Public Opinion and Parties*, and in the *Journal of Democracy*. We thank the editors of those journals—Tom Kecskemethy; Susan Banducci, Jae-Jae Spoon, and Daniel Stevens; and Larry Diamond, respectively—for the opportunity.

Obviously, this project would not have been possible without the ongoing and extraordinary support (and patience!) of Princeton University Press, which dates to the publication of Sides and Vavreck's *The Gamble*. We thank them for continuing to publish a more academic account of a presidential election for a wider audience. We especially thank Eric Crahan, John Donohue, and Terri O'Prey.

This project, like so much else that is central to our lives, has depended on the support of our families: Jeff Lewis; Mary McThomas; and Serena, Ethan, and Hannah Sides. Most people who lived through the 2016 campaign thought that once was enough, but our spouses and children relived it with us every day for two more years. Somehow,

Mary and Jeff never, not a single time, asked Michael and Lynn to turn the cable news off. We are all extremely lucky people.

Finally, we have dedicated the book to our graduate school advisers. Dick Fenno (for Lynn Vavreck), Henry Brady and Jack Citrin (for John Sides), and David Sears (for Michael Tesler) were instrumental in our development as scholars, and being their students motivates us to do good work every day. Their research and guidance have been invaluable—not only to us, but to the study of politics.

INDEX

Note: Page numbers followed by "f" or "t" indicate figures and tables, respectively.

2012 election: economic conditions, 161; lessons for Republican Party, 35–37, 38, 68, 95, 130, 215; Republican candidate endorsements, 43–44, 224f; Trump quotations, 82; voting choices, 157–159, 163f

2016 Democratic primary season, 97–129, 160t, 230–234; candidates and identity, 8, 99–100, 123–127, 124t, 126f; delegates in, 97–98, 98f, 111; endorsements during, 100–101, 101f, 102, 103, 104f, 112, 231; party leadership unity, 97–98, 100–101, 101f; voting issues and factors for, 8, 99, 123–127, 124t, 126f, 128–129, 232–233t

2016 presidential election: campaigns' platforms and fundamentals, 6, 10, 131, 134, 220; economy as factor in, 7, 8, 9, 10, 13, 14–22, 31, 70, 74, 75f, 76, 92, 124t, 128–129, 132–133, 157, 158f, 172–177, 174f, 226, 228, 232t, 236–240, 239t; forecasts and indicators before and during, 9, 13, 21–22, 32, 131, 135, 152–153, 157, 161–162, 162f, 190, 221–223, 251n22, 251n27; group identities' power in, 2–3, 4–5, 6–11, 71, 90–95, 100, 165, 169–172, 178–179, 184; national conditions, 4, 7, 13, 20–21, 31–32; polls in, 8–9, 135, 137f, 140–141, 145, 147–148, 150–151, 151f, 159, 161, 190; results and aftermath, 9, 154–155, 189–197, 200; voting issues and factors in, 4, 6, 9, 70, 130–153, 151f, 152f, 155–200, 225–226, 227.

See also Clinton, Hillary; Electoral College and vote; popular vote; Trump, Donald

2016 Republican primary season, 7–8, 33–35, 34f, 40–46, 48, 93, 128–129, 160t; debates during, 46, 51f, 54, 57f, 58–59, 64, 65, 67–68, 82, 263n24; delegates in, 33–34, 34f, 36; differences from 2008/2012, 2–3, 8, 9, 43–44, 46, 61, 224f; endorsements during, 42–44, 43f, 45f, 58, 223, 224f, 258n30; party divides and fractures, 7–8, 10, 40–46; Trump media attention, 7–8, 35, 48–68, 51f, 52f, 57f, 69, 278n16; Trump racial rhetoric and differentiation, 5, 6, 10, 54, 71, 81–82, 83, 84–85, 87–90, 93; voting issues and factors in, 8, 70, 74–76, 78–79, 82–85, 87. *See also specific candidates*

Abedin, Huma, 146
Access Hollywood tape, 140, 141, 143–144, 185–186
Achen, Christopher, 16–17, 125
activation of group identities: and economic anxiety, 172–173, 175; in general elections, 153, 156, 159, 161; and modern sexism, 187–188, 240–241, 301n58; political predispositions, 152–153; in primary elections, 70, 71–73, 95; of racial groups, 81, 85–86, 88, 89–90, 169–170, 178–179, 234–236